Dissident Histories in the Soviet Union

Library of Modern Russia

Advisory board

- Jeffrey Brooks, Professor at Johns Hopkins University, USA
- Michael David-Fox, Professor at Georgetown University, USA
- Lucien Frary, Associate Professor at Rider University, USA
- James Harris, Senior Lecturer at the University of Leeds, UK
- Robert Hornsby, Lecturer at the University of Leeds, UK
- Ekaterina Pravilova, Professor of History at Princeton University, USA
- Geoffrey Swain, Emeritus Professor of Central and East European Studies at the University of Glasgow, UK
- Vera Tolz-Zilitinkevic, Sir William Mather Professor of Russian Studies at the University of Manchester, UK
- Vladislav Zubok, Professor of International History at the London School of Economics, UK

Building on Bloomsbury Academic's established record of publishing Russian studies titles, the *Library of Modern Russia* will showcase the work of emerging and established writers who are setting new agendas in the field.

At a time when potentially dangerous misconceptions and misunderstandings about Russia abound, titles in the series will shed fresh light and nuance on Russian history. Volumes will take the idea of 'Russia' in its broadest cultural sense and cover the entirety of the multi-ethnic lands that made up imperial Russia and the Soviet Union. Ranging in chronological scope from the Romanovs to today, the books will:

- Re-consider Russia's history from a variety of inter-disciplinary perspectives.
- Explore Russia in its various international contexts, rather than as exceptional or in isolation.
- Examine the complex, divisive and ever-shifting notions of 'Russia'.
- Contribute to a deeper understanding of Russia's rich social and cultural history.
- Critically re-assess the Soviet period and its legacy today.
- Interrogate the traditional periodizations of the post-Stalin Soviet Union.
- Unearth continuities, or otherwise, among the tsarist, Soviet and post-Soviet periods.
- Re-appraise Russia's complex relationship with Eastern Europe, both historically and today.
- Analyze the politics of history and memory in post-Soviet Russia.
- Promote new archival revelations and innovative research methodologies.
- Foster a community of scholars and readers devoted to a sharper understanding of the Russian experience, past and present.

Books in the series will join our list in being marketed globally, including at conferences – such as the BASEES and ASEEES conventions. Each will be subjected to a rigorous peer-review process and will be published in hardback and, simultaneously, as an e-book. We also anticipate a second release in paperback for the general reader and student markets.

For more information, or to submit a proposal for inclusion in the
series, please contact:
Rhodri Mogford, Publisher, History
Rhodri.Mogford@bloomsbury.com

New and forthcoming

Fascism in Manchuria: The Soviet-China Encounter in the 1930s, Susanne Hohler

The Idea of Russia: The Life and Work of Dmitry Likhachev, Vladislav Zubok

The Tsar's Armenians: A Minority in Late Imperial Russia, Onur Önol

Myth Making in the Soviet Union and Modern Russia: Remembering World War II in Brezhnev's Hero City, Vicky Davis

Building Stalinism: The Moscow Canal and the Creation of Soviet Space, Cynthia Ruder

Russia in the Time of Cholera: Disease and the Environment under Romanovs and Soviets, John Davis

Soviet Americana: A Cultural History of Russian and Ukrainian Americanists, Sergei Zhuk

Stalin's Economic Advisors: The Varga Institute and the Making of Soviet Foreign Policy, Kyung Deok Roh

Ideology and the Arts in the Soviet Union: The Establishment of Censorship and Control, Steven Richmond

Nomads and Soviet Rule: Central Asia under Lenin and Stalin, Alun Thomas

The Russian State and the People: Power, Corruption and the Individual in Putin's Russia, Geir Hønneland et al. (eds)

The Communist Party in the Russian Civil War: A Political History, Gayle Lonergan

Criminal Subculture in the Gulag: Prisoner Society in the Stalinist Labour Camps, Mark Vincent

Power and Politics in Modern Chechnya: Ramzan Kadyrov and the New Digital Authoritarianism, Karena Avedissian

Russian Pilgrimage to the Holy Land: Piety and Travel from the Middle Ages to the Revolution, Nikolaos Chrissidis

Dissident Histories in the Soviet Union

From De-Stalinization to Perestroika

Barbara Martin

BLOOMSBURY ACADEMIC
LONDON • NEW YORK • OXFORD • NEW DELHI • SYDNEY

BLOOMSBURY ACADEMIC
Bloomsbury Publishing Plc
50 Bedford Square, London, WC1B 3DP, UK
1385 Broadway, New York, NY 10018, USA
29 Earlsfort Terrace, Dublin 2, Ireland

BLOOMSBURY, BLOOMSBURY ACADEMIC and the Diana logo are trademarks
of Bloomsbury Publishing Plc

First published in Great Britain 2019
Paperback edition published 2021

Copyright © Barbara Martin, 2019

Barbara Martin has asserted her right under the Copyright, Designs and Patents Act,
1988, to be identified as Author of this work.

For legal purposes the Acknowledgments on p. xii constitute an extension of this
copyright page.

Cover design by Simon Goggin

Cover image: Alexandr Solzhenitsyn in Zurich, 1974. (© James Andanson/Getty Images)

All rights reserved. No part of this publication may be reproduced or transmitted in any
form or by any means, electronic or mechanical, including photocopying, recording,
or any information storage or retrieval system, without prior permission in writing from
the publishers.

Bloomsbury Publishing Plc does not have any control over, or responsibility for, any
third-party websites referred to or in this book. All internet addresses given in this
book were correct at the time of going to press. The author and publisher regret any
inconvenience caused if addresses have changed or sites have ceased to exist, but
can accept no responsibility for any such changes.

A catalogue record for this book is available from the British Library.

A catalog record for this book is available from the Library of Congress.

ISBN: HB: 978-1-78831-053-6
PB: 978-1-35019-244-7
ePDF: 978-1-35010-680-2
eBook: 978-1-35010-681-9

Series: Library of Modern Russia

Typeset by Deanta Global Publishing Services, Chennai, India

To find out more about our authors and books visit www.bloomsbury.com
and sign up for our newsletters.

To My Mother

Contents

List of Illustrations	xi
Acknowledgments	xii
Note on Transliteration and Abbreviations	xiv
Introduction	1
Note on methodology and sources	6
1 The Party's Call to Denounce Stalin's Crimes	11
Anton Antonov-Ovseenko's duty to his father	13
Roy Medvedev: Writing for the Party	22
Aleksandr Nekrich: Pushing the limits of de-Stalinization	31
2 From a Reopening of the Stalin Question to a Closure of the Ideological Lid	39
A Mandate to end de-Stalinization	40
Opposition on the historical front	47
The Brezhnev compromise	56
3 Voicing Opposition to Stalin's Rehabilitation	61
A rebellious intelligentsia	62
From the Gulag to the anti-Stalinist barricades	69
The Nekrich Affair	75
4 Writing History through the Voice of the Repressed	83
The Gulag Archipelago	85
Let History Judge	94
5 Exiting the System	109
From the official field to the underground publishing world	109
Expulsion as a tool of repression	117
6 From "Inner Emigration" to Exile	133
Living in "Inner Emigration": Medvedev's fragile compromise with the authorities	135
Exile as the ultimate form of exit	145

7	Diverging Truths	157
	Two truths about the Soviet past	159
	Skirmishes on the historical battlefield	164
	Between history and folklore	172
	Dissident histories as ethical manifestos	179
8	Unleashing the Past	183
	Perestroika and the resurgence of history	183
	The belated return of dissident histories to the Soviet public	189
	Questioning dissident histories' factual accuracy	197

Conclusion	205
Notes	211
Timeline of Events	256
Bibliography	264
Index	277

List of Illustrations

Figure 1.1	Anton Antonov-Ovseenko with his father's portrait by Iurii Annenkov in the background, 1985. Courtesy of the Gulag Museum	14
Figure 1.2	Roy Medvedev in his home office in Moscow, 1973 © Margarita Medvedeva. Courtesy of Zhores Medvedev	24
Figure 1.3	Zhores Medvedev in his home office in England, 1987 © Margarita Medvedeva. Courtesy of Zhores Medvedev	25
Figure 1.4	Aleksandr Nekrich, n.d. Courtesy of Hoover Institution Archives, Aleksandr Moiseevich Nekrich Papers, Box 62, Folder 1, Hoover Institution Archives	33
Figure 4.1	Aleksandr Solzehnitsyn, 1970. Courtesy of Mezhdunarodnyi Memorial Archive, Moscow	86

Acknowledgments

As a francophone historian writing in English about Soviet history, I have striven to reflect in my work the various academic influences and historiographical traditions to which I was exposed. While the initial spark of inspiration came while I was doing an exchange semester at Yale University in 2010, the bilingual and multicultural setting of the Geneva Graduate Institute of International and Development Studies provided me with a stimulating environment to conduct research at the crossroads of the Francophone and Anglo-Saxon academic cultures. Several research stays in Moscow and Bremen made me more familiar with the Russian and German historiography on Soviet dissent and with research communities in these countries.

In the process of conducting research over and writing this book, I benefited from the support and kind assistance of many scholars. My deepest gratitude goes to Andre Liebich, who not only provided me with patient, committed, and yet flexible guidance, but also shared with me his deep knowledge of the Soviet and post-Soviet world and taught me to look at the past with a critical and dispassionate eye. Davide Rodogno and Kathleen Smith have also provided me with invaluable comments and advice. As I presented my research in Europe, Russia, and the United States, I made connections and received valuable feedback from colleagues, which contributed greatly to my reflection. I am grateful, among others, to Allen Lynch, Ann Komaromi, Stephen Cohen, Benjamin Nathans, Peter Reddaway, Gabriel Superfin, Vsevolod Sergeev, Clemens Günther, Roman Khandozhko, and my Bremen colleagues. Finally, I thank the anonymous peer reviewers and my former editor Thomas Stottor for their constructive critique of my manuscript in the final stages of publication.

A Western research on Soviet history requires more than a whiff of Russian fragrance, and my stays in Moscow between 2012 and 2017 and contacts with local historians played a crucial role in forming my perceptions about the past. In particular, I greatly benefited from my repeated contacts with the research and information center of "Memorial." Konstantin Morozov kindly provided me with the necessary contacts and introduction to Memorial's staff and helped organize my first six-month stay in Moscow. Besides the archivists Aleksei Makarov and Tatiana Bakhmina and the librarian Boris Belenkin, I would like to thank most warmly Gennadii Kuzovkin, head of Memorial's Program on the History of Soviet Dissent, for his invaluable help. These close contacts with Memorial also intensified with my work over the dissident historical collection *Pamiat'*, which evolved into a separate book project in collaboration with Anton Sveshnikov.[1]

My gratitude also extends to the staff of other archives that I visited. I thank the staff of the Hoover Institution Archives; the Open Society Archives; the Bibliothèque de Documentation Internationale Contemporaine; and Maria Klassen from the Forschungsstelle Osteuropa archive. In Moscow, I thank the staff at the Russian State

Archive of Contemporary History and the Russian State Archive of Socio-Political History. My warmest appreciation goes to the staff of the Department of Conservation of Documents of Private Collection at the Moscow City Archive for doing everything in their power to facilitate my access to Roy and Zhores Medvedevs' personal papers.

Because this research is partly still living history, I was most fortunate to meet with some of the characters in this story and those who had known them. The late Anton Antonov-Ovseenko generously hosted me for several days at his country dacha in June 2012 and opened his personal papers to me. His son Anton and his foster sister Valentina Tikhanova also kindly assisted me, as did Roman Romanov, director of the Gulag Museum, originally founded by Antonov-Ovseenko. Roy and Zhores Medvedev both welcomed me for several interviews in Moscow and London, and helped me get access to their personal papers and their memoirs. Moreover, Zhores was kind enough to review the chapters concerning his brother and offer corrections and feedback. I would also like to thank Natalia Solzhenitsyna for her assistance in putting me in contact with two admirable elderly ladies, whose voices were living links to Solzhenitsyn's past: Nadezhda Levitskaia and the late Elena Chukovskaia.

Funding from the Swiss National Foundation for Science allowed me to spend a total of twelve months at the Higher School of Economics in Moscow and thirteen months at the Research Centre for East European Studies (FSO) at the University of Bremen in 2014–15 and 2017–18. Without this generous assistance, this book would probably not have seen the light of day. I also greatly thank Kirill Levinson and Susanne Schattenberg for helping to organize my stays at their respective institutions. In addition, a grant offered by the Zeit Stiftung Ebelin und Gerd Bucerius in the framework of the program "Trajectories of Change" allowed me to write up my manuscript and to attend the Foundation's stimulating conferences. Finally, funding from the History Department at the Geneva Graduate Institute allowed me to travel to the Hoover Institution Archives.

I would like to address special thanks to my Russian and Ukrainian friends, for hosting me during my research stays in Moscow and for their assistance with interview transcriptions: Katia Nazarova; Katia Samarina and her parents; Mariia Burtseva.

Finally, I am most grateful to my husband Pierre for his patient support and love.

Note on Transliteration and Abbreviations

Note on Transliteration

The system of Romanization of the Cyrillic alphabet used here conforms to the most recent standards of the Library of Congress (LOC), commonly used in English. However, as a matter of convenience, and in keeping with the common usage, the diacritic signs such as ĭ (for й) or t͡s (for ц) have been omitted.

Nevertheless, in the body of the text, some commonly known names whose standard spelling differs from the LOC standard have been written using the spelling most familiar to the readers (e.g., Roy Medvedev instead of Roi Medvedev; Trotsky instead of Trotskii).

Bibliographical references in Russian have also been transliterated using the LOC standard, whereas Russian names in non-Russian references have been left in the transliteration system chosen by the publisher.

Note on Abbreviations

Archive denominations

Conventional archival abbreviations in Russian: F. (*fond*): Archival fond; Op. (*opis'*): finding aid; D. (*delo*): file; l. (*list*): page.

BDIC:	Bibliothèque de Documentation Internationale Contemporaine, Université de Nanterre (France).
HIA:	Hoover Institution Archive, Stanford University, California (United States).
HU OSA RFE/RL RI:	Open Society Archive, Central European University, Budapest (Hungary); Radio Free Europe/Radio Liberty Research Institute.
OKhDLSM:	Otdel Khraneniia Dokumentov Lichnykh Sobranii Moskvy (Department of Conservation of Documents of Private Collection of Moscow), part of the Moscow City Archive (Russia). The references given for the Fond 333 (Roi i Zhores Medvedevy) are not permanent references, but are based on the "*sdatochnye opisi*" (sd. op.) ("submission inventories") and the files are "*uslovnye dela*" (u.d.) ("provisional files").

Personal Papers
of A.V. A-O: Personal papers of Anton Vladimirovich Antonov-Ovseenko. At the time of this research, these papers were not part of an archive but were made available to me by Antonov-Ovseenko himself. The references are therefore limited to a short description of the document and its date.
RGANI: Rossiiskii Gosudarstvennnyi Arkhiv Noveishei Istorii (Russian State Archive of Contemporary History), Moscow (Russia).
RGASPI: Rossiiskii Gosudarstvennyi Arkhiv Sotsial'no-Politicheskoi Istorii (Russian State Archive of Social-Political History), Moscow (Russia).

Other abbreviations

APN: *Agentstvo Pechati "Novosti"*: Soviet Publication Agency "News" in charge of publishing propaganda material aimed towards the Western bloc.
CPSU: Communist Party of the Soviet Union.
IML: Institute of Marxism-Leninism.
KGB: *Komitet Gosudarstvennoi Bezopasnosti*: Committee of State Security (Soviet political police, also called Cheka, OGPU, NKVD).
NKID: *Narodnyi Kommissariat Inostrannykh Del*: People's Commissariat (Ministry) of Foreign Affairs.
NKVD: *Narodnyi Kommissariat Vnutrennykh Del*: People's Commissariat (Ministry) of Internal Affairs (Soviet political police, also called Cheka, OGPU, KGB).
PCC: *Komitet Partiinogo Kontrolia*: Party Control Committee.
POUM: *Partido Obrero De Unificación Marxista*: Workers' Party Of Marxist Unification (Political Party During The Spanish Civil War).
RSFSR: Russian Soviet Federative Socialist Republic.
TASS: *Telegrafnoe Agentstvo Sovetskogo Soiuza*: Soviet News Agency.
TsK: *Tsentral'nyi Komitet*: Central Committee of the Communist Party of the Soviet Union.

Introduction

On January 18, 1974, Aleksandr Solzhenitsyn made a public appeal protesting the media hate campaign against him and *The Gulag Archipelago*. A few months earlier, the KGB had seized a copy of the manuscript, after brutally interrogating and driving to suicide one of the writer's assistants. Within a few days, Solzhenitsyn had been informed of the tragedy and had sent word to the West for the publication of his book. On December 28, 1973, the first volume of this 1,800-page literary research appeared in Paris, making headlines worldwide. In the Soviet Union, however, the media branded Solzhenitsyn as a traitor, grossly misrepresenting his work, which remained inaccessible to Soviet readers. In his appeal, Solzhenitsyn expressed his disbelief in the face of this public outpouring of hatred. He had not expected such a radical renunciation of previous acknowledgments of the regime's crimes. The campaign against him showed "how tenaciously [the Soviet leaders] cling to the bloody past and how they want to drag it with them, like a sealed up pack, into the future."[1] A few weeks later, the writer was arrested and deported from the USSR—a measure applied for the first time against a political opponent since Lev Trotsky's expulsion in 1929.

With *The Gulag Archipelago*'s publication and Solzhenitsyn's arrest, the confrontation between the Soviet regime and the man who had become its dissident number one reached its peak. At stake in this conflict was the monopoly over history, which the Soviet leaders sought to enforce in the face of mounting challenges from dissident authors who circulated their writings underground and published them in the West. With the denunciation of Stalin's "personality cult" at the 20th Congress of the Communist Party, in 1956, Nikita Khrushchev had sought to control a process of revelations about the regime's past crimes, which he knew could not be evaded. Instead of neutralizing a dangerous theme, however, he opened a Pandora's box, which soon escaped his control. By the 1960s, following the bolder de-Stalinization course launched by the 22nd Party Congress, professional historians, writers, and philosophers, had begun to study the so-called blank spots of Soviet history and to draw embarrassing conclusions. In the first half of the 1960s, new publications in the literary and historical fields opened up hitherto taboo pages of the past to Soviet readers, from the history of the Gulag camps to the early Soviet defeats in the Second World War.

As Leonid Brezhnev replaced Khrushchev at the Party's helm in 1964, however, a new ideological wind began to blow. Despite persistent rumors concerning the new leaders' alleged plan to rehabilitate Stalin at the 23rd Party Congress, the Stalin question remained unsettled, and past Congress resolutions continued to apply. Nevertheless, literary works depicting the Stalin era in dark shades were progressively excluded from print and the meager flow of revisionist historical publications dried up. As repression against historians increased, most of them toed the line and relegated their unpublished manuscripts to the drawer, fearing dismissal from comfortable positions. Yet a minority of authors refused to renounce the prospect of publication and turned their sights to the West. This choice was not without consequences and could potentially trigger repression. Over time, many dissident authors published in the West would be compelled to emigrate or be arrested.

The history of Soviet dissent has traditionally been studied through the deformative lens of Soviet repressive policies, portraying dissidents both as heroes and victims. This research offers a new approach and characterizes the relationship between the authorities and dissident researchers as one of progressive mutual estrangement, conditioned both by a change in official policy and a radicalization of dissident discourse. Initially, historical research on the dark pages of the Soviet past benefited from an incontrovertible legitimacy, born from the resolutions of two Party Congresses. However, as censorship tightened, and pro-Stalinist discourse became ubiquitous in Soviet press, dissident researchers radicalized their discourse, greatly expanding on Khrushchev's limited critique, and eventually turned to the West to publish their works. I argue that it was thus a self-reinforcing dynamic of estrangement, rather than a purely repressive policy, that turned these authors into dissidents.

By renouncing any overt ideological revisionism on the Stalin question, the Brezhnev leadership adopted a posture of ambiguity, which served its stabilization objectives and endowed it with greater flexibility to chart a compromise course in the moving ideological sands of the post-Khrushchev era. Yet, ironically, dissent could also thrive on such spaces of ambiguity and harness the legitimizing potential of official discourse for its own aims. Just as human rights activists followed the "legalist" strategy of "civil obedience" launched by Aleksandr Esenin-Vol'pin, calling on the authorities to abide by their own laws, anti-Stalinists and dissident researchers who wished to shed light on Stalin's crimes could call on the Party to observe its past Congress resolutions.[2] Thus doing, dissidents acted upon official discourse in creative ways, which hardly coincided with the regime's stated and implicit objectives. Nevertheless, the dissidents' legitimacy claim allowed them to federate largely around their projects and to enlist as supporters countless intellectuals and Party members. This strategy, coupled to the divisive nature of the Stalin question and the authorities' misgivings about fully belying their past anti-Stalinist verve, conditioned the state's response to the dissidents' action. As long as they remained within a gray zone and adhered, at least in words, to the canons of past Congress resolutions, dissident researchers could hope to avert repression and get away with mere intimidation measures. However, when they turned to the West as an outlet for their works after being excluded from print in the USSR, they incurred accusations of instrumentalization by the adverse ideological camp—an indictment with potentially severe consequences. It would take two decades and the advent of Perestroika for the Soviet regime to fully acknowledge again the legitimacy of anti-Stalinist narratives and for the works of dissident researchers to be allowed into print in the Soviet Union.

Dissident historians therefore deserve attention not only as individuals, but also as a group, which collectively challenged the Soviet authorities to pursue the de-Stalinization course launched by the Khrushchev leadership and to abide by its past promises in relation to Stalin's victims. This study is the first to identify this group and to examine these figures jointly. In addition, this research also adds up to our reflection on Soviet dissent as a historical phenomenon and offers a new lens of analysis, by examining the process of *becoming* a dissident. I argue that dissent was not a state of mind, a set of views or actions, but a personal trajectory, which was determined both by an individual's *persistent* will to act according to his/her consciousness and by the evolution of the political context, which determined the labeling of such actions as subversive and the degree of repression to be meted out to their authors. This dynamic approach to dissent allows me to account for the existence of a variety of degrees and stages of dissent, which have hitherto eluded any consensual definition. As I examine the trajectories of four dissident authors from the early 1960s, when they were, or hoped to be published legally in the USSR, to the 1970s, when they faced repression for publishing more radical works abroad, I interrogate the interaction of personal and political factors that led to this dramatic shift. Why did these authors, who chose a strategy of legality in the early 1960s, refuse to toe the line when the ideological climate changed in the mid-1960s? Which stages did they go through, as they progressively became estranged from the system they had once been part of? And how did their eventual exit from the official realm, through inner emigration or exile, influence their work conditions? I argue that Khrushchev's policy of de-Stalinization was initially a potent trigger for the emergence of these works, but that the more repressive climate of the late 1960s, while it effectively muzzled the majority of dissenting voices, only emboldened the subjects of this research. Expulsion from the Party and from professional unions or the loss of employment were warning signals, which dissidents chose to disregard, exposing themselves to further repression. Eventually, the only alternative was between exile and inner emigration, the latter option being, more often than not, an antechamber to arrest.

Second, this study contributes to scholarship on Soviet historical writing by identifying dissident historical research as a specific genre, distinct both from Soviet revisionist historiography of the 1960s, which Roger Markwick has examined,[3] and from literary and autobiographical dissident works dealing with the same subjects. Western historiography, while praising the courage of dissident authors, has generally been dismissive of this body of texts, which did not fit traditional scholarly standards, failing to grasp the specificity of their ethical and political functions as devices of "truth-telling." How can we explain the emergence of this genre and which personal and political circumstances influenced it? What were its main defining characteristics and to what extent did it differ from traditional historiography, both Western and Soviet? And given the specific functions of dissident histories, how successful were they in achieving their authors' aims? I argue that an important defining characteristic of such works was the heavy reliance on oral testimonies and memoirs, particularly of victims of political repression. These oral and written accounts not only allowed dissident authors to supplement the lack of access to archives, but also endowed these histories with greater symbolic legitimacy and moral weight as collective monuments to the Stalin-era victims.

Filtered through the authors' own subjectivities and political views, these testimonies also gave dissident works a particular ideological coloration. Dissident authors claimed to be "restoring historical truth," but these truths were often at odds with each other, incomplete, subjective, and sometimes self-censored to fit the author's political or personal agenda. As I evaluate the impact of dissident histories on Soviet society, I argue that their significance was eventually more moral than political. Politically, these works conveyed diverging messages, which sometimes undermined their claim to truth-telling. Their moral dimension, however, was obvious both to Soviet and Western observers, and it superseded concerns for factual accuracy, which did surface in scholarly critiques of these works. Their reception during Perestroika confirms this eventual supremacy of the moral over the political: dissident histories were belatedly published in the USSR and could hardly offer any new revelations. They did not shake the political system the way they would have a decade earlier. Yet their moral weight, reinforced by the status of outcast of their authors, remained intact.

Finally, this research contributes to a reevaluation of the history of late Soviet society and politics. Since the end of the Cold War, newly available archival sources and new scholarly approaches have allowed for a collective reexamination of the Khrushchev and Brezhnev eras, making place for greater nuances and calling into question both the alleged "liberalism" of the Khrushchevian "Thaw" and the "stagnating" nature of the Brezhnev years. In the study of Soviet dissent, once a highly ideologized question, black and white tones have also given way to a grayscale. While I still find the ideological rupture between the two periods relevant for the question of historical writing on the Stalin era, I also underscore the societal dynamism of the Brezhnev years. By calling attention to the question of dissident networking within the Soviet Union, I question traditional representations of dissidents as courageous but isolated individuals fighting single-handedly a monolithic authoritarian state. While networks of dissidents in relation with the West, such as the Helsinki Watch groups,[4] have been the object of much scholarly attention, the interactions between open dissidents and figures of the Soviet political and intellectual establishment have remained out of focus. This study is therefore original in examining these networks and in interrogating how these relations influenced the content of dissident histories, but also the fate of their authors. In my analysis of protests against Stalin's rehabilitation in the 1960s, I show how the support of prominent figures of the intelligentsia initially lent weight to what was widely considered a legitimate political cause, but I also argue that these protests were most effective when they aimed at shielding an individual from repression, such as was the case in the Nekrich Affair. Another finding of this research is the personal contacts between reformists within the Communist Party apparatus and such a dissident as Roy Medvedev, which testify to the ideological affinities between individuals with seemingly opposed trajectories.

In my analysis of the shift of the ideological line on the Stalin question in the early Brezhnev era, I also bring new nuances to this widely discussed question, on the basis of some new archival sources and testimonies. While the dissident narrative according to which Brezhnev had sought to rehabilitate Stalin generally went unquestioned in the West, I draw attention instead to the conflicts between various factions within the leadership and to the ultimate role of Brezhnev as consensus-builder. While flirting with pro-Stalinist elements whom he appointed to key positions in the ideological field, Brezhnev fell short of rehabilitating Stalin, anticipating the divisive nature of this move, but he did exclude from the public space discussion about the most embarrassing pages of the Soviet past, in order to safeguard the regime's internal stability. And yet these struggles behind the scene are significant for the fate of dissident historians, as they underscored the lasting ideological legitimacy of anti-Stalinism and the ideological proximity between in-system reforming elements and dissidents on this federating question.

Still, repression against dissident historical research was the logical outcome of the reaffirmation of the state's monopoly over history. The study of archival documents now allows for a partial reconstruction of Soviet decision-making in relation to dissident authors, revealing the complexity of handling high-profile cases in a context of political détente with the West and the diverse approaches to some divisive cases among Soviet leaders. While many dark zones remain, these sources allow us to go beyond the apparent contradiction between the treatment of Solzhenitsyn, branded as traitor in the press and expelled from the Soviet Union, and of Medvedev, a more moderate critic, who was de facto allowed to publish his works in the West for decades. Indeed, repression was never indiscriminate, and depended on such factors as the degree of radicality of the published works, but also the dissident's popularity in the West and within Soviet society.

Four figures occupy the center-stage of this research: Aleksandr Solzhenitsyn, Roy Medvedev, Anton Antonov-Ovseenko, and Aleksandr Nekrich. They constitute a heterogeneous body of authors, with diverse professional and personal backgrounds, different life trajectories, and various ideological proclivities. What did unite them, however, was a striving to publish their research on the so-called blank spots of the Soviet past, first by seeking to push back the limits of what could be legally published in the Soviet Union, and then, when censorship was tightened, by turning to the West as an outlet for their research, either in *tamizdat*, the publication by Western editors of uncensored Soviet works, or from exile. Moreover, theirs were ambitious studies based on a substantial body of sources collected for the most part within the USSR, and not mere political, philosophical, or historical essays of the kind that then flourished in *samizdat*, the underground network of diffusion of uncensored literature. As I chose to restrict myself to Soviet dissident authors from the Russian Soviet Federative Socialist Republic, having published original research on Stalin-era history in the West from the 1960s to the 1980s, these four researchers stood out as the most significant figures of the period, both in terms of their fame in the West and popularity within the Soviet Union during Perestroika. They were certainly not the only ones involved in uncensored historical writing, but their works reached a much broader audience, received international acclaim, and had some degree of influence.

Yet the differences between these figures are no less significant than what unites them. Their experience of Stalin-era terror, direct for Solzhenitsyn and Antonov-Ovseenko, who were former political prisoners, and indirect for Medvedev, whose father died in the Gulag, influenced the radicality of their writings. Their professional background also determined their degree of adherence to scholarly norms: Nekrich was a professional historian, while Solzhenitsyn was a writer; Medvedev had a training in history and philosophy and a PhD in pedagogical sciences; Antonov-Ovseenko studied history before his arrest but remained an independent scholar. Their political convictions, ranging from Medvedev's reformist communism to Solzhenitsyn's Orthodox Russophile views, also had a pervasive influence on their writings. Finally, as individuals, their diverse life choices and strategies of action influenced their trajectories: Nekrich privileged legality and emigrated before giving free rein to his scholarly ambitions; Medvedev chose inner emigration but navigated skillfully, keeping sight of the "red line" at all time to evade repression; whereas Solzhenitsyn willfully ignored any warning and defied the leadership until his expulsion from the USSR. The differences between these authors show the various ideological, personal, and ethical motivations that led individuals to undertake research on the dark pages of the Soviet past and the different forms that their search for "historical truth" took. Although all of them reacted to what they perceived as a falsified official history, their understanding of "truth" varied, triggering conflicts of interpretation based on their political views and different levels of adherence to scholarly norms. Yet such divergences were also the reflection of a broader intellectual search for new meanings and new identities that would blossom in Soviet print during Perestroika. Making sense of the Stalin-era terror was a fundamental task for Soviet society, and the various responses dissident researchers offered to this question also pointed to different political models they aspired to.

Beyond these differences, the similarities of trajectories of dissident researchers also hint to what set them apart from the human rights movement, with which they had personal connections and affinities. While both groups were driven by ethical motives, dissident historians did not consider themselves as activists, but primarily as authors and researchers, whose instrument of action was the written Word. They chose to engage in an activity they perceived as legitimate, politically and morally necessary and significant. What influenced their trajectory, then, was the interaction between a personal experience of Stalin-era repression, an intellectual background, often coupled to a historical training, and strong political and moral convictions. In my portrayal of dissident authors, I sought to go beyond Cold War era clichés, conveyed not only by Western media, but often by the dissidents' own memoirs, framed in the dominant "David against Goliath" narrative. Indeed, beyond their astounding courage and moral stance, dissidents were sometimes driven by less avowable motives, such as the thirst for revenge, and blinkered by ideological biases.

Note on methodology and sources

Despite its ideological coloration and lack of a consensual definition,[5] I have used the term "dissident" to qualify my research subjects. Indeed, they were not simply researchers writing about Soviet history in the absence of access to archives. They were politically active citizens who considered that shedding light on the past was a significant contribution they could make to the struggle for the democratization, or the abolition, of the Soviet regime. By deliberately challenging the state monopoly on history production, and by taking up this self-assumed role, they de facto adopted a posture of dissent. Because they considered that state-controlled history had failed to tackle crucial spheres of the past, they felt the duty to endorse a role for which they understood that they were not the best equipped, but that they nonetheless were the only ones willing to perform.

Two dimensions of dissent are significant for this research. The first is the personal dimension, the impact of dissent on the life of individuals. At this level, a "dissident" is someone who repeatedly and consciously violates the regime's legal norms or accepted rules of social behavior out of moral, political, religious, or ideological motives, deliberately incurring political repression.[6] Dissidence is thus a *type of behavior*, rather than a *way of being or thinking*, as implied by the Russian term *inakomysliashchii* (literally: "one who thinks differently").

The second is the collective dimension, the transformative effects on society. From this point of view, dissent is constituted, following Detlef Pollack's and Jan Wielgohs's definition, by "all discourses and activities critical of the regime that constituted, or wished to constitute, an autonomous sphere of public, political and cultural communication outside of the official institutions of the party state and which in so doing openly denied the claim of the regime to full control of public life."[7] In other words, collective dissent creates alternative public spheres of communication, breaking the monopoly of the totalitarian regime over the production of public discourse.[8]

Nevertheless, I also understand the limitations of the term, which implies the existence of strict binaries, whereas the image of a continuum from loyalty to dissent would be more accurate. As Roger Markwick has pointed out in his study on Soviet revisionist historians, the more vocal dissent of such actors as Roy Medvedev or Aleksandr Solzhenitsyn emerged on the fertile ground of intellectual nonconformism of the 1960s.[9] This research underscores this deep connection, by showing the link between the action of dissident researchers and developments within Soviet intellectual life. The figure of Aleksandr Nekrich, a nonconformist professional historian, conveniently bridges these two worlds. The "Nekrich Affair" constitutes a central focal point of this research: protests against the historian's exclusion from the Communist Party within the academic community and beyond thus demonstrated the porosity and mutual interactions of groups variously integrated into the system. Furthermore, Nekrich himself wavered between the poles of loyalty and dissent, showing the need to go beyond dichotomous categories.

Another important concept for this research is that of the intelligentsia, a collective designation which also lacks a consensual definition. In the nineteenth century, the intelligentsia was defined as "the educated critics of the Russian social and political order,"[10] playing the role of "conscience of the nation"[11] and "spokespersons of the masses."[12] Or, in Inna Kochetkova's more succinct definition: "A group of people who saw themselves as separate and alienated from the rest of society due to their higher level of education and the progressive ideology they subscribed to."[13] In the Soviet Union, however, the intelligentsia was redefined and broadened, to include all "people who are occupied professionally with mental labor."[14] This group swelled both as a result of mass access to education and of the growing need of an industrializing state for technical and administrative cadres. Consequently, the intelligentsia lost its potential for protest and thirst for truth, as it became diluted in a broader white-collar stratum. I would argue for a definition straddling these two extremes and allowing for greater ideological diversity: not all white collars belonged to the intelligentsia, but not all intellectuals were liberal. The intelligentsia, then, could be defined as being formed by individuals who, by their intellectual profession, by their higher education, or by their social origin, were inclined to critically engage in, and contribute to current social, political, cultural, and philosophical debates. Dissident authors were thus by definition members of the intelligentsia, and so were, as a rule, their readers, at least in the Brezhnev era, when the circulation of samizdat and tamizdat was largely limited to intelligentsia circles.

As intellectuals, dissident researchers left an abundant trail of memoirs, correspondence, essays, drafts, and other writings, which constitute precious sources for the historian. Research over the very rich Roy and Zhores Medvedev archival fond at the Moscow City Archive and the Aleksandr Nekrich papers at the Stanford Hoover Institution Archives was completed by the Medvedev brothers' autobiographical writings and interviews with them, as well as Nekrich and his colleagues' memoirs.[15] When I started this research, I also had the chance of meeting Anton Antonov-Ovseenko, who was in the last year of his life. He gave me an interview and access to his personal papers, which yielded some very interesting sources. One of the limits of my work, however, was the lack of access to Aleksandr Solzhenitsyn's papers, although this was partly supplemented by published archival sources and interviews with two of his closest assistants, Elena Chukovskaia and Nadezhda Levitskaia.[16] Finally, these personal sources were supplemented by research in Russian state archives and samizdat depositories at "Memorial" in Moscow and at the Open Society Archives in Budapest.

The necessity of relying on such subjective sources as memoirs and interviews, admittedly, presents some pitfalls. In Medvedev's case, his words can often be checked against written documents from the time, especially his very extensive correspondence with his brother for the years 1973–89. The same applies to the Medvedevs' memoirs, which were written on the basis of primary sources, heavily quoted from and footnoted. This is not the case for Antonov-Ovseenko, whose oral and written recollections can rarely be checked against alternative sources and are clearly to be handled with caution. Whenever necessary I have made it clear that the information provided was open to questioning and that I was unable to verify it. Interviews with two of his relatives helped clear some of these blind spots, though by far not all of them, and documents from state archives provide a more objective account of some episodes. Nekrich's memoirs are also an ambivalent source. While they were certainly written with a historian's concern for factual accuracy, close enough to the events related, in the early 1970s, the context of their publication probably influenced their tone. At the time, Nekrich was applying for political asylum in the United States and seeking to demonstrate that, despite his past Communist Party membership, he had indeed been a dissident. This likely led him to overemphasize his past record of dissent. Finally, Solzhenitsyn's memoirs are also a source to be considered with circumspection, as they sometimes conflict with the evidence we have, but they do offer his own perspective on events.[17] More reliable, or at least more dispassionate, are his memoirs on his secret helpers, his "invisible allies."[18]

This study is structured along the main argument and follows the evolution of dissident researchers through various stages: from the official realm to the underground publishing world, and from an exit from the system through exile or inner emigration to a reintegration into the Soviet official sphere. The structure is both chronological and thematical: while the first chapter focuses on dissident researchers' attempts at finding an accommodation with censorship, Chapters 2 and 3 examine changes in the political and societal sphere, which in turn triggered a radicalization of the discourse of dissident authors, a phenomenon examined in the fourth chapter. The process of exit from Soviet official sphere is examined in Chapters 5 and 6, which focus on samizdat and tamizdat as manifestations of authors' and readers' desire to counter censorship, but also the sanctions incurred by authors who published in tamizdat. Life in exile and inner emigration then constituted the ultimate stage of this process. Chapter 7 examines the conflicts between dissident researchers and reactions of Western audiences to these works, emphasizing the characteristics of dissident histories as a specific genre, a theme already broached in Chapter 4. Finally, the eighth chapter examines the reception of dissident histories in the Soviet Union during Perestroika.

This account may not fully do justice to the multifaceted trajectories of these four authors. It has been my objective to go beyond the binary Cold War lens, with its focus on embattled dissidents allied with the West against Soviet totalitarian rulers, leaving Soviet society out of the picture altogether. Instead, I show how these researchers only progressively drifted into dissent, as a result of their determination to shed light on the past, out of personal, moral, or political reasons. Inserted within networks of supporters on both sides of the Iron Curtain, they played an astute game between East and West, using publication in tamizdat to reach their target audience in the Soviet Union. Neither victims nor heroes, they were courageous bearers of their own "truth" about a traumatic past that continued to weigh down on Soviet society, despite attempts to hush it up.

1

The Party's Call to Denounce Stalin's Crimes

In the spring of 1956, Roy Medvedev, then a young school headmaster, was among millions of Party members, communist youth (Komsomol) activists, civil servants, and workers summoned throughout the country to a reading of Nikita Khrushchev's report "On the Cult of Personality and Its Consequences."[1] For four hours, the dumbfounded audience stood listening, frozen in horror, before dispersing individually without a word.[2] Medvedev was not the only one confused by the revelations. In the coming months and years, Soviet society was confronted with a reappraisal of two decades of its history, to a reassigning of labels and moral assessments: if the "enemies of the people" were innocent victims, then who was to blame? Could the guilt for the death of millions really be assigned to a single figure? And how was the responsibility of the Party to be evaluated?

Nowhere was the confusion concerning the revision of the past greater than among historians. Until then, the field of "Party history," dealing with the post-1917 period, had been entirely dominated by Stalin's *Short Course on the History of the Communist Party (Bolsheviks)*. This textbook, published under Stalin's name and close supervision in 1938, glorified the Soviet leader's victory over his political opponents and exalted his alleged achievements. From then on, according to Roger Markwick, the *Short Course* achieved "biblical status" and "established the *paradigm* within which all other historical writing was confined."[3] Crucially, in the Secret Speech, Khrushchev directly attacked the *Short Course* as an embodiment of Stalin's personality cult, and argued for the need to write "a new textbook on the history of our party."[4] And he had precise guidelines for historians: Stalin's personality cult was a distortion, an "illness," which had to be cured for the Party to move forward. Not only was there a stark boundary separating Leninism from Stalinism, but the Stalin era was divided between an early period, until 1934, when Stalin played a positive role in his struggle against the intraparty oppositions, and a later period, dominated by the excesses of the personality cult. By shedding the most obvious distortions that had discredited Party history, Khrushchev wished to reclaim for history the central role in Party politics and propaganda that it had played under Stalin and enhance its power of indoctrination. Thus doing, however, he was opening a "Pandora's Box."[5] He envisioned a controlled shift of narrative within a fundamentally unchanged framework, whereas a number of historians interpreted de-Stalinization as a liberalization of the historical field.

The 22nd Party Congress, in 1961, took de-Stalinization one step further, giving anti-Stalinists new grounds for hope. This time, Khrushchev denounced Stalin-era crimes openly and unequivocally. The newspapers were filled with the fiery speeches uttered at the Congress. Nevertheless, the First Secretary was careful to subsume the history of repression under an optimistic narrative involving the guiding hand of the Party, leading Soviet society along the glorious path to communism.[6] Through the unveiling of "historical truth," the Party would emerge fortified and cleansed: it was necessary to "record truthfully" all past crimes "so that phenomena of this sort can never be repeated in the future."[7] Turning words into deeds, the Congress ordered that Stalin's remains be removed from Lenin's Mausoleum on Red Square and reburied by the Kremlin wall.[8] Soon afterward, cities throughout the USSR were stripped of Stalin's name and those of his closest collaborators': most notoriously, the glorious city of Stalingrad became Volgograd.

In the historical field as well, the wind of change was blowing. In December 1962, an "All-Union Conference to Improve the Training of Scientific-Pedagogical Cadres in the Historical Sciences" was convened in Moscow.[9] Two thousand historians attended this unprecedented event, which gave a forum to many grievances relating to the state of the historical field in the post-Stalin era. The very fact that such a diversity of opinions was given free expression in an official framework was in itself remarkable. Yet the divisions and the pessimistic observations on the state of historical scholarship testified to a failure of the profession to face up to the challenges of a change of paradigm.

The 20th and 22nd Party Congresses established the legitimacy of anti-Stalinist narratives. Yet from the onset the discrepancy between the official objective of affirming a new, unified, and ideologized discourse about the Stalin era, and the desire of historians to free themselves from the shackles of Stalin's *Short Course* conditioned the birth of dissident histories. Whether they were professional historians, like Nekrich, or independent researchers, like Roy Medvedev, the authors examined in this chapter felt inclined to interpret official calls for new narratives about the Stalin era in creative ways. In rupture with previous practices, they understood Khrushchev's speech not as a final document, a catechism to be memorized and repeated unreflexively, but as an impulse for further research. Moreover, they sought to expand the scope of what remained a selective indictment. Khrushchev had targeted only crimes committed between 1934 and 1953, at the height of Stalin's personal power. He could not afford to question the ruthless collectivization of Soviet agriculture with the arrests of millions of "kulaks" (rich peasants), which had triggered a devastating famine. Nor did he have the courage to rehabilitate Stalin's opponents: the "Leftist" opposition of Grigorii Zinoviev and Lev Kamenev, the "Rightist" opposition of Nikolai Bukharin, and the archenemy, Lev Trotsky. No less problematic was Khrushchev's attempt to whitewash the Party itself by attributing the responsibility for political repression solely to Stalin and, to a lesser extent, Beria.

Even as they ostensibly played by the rules, seeking publication in the Soviet Union, dissident researchers already acted as independent players, for aims they had self-defined. Nekrich published his study on the onset of the German attack on the USSR outside of his institute's publishing plans. Medvedev undertook his research on Stalinism in his free time. Antonov-Ovseenko wrote of his own initiative a biography of his father to commemorate the repressed revolutionary. They acted out of political, memorial, and ethical motives. Yet their willingness to play by the rules of the system also conditioned the limits of their independence: those imposed by censorship, self-censorship, and the use of censored sources. Their narratives may strike us as tame or even strikingly orthodox, yet for the time they raised bold questions, only sugarcoated in the appropriate ideological formulas. While Nekrich and Antonov-Ovseenko passed the test of publication before a change in the official line, Medvedev did not, probably because the scope of his research was the most ambitious of all and asked bold questions, not only about the past, but also about the future politics of the Party, which the Soviet leadership was not prepared to answer.

Anton Antonov-Ovseenko's duty to his father

"A son does not answer for his father"

Anton Antonov-Ovseenko was born in 1920 with a glorious surname. His father, Vladimir Antonov-Ovseenko (1884–1938), was a famous revolutionary who had led the storming of the Winter Palace in Petrograd on October 25, 1917, and arrested the Provisional government. Active in the revolutionary movement since he was seventeen, he joined the Russian Social Democratic Labor Party (RSDRP) a year later. By the time he joined the Bolsheviks in 1917, he had survived several arrests and a death sentence, performed a spectacular prison escape, and spent seven years in emigration in Paris. His organizational and oratorical skills were soon acknowledged: elected head of the Executive Committee of the North Region at the Congress of the Soviet of Workers' and Soldiers' Deputies, he played a prominent role in the organization of the October Revolution in Petrograd.[10] After the Revolution, he took an active part in the struggle against anti-Bolshevik forces on the Ukrainian and Southern fronts, but also internally, in Tambov, where he participated in violently crushing Antonov's peasant rebellion.[11] As the Civil War came to an end, he organized famine relief in the Samara region. Eventually, Trotsky placed him as the head of the Revolutionary Military Council's Political Department. This proximity with Stalin's future number one opponent proved fateful: in 1923, Antonov-Ovseenko signed Trotsky's appeal, later known as the "Declaration of 46," calling for greater party democracy. The consequences were soon to be felt: in 1924, the revolutionary was appointed Soviet consul in Prague, and subsequently in Lithuania and Poland—a diplomatic exile that did not end with his public repentance, in 1928.

By 1934, however, Antonov-Ovseenko had regained his political clout and returned to Moscow as chief prosecutor of the Russian Soviet Federative Socialist Republic (RSFSR). His revolutionary memoirs, published in 1933, reflected his complete submission to Stalin's rule, with a due indictment of Trotsky and genuflection before Stalin's "huge role" in the Revolution's success.[12] During the Spanish Civil War, he was appointed Soviet consul in Barcelona, serving as an adviser and supervising weapon deliveries to the Popular Front, while demonstrating his anti-Trotskyite zeal against the POUM.[13] Yet this did not save him from sharing the fate of his revolutionary comrades. The summons to Moscow and appointment as People's Commissar for Justice of the RSFSR in September 1937 proved a mere diversion tactic. Arrested a month later,

Antonov-Ovseenko was tried in February 1938 by a military court (*voenkollegiia*). He recanted previous confessions given during the investigation, probably under torture.[14] Before being led away to execution, in February 1938, as his young cellmate Iurii Tomskii recalled, he solemnly proclaimed: "I ask whoever recovers liberty to tell the world that Antonov-Ovseenko was a Bolshevik and remained a Bolshevik until the last day."[15]

His son Anton grew up abroad, with his father's second family, having lost his mother early on: this fiery, possibly mentally ill, woman was arrested in 1929, and committed suicide in prison seven years later.[16] The young man was studying history at the Moscow Pedagogical Institute when his father was recalled from Spain and arrested. His expulsion from the Komsomol, following his refusal to condemn publicly his father, might have led to further retributions. However, he claims he was saved by Stalin's latest slogan: "A son does not answer for his father," and the attempt to exclude him from the Institute failed. Unaware of his father's execution and convinced that his condemnation resulted from a mistake, Antonov-Ovseenko still revered Stalin. Ironically, in 1939, he worked as an art museum guide and oversaw the preparation of an exhibition in honor of Stalin's sixtieth birthday. "The victory of Stalinism, the unity of the party and the people, the warmest patriotism—all of this I perceived as the only possible reality," he recalled.[17]

In 1940, Anton Antonov-Ovseenko was arrested on criminal charges, for his alleged complicity in two comrades' shady business transactions.[18] First condemned to an eighteen-month prison term, he was released on November 1, 1940, after his sentence was annulled by an appeals court. Yet the judgment was overturned by the Supreme Court of the Republic and on June 22, 1941, he was rearrested and served his sentence in the Gulag.[19] Liberated in January 1943, the young man took the risk of returning to

Figure 1.1 Anton Antonov-Ovseenko with his father's portrait by Iurii Annenkov in the background, 1985. Courtesy of the Gulag Museum.

Moscow, only to undergo a second arrest in August. This time, as the son of an "enemy of the people," he faced political charges: article 58, points 10 (anti-Soviet agitation) and 8 (anti-Soviet terror activity). However, Antonov-Ovseenko protested the charges, pointing out his near blindness.[20] The accusation of terrorism was eventually dropped, but he received an eight-year term, based on incriminations of a prison cellmate and of his former roommate, Sergei Fukel'man, employed by the NKVD to inform on him since 1938, as Anton found out half a century later.[21]

Antonov-Ovseenko eventually spent ten years in the Vorkuta and Pechora Gulag camps, in the Great North. Paradoxically, he attributed his survival to his invalidity, but also his story-telling, singing, and acting skills, which mostly kept him from the deadly "common works," such as wood felling.[22] When he was liberated, in 1953, his passport contained a stamp forbidding him from living in the thirty-nine largest Soviet cities. His narrative of those years emphasizes the instability of his situation, as he moved from Pechora to the Crimea, where he worked as cultural activities organizer in several resorts, "losing" his passport several times to avoid being identified. Finally, in Abkhazia, he claims that he somehow managed to obtain a "clean" passport and recovered some peace of mind.[23]

It was there that, in 1956, he heard that Anastas Mikoian had publicly rehabilitated Vladimir Antonov-Ovseenko at the 20th Party Congress, anticipating Khrushchev's Secret Speech.[24] This opened the way for Anton's own rehabilitation, but did not help him obtain the Moscow registration he had lost following his arrest. "Moscow is not made of rubber," allegedly replied the Soviet official he solicited.[25] Until 1963, Antonov-Ovseenko lived in Tambov, where his son Anton was born in 1962.[26] Only belatedly did the historian decide to lobby higher instances to obtain an apartment and a registration in the capital. Although he arrived well after the short-lived wave of compensations in regard to victims of political repression, he eventually received a one-room apartment.[27] As a personal pensioner of All-Union importance, member of the All-Union Society of the Blind, he could live on his small pension.[28] Yet he remained unsatisfied by the meager compensations received for the loss of his youth and his father's execution.

Half-measures in the public rehabilitation of victims of terror

In the early 1960s many rehabilitated Old Bolsheviks—veterans of the Revolution who had been unjustly repressed during the Stalin era—were symbolically reintegrated into the public sphere. Those famous names that had vanished from print for several decades now reappeared: the press commemorated their birthdays, resurrecting to public memory their revolutionary achievements, and museums or exhibitions opened in their native towns. However, this posthumous public rehabilitation concerned only a portion of the purge victims, and mostly resulted from lobbying from relatives and groups of Old Bolsheviks. Each case was the object of thorough discussion in higher Party instances: did their past merits outweigh their errors, or was their biography permanently stained by past incriminations, regardless of their official rehabilitation?

Such was Vladimir Antonov-Ovseenko's case. Although he was generally acknowledged as one of the outstanding figures of the Revolution, and his memoirs on this period had been reissued in 1957, the labels of "Menshevik" and "Trotskyist" continued to be attached to him. In 1963, for the eightieth anniversary of his birth, a group of Old Bolsheviks headed by Elena Stasova petitioned Leonid Ilichev, Central Committee secretary in charge of Ideology, to obtain a series of commemorative publications and events in Moscow, Leningrad and Antonov-Ovseenko's hometown Chernigov. The signatories emphasized the exceptional record of "one of Lenin's close disciples," who had played an "outstanding role in the preparation and realization of the October Revolution, the Civil War and the construction of the socialist state."[29] In reaction, the Ideological Department commissioned a biographical notice of Antonov-Ovseenko. It emphasized his participation in the Trotskyist opposition, which the revolutionary had subsequently justified as an attempt to conciliate Trotsky and Stalin to avoid a scission of the Party. This mixed record explains the Ideology Department's recommendation that a commemorative article be published in a second-tier newspaper, *Krasnaia Zvezda*. Despite being much less than required by the letter's signatories, it was still a partial success.[30] Similar decisions were usually taken in relation to rehabilitated Old Bolsheviks, whereas those who had never been repressed could expect greater recognition of their accomplishments.

Anton Antonov-Ovseenko, however, was frustrated by this modest response. On April 5, 1963, he wrote a letter to Anastas Mikoian, enclosing a copy of Stasova's letter, and complained that the commemoration of his father's eightieth birthday had been all but ignored. Although he had sent an article to *Izvestiia*, the article in *Krasnaia Zvezda*—also an initiative of his—had remained the only publication on Antonov-Ovseenko, and none of the commemorative measures initially planned in his honor had been allowed to take place. Anton concluded with a plea for intercession: "It is hard to believe that someone is deliberately stifling the memory of the honest disciple of Lenin (*leninets*) V.A. Antonov-Ovseenko. But if this sacrilege is indeed taking place, then I ask you and Nikita Sergeevich Khrushchev to intervene in this unsavory affair."[31]

Antonov-Ovseenko had more success in his lobbying of regional officials. In his father's hometown, Chernigov (Ukrainian Soviet Republic), he wrote to the head of the regional archive to ask for the commemoration of his father's birthday. He received a warm answer: besides a commemorative exhibition and the publication of an article in the local newspaper, the archivist mentioned the project of naming one of Chernigov's streets after V. A. Antonov-Ovseenko.[32] Throughout the country, and particularly in the cities where the revolutionary had lived, museums organized exhibitions in V. A. Antonov-Ovseenko's honor, with his son keenly offering to send historical documents and material. In 1963–65, he thus corresponded with the Kharkov historical museum, a Sevastopol' factory museum and the museum of the Black Sea Fleet, a military museum in the Leningrad region, a historical museum in Odessa, Kuibyshev (Samara)'s Museum of Local History, and Tambov's Museum of the Great Socialist October Revolution.[33]

However, even this half-hearted rehabilitation raised criticisms. In August 1965, the newly appointed head of the Central Committee Department of Science and Higher Education and notorious pro-Stalinist Sergei Trapeznikov and his colleague in charge of Ideology Vladimir Stepakov wrote a letter to the Central Committee protesting against the publication of "one-sided" commemorative articles of rehabilitated figures, which overemphasized their accomplishments, while silencing their mistakes. These publications led "immature" Party members to raise the question of the rehabilitation of the Party's oppositionists Lev Trotsky, Nikolai Bukharin, or Lev Kamenev. They proposed that such publications be in the future authorized only by the secretariat of the Central Committee, after evaluation by the IML.[34] While this proposal may not have been adopted, such publications clearly abated in the following years. Vladimir Antonov-Ovseenko was among the rehabilitated revolutionaries, the commemoration of whom Trapeznikov judged undesirable. During two conferences on the state of social sciences which he presided over in June and November 1965, several historians criticized Antonov-Ovseenko's public rehabilitation. A. V. Likholat thus complained that "the fact that he was an active Trotskyite and led a struggle against Lenin before the October Revolution, that he participated in the Trotskyist opposition, made serious mistakes in the Ukraine during the period of the Civil war, is concealed."[35] V. S. Aleksandrov also expressed dismay at the depiction of Antonov-Ovseenko in the press as "faithful, steadfast Leninist," when his participation to the Trotsyist opposition was well-known. He concluded that "we have to show their mistakes, as much as their positive role. It will show the objective path of development of the history of the Party."[36]

Anton Antonov-Ovseenko saw it as his duty to fend off such attacks against his father. In April 1966, he protested a statement made by the historian Dmitrii Oznobishin during a working session at the Institute of History of the Academy of Sciences. Oznobishin had allegedly assigned to Vladimir Antonov-Ovseenko the label of "Trotskyite" in relation to the Civil War period—an obvious anachronism—and accused him of disregarding Lenin's orders. Anton found the accusation both unfounded and "unbearable" from a political point of view. Vladimir Antonov-Ovseenko had been "rehabilitated both as a citizen and as a communist," and Oznobishin's statement had "an offensive character for his memory." For this, his son demanded public apologies during the next meeting of the Institute's staff.[37]

The results of this protest letter are unknown, but, at that time, Anton Antonov-Ovseenko seems to have been tilting at windmills, without much result. In February 1965, he complained bitterly in a letter to Mikoian about the various attacks against his father and the official refusal to commemorate his eightieth birthday. He concluded: "I consider the rehabilitation of the name of my father as my civil duty."[38] This, he believed, implied reclaiming history from those who falsified it for political aims. To this end, Anton Antonov-Ovseenko had long ago decided to write his father's biography.

"In the name of the revolution"

In October 1964, Anton Antonov-Ovseenko received a letter from A. Ianin, head of the Committee of Veterans of the October Revolution for the Tambov and Riazan regions. Ianin explained that he had been looking for a long time for relatives of Vladimir Antonov-Ovseenko, with whom he had worked in Tambov at the time of the struggle against the Antonov rebellion. The veteran noted that, while a lot of books were being published in Moscow about victims of the personality cult, he had not found a single brochure on Antonov-Ovseenko's revolutionary activity. Ianin complained bitterly about attempts from a number of "Stalin's heirs"[39] to silence the names of such "great heroes" as Antonov-Ovseenko. With the forty-seventh anniversary of the Revolution approaching, Ianin had decided to contact publishing houses in Moscow to urge them to publish a book about the glorious revolutionary. He therefore turned to Anton to ask if he had documentary material he could share to allow for such a publication.[40]

Not only did Antonov-Ovseenko have material for such a book, but he was actively involved in fulfilling his "civic duty" and rehabilitating his father's reputation in Soviet history. Despite his near blindness, which considerably complicated his research work, he set out to gather all available historical material on his father's political career, from the prerevolutionary period to his tragic end. He drew heavily on the latter's autobiographical writings: *Under the Banner of October* (1923); *In the Year 1917* (1933); and four volumes of *Notes on the Civil War* (1924–33). V. A. Antonov-Ovseenko's papers had been seized when he was arrested in 1937, but they had then been transferred to the Central State Archive of the October Revolution and Socialist Construction (TsGAOR). Although these sources were initially unavailable, Anton managed to get access to the TsGAOR fond in 1973, as he was working on a revised edition of his book, published in 1975.[41] However, early on, he was able to gain access to the Central Party Archives (TsPA), hosted by the IML. Libraries and regional archives, in Tambov for instance, provided him with additional material.

The testimonies of Old Bolsheviks who had known his father before, during and after the Revolution were also a valuable source of information for Antonov-Ovseenko. One such encounter was fortuitous: he once received a letter from Andrei Chekotillo, a retired scientist who had been his father's cellmate in Sevastopol' in 1906 and who asked him whether the latter was still alive, expressing the wish to exchange memories about the past.[42] In other cases, the historian actively sought out witnesses of the past, with varying results. In 1964, he wrote to the City Party Committee of Kraslava, a Latvian town where his father had received assistance after his arrest in Moscow, to ask if witnesses of the events could still be found—without success.[43] In Riga, however, he found Ivan Iakovlev, a former sailor who had listened to Antonov-Ovseenko's fiery speeches in Helsingfors (Helsinki) in 1917.[44] In Tambov, where Anton lived in the early 1960s, he found a circle of witnesses and sympathizers, including the head of the local literary museum N. A. Nikiforov, as well as locals who had known his father, such as Semen Evgenov or the writer Boris Dal'nii.[45]

On November 7, 1963, the forty-sixth anniversary of the October Revolution, the local newspaper *Tambovskaia Pravda* published a chapter of Antonov-Ovseenko's future book, *In the Name of the Revolution* (*Imenem Revoliutsii*). It was preceded by an introduction by Elena Stasova. As a Central Committee secretary at the time of the October Revolution, she had known V. A. Antonov-Ovseenko well and remembered him "as a man of passionate revolutionary temperament, inexhaustible energy," whose "qualities of fighter found their strongest expression in the days of the October storming [of the Winter Palace]." She concluded that his name had been "unfairly forgotten and calumniated. Today he is back among us, with the people, to whom he has given his whole life."[46]

Later on, Anton Antonov-Ovseenko reflected that, ideally, he would have liked to write more than just a biographical essay and compile a collection of testimonies about his father, to give a more complete portrait of the man.[47] However, in a changing political context, he was running out of time and faced increasingly adverse winds. In November 1964, the historian published in *Novyi mir* a series of documents about his father's life in emigration, along with Stasova's foreword to his book.[48] The publication ended with Iurii Tomskii's recollections about Antonov-Ovseenko's last days in prison and was signed "Anton Rakitin," a pseudonym he would later use for the book as well. He claimed he did not hide behind a pseudonym out of fear of repression, but in order to enhance readers' trust in the author's objectivity.[49]

While *Novyi mir* was well-known as a liberal journal, it was another challenge to publish with the more orthodox Politizdat. Yet, the state publisher had at the time begun refashioning its publishing identity: in order to attract a younger public, it sought to publish lively and entertaining prose about heroes of the Soviet past. This evolution would later lead to the founding of the biography series "Fiery Revolutionaries," the first title of which came out in 1968. By calling on professional writers of talent, some of whom were less than orthodox from a political perspective, Politizdat hoped to reconquer an ideologically disaffected readership.[50] Polly Jones argued that first experiments with the biographical genre had proven that it "serves as a successful form of propaganda of the heroic traditions of Bolshevism" and that biographies "enjoy especially large popularity when written artistically, in a lively way, emotionally."[51] In the context of this identity mutation, Anton Antonov-Ovseenko must have appeared as a suitable author: he coupled the training of a historian with the literary verve of a writer, and as the son of a Bolshevik leader, he could write from a unique vantage point.

Anton submitted his manuscript in September 1964. Within a month, following Khrushchev's ouster, a new wind was blowing. A meeting was called at Politizdat on November 20 to discuss the manuscript. The discussion took place in presence of the author and a dozen other participants, mostly historians and writers. The first speaker, M. S. Maiorov pointed to the manuscript's political flaws, which made it impossible for him to review the book: the author reflected Lenin's and the Central Committee's roles weakly and, conversely, overemphasized Antonov-Ovseenko's personality and actions. The Bolshevik revolutionary's personality did not need to be excessively highlighted, nor should the author downplay Antonov-Ovseenko's mistakes by attempting to justify his Menshevik and Trotskyist past.[52]

Some other participants in the meeting agreed with this evaluation and reproached the author with exaggerating Antonov-Ovseenko's role in the socialist prerevolutionary émigré press in Paris and concealing that he was then a Menshevik. As Vladlen Loginov put it, "Antonov-Ovseenko led revolutionary work, but in this period, he was no Bolshevik, and only after a long, winding path did he finally join the Bolsheviks' party. It will not undermine his prestige in the least. It is better to say the truth, indicating that he always remained a revolutionary."[53] Others were more severe and called on the author to accept the label of Trotskyite as an objective statement. Only two speakers contested this characterization. S. N. Ivanov recognized that, having studied the documents in greater detail, he had begun to question Antonov-Ovseenko's characterization as Trotskyite. Admittedly, he had signed the "declaration of 46," but he had done this less in agreement with Trotsky than in opposition to the Central Committee's line; eventually, it was his strong character and idealism that had "betrayed him." V. G. Iasnyi supported this point of view, emphasizing that while only a handful of people had voted in favor of Trotsky's resolutions, in 1938 "hundreds and hundreds of people" had been accused of Trotskyism and been repressed. He concluded that "it was just one of the methods of the time. . . . Why should we just give away to Trotsky so many revolutionary heroes? Our readers and readers abroad just won't understand us."[54]

However, for the majority, accusations of Trotskyism remained the ultimate sin, one that they would certainly not dare trifle with. The 20th Party Congress had not rehabilitated any leader of the innerparty opposition, and the condemnation of Stalin's personality cult did not amount to a vindication of his adversaries. Z. N. Politov made this point very clear: Antonov-Ovseenko could not be exculpated from the accusation of Trotskyism on the basis of his opposition to Stalin in 1923. "If we go this way, we will distort the whole history of the Party," he sententiously warned.[55]

The participants also criticized the author's decision to hide behind a pseudonym. M. P. Kim feared that the readers would be surprised by the writer's tone: his warm praises in relation to the hero "will be clearer if the reader knows that the author is Vladimir Aleksandrovich's son." The subjective approach to some elements of Antonov-Ovseenko's biography was comprehensible, coming from his son, but seemed incongruous on the part of an unrelated author. Of course, a son could "hardly write about his father coldly," especially given the latter's merits, and his enthusiasm was comprehensible. But "if the author wants to be more objective in the eyes of the reader, then he will have to remove some moments of excessive exaltation. The manuscript will only gain from this."[56]

To these criticisms, Anton Antonov-Ovseenko replied in detail, without conceding any ground and emphasizing that he considered himself as a historian, working with archival sources and seeking to attain maximal objectivity. He agreed to remove from the manuscript elements concerning the history of the Civil War in Ukraine and the role of the anarchist Nestor Makhno that had been criticized. "But there are questions on which, as a historian, I disagree. I think that in the coming years I will be proven right, and the history of the Civil War in Ukraine will be studied differently." On some other questions, however, he was inflexible. "First of all, on Trotskyism. If in the book the word Trotskyite or Trotskyist views is to be used in relation to Antonov-Ovseenko, then I renounce this book categorically. I can agree with anything, but I categorically object to the label of Trotskyite." Antonov-Ovseenko then went on to lay out his "short theses" about the book. First, his father had fought for the unity of the Party and had been misunderstood in this regard. His fiery character had sometimes caused him to make mistakes. Second, only in this one instance had he stood up against the Central Committee's organizational line, and this was the only reason why he was said to have joined the opposition. Third, he had never led any fractional struggle and had always disagreed with Trotsky on fundamental questions. This was both a "personal antipathy" and political opposition, as they held radically different views on the peasant question. The historian concluded that he would not tolerate "this –ism of Trotskyism, this stigma next to Antonov-Ovseenko's name."[57]

Moreover, he felt the acute need to defend himself against accusations of partiality. Not a single fact that he had brought up was invented, he claimed, and, as a historian, he strove to maximal objectivity. Nevertheless, he admitted that it was "very difficult not to write with enthusiasm" about his father, who was both a military commander and a writer, and whose activity, particularly in the military field, had been so unjustly denigrated. He tried to show Antonov-Ovseenko's impressive revolutionary record "in all of its diversity," without, however, "placing him on a pedestal." And he felt that, on the whole, he had succeeded.[58]

In spite of these disagreements, *In the name of the Revolution* did come out in July 1965. Anton recalled bringing an autographed copy to the head of the Central Party Archive, who expressed his disbelief that the book had been published.[59] Always skillful at negotiating with higher-ups, Anton claims that he convinced the two old ladies in charge of censorship at Politizdat, who accepted to approve his manuscript for publication.[60] It is unlikely, however, that decisions of this kind were taken only at the level of the publishing house. Antonov-Ovseenko's good fortune had probably more to do with the lack of clear directives from above in the year following Khrushchev's removal. Still, he was forced to cut a "biting concluding paragraph," leaving only an innuendo to his father's death.[61]

The book was a success. A review of *Imenem Revoliutsii* appeared in *Kommunist* in August 1965, signed by the historian V. Pogudin.[62] It quoted from the introduction by Stasova, who enjoyed general respect as "one of the oldest members of the Party." Her warm praise of the revolutionary was echoed by the reviewer, who noted in a nuanced way:

> Antonov-Ovseenko lived a short life, but a complex one, full of events. It cannot be painted in just one color. Alongside periods full of revolutionary fire (*gorenie*), there were also some sad episodes in this life. From 1910 to 1917, being in emigration, he found himself temporarily in the camp of the Mensheviks-liquidators. From 1923 to 1927, he joined the Trotskyite opposition, although he did not lead any fractional struggle. But these were indeed just episodes, which were not characteristic of Antonov-Ovseenko's whole life path.[63]

Other reviews appeared in *Novyi mir* (n° 12), *Nauka i zhizn'* (n° 7), *Izvestiia* (July 18), *Krasnaia zvezda* (September 10), *Moskovskii komsomolets* (November 27), and many provincial newspapers. The book was also a success with the public. Despite a large print run, all issues were soon sold out.[64] A testimony to the public interest raised by the book, and by the figure of Antonov-Ovseenko, was a letter from a young pioneer leader from Leningrad, dated from October 1967. She explained how her group had discovered the figure of the great revolutionary, had collected information about him and read Anton's biography, and would now seek to be attributed the name of Antonov-Ovseenko. She invited Anton to join them for the forthcoming neighborhood pioneers' celebrations, during which they planned to tell other pioneers about Antonov-Ovseenko.[65] In the following years, the historian continued to publish historical articles and essays on Vladimir Antonov-Ovseenko.[66]

At the time, Anton remembered, his paramount goal was to fulfill his duty of memory toward his father. This constituted a legitimate objective both from the point of view of the Khrushchev leadership and Soviet society. Such publications could easily fit with the Party's political objectives of youth indoctrination and propaganda of the history of the Revolution, as long as the question of the annihilation of Antonov-Ovseenko's generation of revolutionaries could be evaded. Yet there was a profound disconnect between Anton Antonov-Ovseenko's thirst for justice and compensation and the dissatisfying middle ground that Khrushchev's de-Stalinization offered. These contradictions, however, would only come into the open in the Brezhnev years.

Roy Medvedev: Writing for the Party

Genesis of a history of Stalinism

Born in 1925 in Tbilisi, the twin brothers Roy and Zhores Medvedev had a short, yet happy childhood. They looked up to their father with adoration: Aleksandr Medvedev had the military chic of the Political Commissar of the 1930s, coupled with the sharp mind of the philosopher, top lecturer of dialectical and historical materialism at the Tolmachev Military-Political Academy and at Leningrad University.[67] His sudden arrest, in August 1938, and his condemnation to eight years of camp, from which he would never return, left a deep, traumatic imprint on the two brothers' lives. They had not yet turned thirteen when the family was evicted from its Moscow apartment. Their father's manuscripts, all that remained of decades of philosophical reflections, were seized by the NKVD, and the thousands of books from his personal library disappeared in the whirlwind of the war years. Throughout their wanderings, from Moscow to the Smolensk region, from Leningrad to Rostov-na-Donu, Roy and Zhores continued to receive letters from their father, sent from the Kolyma camps. Until one day, in March 1941, one of their letters was returned with the mention "undelivered because of the death of the addressee." After the German invasion, in September 1941, the Medvedev family was forced into evacuation. Back in Tbilisi, they lived with relatives for a few years. In February 1943, the seventeen-year-old twins were mobilized to defend their Fatherland.[68] Roy had just managed to graduate from secondary school one semester early, which qualified him to enroll in an officers' school. However, because of his unfavorable family background, he was sent to the rear to work in an artillery arsenal. Zhores was sent to the front but was demobilized a few months later, following a foot injury. In 1944, he started studying biology at the Timiriazev Agricultural Academy.

Roy leaned toward philosophy and history, and despite his mother's warnings, decided to enroll in Leningrad University, where his father had once lectured. "Biology seemed to my mother the safest of all sciences," he remembered. Admittedly, his brother's experience showed that being an honest biologist, in the context of Trofim Lysenko's sway over Soviet sciences, could also be dangerous. Being an honest philosopher or historian, on the other hand, "was then all but impossible." Yet Roy said he had "learned the rules of sensible caution early on. I strove to learn my father's profession but was not eager to share his fate."[69] This caution, seemingly incompatible with the expression of dissenting views, remained in fact the hallmark of Roy Medvedev's career as a dissident.

The young man graduated in 1951 with honors, but as the son of an "enemy of the people," he could neither teach in university nor start a doctoral degree. He was appointed as a history teacher in a school in the Urals. Interested in pedagogy, he became a school headmaster to experiment with pedagogical methods. A few years later, he moved back to the Leningrad region, where he worked in a fishermen's village by the Gulf of Finland. It was there, in February 1956, that he heard the Secret Speech, read out during a Party meeting, which he was called upon to attend as part of the school teaching staff. Roy knew about the crimes perpetrated during the Terror and was aware that his father had been tortured. In the late 1940s, he had met Ivan Gavrilov, a friend of his father's, who had seen Aleksandr Medvedev in the Gulag and told his son about life in the camps. But there was much that the young man still ignored, and the Secret Speech had a dramatic eye-opening effect on him. He had been oblivious to the sheer scale of repression of Party members and had believed official propaganda on a number of key issues: Sergei Kirov's death, the guilt of the oppositionists Nikolai Bukharin, Grigorii Zinoviev, Lev Kamenev, and Aleksei Rykov. And although he believed in his father's innocence, he also believed that Stalin was unaware of life conditions in the camps. Nor was Roy aware of Stalin's responsibility in the early defeats in the war, or his encouragement of his own personality cult.[70] In September 1956, after two years of administrative procedures, Aleksandr Medvedev was finally officially rehabilitated. This removed the last obstacle that still prevented Roy from joining the Party.[71] From the outset, however, Medvedev joined the Party with a critical mindset: for him the Secret Speech was a source of new interrogations, which triggered in him the desire to reflect upon the nature of the phenomenon that had left such a deep and tragic imprint on Soviet society.

Although Medvedev turned to pedagogics as his field of specialization, defending his candidate (*kandidatskaia*) dissertation (roughly the equivalent of a PhD) in this field in 1959, he retained his interest in history and politics. His promotion to the rank of full Party member the same year accelerated his promotion to the position of deputy editor in chief of the Moscow publishing house "Uchpedgiz," where he had started working in 1958 as editor of the journal "Polytechnic Education." Two years later, however, he resigned from this position; from August 1961 onwards, he worked as a researcher at the Institute of Research for Polytechnic Teaching, Production Teaching, and Professional Orientation at the Academy of Pedagogical Sciences. This new job left him enough time to start working on a new parallel project: a history of the origins and consequences of Stalinism.[72]

The son of a philosopher, with a degree in history and philosophy, Roy Medvedev said he had always felt inclined to write an analysis of Soviet society. Khrushchev's calls to historians, from the tribune of the 22nd Party Congress, to study Stalin's personality cult lent full legitimacy to the project that Medvedev had conceived after 1956. In the early 1960s, an increasing number of articles had begun to appear in newspapers and journals, offering daily new revelations about the past. Medvedev started gathering them methodically for his research. As an editor and then as a researcher at the Academy of Pedagogical Sciences, he could subscribe to a service providing newspaper cuttings from national press and about a hundred regional newspapers on given themes. He had thus subscribed to such keywords as "rehabilitations," "Stalin," or "personality cult," and received numerous articles or obituary notices published on birth anniversaries of recently rehabilitated local figures. This allowed him to grasp the sheer scale of Stalin-era political repression.[73]

Yet a comprehensive synthesis and analysis of these events remained to be written, and official historians did not seem up to the task. Years later, upon interrogation by the PCC, Roy Medvedev would justify his decision to engage in historical research with the following metaphor:

> If I felt that our history institutes really studied the nature and history of Stalinism and Stalin's crimes, I wouldn't have written my book. But I know that they don't do any research on that subject. . . . Look here, if Moscow's bakers stopped baking bread, then certainly home bakeries would sprout up everywhere, or people would begin baking their own. But no less than bread, our people needs the truth about our country's past; they must know why they suffered such tragedies. Therefore, I had to search for the truth, but using the methods of a craftsman.[74]

The "bread" that Medvedev offered to feed the people would be baked from wheat grown by the Party, albeit seasoned with Medvedev's own salt. Although by 1967 he presented his activity as necessary for Soviet society, in the early 1960s he strategically fashioned himself as an interpreter of the Party's new line, offering his political and philosophical conclusions as an independent and, as it turned out, unrequited, consultant (see Figures 1.2 and 1.3).

More polemical was the research of his brother Zhores on a highly controversial figure of the history of Soviet science: the biologist Trofim Lysenko. Lysenko was a

Figure 1.2 Roy Medvedev in his home office in Moscow, 1973 © Margarita Medvedeva. Courtesy of Zhores Medvedev.

Figure 1.3 Zhores Medvedev in his home office in England, 1987 © Margarita Medvedeva. Courtesy of Zhores Medvedev.

pseudoscientist who had carved his way to the top of Stalin-era biology by eliminating from science—and often from life—his more brilliant competitors, practicing classical genetics. Despite the onset of de-Stalinization, his phony theories about the inheritance of acquired characteristics continued to enjoy a dominant position in Soviet biology. Confronted with the rejection of his own research, which contradicted Lysenko's theories, Zhores set out to write a history of the Lysenko phenomenon in Soviet sciences. The manuscript began to circulate widely within the scientific community. Thanks to the comments, testimonies, and additional materials provided by his readers, the biologist improved and considerably enlarged his initial work.

Roy Medvedev was inspired by the efficiency of this method and decided to proceed similarly with his own work. A prolific author and a hardworking researcher, he could combine successfully his underground activities with professional career growth: from 1962 to 1965, he published over forty articles in his field, was promoted head of his department, and was elected secretary of the Institute's Party organization, while devoting up to eight hours daily to historical research. By the beginning of 1963, his manuscript had grown to 200 pages. A year later, its volume had doubled.[75] Over the following years, his work would grow up to a thousand typographed pages, thanks to numerous additions provided by friends and Old Bolsheviks of his acquaintance. Medvedev's original work method consisted in an incremental, progressive revision of his manuscript based on direct feedback and additions from readers. As word of his research spread, he received an increasing number of requests from potential reviewers. He gave his manuscript to read for a limited time and asked readers to make additions, remarks, express wishes. In the second stage, Medvedev would visit his informants again and record their discussion on tape. Based on this new information, the historian would amend and enlarge his manuscript, and, twice a year, he would type a new version of it.[76]

The first version, completed in 1964,[77] was initially entitled *Before the Tribunal of History* (*Pered sudom istorii*). Divided into seven chapters, Medvedev's study adopted a time frame that was very similar to that adopted by Khrushchev in the Secret Speech: Kirov's murder, in 1934, constituted the starting point of a wave of Terror that peaked in 1937–38 and affected primarily former oppositionists and state and Party cadres. Chapter 4 was dedicated to the reasons for political repression; chapter 5 offered a reflection on the factors that had facilitated Stalin's power usurpation; and chapter 7 examined some "dangerous consequences of the personality cult." So strong was the focus on the 1930s that a decade and a half of Stalin's wartime and postwar rule were lumped together in one chapter (the sixth), while the 1920s were only briefly dealt with in the first chapter.

In the following years, Medvedev would considerably amend and enlarge this first version, especially chronologically, but the central questions of the fourth, fifth, and seventh chapters would remain fundamental to his study. Indeed, his was never a purely historical inquiry. It was essentially a work of political philosophy investigating the origins, causes, and consequences of Stalinism—a phenomenon which Medvedev posited to be alien to the ideology, values, and practice of the Soviet regime, as defined by its founding figure, Lenin. Medvedev adopted both the language and the political framework of Khrushchev's Secret Speech: beyond Stalin's figure, what was to be denounced was the "personality cult" as a broader phenomenon. The inquiry's goal was to identify factors that had facilitated the establishment of the personality cult. The implicit logic was that the Soviet regime could be purged from these politically alien elements and distortions.

Because Medvedev seems to have seriously envisaged the publication of his book in the Soviet Union, he adapted the style and content of this 1964 version to meet the expected demands of censorship. And in order to gain acceptance for his treatment of some particularly sensitive topics, the author had to inscribe his research within the official boundaries of Khrushchev's limited de-Stalinization, not sparing his praises for the work accomplished by the Soviet leader. This was visible for instance in his overly optimistic appraisal of the changes brought about by the 20th Party Congress: following the Party's categorical denunciation of the "ideology and practice of the personality cult" and severe condemnation of Stalin's crimes, "Lenin's norms of Party life" had been restored, and the "victims of the bloody arbitrariness" had been rehabilitated.[78] Medvedev also demonstrated his ideological credentials by attacking China and Albania, echoing Khrushchev's charge against these rival communist regimes. Tirana and Beijing had claimed that the relation to Stalin constituted a line of demarcation between "true Marxist-Leninists" and "contemporary revisionists." Medvedev agreed that the relationship to Stalin constituted a dividing line within the international communist movement, but he believed that facts would show "who stands on true Marxist-Leninist positions." It was with this goal in mind that he had written his book.[79]

The book opened with a chapter on "Stalin's first crimes," covering the prerevolutionary period and the first two decades of Soviet power, up to and including Kirov's murder, in 1934. Although this contradicted his heavy emphasis on the 1930s and the official chronology of the Terror, Medvedev concluded that "the opinion according to which there were two entirely different periods in Stalin's life and activity, before 1934 and after 1934, is absolutely untrue."[80] Yet he failed to substantiate this claim other than by pointing to Stalin's character flaws and listing political divergences between him and Lenin. By neglecting these early warning signs, he argued, the Party leadership had made the birth of Stalin's personality cult in the 1930s possible.

The second chapter, on the "destruction of former oppositionists," reflected by and large the official line regarding the innerparty oppositions. Medvedev saw "no ground whatsoever to revise the fundamental and important results of the intraparty struggle of the 1920s."[81] However, the historian severely condemned the use of torture, which placed the Soviet NKVD on a par with the German Gestapo, and denounced the falsification of the political trials of the 1930s. "These trials were a monstrous representation, a scary show, which obviously had to be rehearsed many times before it could be shown to the public."[82] Although the fantastic charges against the oppositionists had been dropped after the 20th Party Congress, Medvedev noted, no official acknowledgment of their civil rehabilitation had occurred, and history textbooks still avoided the question. A perverse result of this was that "the shameful and illegal trials of the 1930s have turned into martyrs people who, in their majority, had been justly and severely condemned by our party."[83] Behind the repression of former oppositionists, Medvedev identified Stalin's hand. He had seized this opportunity to take a personal revenge and to reinforce his personal power while blaming political and economic difficulties on his adversaries. But the "logic of the struggle" dictated that Stalin would go further and get rid of all Leninist cadres in the Party under the cover of political trials.

The repression of party and state cadres constituted the subject of the third chapter. Very factual, at this stage it consisted largely of long lists of names at the various levels: within central state and party organs; within party committees at the regional, local, and republican levels; in trade unions and the Communist youth organs; within the Red Army; within foreign Communist parties and the Komintern; in sciences; in arts and literature; and among the masses. Medvedev emphasized that most of them had never taken part in any opposition. Theirs was "the pointless and merciless annihilation of the best people of our party and state. This was the most terrible act in the tragedy of the 1930s."[84] On the repression of rank-and-file party members and noncommunists, Medvedev remained vague, probably because he lacked precise data. He estimated the number of Soviet citizens repressed in the prewar period to "at least two million" and sententiously concluded that "none of the despots and tyrants of the past had ever persecuted and destroyed such a great number of their compatriots."[85]

The sixth chapter completed this chronological overview by examining Stalin's personal power and repressions in the 1940s and early 1950s, in the USSR and in

Eastern Europe. Using the same metaphor as Solzhenitsyn in *The Gulag Archipelago*, Medvedev compared the growth of the repressive apparatus to that of a cancer tumor, with NKVD departments creeping into all cities and work structures, relayed by a network of informers. This huge apparatus, which no foreign threat could vindicate, justified its own existence by hunting down "enemies of the people."[86]

The three analytical chapters were undoubtedly the most provocative, as they raised issues with potential implications for the current regime. First, he attempted to answer the question of Stalin's responsibility for the crimes committed under his leadership. Medvedev concluded that none of the excuses usually given to the Soviet leader were valid. Stalin had not been deceived by his subordinates and was indeed the main driving force behind the Terror. He might have been paranoid, but this circumstance did not exempt him of responsibility for his actions. Stalin had mostly acted out of vainglory, concluded the author. He had only eliminated the Old Lenin Guard, constituted of proud and unbendable personalities, because their revolutionary record overshadowed his.

The object of the sixth chapter was to identify factors that had facilitated Stalin's usurpation of power, and which should be addressed in order to avoid a reoccurrence of Stalinism. The most prominent factor, which explained the lack of popular resistance to his crimes, had been the "quasi-religious" character of the cult of Stalin's personality. This posed questions in terms of the functioning of the party: there had to be safeguards against abuses of power, if the life and death of citizens was not to depend on "the party leader's personal qualities."[87] Other political issues to be remedied included the "absence of transparency and freedom of criticism in our country," but also the centralization of power, which had turned from a temporary into a long-term factor; and, finally, the lack of a mechanism to limit in time a leader's mandate. The historical context, and in particular the USSR's internal and external situation in the 1930s, had also contributed to the catastrophe. Finally, Medvedev pointed to the lack of unity within the party, which "was ready for the struggle with any enemies" but proved "defenseless in the face of blows inflicted by the hand of its own leaders."[88]

These divisions were made more acute by what Medvedev called the "petty bourgeois transformation" (*pererozhdenie*) of some of the Party and Soviet cadres. Under this ideological label, he designated an opportunistic career strategy. Mass political repressions had allowed for the promotion of a new generation of cadres who had a personal stake in Stalin's dictatorial rule. This new generation of "Stalinist" cadres had then dominated the country's leadership from the 1930s onwards.[89] This was a clear hint to the shady political past of many current Party leaders who had begun their careers during the Stalin era and had occupied positions left vacant by the purges. Some of them had never freed themselves from the political thinking of the Stalin era. Medvedev pursued his attack against "Stalinists" in the seventh chapter, which dealt with the consequences of the personality cult. Stalin's system had relied on this new type of young party workers: "Disciplined and commanding, indifferent to the people and their needs, but attentive to their superiors, rude and not standing any criticism from below, saying one thing and doing another." "Cruel" and "removed from the masses," they resorted to force and terror, rather than words, to convince others.[90]

In the last chapter, behind a criticism of Stalin's system of power, Medvedev denounced practices that survived into the post-Stalin era. He denounced the dangerous tendency to let one ruling figure take crucial decisions for the life of a country without consulting others, leading to catastrophic errors. Although his examples were from the Stalin era, his critique could well have applied to Khrushchev's harebrained strategies in the foreign policy field.

> At the moment, there cannot be and should not be any situation when a man can single-handedly decide on the fate of a great state, is the chief referee for all main questions in the military, political, scientific and economic fields, when this person's tastes become the norm in literature, art, painting—in short, when a given personality concentrates in his hands an immense power and a decisive influence in all spheres of society's life. Such a form of government would find itself in total contradiction with the current level of development of production forces and would unfailingly lead to the most serious and significant mistakes.[91]

In addition, the establishment of Stalin's rule dealt a fatal blow to intraparty democracy and the participation of masses and caused the bureaucratization of the system. In the sciences, bureaucratism and a dangerous form of monopolism imposed from above replaced the healthy pluralism necessary for the development of research. In political and social life, Stalin's tendency toward "sectarianism" led to his pathological mistrust of whole categories of citizens, such as Jews. The gap, and even blatant contradiction, between words and deeds was another characteristic of Stalin's rule: the discrepancy between the good measures adopted and their failure to be implemented inspired mistrust from the people. Finally, Medvedev reproached Stalin with usurping a place he did not deserve in official history, thus diminishing Lenin's role. This also applied to the fields of ideology and Marxist philosophy, where Stalin's works, despite lacking originality, had become classics.

In his conclusion, Roy Medvedev justified his decision to write the book. Foremost were political, but also ethical reasons. If he listed the crimes committed by Stalin and his henchmen, it was "primarily out of respect for the memory of our deceased fathers and brothers, hundreds of thousands, and maybe millions of people, the best people of our land, who became victims of the arbitrariness and lawlessness caused by Stalin." But the truth was also a political necessity, for the harmful consequences of the personality cult could only be uprooted by telling the workers about them.[92]

Medvedev also preempted future critiques: he recognized that fears that "enemies" of the USSR might pick up on any displayed weakness or acknowledgment of mistake were justified. Nevertheless, it was precisely through self-criticism and the correction of distortions of socialism that the Soviet Union would be able to "cut the ground from under the feet of bourgeois propaganda, which has been using these distortions for many years in its struggle against socialism."[93] Refuting the equation of Stalinism with Communism, Medvedev claimed that the former was a phenomenon "deeply foreign to Marxism-Leninism." Nor could Stalin's crimes be canceled out by the Soviet people's and Communist Party's accomplishments during his rule. "Yes, Stalin was our leader in difficult years. This is a fact that we cannot change anymore. But he was a poor leader, and he made these difficult years even more difficult."[94] Finally, Medvedev concluded that although Stalin had sought to control his own legacy, "no one has power over the judgment of history. It has severely condemned Stalin, as it will condemn all those who attempt to heed the same path of lawlessness."[95]

Pered sudom istorii was a bold research if one considers the author's intention of soliciting party support and seeking publication in the Soviet Union. Such expectations were justified by the radical speeches of the 22nd Party Congress and Medvedev's belief that the topic of his research was legitimate, yet he also remained cautious as he treaded a new path. To the Western reader, or even in comparison to subsequent versions of *Let History Judge*, this manuscript appears strikingly orthodox in its treatment of key questions and in its language. Most importantly, at this stage, Medvedev did not question the politically biased chronological frame defined by the Secret Speech and did not fill the "blank spots" Khrushchev had left out. This is unsurprising, since Medvedev needed to "speak the party's language" in order to earn the trust of Soviet leaders. But it also testifies to his heavy reliance at this stage on published primary sources, which were bound to convey the party's line. In the 1960s, the Soviet press could mention in print only rehabilitated party leaders, leaving aside unrehabilitated accused of early political trials and the silent masses of victims of countless repressive actions of the Stalin era.

Submission of a first version of the manuscript to the Party

By the spring of 1964, rumors about Roy Medvedev's historical study had reached the Central Committee of the CPSU. When he received a request from Politizdat to send his manuscript, Medvedev argued that his book was not yet ready for publication. However, when the editor insisted that the request originated with Central Committee Secretary Leonid Il'ichev, the historian agreed to send a copy. A similar demand came around the same time from Iurii Andropov, through his aide Georgii Shakhnazarov. The future KGB boss (1967–82) and General Secretary of the CPSU (1982–84) was then head of the Central Committee International Department in charge of relations with socialist states, a department with a liberal reputation in which several of Medvedev's former university classmates were employed.[96] Andropov summoned Medvedev for a talk and told him he found his work "interesting," then asked if he could keep the manuscript.[97] The historian refused a third request, however, from another Central Committee Secretary, Boris Ponomarev, who solicited him anonymously through his aide. The historian retrospectively justified this refusal by his rule to give his book to read only to those who agreed to contribute something in exchange: either remarks, corrections, or their own manuscripts, memoirs.[98] Indeed, Medvedev refrained from letting the book circulate freely in samizdat, having witnessed how far his brother's manuscript on Lysenko had circulated. From thirteen copies initially distributed to fellow scientists, *Biology and the Personality Cult* spread to the whole country, with up to several thousand copies in circulation.[99]

At the time, Roy Medvedev did not feel he was stepping out of the realm of legality. His 400-page manuscript remained carefully inscribed within the official narrative and could arguably have been published in the Soviet Union, had Khrushchev or his successors deepened the de-Stalinization course. It would take Khrushchev's ouster and the radical change of ideological line in the late 1960s to turn him into a dissident, as he continued and enlarged his research despite clear signs that the tide was changing, and as his views began to diverge increasingly from the official line.[100]

In September 1965, Politizdat returned Medvedev's manuscript *Pered sudom istorii,* submitted a year earlier, presumably on the editor's insistence. It came with a letter of refusal and a six-page review by A. Kotelenets.[101] The reviewer acknowledged the legitimacy of studying this important topic. Without a "truthful study" of the consequences of Stalin's personality cult, no deep study of the history of Soviet society could take place. Such a reexamination was also necessary "for the denunciation of the Chinese, Albanian and other dogmatists who defend Stalin."[102] However, Kotelenets noted that the manuscript, overall, "raised great doubts." He questioned the title "Before the Judgment/Tribunal of History," noting: "A judgment can only be just, real when each word of accusation is buttressed by facts, proofs." This, claimed Kotelenets, was not the case in Medvedev's study, which unnecessarily exaggerated negative aspects and launched unverified accusations on such sensitive questions as the history of collectivization or relations with Eastern European communist regimes. The absence of bibliographic references and the reliance on oral testimonies further demonstrated the author's "superficial" (*legkovesnyi*) approach to questions of primary political importance. In particular, the reviewer criticized Medvedev's claim that the best elements in the Party had been repressed and replaced by unprincipled careerists. This contradicted the official narrative, conveyed in the June 30, 1956 TsK resolution, according to which a "healthy Leninist core" had remained within the Party throughout the Stalin era.[103] The historian could not tackle such questions "from the position of a skeptical outsider" and had to approach this theme "fully armed" (*vo vseoruzhii*).[104]

Kotelenets's review offered a good reflection of the situation on the ideological front a year after Khrushchev's ouster. He may not have received new instructions yet, but he could tell that the time for anti-Stalinist publications had passed and that the policy of de-Stalinization was about to be rolled back. Less cautious editors later had to pay the price for their lack of ideological "vigilance." His acknowledgment of the legitimacy of the topic of Medvedev's research was also revealing. Yet in Medvedev's case more than in any other, there was a striking gap between the author's creative interpretation of what he perceived to be his legitimate task and the Party's strict ideological requirements in relation to Party history.

Aleksandr Nekrich: Pushing the limits of de-Stalinization

From the front to the archives

As a professional historian, Aleksandr Nekrich was keenly aware of the disconnect between his scholarly aspirations and the official line. Yet his strategy was precisely to start from Khrushchev's critique of Stalin's wartime "mistakes" and to broaden the indictment as far as possible within the limits set by censorship. Revisionist historians such as himself could thus contribute to expanding the scope of de-Stalinization. Yet this strategy was dependent on a continuation of this policy at the highest level. In the aftermath of Khrushchev's ouster, there was no certainty that this would be the case, and Nekrich therefore hurried to get his latest monograph *June 22, 1941* past censorship and into print. Although new guidelines still had to be enacted, Brezhnev's mention of Stalin during the celebrations of the twentieth anniversary of the war seemed a bad omen for Nekrich, who felt that "a race against time had begun, and that [he] could easily lose the contest."[105]

Born in 1920, Nekrich belonged to the first generation grown up in the Soviet Union, which had answered the call to defend its Fatherland in the "Great Patriotic War." As he made his way home, in September 1945, he left behind the sacrificed lives of his brother and several fellow students.[106] Yet he stepped forward, as a freshly accepted Communist Party member, toward the promising career of a historian at the Institute of History of the Academy of Sciences of the USSR. His wartime experience and deep interest for politics led him to the study of British foreign policy on the eve of the Second World War, despite warnings by sympathizing professors against studying events not yet considered as history.[107]

In the troubled waters of the late Stalin era, the young man indeed stumbled upon hostility from more ideologically orthodox elements within the Institute. First, they sought to hinder the defense of his dissertation, and then its publication. During the campaign against "cosmopolitanism," his Jewish origins were the basis for countless attacks.[108] In his memoirs, the historian would depict these trials as a confrontation of enlightened and obscurantist forces, thus downplaying the question of his own eventual submission to the dictate imposed from above. Among the enlightened victims of Stalin's arbitrariness with whom Nekrich's fate was tied were his friend, the philosopher Abram Deborin, branded since the 1930s as "Menshevik idealist," and Nekrich's academic adviser Ivan Maiskii, a former Menshevik and prominent diplomat. Confronted with the prospect of losing his employment, and perhaps facing arrest, Nekrich opted for capitulation. In October 1952, in a three-page letter of "self-criticism," he admitted to a number of mistakes of his book, then entitled *Pro-Fascist Politics of English Imperialists in Europe*, while disputing some accusations leveled at his work. He concluded with a self-abasing statement, underscoring the pivotal role of "I.V. Stalin's brilliant work *Economic Problems of Socialism in the USSR*" and promising to revise his own work "very accurately and self-critically" to make it conform "to the demands of Marxist-Leninist methodology and the high level of our Soviet scholarship."[109]

By February 1953, things had taken a turn for the worse, however, as Maiskii was arrested and accused of being a "British spy."[110] Aware that his name stood on a list of staff to be fired, Nekrich had to undergo the humiliating ritual of condemning his former adviser publicly. He later wrote that he felt he had "no other choice if [he] didn't wish to challenge the state, with all the consequences that implied."[111] Stalin's death reshuffled the cards unexpectedly. Yet as his position was on the line again in March 1953, the historian got away by acknowledging the "essential methodological drawbacks" of his work.[112] His reluctance to confront the state openly would remain constant, even as Nekrich took greater risks in the post-Stalin era. Despite a burning desire to bring his actions in greater concordance with his convictions, he would

Figure 1.4 Aleksandr Nekrich, n.d. Courtesy of Hoover Institution Archives, Aleksandr Moiseevich Nekrich Papers, Box 62, Folder 1, Hoover Institution Archives.

always shy away from undertaking actions that the authorities might have deemed illegal (see Figure 1.4).

The end of the Stalin era, however, heralded momentous changes. In 1955, Nekrich's first monograph finally appeared in print under the ideologically "rebranded" title *The Policy of British Imperialism in Europe, October 1938-September 1939*.[113] Historical research also began to shed its shackles and Nekrich uncovered with excitement the newly available possibilities in terms of archival research. Although a trip to England remained beyond the imaginable, he could find palliatives by accessing Baltic archives and German archival documents captured during the war. From a political point of view, Khrushchev's Secret Speech represented a source of inspiration and hope. "It seemed at the time that socialism was not a mistake, that the 'great experiment' had been a success, in spite of all the horrors, all the blood and grime. The party had told the truth, the whole truth." Or if not exactly the whole truth, then, at least, it seemed that, once set in motion, the process would lead to further investigation and indictment of crimes and, eventually, the condemnation of the guilty.[114]

The years of the Thaw were productive ones for Nekrich, who wrote and coauthored several books about the war. At a time when many historical studies were written in a stiff, dull scholarly style, Nekrich was one of the few historians to write popularization works in a lively and accessible manner.[115] Starting from 1958, he also coedited the ten-volume edition *World History*. Yet his hands remained tied by self-censorship, ideological peer control from his coauthors and Institute colleagues, and *Glavlit*, the official censorship organ. In relation to his first study on the beginning of the Second World War, coauthored with V. M. Khvostov, head of the Institute of History, Nekrich later admitted: "We continued to avoid discussion of one of the major issues: the role of the Soviet-German pact of 1939 in unleashing the war."[116] In 1963, he published a new monograph, *British foreign policy during the Second World War*, which had earned him the title of "doctor of historical science" the year before.[117]

Nekrich understood that to fully "overcome the consequences of the personality cult," as the label then in fashion went, implied shedding "dogmatic views of history and historical events which had been embedded in our consciousness." This was a daunting task, especially in the historiography of the Second World War. Thus the historian was undergoing an emancipation process as much in relation to official canons as toward his own previous beliefs, resulting from decades of indoctrination. As new facts came to light, but numerous topics remained out of reach, Nekrich's priorities shifted from determining the real scale of casualties in the war to the politically highly sensitive question of "why it was so high." This was becoming "a matter of concern to many, not just to historians but to people in the Soviet Union far outside the field of history."[118]

A bold step: The publication of *June 22, 1941*

The monograph *June 22, 1941* was the result of these reflections. As its title indicated, the focus was on the German attack on the Soviet Union, from the early signals of an impending reversal of alliances to the first catastrophic weeks of Soviet defeats on the Eastern European front. Although Nekrich had conceived of the book in 1945, drawing inspiration from his own wartime experience, he did not realize his project until Khrushchev's de-Stalinization turned it into a legitimate object of inquiry. Yet the foreword already reflected the more uncertain climate reigning after Khrushchev's ouster. Anticipating possible criticism for focusing on dark pages of the past, and possibly answering an April 1965 article by sculptor Evgenii Vuchetich,[119] the author argued that, although it was easier to speak of victories, "a historian who has taken on the task of studying the war is obliged to remember not only the way it ended but how it started," the two events being "inseparably connected."[120] Failing to analyze the reasons for the Soviet Union's initial defeats in the war "not only damages historical truth, not only minimizes the heroism shown by Soviet soldiers in the initial period of the war and the grandeur of our victory in the war which began under such extraordinarily unfavorable circumstances, but also objectively harms the interests of our state, leading to incorrect conclusions from the lessons taught us by history."[121]

According to Leonid Petrovskii, a historian who later became a key protagonist of the "Nekrich Affair," *June 22, 1941* was a solid study. It drew on a wide base of primary sources, both Soviet and Western, some of them appearing in print for the first time, as well as extensive secondary literature. "The author offered a new approach to a series of questions of the pre-war period, he based his argumentation solidly on facts, the newest data, archival documents. The sections devoted to the influence of Stalin and Stalinism on the military preparation of the Red Army were particularly convincing."[122] But rather than adding to existing research on the subject, *June 22, 1941* was intended for a wide audience: it had to be "compact, so that any individual, regardless of profession, might find it easy to read."[123] Indeed, the book's powerful impact lay more in the effectiveness of the form, which remained intact even after five sets of censors had trimmed the text thoroughly, than in the novelty of the content itself. In Nekrich's view, "Since the book was written in one stretch, while it may have been possible to cripple it, the ideas it contained could not be eliminated altogether."[124]

And the ideas were provocative, despite having to be coated in thick layers of ideologically palatable and politically correct concepts and interpretations. Admittedly, Nekrich remained disconcertingly orthodox in his interpretation of the conclusion of treaties of mutual assistance with the Baltic states. They "had for two decades served as centers for the anti-Soviet intrigues of the imperialist countries" and threatened to become "an anti-Soviet bridgehead" under Nazi control.[125] As a result, "The workers of the Baltic area, worried by the strengthening of Germany, demanded the transfer of power to genuine people's representatives. In June 1940, people's governments came to power in Estonia, Lithuania and Latvia."[126] This traditional narrative could clearly not be questioned, since doing so could open the door to Baltic claims to self-determination. Neither could Nekrich afford to criticize the Nazi-Soviet pact in principle, or to mention its secret protocols. The "reunion" of territories of Western Ukraine and Byelorussia to the Soviet Union was presented as a measure "to strengthen [Soviet] territory," which also allowed "more than twelve million inhabitants from these regions [to be] saved from the danger of fascist enslavement."[127] His presentation of the Soviet-Finnish war as having been initiated by Finland, Nazi Germany's aggressive ally, was also highly conventional.[128]

Yet Nekrich's convincing demonstrations of the Soviet leadership's failure to prepare the country for the war and active undermining of the Red Army's defense through purges of its best commanders in 1937 had a corrosive effect on the reader's deeply ingrained certainties. In the third part, entitled "Warnings That Were Disregarded," he clearly pointed to the responsibility of the Soviet political leadership for the tragic events of the summer of 1941. Nekrich rendered homage to the Soviet people and duly paid tribute to the heroism of Soviet soldiers. However, he noted that their desperate and heroic resistance failed to represent a significant challenge to the German Wehrmacht.[129]

Originally, Nekrich had used a weighty testimony to buttress his accusations against Stalin for disregarding warnings about the imminent German attack: that of Marshal Filip Golikov, head of the Central Intelligence Directorate during the war. Golikov answered Nekrich's questions openly and unequivocally. He affirmed that the work of Soviet military intelligence was undermined by Stalin's conviction that all the data confirming the impending attack were part of a disinformation scheme by "British imperialists" to pit Moscow and Berlin against one another, but also by his "cautious attitude toward all intelligence data" and his refusal to acknowledge any elements that might contradict his "erroneous assessments of the military and political situation."[130] But Golikov also pointed out a third factor: the massive purges in the party, state, and military apparatuses and the atmosphere of mistrust fostered by the personality cult. Seeking to clarify Golikov's point of view, Nekrich asked at the end of the discussion:

> At about what time did you . . . no longer have any doubts that the Germans were preparing to attack?
> I should think as far back as before the end of 1940.[131]

This interview, which Golikov authorized, should have become a central piece of evidence of the book. However, KGB censorship singled out this testimony, demanding its removal on the grounds that "these are subjective impressions and cannot serve as a basis for scientific conclusions." The KGB report concluded that it was "inexpedient" to publish the book, arguing that the author had failed to provide "a correct analysis of some of the most important events of that period," and interpreted many events subjectively.[132] How can we explain that the book was nevertheless published? According to Nekrich, at the time, the KGB no longer had the last word, especially if its evaluation was counterbalanced by positive reviews from other organs. Perhaps more decisively, Nekrich gave up the fight with censorship and agreed to trim down drastically mentions of his interview with Golikov to ensure the speedy publication of his book. Finally, the monograph came out in October 1965 under the auspices of the publishing house "Nauka."[133]

In three days, 50,000 copies of *June 22, 1941* were sold out, and potential readers started flooding the author with requests for the book. Translations into Czech, Polish, and Hungarian began, and some excerpts were published in Yugoslavia.[134] However, in the Soviet Union, not a single historical journal commented on the work. Apart from a review in a Central Asian newspaper, the only other echo was a review in *Novyi mir*.[135] The author, G. B. Fedorov, a friend of Nekrich's, praised the author not only for his knowledge of the topic, but also for his truthful rendition of contemporary events he had experienced, which gave the book "an enormous force of emotional influence." Nekrich's voice was that "of a patriot of his country, its historian and its defender, an officer who has returned to his peaceful scholarly profession after the victorious war, who has not forgotten or lost part of the thoughts and feelings which had consumed him while the war was still on."[136]

Fedorov's warm praise, however, remained disconcertingly isolated. This silence betrayed the lack of official ideological orientation, in the months preceding the 23rd Party Congress. The research of Nekrich, Antonov-Ovseenko, and Medvedev had been inspired and legitimated by the 20th and 22nd Party Congresses, yet their broad interpretations of de-Stalinization was increasingly at odds with the changing ideological climate of the mid-1960s. For a time, these narratives remained within a grey zone and, in the ideological hiatus of 1965, two of these works made it into print. Nekrich's work, in its censored version at least, remained within the boundaries of acceptable discourse by the standards of the early 1960s. Khrushchev had, after all, singled out Stalin's military command for criticism in the "Secret Speech." The same went for Antonov-Ovseenko's biography of his father: the revolutionary had been officially rehabilitated, and although his past political record remained the object of controversy, this was considered a legitimate object of study. As for Roy Medvedev's research on Stalinism, it occupied, even in its earliest version, a precarious position on the boundary of the permissible. Andropov and Ponomarev might have considered it legitimate in 1964, but by the late 1960s, the political context had changed, and Medvedev had greatly expanded the scope of his study, making it unpublishable in the Soviet Union. In these authors' dissident trajectories, the years prior to 1965 stand out as an unsuccessful attempt to find common ground with the authorities. Yet it was precisely this misunderstanding, this misplaced hope for an overlap between the

Party's objectives and Soviet intelligentsia's expectations, which provided the initial spark, the impetus for these works. None of these researchers had planned from the onset to publish abroad or to emigrate. However, once they had embarked on a course they perceived as legitimate, they felt vindicated in pursuing their journey, regardless of possible sanctions.

These works did not emerge in a vacuum, but in the context of a broad debate on the Stalin question within the intelligentsia and in political spheres. Although the legitimacy of such discussions on the meaning of the Stalin era was never denied, the shifting balance of forces determined which narratives would be given predominance and which would disappear from print. Dissident researchers sided with the anti-Stalinist camp, defending Khrushchev's legacy, but they were outnumbered by the coalition formed by the conservatives, favoring a return to "order" in a broad sense, and the pro-Stalinists, who lobbied for Stalin's rehabilitation. The outcome of these struggles of influence would be crucial for the fate of dissident researchers and their works.

2

From a Reopening of the Stalin Question to a Closure of the Ideological Lid

In the late 1960s, a document became ubiquitous in samizdat and was published in many Western journals: in this "short transcript" of a discussion at the IML, a group of Old Bolsheviks and dissidents loudly praised Aleksandr Nekrich's book *June 22, 1941* and condemned official falsifications of the history of the war. This mythic discussion, which is discussed in this chapter, played a fatal role both for Nekrich and his book, less because of the actual content of the debate than because of the broad publicity that it received in Western media and the interpretations that it elicited. This chapter thus gives a new appraisal to the event, offering a corrective to Nekrich's and his supporters' narrative. Indeed, this discussion was not isolated; it took place in a broader context of debate on the Stalin question, not only in the academic community, but also on the highest echelons of power. How was the new official stance on the Stalin question elaborated? Which role did the lobbying of anti-Stalinist and pro-Stalinist groups play in the elaboration of a new line? How did professional historians, and in particular the academic community to which Nekrich belonged, participate in and react to these debates? These questions and the eventual compromise reached by the Brezhnev leadership are examined in this chapter. I argue that the anti-Stalinists, a group to which dissident historians and their supporters belonged, played an active role in reaffirming the legitimacy of de-Stalinization, which counterbalanced the revisionist zeal of pro-Stalinists, who actively lobbied the leadership to obtain Stalin's rehabilitation at the time.

Khrushchev's policy of de-Stalinization had never been an object of open discussion; like most of his controversial policies, the Soviet leader had imposed it from above, disregarding or crushing any opposition. Susanne Schattenberg has argued that Khrushchev's replacement was reflected less in policy content than in leadership styles. By the mid-1960s, Khrushchev's fellow Presidium members were getting increasingly resentful of his unpredictable and authoritarian style of leadership, reminiscent in some ways of Stalin's personality cult.[1] The result of this widespread exasperation was the coup orchestrated against him, at the October 1964 Central Committee Plenum. Unsurprisingly, following his ouster, latent discontent concerning de-Stalinization surfaced and coalesced, and two opposed fronts on this question reappeared. As a result, the early Brezhnev era was characterized both by discussions, sometimes even confrontations on the Stalin question, and by the search for consensus.

Restoring actual collective leadership while stabilizing his own power at the top were key goals for Brezhnev, if he wished to avoid the fate of his predecessor. For Edwin Bacon, the notions of compromise and agreement within the leadership and "social contract" with the people have long been commonly used to evaluate Brezhnev's leadership style.² As General Secretary, he was careful to always solicit, not only the approval, but also the direct input of his colleagues. Although he retained ultimate authority, he presented his decisions as the outcome of collective discussion and fashioned himself as a consensus-builder and arbitrator. At the same time, he secured his ruling position through extensive patronage networks and by building coalitions with other factions within the leadership.³

Reaching consensus on the Stalin question, however, was not an easy task. Contemporaries, such as Georgii Arbatov, thus remembered a "struggle, sometimes quite sharp, although mostly led behind the scenes," between opponents and proponents of de-Stalinization.⁴ Changes at the party's helm were not followed by an automatic replacement of top executives in the state and party apparatus, which imposed significant checks on the new General Secretary's freedom of maneuver.⁵ On the question of de-Stalinization, Brezhnev had to contend with his colleagues in the Politburo, who seem to have been generally hostile to a rehabilitation of Stalin, but he also brought more radical pro-Stalinist elements in his political "suite," from his earlier patronage networks. The Soviet leader could in no way be described as a Stalinist; he stood, in this matter as in many others, in favor of striking a consensual middle course between the two extremes. Regardless of his own views, he did not deem the Party ready for an ideological U-turn and preferred to revert to a more conservative appraisal of the Stalin era, balancing out achievements and "mistakes."⁶ It seems that he never intended, as has often been assumed, to rehabilitate Stalin officially. Nevertheless, the need to rely on his patronage networks in order to neutralize potential rivals may have led him to give some considerable leeway to his pro-Stalinist protégés, particularly Sergei Trapeznikov, who enjoyed crucial influence over the field of history after 1965. Trapeznikov's controversial initiatives thus aroused widespread fears of an impending reversal of the official course in relation to Stalin. Ultimately, however, he was kept in check both by anti-Stalinist protests and by the enduring legitimacy of the 20th Party Congress.

A Mandate to end de-Stalinization

A decade of upheavals

A salvation for millions of prisoners who were liberated from the camps in the 1950s, de-Stalinization nevertheless proved early on destabilizing for the Soviet order. Public readings of the Secret Speech triggered a flood of unsettling interrogations about the origins of Stalinism and its relationship to socialism as a whole.⁷ Instances of dissent were rife in this period of disorientation, when the boundaries of the criticism allowed were not yet clearly set.⁸ Although they were sometimes labeled as such, critiques voiced at official meetings were hardly ever "anti-Soviet": they often arose from a tendency to take Khrushchev's call for a return to Leninist legality too earnestly.[9] Yet the Soviet leadership felt threatened by these incontrollable outbursts.

With the June 30, 1956 Resolution "On the Overcoming of the Personality cult," the Party sought to reestablish its control over a process that seemed to have gone out of hand. It offered a more balanced vision of the Stalin era, weighing accomplishments against mistakes, and rebutting allegations about the systemic causes of the Terror by claiming that a healthy "Leninist core" within the Central Committee of the Communist Party had sought to oppose Stalin's actions. However, both the Secret Speech and the new resolution contained contradictions and ambiguities, and the new narrative, insisting on the regime's accomplishments, failed to assuage public doubts.[10]

The June 1956 Poznań protest in Poland and the Hungarian Revolution, which triggered Soviet intervention in November, testified to the widespread confusion engendered by the denunciation of Stalin's crimes within the international Communist movement. On the home front as well, a more decisive response was needed: Soviet intelligentsia, in particular, was to be reminded of the boundaries of acceptable criticism. A December 19, 1956 closed letter from the Central Committee warned party organizations against "the emergence of anti-Soviet elements" and pointed to recent excesses in the literary, historical, and educational fields. Shortly thereafter, the Soviet leadership launched an anti-revisionist campaign, targeting anti-Stalinist writers and historians.[11]

Among the victims of this campaign were the journal *Vosprosy istorii* ("Questions of History") and its editors Anna Pankratova, a Central Committee member, and Eduard Burdzhalov. In the wake of the Secret Speech, the editors had sought to bolster the liberalization of historical discourse through revisionist publications and by organizing readers' conferences, which offered a forum for the discussion of revisionist views. Burdzhalov's advocacy of radical reform in historical scholarship and questioning of established views about Trotskyites and other oppositionists aroused increasing criticism, justifying his dismissal from the journal's editorial board in March 1957. As for Pankratova, she died two months later. In January 1957, the Central Committee created a new historical journal under the direct control of the IML, *Voprosy istorii KPSS* (Questions of CPSU History), in order to break *Voprosy Istorii*'s monopoly over Party history.[12] This was but one example of the upheavals provoked by the Secret Speech. The Krasnopevtsev Affair, and trials over other underground Marxist revisionist groups, constituted another manifestation, albeit clandestine, of the repercussions of de-Stalinization on the academic community.[13]

The backlash of 1956 was no accident. Over the course of the following years, Khrushchev seemed to show little consistency in his debunking of the personality cult, attempting to retain a balance between opposed currents within Soviet society and at the top of the Soviet leadership. Despite what sounded like a call for reform in historical scholarship, many historians remained confused by the lack of clear party guidelines, stuck between the devil of "dogmatism" and the deep blue sea of excessive "revisionism." While the new line of criticism of Stalin was swiftly implemented in a revised edition of *The History of the Communist Party of the Soviet Union*, internal opposition to de-Stalinization remained strong in certain conservative academic circles and institutions.[14]

This resistance reflected the opposition that Khrushchev's policy of de-Stalinization met within Soviet society at large, not just from past informers, perpetrators, and accomplices of Stalin's crimes, but from a broader conservative majority. Those who had silently endured hardships for the sake of "constructing socialism" and had selflessly fought in the Great Patriotic War in Stalin's name found Khrushchev's critique hard to swallow. They had sacrificed too much to see the fruits of their efforts denigrated. They could not see their lives inscribed within a fundamentally negative narrative, which divided their generation between perpetrators, bystanders, and victims.[15]

Khrushchev was not insensitive to these moods, even as he moved on to crush resistance to de-Stalinization at the 22nd Party Congress, in 1961. He remained ambivalent about the ways in which Soviet intelligentsia was taking advantage of the relative liberalization. After authorizing a small wave of publications on the Gulag camp theme in the early 1960s, the Soviet leader moved swiftly to prevent an incontrollable growth of the flow. He would not let the "camp theme" turn into "ammunition for our enemies," and warned that "huge, fat flies will fall on such materials like dung."[16]

Brezhnev used a less crude language, but he could arguably have subscribed to these ideas. In his first years in power, he would progressively let the opponents of de-Stalinization regain lost ground.

The pendulum swings back

The years 1965–66 constituted a turning point regarding the Stalin question, a period during which a new line was progressively formulated. Stephen Cohen saw the Communist Party as being divided between reformers and conservatives, with the liberals and the neo-Stalinists constituting the two fringes of either wing.[17] The fall of the reformist Khrushchev had led to a "swing of the pendulum" in the other direction—a backlash usual for bipartisan systems—which had fallen short, however, of a return to Stalinism.[18] Roy Medvedev, on the other hand, described neo-Stalinists as a distinct group struggling for influence within the Party. While the conservative majority within the Soviet leadership was generally hostile to de-Stalinization but equally averse to any radical ideological shift, the active pro-Stalinist minority lobbied intensively for Stalin's rehabilitation. Both groups agreed, however, on the need to end what they considered an excessive "blackening of Soviet history," which they felt had taken place under Khrushchev. This implied silencing the less glorious pages of the Soviet past, and, in particular, Stalin-era repression.[19] Medvedev's perspective is borne out by the accounts of Arbatov and Aleksandr Bovin, two former members of Andropov's Central Committee international department, a haven of reformist thinking at the time, and of Fedor Burlatskii, political analyst for *Pravda* in 1965–67.[20] The existence of these factions, and the prominent influence that pro-Stalinists enjoyed under Brezhnev, explains why, despite the enduring political legitimacy of anti-Stalinism, dissident researchers studying these questions did fall prey to political repression. At the same time, the existence of an anti-Stalinist minority within the Party gave more weight to the coalition of dissident researchers and prominent members of the liberal intelligentsia who voiced their opposition to Stalin's rehabilitation in the late 1960s—a process examined in the next chapter.

Burlatskii thus recalled the hefty debate surrounding Brezhnev's speech for the twentieth anniversary of Soviet victory over Nazi Germany in May 1965. In April, a wave of positive mentions of Stalin by prominent military figures in Soviet media seemed to herald the Generalissimus's public rehabilitation.[21] Burlatskii and his colleagues had been tasked with drafting Brezhnev's speech, but they were confronted with an alternative draft, produced by Aleksandr Shelepin, then one of the most influential party leaders. Appalled by the pro-Stalinist orientation of the text, they convinced Brezhnev not to use it.[22] Yet they had to submit their own draft to the judgment of the Presidium and Central Committee Secretariat and take their suggestions into account. According to Burlatskii, the "overwhelming majority" was in favor of giving Stalin a more positive appraisal, and some even suggested removing any reference to the "personality cult." Andropov, however, proposed to avoid any mention of Stalin whatsoever, since this question was a factor of division, not only within the leadership, but also within the Party and Soviet people at large.[23] Eventually, Brezhnev adopted a formula close to Andropov's recommendation: his speech mentioned Stalin only once, insisting instead on the crucial role played by "the Soviet people, its glorious heroic army, guided by Lenin's party of communists."[24]

Arbatov and Bovin pointed to the crucial influence of the neo-Stalinist lobby constituted around the historian Sergei Trapeznikov, who became in April 1965 head of the Department of Science and Higher Education of the Central Committee, and Viktor Golikov, Brezhnev's longtime aide for questions of ideology and agriculture. Both had been protégés of Brezhnev since his time as First Secretary of the Moldavian Republic in the early 1950s. They were also old Stalinists who yearned for a return to the old orders. Arbatov claims that they gathered around them a group of like-minded figures, such as Konstantin Chernenko or Nikolai Tikhonov, and sought to exploit Brezhnev's indecisiveness and their influence in order to effect a radical ideological turn. Not only did they have his ear, but they also had a direct influence on the content of some of his speeches and Party documents.[25] Reflecting the general hostility of the liberal intelligentsia toward Trapeznikov, Roy Medvedev described him as "a staunch and smug dogmatist and Stalinist." Devoid of "any serious knowledge either in the field of Marxism or the field of social sciences, either in history, or in philosophy," he had repeatedly failed to be elected to the Academy of Sciences.[26] The hostility seems to have been mutual, as Trapeznikov's role in Nekrich and Medvedev's later exclusion from the Party shows. Indeed, at this historical juncture, he enjoyed a crucial influence.

In June and November 1965, Trapeznikov presided over a series of two conferences convened by the Ideological Commission of the Tsk to discuss the situation in the social sciences and draft recommendations to solve the "significant problems" uncovered in this field, in particular that of Party history. Although the discussions showed that a diversity of points of view still existed on the Stalin question, the conclusions Trapeznikov drew from them were clear: a new line had to be imposed and the criticism of Stalin's personality cult should end.

Encouraged by the changes triggered by Khrushchev's ouster, the participants expressed their opinions relatively freely during the sessions and voiced their irritation with the crude carrying out of Khrushchev's de-Stalinization campaign. Many of the grievances that social scientists and historians voiced concerning the constraints they faced in their work echoed those expressed at the 1962 All-Union Conference of Historians. Some speakers still seemed to entertain hopes for far-reaching liberal reforms. Overall, however, the political balance had shifted from the criticism of Stalin's personality cult to a critique of Khrushchev-era "subjectivism" in the historical field.

During the June meetings on Party history (June 21) and History of the USSR and General history (June 23), a few speakers were invited to present ideas to direct the work of the future commissions. Some of them, following Trapeznikov's explicit injunction, denounced the "subjectivism, which was to a large degree linked with such a phenomenon as the struggle against the personality cult."[27] Vladimir Khvostov, director of the Institute of History of the Academy of Sciences, thus offered an example of the kind of casuistic thinking that was to prevail in the following years. He regretted the political damage inflicted to the Party through the "blackening of Soviet reality" and the discarding of the whole Stalin era from Soviet history. Stalin, once so powerful, had been evicted from historiography "as though he did not mean anything, or never even existed at all."[28] "Historical truth" was the only criterion to apply. Yet Khvostov recognized that it was "inexpedient" to write about some historical questions of the recent past. "Why? First and foremost because we live in a hostile world, a great part of the world is still in the hands of imperialism and is hostile to us." Still, historians should "strive to approach [historical truth] to the maximum," through a "multisided approach," by concentrating not only on the negative aspects of a problem but also on the achievements of the process as a whole.[29]

Khrushchev did not bear alone the responsibility for this state of affairs. Other participants also pointed to the guilt of writers and historians who had overemphasized in their works the negative aspects of the Stalin era. As a result, according to one speaker, the new generation grew up in a spirit of nihilism and tended to condemn their fathers' generation for having failed to struggle against the personality cult.[30] They did not see the older generation as having accomplished "anything heroic, since it was a period of almost uninterrupted mistakes."[31] Therefore, it was crucial to educate youth in a spirit of patriotism and to restore the people's trust in history. At fault was the "dry, boring style" of historical scholarship and textbooks, the failure to popularize history. As a result, writers often filled the void, writing popular history in a lively, entertaining fashion, but far from the standards of orthodoxy expected from historians themselves. The main source of preoccupation, however, was the people's mistrust toward history fed by historians' excessive submission to immediate political aims. The constant rewriting of history books to fit an ever-changing political conjuncture—"*kon"iunkturshchina*"—and the turn toward a new personality cult of Khrushchev in historiography were singled out as the most negative manifestations of this tendency. The difficulty lay in combining responsiveness to the changing imperatives of politics, dictated by "party spirit" (*partiinost'*), with "historical truth."

In his final instructions to guide the work of the newly created commissions, Trapeznikov identified the main issues on the agenda: "The criticism of subjectivism and voluntarism"; "the intensification of the struggle with bourgeois falsifiers of history" and against "bourgeois apology, ideological and political indifference." Finally, he insisted on reflecting on ways to improve the propaganda of history, to enhance the prestige of Soviet history and social sciences in general within the population. He proposed getting inspiration from the 1938 Party resolutions and raising interest for scholarship through propaganda, as the Party had once done with Stalin's *Short Course*.[32]

On November 15–18, the Ideological Commission organized a joint session to discuss the results of the work of the four ad hoc commissions. In his presentation, Evgenii Zhukov, head of the Commission on History of the USSR, drew the lines of what would become in coming years the new official course on historical scholarship. History, he explained, was a political science, and, as they handled materials "of a great political acuteness," historians faced a crucial responsibility. While "truthfully exposing history," they had to "avoid straying into objectivistic positions." In a class society, historical truth could only relate to social classes, and there could be no "non-party relation to history."[33] He went on to attack the "subjectivist influences, foreign to Marxism" that characterized the denunciation of Stalin's personality cult. Stalin had been accused of all possible sins and had been blamed for all the negative developments within Soviet society. Zhukov assigned blame for this state of affair to "people who virtually specialized on nit-picking criticism of Stalin's political and theoretical mistakes, striving to blacken his activity in its entirety."[34] Trapeznikov concurred entirely with Zhukov, condemning "the blackening, groundless criticism of whole periods of the life of our party and people." This had triggered ideological disaffection and even "admiration for bourgeois ideology," which had undermined the authority of Soviet scholarship.[35] While the Central Committee Resolution of June 30, 1956 had offered a clear orientation to the Party, Trapeznikov deplored ulterior developments, which he dismissed as "serious subjectivist mistakes."[36] This emphasis on the June 30 Resolution would become one of the key arguments of the adversaries of de-Stalinization: ignoring the radical resolutions of the 22nd Party Congress, they conveniently stuck to the more moderate and balanced compromise of 1956.

In stark contrast with these evaluations, the general discussion revealed a variety of dissenting opinions, often coming from non-historians who held severe views on the state of historical scholarship. The academician Pavel Iudin, head of department at the Institute of Philosophy of the Academy of Sciences, once a Stalinist,[37] began by thanking "the comrades from the Presidium" for removing Khrushchev from power. He criticized the defeated leader's lack of respect for the intelligentsia, his simplistic approach to theory, and, more generally, the new personality cult that he had installed. This was reflected in a recently published *History of the Great Patriotic War* in six volumes, in which Khrushchev's military role in the victory was preposterously exaggerated, with hundreds of mentions of his name. And then suddenly, in the sixth volume, published after Khrushchev's ouster, the Soviet leader's name had all but disappeared.

> What kind of a science is this, comrades! This is some kind of slyness, petty peasant slyness. At first, they lied, lied, and then somehow tried to sweep away the traces. . . . Clearly, they think that no one will ever write history after them. [But future historians] will, and they will write honestly, genuinely and will condemn you in the most merciless way. . . . One cannot write history like this.[38]

Iudin then contrasted this Soviet multivolume series with Alexander Werth's work *Russia at War 1941-1945*. As vexing as it sounded, Iudin had to recognize that it made "a better impression than our *History of the Great Patriotic War*," providing "a fair, objective picture" of events. Despite being from the adverse camp, Werth had a positive attitude toward the Soviet Union, and analyzed events quite objectively, on the basis of British, French, and Soviet sources. It was comforting to think "that there are still some people on earth who know how to write history," Iudin bitterly concluded.[39]

The next speaker, Konstantin Ostrovitianov, vice president of the Academy of Sciences from 1953 to 1962, expressed regret that most historians followed the principle: "History is politics projected onto the past." He had experienced this as he wrote a history of Soviet economic thought: he found out that many economists he wanted to mention were on the list of authors who could only be criticized, but neither read nor quoted. But how could one offer a serious critique of "hostile theories" without reading or quoting from the original texts?[40] Both speeches were greeted with applause.

The only historian to confront Trapeznikov's new course openly was Andrei Kuchkin, an Old Bolshevik who had participated in the elaboration of two successive editions of *The History of the CPSU*, from 1959 to 1962.[41] He had fixed upon Trapeznikov's positive mention of the *Short Course*, a textbook which many used to "furiously tear to pieces." Now, Kuchkin fulminated, some comrades launched trial balloons, to test the Party's reaction, as they strove to revert to the cult of Stalin's textbook. Although he agreed that the critique of Stalin had gone too far, Kuchkin asked Zhukov to clarify his position: Did he consider that the task of condemning Stalin's cult still stood, or was it being repealed? Maintaining an ambiguity on this question and simply calling for an end to "nit-picking criticism of Stalin" meant "justifying Stalin's personality cult to a certain extent."[42] He concluded by asking the Ideological Commission to put a few speakers in their place "for turning their coats" (*za ikh sharakhanie*).[43]

These 1965 meetings of the Ideological Commission illustrate the debates agitating the Communist Party and the community of historians in the wake of Khrushchev's ouster. They revealed the widespread dissatisfaction with the current state of historical scholarship, eliciting diverging responses. While a minority still hoped for a deepening of de-Stalinization, Trapeznikov and those who had seized the opportunity to "jump ship" were intent on imposing a new reading of Soviet history. Yet they had to contend with Brezhnev's aspiration to consensus and the enduring legitimacy of de-Stalinization.

The 23rd Party Congress

On January 30, 1966, *Pravda* published an article signed by Evgenii Zhukov, V. Trukhanovskii, and V. Shchunkov entitled "The High Responsibility of Historians."[44] According to Nekrich, Zhukov and Shchunkov later claimed that the article had been inspired by Trapeznikov.[45] This seems likely, given that it drew heavily on Zhukov's speech in front of the Ideological Commission. The article clearly pointed out new orientations and boundaries in the historical field. After paying lip service to the necessity of past denunciations of the personality cult, Zhukov et al. denounced the "subjectivist influences alien to Marxism" that had surfaced in some historical works. In particular, they deplored the widespread use of "the mistaken, un-Marxist term 'period of the Personality cult'" and the exaggeration of Stalin's role in Soviet history.

These tendencies had "led, whether voluntarily or not, to the depreciation of the heroic efforts of the Party and people in the struggle for socialism, to an impoverishment of history."[46] One way to overcome these flaws was through the critical evaluation of all Soviet historical scholarship published. Confronted with the publication of "all kinds of reactionary distortions" of history, particularly coming from the bourgeois camp, the historians' duty was "to denounce such inventions, assert truth."[47]

Aleksandr Nekrich knew the danger that the affirmation of such views represented for the fate of his work. In February 1966, he was among six historians and philosophers to write a letter of protest to Mikhail Suslov, Central Committee Secretary in charge of Ideology, in reaction to Zhukov et al.'s article.[48] The signatories contested the attack against the term "period of the personality cult," which had been used in several resolutions of the 22nd Party Congress. Since a Congress resolution could only be amended or canceled by a new Congress, the characterization of this term as "unmarxist" was a direct violation of the Party's rules. Moreover, the signatories claimed that the formulation was "absolutely exact, precisely because it *limits in time* the existence of lawlessness and arbitrariness and shows that the Party was able to put an end to this period."[49] However, their request for publication of their letter was rejected, after examination by Trapeznikov and Stepakov.[50] Nekrich, on the other hand, writes that he and his cosignatories received confirmation that Suslov agreed with their letter and would raise the matter in front of the forthcoming 23rd Party Congress.[51] However, despite persistent rumors to this effect, the question of Stalin's rehabilitation was eventually kept off the Congress's agenda. Nekrich judged that Trapeznikov had been "too hasty." He had sought to "confront the party leadership with the 'fact' that authoritative historians were opposed to the term 'Personality cult,' and that the term should be revised, followed by a revision of decisions made at the 20th Party Congress."[52]

We can indeed interpret this article as part of a lobbying action by the pro-Stalinist faction pushing for Stalin's full rehabilitation. Nekrich's allegation that Suslov, a conservative Politburo member, opposed it, points to the divisiveness of the subject and continued legitimacy of de-Stalinization for Khrushchev's former ideology boss. It seems unlikely, however, that Zhukov's article was published without Brezhnev's approval. The preceding months has seen a renewed crackdown on dissent, with the arrest of the writers Iulii Daniel' and Andrei Siniavskii, and Brezhnev may have seen the Zhukov et al. article as a warning to liberal historians that de-Stalinization was over, and that a tougher line would henceforth be applied in the historical field.

Opposition on the historical front

The discussion of Nekrich's book

It was in this tense context, on February 16, 1966, that the Section of History of the Great Patriotic War at the IML organized a discussion of *June 22, 1941*. Planned since December 1965 by the section's head, Major General Evgenii Boltin, with Nekrich's agreement, its original purpose remains unclear. Was it intended, as Nekrich claims in his memoirs, as part of a "full-scale attack" on his book?[53] Or was it justified by "the exceptional interest in A.M. Nekrich's book," as Boltin himself stated in a letter?[54] According to Nekrich, rumors had been circulating since January that "Stalinist-minded historians, with the support of the Soviet army's central political office, the publications' committee of the council of ministers, and the science department of the Central Committee, were preparing a broad campaign" against *June 22, 1941*.[55] Other participants in the IML discussion[56] have upheld this version, which seemed particularly convincing in retrospect. However, evidence of such an early intent on the authorities' part is lacking.

Nekrich justified his concern by a letter of Boltin he had been shown: the Publications Committee of the USSR Council of Ministers had apparently asked several institutions and specialists to communicate their views on *June 22, 1941*. In his reply of January 2, 1966 to the Committee, Boltin conveyed his comments and gave the book a positive appraisal, mentioning the discussion the IML planned to organize the following month.[57] In another letter to the Publications Committee, dated from November 1966, Boltin explained he had organized the discussion in the context of the preparation of a new edition of *The History of the Great Patriotic War of the Soviet Union*. Nekrich's book presented "undeniable interest and raised a lively discussion within the editorial committee," which justified the organization of the discussion with the author.[58] Nevertheless, Boltin emphasized that already in January, he and his colleagues had voiced their critiques of the book, which provided the basis for the public discussion. What was initially intended as an "internal event," however, took an unexpected turn when Nekrich "misused" the permission he had received to invite a few colleagues and spread rumors about the authorities' intention "to 'crush' (*razgromit'*) the book and declare a 'new conception' of the pre-war period."[59] Nekrich confirmed that he spread the word about the debate at the IML, repeating that only "openness" could help avert the carrying out of "evil deeds."[60]

The history of this discussion has hitherto been written chiefly from the point of view of Nekrich himself and the anti-Stalinist historians who came to his rescue to avert the planned *razgrom*.[61] This can be explained by the fact that the discussion was documented at the time solely on the basis of a "short transcript" selectively compiled by Leonid Petrovskii, a young historian affiliated with the Museum of the Revolution. This text circulated in samizdat and was rapidly published in the West, mainly as an appendix to Nekrich's book.[62] In the 1990s, Petrovskii would also write several articles about the "Nekrich Affair."[63] However, the full official transcript, published in the 1995 Russian edition of *June 22, 1941*, presents a more nuanced vision of this discussion.[64]

The attendance was between 100 and 200 participants, mostly from the IML, the Institute of History and other academic institutes and from the military; some Old Bolsheviks and dissidents were also present.[65] The five-hour discussion started out on a peaceful note: Boltin, acting as a moderator, reassured the audience: no one intended to "crush" Nekrich's book and the discussion would be "absolutely free." The first speaker, Grigorii Deborin, discussed the book on behalf of the editorial team of the first volume of the *History of the Great Patriotic War*. The main criticism he addressed to Nekrich was his exclusive focus on Stalin's guilt for failing to listen to his advisers' warnings. Falling short of justifying Stalin, Deborin insisted on shifting the focus from the personality of the leader to a more comprehensive criticism of the personality cult that had triggered these errors. If the key to past abuses lay solely in Stalin's character flaws, then his death should have closed the door on any further reflections and no lessons were to be learned. But this was not the case. Deborin also reproached Nekrich with relying uncritically on memoirs and testimonies, particularly Marshall Golikov's. In Deborin's view, Golikov was guilty of "disinforming" Stalin, by describing the information he fed him concerning Germany's impending attack as "dubious." The harmful effects of the personality cult thus derived not only from Stalin's own actions and personality, but also from the actions of his subordinates, who deemed it necessary to alter facts to please the Soviet leader, "thus feeding and supporting his devastating ego."[66] This critique was certainly ambiguous. Many participants interpreted it as a call for a more thorough criticism of Stalin's collaborators, but also of the very nature of Stalin-era decision-making processes. However, some took the logic a step further, interrogating the functioning of the Soviet system at large. Clearly, it was not Deborin's intention to push the discussion onto this ground.

The ensuing debate initially proceeded smoothly. The first two-thirds of the discussion saw predominantly interventions from professional historians, balancing criticism and praise of *June 22, 1941*, with varying degrees of support for the author or his opponent, Deborin. All speakers praised warmly Nekrich's work, before making criticisms or suggestions in the perspective of a second edition. The historians spoke freely, avidly seizing this opportunity to discuss significant issues in an open forum, at a turning point in Soviet historical scholarship. However, toward the end, the debate took on a more confrontational turn, with several polemical interventions by dissidents and Old Bolsheviks in support of Nekrich, which met with a clear rebuttal from the organizers.

Most professional historians who took the floor were supportive of Nekrich. According to Viacheslav Dashichev, *June 22, 1941* was written "with a high civil pathos" and appealed to "the feeling of duty towards the people and history."[67] Daniil Melamid praised Nekrich's very good use of a large range of German sources. Although it was intended for a broad audience, it was at the same time "a scrupulous scholarly study."[68] Even Boris Tel'pukhovskii, who would later on coauthor a scathing critique of *June 22, 1941*, found it a "useful," "interesting read," which would raise interest not only among Soviet readers, but also abroad. He did find it "one-sided," though, in its sole emphasis on Stalin's personality.[69] Some participants, forgetting that Nekrich's hands had been tied by censorship, regretted the moderation of his critique. Dashichev criticized the lack of Soviet sources in Nekrich's book, although he recognized that this was primarily due to their inaccessibility to historians.[70] Only two interventions could be described as directly critical of Nekrich's book. M.Ia. Raskat reproached the author with mentioning too superficially the construction of socialism in the USSR and failing to emphasize the role of the masses.[71] As for Telegin, despite praising the book and calling for a second edition, he blamed Nekrich for his excessive reliance on foreign sources, untrustworthy memoirs from military commanders, as well as Khrushchev-era historical works, which, in his view, lacked objectivity.[72]

The participants also abundantly commented on Deborin's intervention, which they interpreted in various ways. Viktor Anfilov warned against Deborin's attempt to "whitewash" Stalin.[73] Melamid refuted some of Deborin's affirmations and stated his opposition to the general orientation of his remarks. It was precisely Stalin that stood at the center of the game. And he was guilty, not of miscalculations, which were, after all, human, but "an obstinate, stubborn ignorance of clear facts."[74] Yet several participants also heeded Deborin's call for a more comprehensive analysis of the effects of the personality cult on decision-making. Dashichev and Anfilov thus pleaded for a deeper examination of the respective shares of responsibility of Stalin and his staff. The atmosphere of fear within the country had led Golikov and others to lie to Stalin, but it was important "to avoid giving the impression that Stalin was simple-minded" and was simply fooled by his subordinates.[75] Vasilii Kulish, however, drew opposite conclusions: he observed with satisfaction "the birth of a new conception of the reasons of our defeats in 1941," which displaced the emphasis from Stalin to the disinformation by Golikov and others, "which led Stalin into error." Kulish also argued that the other speakers' exaggerated emphasis on personalities in the historical process, whether with a negative or positive lens, was a remnant of "the ideology and psychology of Stalin's personality cult," contrary to Marxism-Leninism.[76] Tel'pukhovskii, however, disagreed that Stalin's advisers had deliberately misinformed him, and called for reexamining the circumstances of this collective misevaluation of the international situation. He ended by chastising those speakers who had overstepped the limits of the criticism of the personality cult and put into question the Soviet state's political system.[77]

For the last third of the discussion was characterized by a more polemical tone and sometimes seemed to be getting out of hand, as the speakers directly attacked various taboos of Soviet historiography. These were precisely the speeches, emphasized in Petrovskii's transcript, that later raised the interest of samizdat readers and caused the discussion to be labeled as subversive.

Evgenii Gnedin, who had himself been in charge of providing the People's Commissariat of Foreign Affairs with information before the war, explained that Golikov's maneuver of presenting information about the impending attack as "dubious" was actually a way to bring Stalin's attention unto it. Indeed, only items identified as "dubious or false" raised interest, but it would be underestimating Stalin to think that he could be fooled by such labels. Answering Deborin's call to "to discuss not only Stalin's mistakes, but the system of government of the state," Gnedin provocatively agreed "that Stalin's mistakes and his faults or aspirations derived from the previous development." Finally, he pointed out a major flaw, which he believed was responsible for the defeats of 1941, and remained "relevant to this day": the lack of freedom of information, at least within the state apparatus.[78]

Lev Slezkin, a close friend of Nekrich from the Institute of History, warmly praised the book for its "timeliness" and set out to discuss the question of guilt. Although guilt could be assigned not only to Stalin and his accomplices, but even to Soviet society at large, if we reasoned in terms of degrees of responsibility, then Stalin certainly crowned the list. As for the 1939 German-Soviet pact, although it might have been necessary, its "pro-German" interpretation by the Soviet regime could not be justified. As a nineteen-year-old Komsomol "who considered himself called on to fight against the black forces of fascism," Slezkin remembered the "dispiriting effect" the pact had on him.[79]

Petr Iakir, the next speaker, was a historian affiliated with the Institute of History and the son of Commander-in-Chief Iona Iakir, executed during the Red Army purges in 1937. He commented on the question of the purges in the Red Army and among technical cadres, then voiced his opposition to the use of the expression "comrade Stalin." "It is not personal, but I don't understand how we can call 'comrade' a man who has caused so much harm to our state." In conclusion, Iakir mentioned the waste of combat forces represented by a huge number of healthy young men, wrongly sentenced to death by the NKVD's "troikas," condemned to sitting behind bars during the war, or guarding prisoners in the Gulag camps, while they could have been put to a better use on the frontline.[80]

The discussion ended with two radical speeches, which subsequently raised the most criticism. Leonid Petrovskii, another son of an "enemy of the people" executed in 1937, began with a harangue to the speakers: How could they "speak on this tribune and justify the man who committed such crimes, unheard of in history? How can we educate our youth with the name of a criminal, guilty of the death of millions?"[81] Boltin interrupted Petrovskii to remind him that the subject of the discussion was Nekrich's book and that he did not know of any Party resolution in which Stalin would be declared a criminal. "The resolution of the 22nd Party Congress concerning the removal of Stalin's body from Lenin's Mausoleum for mass crimes against the people and Party has not yet been cancelled"—sententiously replied Petrovskii.[82] Following a somewhat incoherent speech, Petrovskii seems to have been eventually bundled off from the tribune, leaving the floor to no less a fiery speaker, the Old Bolshevik Aleksei Snegov.

Himself a victim of political repression and an ardent lobbyist in favor of their rehabilitation,[83] Snegov qualified Nekrich's book as "honest, truly scientific work" and praised him for "accomplishing a civil feat in a specific, difficult scholarly field."[84] Comparing Stalin to a regiment's commander, Snegov rhetorically asked what fate should await the commander who leaves the front unprotected and lets the enemy through. He would be judged for treason. "We are now discussing this question on a greater scale, we are talking about the commander not of a regiment, but a whole country. . . . How can you, respected comrade Deborin, attempt to take the defense of the real culprit?"[85] Oblivious to Deborin's protests, Snegov set out to indict Stalin's actions from the mid-1930s onwards. A particularly sensitive question was that of the Soviet-German pact. In this regard, Snegov called on the audience to answer honestly: "Would Lenin have made a deal with Hitler, would he have begun to divide and share Europe on the basis of this pact? Just think about it! To perpetrate the fourth division of Poland!"[86] Refuting the term "reunification" in relation to Stalin's annexation of Western Ukraine and Belarus in 1939, Snegov fulminated: "They [just] sat with a map and shared: this is for you, this is for me." He condemned the repression of Polish communists in the 1930s, which had constituted a prelude to the Soviet-German Pact. The Old Bolshevik concluded by indicting the historians' recent tendency to justify Stalin's crimes. They were still under a terrible "hypnosis," which led them to believe that Stalin, not the Party, had been the chief architect of the country's industrialization and collectivization of agriculture.[87]

In reaction to this last speech, Deborin gave a concluding evaluation to the discussion. He first contested the rumors, which had been circulating for ten days and that Kulish had brought up, that "a new doctrine" was in the making. However, he then proceeded to summarize what he considered as the right approach to the questions raised in Nekrich's book: the responsibility for mistakes was shared by those who, whether wittingly or not, heeded and followed Stalin's mistaken path. Deborin contested that he had attempted to defend Stalin and claimed that he had only followed his "party conscience" and sought to "sort things out objectively." Finally, he condemned Snegov's appraisal of the Soviet-German pact, which only repeated the discourse of "our fiercest enemies." He concluded sententiously: "Snegov should think about the camp in which he finds himself." The Old Bolshevik then daringly replied: "I am from the Kolyma [Gulag] camp" under indignant cries from the audience.[88]

Nekrich writes in his memoirs that Boltin was shown during the noontime break a denunciation written to the Central Committee by Colonel Andrei Sverdlov. Son of the late revolutionary Iakov Sverdlov and notorious perpetrator during the Great Terror, he had become a researcher at the IML. The letter stated that "an anti-Soviet mob" had assailed the IML. Under increasing pressure, Boltin urged Nekrich to "dissociate himself" from Snegov's statement in his final word. Nekrich failed to abide by this order, but he did express the regret that the debate had become unnecessarily confrontational, adding that he did not consider Deborin's speech as an attack. Answering criticisms from various speakers, the historian explained the absence of many important documents in his book by directly alluding to censorship. The interview of Golikov purged by censorship, in particular, contained both a strict self-criticism and a denunciation of the Red Army's and other state administrations' responsibility for presenting Stalin with partial and selective information. Nekrich ended by answering Telegin's remark about the alleged lack of objectivity of books published after the 20th Party Congress, and his speech was drowned in applause. "What the Party said at the 20th Party Congress is no 'khrushchevism,' it is our party conscience, it is our heart, our blood, what we fought for, what our fathers fought for, what future generations will fight for. I am deeply convinced of this."[89]

Boltin then concluded the session, obviously anxious to "dissociate" himself and his colleagues from the "anti-Soviet" speeches of some participants in the debate. He insisted on the need to approach the problems discussed as "communists, as Marxist-Leninists" and refrain from emotions, "no matter how painfully memories rise before us." He singled out as a "negative example" of overly emotional speech the interventions of Petrovskii and Snegov. "If we give in to emotions, we will end up rejecting, in essence, all the bases on which Marxist historiography of the Great Patriotic War rests."[90] No one would try to justify Stalin's personality cult. However, there were clear limits to the scope of criticism allowed, and historians had to rely on Party resolutions as guidelines and refrain from "entertaining extremist [ideas]." Boltin then concluded with specific recommendations for a second edition of Nekrich's book.[91]

According to Roy Medvedev, a few days later, the Party committee of the IML condemned the excesses which had taken place during the discussion and identified Snegov and Gnedin's speeches as "anti-Soviet." Nevertheless, at the time, no consequences followed.[92] The discussion would probably not have sealed Nekrich's fate, if not for the broad circulation of the "short transcript" compiled by Petrovskii. Released into samizdat, the document soon crossed the Soviet border and was published in Western media in early 1967. This bad press for the regime would prove detrimental to Nekrich, although he was not directly responsible for it.

Revisionist historians at the Institute of History

The confrontation over Nekrich's book was not an isolated event and should be considered in the context of a broader struggle by Soviet revisionist historians to push forth new historical approaches and interpretations. Traditionally independent from the state, the Academy of Sciences employed numerous scholars with reformist views. Within the Institute of History, the spirit of reformism instilled by the Thaw had given birth to several bold projects of rethinking of Stalin-era dogmas in historical thought.

Since the 1950s, the "New Direction" historians under the leadership of Arkadii Sidorov had been reexamining the question of economic relations in prerevolutionary Russia. Sidorov's students, a group of young talented scholars, turned away from the *Short Course* and Stalin's classical work on the question and returned to Lenin's conceptions and the debates of the 1920s. By the mid-1960s, they had invented the concept of "multistructuredness" to characterize the complex economic and social structure of late nineteenth-century Russia—a sheer "paradigm shift" in the field.[93]

Another daring endeavor was the creation in January 1964 of the Sector of Methodology, under the auspices of the Section of Social Sciences. It was led by Mikhail Gefter, one of Sidorov's former graduate students. His goal was to offer a forum for discussion and reflection "to throw off the dogmatism and scholasticism which had encrusted Soviet historiography and to overcome the divorce between the theoretical disciplines . . . and concrete historical research."[94] Seeking to renew Marxism by returning to Leninist roots, Gefter organized conferences that reexamined important questions of Soviet historiography and put into questions the dogmas of the *Short Course*. The Sector of Methodology's seminars regularly attracted about a hundred participants from various disciplines and institutions.[95] The unorthodox ideas discussed in this forum would later on attract the wrath of the authorities, and by 1970, the Section of Methodology had been dissolved.[96]

The third revisionist group was formed around the agrarian historian Viktor Danilov. In 1958, Sidorov mandated the "Group on Soviet Peasantry" to write a history of the collectivization of agriculture in the early 1930s—a highly sensitive political subject that touched on the ideological core upon which the regime rested.[97] The 800-page monograph entitled *The Collectivization of Agriculture in the USSR 1927-1932* was ready for publication at the end of 1964. However, within twenty-four hours of Khrushchev's ouster, the proofs were withdrawn from the publisher. Over the following two years, under close political guidance, the authors produced three amended versions, successively subjected to discussion—to no avail. By November 1966, the monograph had been condemned as revisionist and denied publication.[98]

The battle of reformism against conservatism was also reflected on the local political level, with the confrontation, in the mid-1960s, between the anti-Stalinist Party committee of the Institute of History and higher Party instances. Nekrich was elected to this Party committee three years in a row, from 1964 to 1966. In late 1964, the liberating spirit of the Thaw could still be felt, and, according to Nekrich, the 300 members of the Party organization were "overwhelmingly anti-Stalinist."[99] In Nekrich's words, the newly elected committee "contained, like Noah's ark, every type of animal, two by two—progressives and Stalinists and those who . . . were simply using their status as committee members to advance their careers)."[100] In office, Nekrich and his peers tried to push further the line of de-Stalinization that was progressively being abandoned by the Soviet leadership. They knew, however, the limits of their power.

During Nekrich's first year, the Party committee was confronted with a disturbing instance of dissent within the Institute: Oleg Puzyrev, a scientific-technical senior researcher, was accused of writing an "anti-Party and anti-Soviet" historical essay. A young man with a physical handicap but a sharp mind, Puzyrev was a friend of Petr Iakir's and his ideas on the fifty-year history of the Soviet state were indeed vitriolic. In a thirty-page opus, he shared his sociological conclusions on Soviet society, with an emphasis on economic and productive relations. He characterized the Soviet state as the "collective exploiter" of the peasants and workers.[101] Nekrich, who read the manuscript as a member of the *partkom*, judged that "it was extremely difficult to defend Puzyrev." The young man's critique of the Soviet elite was based on the perspective of a "return to Leninism," but the Soviet leadership still considered it "an act against the party."[102] As a result, after tumultuous debates, Puzyrev was excluded from the Party and eventually dismissed from his scholarly position.[103] However, this affair was not without any consequences for the Institute of History: in June 1965, as Trapeznikov reported to the Central Committee about it, he noted that several members of the Party section where Puzyrev had worked had tried to shield him from punishment and had been reprimanded. As a result, the Moscow City Committee was called in to investigate the situation of the Institute's Party Committee and Trapeznikov called for measures to enhance ideological work within the Institute's staff.[104]

The following year, as a sign of support for the recent publication of *June 22, 1941*, Nekrich was reelected "by an overwhelming majority" to what had by then become a predominantly anti-Stalinist Party committee, with Viktor Danilov as its secretary. Both the director Khvostov and his deputy L. S. Gaponenko refused to become members of this *partkom,* and another deputy director, A. Shtrakhov, had to step in. The lines of confrontation were drawn.[105]

In Nekrich's words, a "cornerstone of the party committee's policy" was to provide the Institute's staff with an atmosphere of "freedom to defend one's scholarly views without fear of being slandered and accused of political crimes." Therefore, the committee's action was directed toward the "democratization of all academic institutions, and especially of our institute."[106] To this end, the *partkom* presented a plan for reform of election rules according to which the director, his deputies, and the heads of sections would be elected by the whole academic body. The procedures of designation of senior and junior researchers would also be made more transparent and open. Although this ambitious plan remained a dead letter, the whole atmosphere at the Institute became freer, and the *partkom* enjoyed support and authority that went beyond the Academy of Sciences.[107]

In prevision for the forthcoming 23rd Party Congress, a clear expression of the committee's orientation was given by a speech[108] made by Viktor Danilov during a closed Party meeting on February 19, 1966. By a twist of the calendar, the meeting took place just a few days after the discussion of Nekrich's book at the IML, but also two weeks after the publication of Zhukov et al.'s article "The High Responsibility of Historians." The speech reflected both the hope for further reforms inspired by the positions gained by anti-Stalinists and the fear of being forced to retreat. Iakov Drabkin, fellow member of the *partkom*, identified himself, Danilov, Nekrich, and others as the authors. The speech contained several bold demands for the time. It was, in Drabkin's words, a call "to the 'leadership' not to prevent historians from continuing their search for truth concerning the cruel era and the crimes of Stalinism."[109]

Danilov began by outlining the positive developments in the historical field since the end of the Stalin era: the steady progress toward new conceptions, democratization through open discussions within large fora, and the abandonment of Stalin's "false theoretical formulas."[110] Addressing the issue of the fall of prestige of historical scholarship within Soviet society, Danilov recognized that historians had "proved incapable of giving satisfying answers, backed up with arguments, to the questions that society is now raising in relation to history."[111] Popularization works were lagging behind new developments in historiography. Moreover, historians had yet to fulfill the Party's orders and study the conditions of emergence of the personality cult and its relation to society's socialist transformations since 1917. Danilov went on to directly attack the article by Zhukov et al. He took issue with their claim that the fall of the prestige of social sciences resulted from the Khrushchev era. Instead, he affirmed that the new flaws identified by the authors were relics of the Stalin era. The 20th and 22nd Congresses had radically changed the situation and ensured that Khrushchev's new excesses were identified and rejected.[112]

Danilov then proceeded to discuss the question of the "figure of silence" (*figura mol'chaniia*) which was still omnipresent in historical scholarship, despite attempts to eradicate it. The silence surrounding the names of the opposition figures Kamenev, Zinoviev, Trotsky, Bukharin had prevented historians from studying the institutions they had once headed. And the same device was increasingly applied to Stalin himself. Danilov argued for the study of past mistakes, not only as a guarantee against their repetition, but also to draw lessons from them, which would allow Communist parties abroad to construct socialism more rapidly and at a lesser cost. Showing the true scale of the obstacles that the Soviet people had overcome in its construction of a new society would only increase the educational potential of historical scholarship. Conversely, the "figure of silence" undermined "trust in educators, their ideology, and arguments among the masses, particularly youth."[113] Therefore, teachers and researchers would only elicit trust when facts would no longer contradict their words. This would also help counter bourgeois historiography, which concentrated precisely on those pages of the past that Marxist historians failed to explore.[114] The *partkom* secretary also attacked the dual conception of truth expounded in recent publications.[115] While party spirit was "the obligatory, indisputable principle of scholarly research," this had "nothing to do with *kon"iunkturshchina*, the distortion of historical truth to satisfy current moods, and even more to satisfy the interests of some people."[116]

The Institute's collective unanimously approved the Party committee's speech. After the 23rd Party Congress, in April 1966, the authors reworked the text and submitted it for publication in an edited volume. However, the contribution was removed by censorship.[117] This was unsurprising, since Danilov and his colleague I. Iakubovskaia had already sought to publish the most politically sensitive sections of the speech, containing the critique of the "figure of silence" in historical science, in a "letter to the editor" of *Novyi mir*, scheduled for publication in February 1966. On the eve of the *partkom* meeting, the head of the Publications Committee of the USSR Council of Ministers wrote a report to the Central Committee to advise against publication of the article, whose first author had already been singled out for his dissenting behavior.[118]

The authority to decide what could be published was in the hands of conservative figures who chased dissenting views wherever they found them. They did not have, however, the power to define positive policies and acted within a framework defined from above. Even Trapeznikov, who had the power to impose a tough line against dissent in the historical field, was eventually unsuccessful in operating an ideological U-turn that the Politburo deemed too radical.

The Brezhnev compromise

In February 1966, as the first Congress of the CPSU since Khrushchev's ouster was approaching, rumors concerning Stalin's impending rehabilitation intensified, and anti-Stalinists began to mobilize. Among numerous protest letters from the intelligentsia and Old Bolsheviks sent to the Soviet leadership, the most famous was a petition initiated by Ernst Genri[119] and addressed to Leonid Brezhnev by twenty-five prominent intellectuals in the field of science, arts, and literature; signatories included Andrei Sakharov, Kornei Chukovskii, Vladimir Tendriakov, Maia Plisetskaia, and many others. Expressing their distress with the frequent interventions in the media "directed, *de facto*, towards the partial or indirect rehabilitation of Stalin," they voiced their opposition to a revision of the resolutions of the 20th and 22nd Congresses. Claiming to speak in the name of many, they argued: "Our people will not understand and will not accept a divergence—even partial—from the resolutions on the Personality cult. No one can erase these resolutions from [our people's] consciousness and memory." Not only would such a decision cause "serious divergences within Soviet society," but it would also be a political blunder, threatening to cause "a new rift within the ranks of the Communist movement, this time between us and the Western Communist parties."[120] A second letter from an additional thirteen signatories followed nine days later. Not only did the letter circulate broadly in samizdat, as the KGB noted in March 1966,[121] but all the members of the Presidium had read it.[122] According to Roy Medvedev, who took part in the collection of signatures on behalf of Genri, this collective letter had been, if not planned, then at least encouraged from above by a few opponents of the rehabilitation of Stalin within the Party apparatus. They did so in reaction to a letter from prominent military leaders, lobbying the Congress to obtain such an official rehabilitation.[123]

Whether these protest letters and the publicity they received in the Western media, including the Italian Communist press,[124] proved decisive, remains an open question. However, the decision of the Soviet leadership not to mention either Lenin or Stalin in the Congress's main report clearly proved that a compromise position was privileged.

According to Arbatov, the liberals interpreted this as a victory for their camp.[125] Bovin, however, considered that the letter signatories had overestimated Brezhnev's "principledness": "At best he closed his eyes on the counter-attacks of Stalinists and on the fact that a significant part of the TsK apparatus encouraged, supported such attacks."[126]

Although it is tempting to ascribe Brezhnev's restraint to the protests of Soviet intelligentsia, Arbatov points to another moderating influence, coming from within the apparatus. The General Secretary, he argued, understood the need to broaden the range of views he was fed and increasingly trusted the advice of two close reformist advisers, Andrei Aleksandrov-Agentov and Georgii Tsukanov. Moreover, under their influence, he also took guidance from Andropov and some of his former collaborators such as Bovin or Shakhnazarov. Through these combined efforts, Arbatov argues, the influence of the pro-Stalinists on Brezhnev was weakened.[127] Nevertheless, this did not happen without confrontations. Arbatov thus recalls the particularly acute conflict that flared on the occasion of Brezhnev's visit to Georgia, in November 1966. A pro-Stalinist speech had been drafted for Brezhnev by Trapeznikov, Golikov, and some Georgian communists. Gorbatov claims he firmly took position against it, warning against the risk of negative reactions among Eastern European, but also Western European Communist Parties, and reminding Brezhnev that many Politburo members had publicly condemned Stalin at the 22nd Party Congress. Did he want to discredit them? Brezhnev, who had also invited Tsukanov and Andropov in his office, agreed to let them rewrite the speech in a softer key.[128] Arbatov's use of the reference to the 22nd Party Congress echoed the letters of protest to the leadership from the intelligentsia: despite Trapeznikov's attempts to strike off the resolutions of this Congress, it remained a legitimate reference point which no Politburo member felt entitled to question.

Nevertheless, the offensives of pro-Stalinists increased in the following years, particularly targeting historians and writers. The bulk of these attacks fell on 1969, the year of celebration of Stalin's ninetieth birthday, which coincided with a new crackdown on dissent in the aftermath of the invasion of Czechoslovakia. Most prominent was an article entitled "For a Leninist Party Spirit in the Treatment of Soviet History" by V. Golikov, S. Murashov, I. Chkhikvishvili, N. Shatagin, and S. Shaumian, published in February 1969 in the journal *Kommunist*.[129] The authors unveiled a program to redress imperfections of recent Soviet historiography. They called for a return to the emphasis on class struggle, for, in a class society, humanities scholars were bound to reflect the class interests of their own society. Marxist-Leninist ideology was the "true compass" of Soviet historians, who should rely on Lenin's works as a fundamental source, offering an ideologically correct scientific model for the history of the CPSU.[130] Unfortunately, some Soviet historians had failed to study the Party's experience in all its aspects. Instead, they had concentrated solely on mistakes and flaws, without placing these errors in the appropriate context, that of the realization of a fundamentally correct party line.[131] Despite the successes of recent historiography, some "weak" works had made their way into print. Under the pretense of revealing new facts, they sometimes sought to revise fundamental "truths" (*istiny*) or important questions, which the Party had settled long ago. Although the resolution of June 30, 1956 had clearly and exhaustively expressed the Party's condemnation of the personality cult, some historians still sought to "blacken the heroic history of our state and Lenin's party in the period of the construction of socialism, depict these years as a continuous chain of mistakes and failures."[132]

The journal *Kommunist* received many protest letters in response to this article. Leonid Petrovskii complained bitterly that although "no one seized historians by the throat to preach false socialism (*lzhesotsializm*)," some continued to attempt to revise "the resolutions of the 20th and 22nd Party Congress and teach how to conceal historical truth."[133] The fact that Golikov et al.'s article had appeared in the official press organ of the Central Committee worried Petr Iakir. He noted that the ongoing pro-Stalinist campaign was now reaching a climax, with the official backing of the central organ of the CPSU.[134] Roy Medvedev shared these concerns: *Kommunist* had launched a concerted attack on the de-Stalinization course, and this article was already becoming prescriptive for press committees, publishing houses, editorial committees, and censorship organs. This was all the more worrying as, according to Medvedev's information, the piece had not been discussed at the highest echelons of power. He therefore denounced the text as a "factionary intervention," which undermined "the unity of our Party and the whole Communist movement."[135]

By December 1969, marking the ninetieth anniversary of Stalin's birth, the Brezhnev leadership found itself compelled to take a stance. Rumors of a series of commemorative events in Stalin's honor were agitating the intelligentsia.[136] Discussions in the Politburo concerning the publication of a commemorative article showed the uneasiness that this question raised. Although Brezhnev initially opposed the publication of an article, he eventually agreed with his colleagues, who favored a short piece, balancing Stalin's errors and achievements. Petro Shelest thus argued that such an article would be well-received, including by the intelligentsia, as a counterpoint to the recent publication of military memoirs about the war, some of which praised Stalin's role. "Stalin made mistakes—we should speak about them. There were some positive aspects—no one denies it, obviously. And we have to say how it was in history. We should not embellish and we should not distort history."[137] Indeed, Medvedev noted in his *Political Diary* that the publication of this article, which "clearly had a character of compromise," was interpreted as a positive signal by anti-Stalinists, who expected a rehabilitation of Stalin. Still, a zone of silence remained over many of his crimes, particularly in the early months of the war, during industrialization or the forced collectivization of agriculture.[138]

Both the discussion of Nekrich's book at the IML and the ideological conferences of June and November 1965 testify to the broad diapason of views on the Stalin question that found expression in the political and academic fields in 1965–66. Critiques concerning Khrushchev-era historical scholarship centered not so much on de-Stalinization itself, which was still considered as legitimate, but on the caricatural denunciation of Stalin, the failure to interrogate the broader causes of his "personality cult" and, in fine, the subjection of historians to new dogmatic schemes, which only further discredited the historical profession as a whole. It may have been to avoid a new turnaround and save themselves from the ridicule of belying their own speeches at the 22nd Party Congress that Brezhnev and his Politburo colleagues renounced any open revisionism in the historical field. But it was also in line with their paramount objective of greater stability: in this sense, shutting the ideological lid over the Stalin question appeared as a more consensual course than the kind of revisionism that Trapeznikov advocated. Maintaining this space of ambiguity gave the Brezhnev leadership more flexibility to carve a middle-of-the-road line, which could be adapted to the circumstances. Brezhnev's silence at the 23rd Party Congress, when both the anti-Stalinists and pro-Stalinists expected him to take position, was in itself a response. In 1969, however, the need was felt for a statement from the leadership on the occasion of Stalin's birthday, which would positively reaffirm the compromise stance adopted.

By emphasizing the importance of debate and lobbying in the formation of Brezhnev's ideological policy, and by presenting the outcome as a compromise far from the expectations of pro-Stalinists, this chapter challenged traditional narratives, which present the General Secretary as the man who sought to rehabilitate Stalin. One can certainly argue that some of these debates were merely staged to create the illusion of discussion, but the reality of the confrontation of views on the Stalin question at this historical juncture, both in the political and societal arenas, can hardly be denied. I argue that the established legitimacy of anti-Stalinism, underscored by the lobbying of the liberal intelligentsia, acted as an inertial force that counterbalanced the revisionist zeal of pro-Stalinists. The almost accidental propelling of Nekrich to the status of figurehead of the struggle against Stalin's rehabilitation occurred in a context of strong academic activism, which coalesced around the consensual cause of anti-Stalinism. By offering a language that was legitimate from the point of view of the leadership and the movement's participants, anti-Stalinism could federate largely within the intelligentsia and the Party. Dissident researchers fully participated of this movement, although it was primarily through their works that they stated their opposition to Stalin's rehabilitation.

3

Voicing Opposition to Stalin's Rehabilitation

One of the reasons why the discussion of Aleksandr Nekrich's work at the IML raised such interest, enthusiasm, and fears was the context of heightened social activism in which it took place, in the weeks preceding the 23rd Party Congress, but also within days of the trial over Iulii Daniel' and Andrei Siniavskii, which is traditionally identified as the birth of the Soviet dissident movement. In September 1965, the writers were arrested after their identification as authors of uncensored works published in the West under pseudonyms. This first trial against writers for the content of their works, less than a decade after Boris Pasternak had been coerced into refusing his Nobel Prize for *Doctor Zhivago*, sent a strong signal to the intelligentsia. In February 1966, Daniel' and Siniavskii received sentences of five and seven years of camp respectively. Their condemnation triggered an unprecedented wave of public protests in the form of collective letters.

Two months earlier, on December 5, 1965, Soviet Constitution Day, a "glasnost' demonstration" demanding a fair, transparent trial for the writers had gathered 100 to 200 people. This first free demonstration in decades lasted only a few minutes but signaled the dawn of a new era.[1] The organizer of the demonstration, Aleksandr Esenin-Vol'pin, developed an original "legalist" strategy of protest based on calls for a strict obedience of Soviet laws, which were more progressive and permissive than their implementation, or rather lack thereof, suggested.[2] Most of the anti-Stalinist letters of protest of the second half of the 1960s which are examined in this chapter followed a similar strategy, by appealing to the observance of the resolutions of the 20th and 22nd Party Congresses. Sergei Oushakine has provocatively pointed out the high degree of proximity of dissident discourse to official Soviet language. He argued that dissidents were constrained by Soviet society's existing "regime of truth": for their own discourse to be perceived as "truthful," they had to "mimetically replicate" the dominant ideological discourse.[3] While I agree that speaking the Party's language was the only way for protesters to get their message across, I find that they identified with this official discourse, but also acted upon it in creative ways, instead of merely "mimicking" official ideological stamps, as Oushakine claims. Certainly, in the 1960s, appealing to the Soviet leaders' party consciousness seemed a more effective strategy than later calls for the respect of human rights, which became associated with Western interference. But beyond the question of effectiveness, anti-Stalinism also constituted a politically legitimate federating language, which could unite broad groups of protesters from the intelligentsia, with varying degrees of conformism and diverse political views.

While anti-Stalinism constituted for some dissidents an Aesopian language, a substitute for more radical grievances and claims, more moderate protesters found it attractive precisely because it was compatible with continued loyalty to the Party. In this sense, Brezhnev's decision not to repeal past congress resolutions provided these activists with a legitimacy for their actions. However, as the 1960s wore on, and in particular after the 1968 invasion of Czechoslovakia, communist rhetoric was increasingly replaced by calls for a moral condemnation of Stalin's crimes. Ethics, rather than politics, became the basis for the dissident movement's actions.

Traditionally considered as the bearer of moral values, the intelligentsia played a prominent role in these written protests. The Old Bolsheviks, veterans of the Revolution who had often suffered in the camps, were among the vocal opponents to Stalin's rehabilitation, but they were also joined by writers, historians, and scientists. Dissident researchers were bridges between these two communities: through their research, they had come into contact with the living witnesses of the past that Old Bolsheviks were, but they were also intellectuals who interacted with the community of writers and historians, as shown in Chapter 4. These connections made them fully part of the campaign of protest letters, which contributed to their shift from conformism to dissent. While these protests may have had only a marginal political impact on the Soviet leadership, I argue that they were not only morally significant, but could also shield individuals from repression. As the Nekrich Affair shows, the scholarly community was indeed prepared to rise up in defense of one of its members when it felt collectively threatened.

A rebellious intelligentsia

The pen is mightier than the sword

In 1961, Richard Pipes noted that "the old cultured intelligentsia has fulfilled its historic role": not only had it lost "enthusiasm for political action" and receded into "a mood of cynicism and pessimism," but it faced a state that was too authoritarian to be vulnerable to its assault.[4] Although Pipes did identify the persistence of a "body of intelligentsia which does retain a sense of civic awareness," instead of "striving to reform the regime," it sought to "escape it"—that is, erect a barrier between public and private life and achieve autonomy in various fields, in particular in culture, science, literature.[5] Indeed, the success of samizdat in the 1960s did testify to a widespread urge to create spaces sheltered from the state's omnipotent and omniscient embrace. However, what Pipes failed to foresee was the rise of a fringe of the intelligentsia, which would shed its passivity and renew its activism in later years.

Pipes's reference to the "old" nineteenth-century intelligentsia was not coincidental. Indeed, one of the most potent formative myths of the liberal intelligentsia of the 1960s was its identification with its prerevolutionary predecessor. The onset of the Thaw, a period of cultural and societal reawakening following Stalin's death, and the 20th Party Congress opened up new spaces of political and cultural expression and new hopes to this group, which had greatly suffered from Stalin's terror, not only individually, but also collectively. Liudmila Alekseeva's memoirs expressed her generation's aspiration in clear terms: "The old intelligentsia no longer existed, but we wanted to believe that we would be able to recapture its intellectual and spiritual exaltation. Our goal was to lay claim to the values left by the social stratum that had been persecuted by the czars and destroyed by the revolution."[6] Born and educated within the Soviet system, the "sixtiers' generation," or *shestidesiatniki*, subscribed to socialist ideals of social justice, but constructed themselves in opposition to revolutionary violence, the degeneration of which they had witnessed during the Stalin era. In Vladislav Zubok's words, theirs was a "search for meaningful social roles and moral values, to replace those, which had been shattered and defiled after Stalin's death."[7]

Despite their strong identification with the prerevolutionary intelligentsia, however, the *shestidesiatniki* differed from them in several respects, as Benjamin Tromly has pointed out. The broadening of this social stratum as a result of mass access to higher education in the Soviet era had considerably diluted the protest potential of this group, and even among educated elites, identification with the "civic, moral or political agenda in implicit or explicit opposition to the authoritarian state" was far from universal. Moreover, the Soviet regime had largely succeeded in reconciling the intelligentsia with the system, and the overall rise in the level of education meant that the Soviet intelligentsia was "far less socially isolated" than its predecessor had been.[8] In addition, the fact that the old intelligentsia had formed the backbone of the revolutionary movement that had seized power in 1917 also made the struggle against the Soviet state undesirable for a generation that still largely subscribed to communist ideals. Many of them, such as Aleksandr Tvardovskii, editor in chief of the liberal literary journal *Novyi mir* who first published Solzhenitsyn and candidate member to the Central Committee of the CPSU in the 1960s, opted for a struggle from within the system.

Endowed with a prestige unequaled in Western societies,[9] Soviet intellectuals could hope to reach a wide audience, both among the literate masses and at the highest echelons of power. Indeed, the regime's attitude toward the intelligentsia was characterized by a fundamental ambiguity: while the educated layers of society fulfilled essential technical and ideological functions that could not be dispensed with, the intelligentsia as a social group was rightly considered as a potential opponent of the established political order. And this opposition was made public in many ways. Not only did the intelligentsia carefully monitor the Soviet leadership's actions, but it also tended to become organized and form independent groups, threatening the Party's absolute monopoly on power.[10]

One important lever of action was the writing of protest letters to the party leadership or to the press. Individual letter-writing to higher instances had always been a common means of public expression, widely used to convey discontent, disagreement, or dismay, as well as admiration, gratitude, or approbation. Letters were commonly addressed to public figures such as writers, to newspapers and literary journal editors, and to political figures or official organs. They constituted, according to Denis Kozlov, a form of "participatory politics."[11] But they could also be used to voice complaints of a private character and seek intercession. The phenomenon of protest letters was not limited to the intelligentsia. Workers and peasants, being traditionally less literate, were arguably less prone to resort to written protests—although recent studies of letters to journal editors during the Thaw show that readers from the broadest social and political spectrum expressed their opinion on current publications.[12] Ekaterina Surovtsevsa has examined letters from Soviet writers to their leaders and identified five main letter types: letters containing complaints or requests of a personal character were the most numerous, whereas letters containing praises, invectives, declarations, or letter-pamphlets were less common occurrences.[13] Most of the letters and petitions examined in this chapter, however, were "letter-pamphlets": their authors directly challenged the authorities, launched accusations, or offered a more moderate but "resolute critique" of institutions or political figures.[14]

Indeed, the post-Stalin era marked a break with the previous period, insofar as political reforms initiated from above bred new hopes concerning the effectiveness of lobbying from below. By the mid-1960s, collective petitions were also becoming more common: they added weight to the grievances expressed, but were also more severely punished, as instances of "organized" illicit behavior. More traditional in form and judged less threatening than other contemporary forms of dissent (such as unauthorized demonstrations or the compiling of samizdat "white books" on political trials), these letters were nonetheless taken seriously by the Soviet leadership, particularly due to their organized character. Those who signed them were designated as *"podpisant"* (signatory), a title of courage, de facto synonymous with "dissident."[15] Emerging as a response to the belief that Khrushchev's successors were orchestrating an official campaign to rehabilitate Stalin, anti-Stalinist collective letters constituted an early focus of the burgeoning dissident movement. Many letters addressed specific cases: they were written in reaction to political trials, arrests, or other instances of repression, with the aim of repealing the sentence or influencing the verdict. Others were protests against pro-Stalinist publications. Increasingly, however, letters ostensibly addressed to the Soviet leadership ended up circulating underground. Together, they participated in creating "imagined communities" of dissent, spreading among broad circles of samizdat publics a consciousness of unity in opposition.

According to Mikhail Meerson-Aksenov, letter-writing fulfilled the same function of free expression as the press in democratic societies, but with a personal tinge: a letter expressed the author's "moral consciousness" and appealed to the addressee's own "moral consciousness."[16] Denis Kozlov has noted the role that letter-writing played in the post-Stalin era as "an established mechanism for influencing politics." As "a tool for social action and participation in power, letter writing was a form of activism that presumed the author's high degree of identification with the existing order—their perception of themselves as its integral part."[17] This was certainly true for a group which was especially vocal in expressing its disagreement with the official line on the Stalin question, the Old Bolsheviks. They had fought for the triumph of revolutionary ideals, and many of them had fallen prey to Stalin's criminal grip. Many of them had modest origins and had been "raised by the Revolution." Yet what inspired them to speak up was a feeling of injustice, inspired by their experience of repression and the state's inappropriate response to this historical failure of a system they had fought to establish. As for the other participants of anti-Stalinist protests, they constituted a group with similar characteristics to those of dissident researchers: they were for the most part intellectuals, who acted out of moral convictions, but also often based on their personal experience of the Terror, through the loss of a relative or their own record of repression.

Anti-Stalinist protest letters

The wave of protest letters sent to the Soviet leadership before the 23rd Party Congress, in February–March 1966, was but the first in a series of written protests against Stalin's rehabilitation. In September 1967, on the occasion of the fiftieth anniversary of the October Revolution, forty-three sons and daughters of repressed Communists called on the Soviet leadership to put an end to the public rehabilitation of Stalin. Among the initiators of the action were Petr Iakir and Leonid Petrovskii, son and grandson of two important Bolshevik leaders, both of them participants of the IML discussion of Nekrich's book. Anton Antonov-Ovseenko was also among the signatories. Expressing regret that the names of the victims of the personality cult had been either forgotten or stained by infamous labels, the signatories called for the construction of the monument in their honor promised by Khrushchev at the 22nd Party Congress.[18] In framing their demands strictly within the confines of past resolutions and promises and in symbolically connecting de-Stalinization to the ideals of the Revolution, the forty-three established a line of continuity between the Khrushchev and the Brezhnev eras, contrasting with the new leadership's marked emphasis on its rupture with Khrushchev's "subjectivism."

The same year, Lev Kopelev commented in an open letter on recent pro-Stalinist publications, such as the memoirs of Kliment Voroshilov, Stalin's right-hand man, or literary works by Viacheslav Kochetov.[19] Kopelev estimated optimistically that the efforts of pro-Stalinists would be vain, for the Soviet people, led into delusion under Stalin, had definitively realized the criminal nature of his regime and understood that "justifying Stalin equals calumniating socialism." He concluded that "after all that became known at the 20th and 22nd Party Congresses . . . the myth of Stalin's cult has been destroyed once and forever."[20] Although Kopelev placed his hope in the moral and political revolution triggered by the 22nd Party Congress, his conservative opponents preferred to appeal to the minimalist compromise of the June 30, 1956, resolution, characterizing ulterior developments as "revisionism."

This opposition could be felt in letters protesting the 1969 article by Zhukov et al. "For a Leninist Party Spirit in the Treatment of Soviet History."[21] In their individual letters of protest, Roy Medvedev, Leonid Petrovskii, and Petr Iakir all contested the depiction by Golikov et al. of the June 30, 1956 resolution as reflecting the Party's position. They believed that the limited compromise reached while Khrushchev still shared power with Molotov, Malenkov and Kaganovich had since been made redundant by the bolder resolutions of 1961. "Who gave the authors the right to teach historians to forget the resolutions of the 22nd Party Congress?"[22] asked Petrovskii indignantly. Iakir confronted the Soviet leaders with their hypocrisy: all current Politburo members had once spoken up in condemnation of Stalin and his henchmen, he claimed, before giving concrete examples from the speeches to the 22nd Party Congress.[23] Medvedev reminded his readers that none of the Secret Speech's accusations had ever been contested; on the contrary, hundreds of publications had confirmed them. *Kommunist* had no right to stand up against party resolutions that remained in force, and to characterize statements made during the congress as "irresponsible inventions."[24]

By 1969, however, many protesters were losing faith in the power of such rhetoric and in their ability to influence the leadership. Increasingly, protests against Stalin's rehabilitation merged with new concerns over political repression and the tightening of censorship. Protest letters began to reflect fears of a rebirth of some aspects of Stalinism, particularly after the Soviet invasion of Czechoslovakia. In their "Address to the figures active in the field of science, culture and arts," Il'ia Gabai, Iulii Kim, and Petr Iakir noted that, in recent years, "the ominous symptoms of a restoration of Stalinism can be observed." This was manifested through the organization of political trials "against people who had the courage to defend their dignity and internal freedom, who dared to think and protest."[25] Calling on their addressees to actively stand up against a rebirth of Stalinism, the authors of the text concluded threateningly: "Each of your silences is a further step towards a new Daniel' and Siniavskii trial. Gradually, with your silent acquiescence, a new 1937 could arise."[26]

Their call was echoed by many expressions of protest, often directed against the return of censorship in the literary field, and the reinforcement of the "figure of silence" in historical publications. The authors of letters insisted on the crucial need for freedom of speech and transparency (glasnost') in relation to the Stalinist past to prevent a return of Stalinism. "Indeed, the murder of the truthful word comes from there, from the cursed Stalin era," wrote Lidiia Chukovskaia in 1968.[27] Lev Kopelev called anti-Stalinists and neo-Stalinists alike to an open dialogue, arguing that what the latter feared most was "the free exchange of opinions, transparency, concrete historical truth, a real Marxist critique."[28] Others were more pessimistic, noting that freedom of speech was only respected in relation to the opponents of de-Stalinization. In January 1968, Grigorii Svirskii thus warned the Moscow section of the Union of Soviet Writers: "The eradication of discussion books is a particularly alarming symptom. It means that thinking people are not needed. A thinking person in conditions of arbitrariness is potentially a dissenter."[29]

Moreover, Stalin's crimes, but also positive appraisals of his historical role, were increasingly criticized from a moral and legal, rather than a political standpoint. Already in 1965, Grigorii Pomerants, in his treatise "The moral make-up of a historical figure" stated that, while support of Stalin in the context of the struggle against fascism could have been justified, his contemporary idolization was intrinsically immoral. "To restore respect for Stalin, knowing what he has done, means to establish something new, to establish respect for denunciations, torture, and executions."[30] The most radical expression of this shift in emphasis was Iakir's letter of protest to the journal *Kommunist*.[31] Placing the accent on the principle of legality, Iakir used the Soviet criminal code to demonstrate that Stalin's crimes fell under specific law articles and, therefore, deserved the corresponding punishment. His goal was to "demonstrate that [*Kommunist*] has taken the defense of a criminal who has deserved four death sentences and, by addition, 68 years of imprisonment . . . if we count these crimes as having been committed once only, but as these were committed constantly, then this punishment should be multiplied thousands of time."[32] Unless the authors of the article offered convincing counterevidence, Iakir considered himself entitled to engage a lawsuit against Stalin for the crimes he had listed. He expressed his conviction that "posthumous condemnation is possible, just as posthumous rehabilitations are possible and legal."[33]

However, beyond judicial decisions, what mattered was the judgment of history, which involved the research of historians, but also the political will to perpetuate the memory of victims. Lidiia Chukovskaia called for establishing a day of commemoration of victims of political repression, and creating monuments and cemeteries, where relatives could openly express their grief. She insisted that she did not call for vengeance and did not have in mind a criminal, but "a societal judgement."[34] She wanted "this machine, which transformed a lively person blossoming with projects into a cold corpse, to be investigated, one little screw at a time." And a judgment should be passed on it, "out loud."[35] Leonid Petrovskii denied that the work of courts and judicial organs should take precedence over that of historians. "It is precisely in front of the tribunal of History that the crimes of Stalin and his accomplices (*oruzhonostsy*) must stand ...! This should be done for the sake of the struggle for Communism, which does not recognize any superfluous and vain sacrifices."[36]

Petrovskii's call to judge Stalin's crimes before the tribunal of history echoed the title of Medvedev's opus *Let History Judge*. For such a judgment to take place, both of them were convinced, the truth about Stalin's crimes had to be revealed. But the notion of "truth" was itself disputed.

The theory of two truths

Indeed, an echo of the discussion on Stalin in the philosophical field was the debate on the notion of "truth" and the role of writers and historians in revealing the "truth" about past events. There was arguably nothing fundamentally new in this debate, except for its implications in a new political context. This multifaceted notion had been central to Russian culture for centuries. The traditional structuring opposition was between the word *pravda*, meaning "truth as justice" (closely related to the notion of *spravedlivost'*: justice, fairness, truth), a concrete, but also subjective truth, and *istina*, designating a more absolute notion of "enlightened truth," reached through the intellect and standing objectively above the human realm.[37] In the Soviet Union, the notion of *pravda* was dominant. Truth could only mean social justice and no truth abstract from social realities could exist. Therefore, ideology was the yardstick according to which it should be measured, and the Party remained its sole interpreter, entitled to guide the people through this dialectical maze. However, maintaining the Party's monopoly on truth could only be achieved by silencing dissenting voices in the chorus. While repression had effectively suppressed alternative discourses in the Stalin era, once this threat declined, alternative "truths" began to bud and blossom. As Philip Boobbyer noted, the Bolsheviks had once used "truth" as a weapon in their struggle against the Tsarist regime, but this was a double-edged sword, which could be turned against the Soviet regime as well.[38]

Khrushchev's de-Stalinization had aimed at reconciling the Party's *pravda* and widely known facts. However, the rejection of previously monopolistic truths only created widespread confusion. As statements of past authorities were declared void, the Soviet people struggled to trust its new leaders. In these moving sands, a cacophony of alternative interpretations emerged, as a result of the relative relaxation of censorship. The Soviet intelligentsia was undergoing a process of reawakening of conscience, after decades of brutal repression against any manifestation of independent thought. In this context, literature took the lead in reaffirming the importance of moral values. In 1953, Vladimir Pomerantsev had published in *Novyi mir* a much-debated essay entitled "Sincerity in Literature," in which he put the outdated canons of Socialist Realism on trial and called for a return to "reason, conscience and inclination."[39] However, some pro-Stalinist intellectuals disagreed with the representation of the Soviet past that *Novyi mir* sought to convey, and they strove to impose their own conceptions.

One of these attempts was Evgenii Vuchetich's article "Let's Introduce Clarity," published in *Izvestiia* in April 1965, on the eve of the celebrations of the twentieth anniversary of the Soviet victory in the Great Patriotic War.[40] This famous sculptor, creator of several renowned war monuments, reacted to an article by *Novyi mir*'s editor in chief Aleksandr Tvardovskii and defined his stance on the question of truthfulness in literature in opposition to the writer's position. He contrasted "truth" (*pravda*) to what was only a "semblance of truth." Only the "artist's acute, piercing sight" could distinguish "the truth of the fact" from the "truth of the phenomenon." Explicating these concepts, the artist took examples from the history of the war:

> Of course, it is true that in the initial period of the war there were instances of disorder, confusion, and sometimes even panic . . . . This is the truth, but only the truth of the event, the fact, and not *the truth of life and of the people's struggle* in one of the most critical periods of its century-long history. The authentic truth (*istinnaia pravda*) consists not only in [the fact] that we retreated to the Volga banks, but that, having broken the fascist beast's spine on the steep banks of the Volga, we then marched on to Berlin and erected our great victory's banner upon the Reichstag.[41]

The dual conception of truth expounded in this article raised much indignation within the anti-Stalinist intelligentsia, and a group of Soviet historians wrote an open letter of protest in reaction. They considered that such an approach to history amounted to a suppression of those historical facts that did not fit the official heroic historical narrative. Were the millions that died during the occupation of the Western regions in 1941–42 "not [part of] the 'truth of life' and just facts, events?" asked the authors of the letter. "We have no right to forget about this, not just because there is no family in the USSR that did not have its victim. But we also have another duty, another obligation: to comprehend historical truth in its whole entirety [*sic*], in the name of the *present* and the *future*."[42]

This question was also central to a series of articles published by Roy Medvedev in his samizdat journal *Political Diary* in early 1967.[43] The historian expressed his disagreement with Vuchetich's approach, which adopted the language of objectivity, but was in fact conducive to censorship and ultimately yielded a distorted picture of reality. All agreed that truth was essential, but there were divergences concerning the kind that was needed.

Why had historical scholarship ceased to study Stalin's crimes? Censors had banned many valuable historical and literary works shedding light on the dark pages of the past, arguing that they did not reflect "the Great Truth of our life and our history, which is needed by the Soviet People."[44] Medvedev recognized that, in theory, the conception of a "truth of life" opposed to the "truth of the fact" made sense. However, what was problematic was the instrumentalization of this theory "to exclude from our books' pages, our cinema screens and theater stages the authentic truth of life, to defend a one-sided and essentially untrue representation of reality." Under the notion of "small truth," pro-Stalinists encompassed "many events and phenomena of our reality of huge importance," in particular Stalin-era crimes. The historian asked rhetorically: "But did [these events] not have an influence on the development of our social life that was at least equal to the successes of the industrial construction and the expansion of public education?"[45]

"On historical truth" was also the title of a lecture that Aleksandr Nekrich gave at the Obninsk Palace of Culture, in November 1966.[46] The speech betrayed the extent to which the historian was still caught up in ambiguities, as he hesitated between shedding the shackles of official ideology and conforming to official canons. Commenting on Vuchetich's conception, Nekrich contested that there could be two truths. There was only one historical truth, which historians, based on their Marxist-Leninist worldview and communist party-mindedness, should fully explore. The Leninist principle of learning from past mistakes dictated precisely such an approach. Not without contradictions, however, the historian asserted that "the search for truth (*pravda*) in historical scholarship is the search for an objective truth (*istina*) independent of anyone's, and even any class's will." Yet he also claimed that this truth could only be fully explored from the proletariat's perspective, and thus drew a distinction between "marxist objectivity" and "bourgeois objectivism."[47]

This debate on truth was thus the philosophical side of the struggle taking part in the political arena and within historical research institutions around the figure of Stalin. This debate revolved around the questions of what to remember and what to forget, what to emphasize and what to silence, whom to commemorate and whom to condemn. Ultimately, the stake of the struggle was not so much to determine who held the "truth" (*istina*) but the highly political choice of which "truth" (*pravda*) to reveal to the people and which to conceal.

From the Gulag to the anti-Stalinist barricades

The Old Bolshevik Aleksei Snegov

The other key actors in the anti-Stalinist campaign were the Old Bolsheviks. This group enjoyed a privileged access to some of the top party leaders, which ensured that their words would be heard. Some Old Bolsheviks had remained staunch Stalinists throughout years of detention.[48] Others, however, had returned from the Gulag with a determination to act for change. Nanci Whittier Heer noted that they constituted an active group unanimously supporting revisionist views at the All-Union Conference of Historians in 1962,[49] but they lobbied for de-Stalinization in numerous other venues.

Most active and influential of all was Aleksei Snegov (born Iosif Izraelevich Falikson). A veteran of the Revolution and Civil War in his native Ukraine, he had only narrowly avoided execution at the hands of Semen Petliura's troops. In the 1920s and 1930s, he occupied various positions in the party apparatus in the Ukraine, the Caucasus, Siberia, and in Leningrad.[50] In May 1936, when Snegov was demoted from his party position, Mikoian, who had known him since 1930, employed him in the fish industry, which fell under his authority. Still, the Old Bolshevik was arrested in July 1937 and was subjected to severe torture—the traces of which he bore forever in his flesh. He signed false confessions but recanted during his trial.[51] Amnestied after Beria's nomination as head of the NKVD, in January 1939, he was soon rearrested and condemned in July 1941 to fifteen years of detention.[52]

Snegov's liberation came only in 1954, after Beria's own arrest. According to Medvedev, while still in detention, the Old Bolshevik managed to arrange for the delivery of letters to Mikoian and Khrushchev's private addresses. He reminded them of their past acquaintance, and shared details of Beria's crimes, offering to provide evidence before the court.[53] However, after testifying at Beria's trial in December 1953, Snegov was re-incarcerated and only a few months later did Khrushchev order his liberation.[54] In March 1954, Snegov was rehabilitated and his party membership restored. Khrushchev subsequently appointed him Deputy Director of the Political Section of the Gulag, a position he occupied for four years.[55] After 1956, placed in charge of the liberation of victims of political repression, the Old Bolshevik advocated an acceleration of the process, knowing not from hearsay what one additional day in detention meant for a prisoner.[56]

For Kathleen Smith, "Snegov's loyalty to the party in spite of great suffering made him the perfect person to persuade Khrushchev that denouncing Stalin could redeem and even strengthen the party."[57] By Anastas Mikoian's own admission, Snegov and another former *zek*, Ol'ga Shatunovskaia[58] "played a huge role in our 'enlightenment' in 1954-55 and in the preparation of the Stalin question at the 20th Congress in 1956."[59] Although Khrushchev fails to mention them, his son confirms that they were one of the main moving forces behind the Secret Speech, offering Khrushchev and Mikoian both their firsthand knowledge of repression and their advice.[60] According to Mikoian's son, Snegov had understood, before anyone else, that the 20th Party Congress should become a "landmark." He justified it in the following words: "If they don't debunk Stalin at this congress, the first one after the tyrant's death, and don't tell about his crimes, they will go down in history as his voluntary accomplices. Only by denouncing Stalin's role will they convince the Party that they were unwilling co-participants."[61]

In the 1960s, as most former political convicts had been rehabilitated, and having himself retired, Snegov continued to speak out against Stalinism. In the wake of the 22nd Party Congress, this gifted orator held speeches on Stalin's crimes in a multitude of venues: at meetings of Old Bolsheviks, at the October Revolution Museum; at military academies; or at research institutes.[62] Everywhere, his daring interventions raised curiosity and triggered controversy. He was also a would-be scholar, who considered it his "duty as a communist" to undertake research on the Soviet past.[63] He did publish several memorial books and articles in the early 1960s.[64] Yet, on the whole, he was less successful in print, perhaps, as Roy Medvedev claimed, because his lack of education kept him from systematizing his knowledge,[65] but also because of the barriers of censorship.

In June 1964, after three years of archival research, Snegov submitted an article on Stalin's opposition to Lenin's course at the 6th Party Congress in 1917 to the journal *Voprosy istorii KPSS*. Despite positive reviews, however, the article was blocked following Khrushchev's ouster.[66] As the overthrown leader's protégé, Snegov could no longer count on the Soviet leadership's leniency. In April 1965, after receiving the instruction to fundamentally revise his work, the Old Bolshevik wrote a letter to his archenemy Mikhail Suslov to protest the IML's monopolization of history and deliberate cover-up of the truth about the 6th Congress.[67] In another letter, he called for the full edition of Lenin's works, criticizing the recently published "Complete works" compiled by the IML. Petr Pospelov, head of the IML, was called upon by the Central Committee to comment on these letters. He vehemently protested against Snegov's accusations and justified the failure to publish his article on the ground of its intrinsic flaws. He concluded by accusing the Old Bolshevik of "blacken[ing] in every possible way the publications produced under the direct leadership of the [Central Committee]" in his letters and public speeches.[68]

Nevertheless, Snegov continued his advocacy unimpeded. Over the years, he sent more than forty letters to the Central Committee, some of which met success.[69] His intervention at the discussion of Nekrich's work at the IML in February 1966 was not the only one of his public speeches to make its way into samizdat. In July 1966, he made a long intervention, greeted with applause, during a discussion of the book project of the third volume of *The History of the CPSU* co-organized by a group of Old Bolsheviks and the IML.[70] According to the samizdat transcript, he spoke for an hour—the majority of the audience having voted in favor of granting him an additional forty minutes. In his speech, he repeatedly attacked Stalin, accusing the authors and editors of the third volume of attempting to conceal the Soviet leader's mistakes. It was only logical, he sarcastically noted, that the authors should have made a positive mention of Stalin's *Short Course* in their introduction, since their own work was "an enlarged and later edition of the *Short Course*."[71] In conclusion, Snegov violently attacked Stalin's work and accused the authors of the third volume of throwing discredit upon scholarship. There had never been "a more anti-Leninist, anti-scientific, anti-historical work than the *Short Course*," which had turned false denunciations and confessions obtained under torture into historical facts.[72]

Unsurprisingly, Snegov eagerly helped fellow anti-Stalinist researchers. He regularly met Roy Medvedev between 1964 and 1969, providing him with a wealth of information, which the historian used for *Let History Judge*, two biographies of Khrushchev and *All Stalin's Men*.[73] In later years, Snegov would also actively help Anton Antonov-Ovseenko write his work on Stalin.

However, the Old Bolshevik's activism was not to the taste of the Brezhnev leadership. On June 7, 1967, he was first summoned to the PCC and asked to provide a written explanation for his repeated "incorrect behavior." However, he failed to send the requested documents and ignored subsequent summons.[74] An April 22, 1969 decision from the PCC stated that Snegov should be warned that his case would be discussed *in abstentia*, should he fail to obey the summons.[75] Attached was a note giving an overview of Snegov's "non-party" conduct. Snegov had assigned himself the role of "protector of the decisions of the 20th Congress," but his overly negative depiction of Stalin's activity amounted to "whitewashing" the Party's opponents.[76] The report went on to indict Snegov's confused and demagogical interventions in front of a multitude of audiences and in collective letters to various institutions. Furthermore, Snegov "sometimes serves as instructor and advisor for Soviet authors, whose anti-Soviet writings circulate illegally within the population."[77] Most irritatingly, these public speeches had earned the Old Bolshevik a solid reputation in the Western "reactionary" press, which called him a "professor," "prominent historian," and used his interventions to attack the Soviet regime.[78]

Yet Snegov's case was not settled for another two years. Sergei Khrushchev claims that, while the Old Bolshevik's exclusion was debated already in 1967, Mikoian talked to Suslov and convinced him of the impact it would have on public opinion if a man who had spent seventeen years in detention were excluded from the Party for voicing an opinion shared by many.[79] According to Roy Medvedev, health problems also explain the delay in expelling Snegov: in 1969, as a result of the PCC's threats, he suffered from heart problems and spent two years in the hospital.[80] In 1971, he was finally expelled by his primary party cell, but the decision was eventually canceled by higher instances.[81] According to Leonid Petrovskii, the head of the PCC Arvid Pel'she was behind this decision: impressed by the show of support of Old Bolsheviks, he convinced Brezhnev to let Snegov "die as a Bolshevik."[82]

A Soviet Don Quixote

Anton Antonov-Ovseenko had in common with Snegov that he belonged to the "aristocracy" of the regime and his numerous letters of protest benefited from a particular attention. As a former prisoner and the son of a renowned revolutionary, he could also count on the backing of many Old Bolsheviks, who trusted him and actively supported him. In July 1965, he began to look for publishers for his father's biography in Poland and in Czechoslovakia. However, he remained frustrated with the concessions he had to make to publish his book in the USSR. This frustration came out with particular force after the publication, in July 1965, of a short note in *Izvestiia*, entitled "History of a Telegram."[83] A. M. Sovokin, a historian and specialist of Lenin, pointed to what he claimed was a mistake in *Imenem Revoliutsii*. The episode concerned a telegram sent on October 24, 1917, containing a coded order to send reinforcements to Petrograd from the Baltic Fleet after the beginning of the October Revolution. Anton Antonov-Ovseenko wrote that his father had sent it to Pavel Dybenko. However, Sovokin claimed that the telegram had actually been sent by Iakov Sverdlov to Ivar Smil'ga in Helsingfors, as the latter's 1919 memoirs attested. But, Sovokin alleged, after Sverdlov's death and Smilga's exclusion from the Party as a Trotskyite in 1927, Dybenko and Antonov-Ovseenko had crossed out Sverdlov's and Smil'ga's names on the telegram and written theirs instead. He concluded sententiously that "this is how a historical document was falsified."[84]

The question of this telegram remains obscure to this day.[85] What is beyond doubt, however, was that Antonov-Ovseenko reacted very strongly to this article, which he considered as "inspired" from above to throw discredit upon his father and his biography of him.[86] A week later, as if to prove that Sovokin's piece did not represent *Izvestiia*'s official editorial line, a very laudatory review of *Imenem Revoliutsii*, written by an Old Bolshevik, appeared on the pages of the newspaper.[87] Nevertheless, Antonov-Ovseenko decided to use all the means at his disposal to obtain Sovokin's public recantation. First, in a letter to the editorial committee of *Izvestiia*, Anton deconstructed Sovokin's argumentation, explaining that he had himself done research on the question, and had concluded that two different telegrams had been sent on October 24: one by Antonov-Ovseenko to Dybenko by radio, the other by Sverdlov to Smil'ga a few hours later by telegraph. The revolutionary's son expressed his indignation that the newspaper should have published Sovokin's note within days of the publication of *Imenem Revoliutsii*, without inquiring into its veracity. He demanded the publication of an editorial refutation of Sovokin's piece.[88] Yet when he met with a responsible figure of the newspaper, he felt he was facing a wall.[89] Two weeks later he wrote to Anastas Mikoian and to Central Committee Secretary Petr Demichev, calling Sovokin's attack "posthumous calumny" and asking for their intercession.[90]

In late August, a recantation from Sovokin appeared in the newspaper.[91] The historian recognized that the "most likely" explanation was that the same telegram had been sent twice, which made his previous accusation of falsification void. However, this failed to appease Antonov-Ovseenko. He complained that the "slanderer" had not even apologized, only citing "new evidence" and recognizing his "error."[92] Antonov-Ovseenko then appealed to a wide circle of acquaintances, primarily among Old Bolsheviks, to write letters of protest to *Izvestiia*, and received support from Kiev,[93] Gomel',[94] Tambov,[95] Leningrad,[96] and Moscow.[97] Despite the broad mobilization, however, no reaction from *Izvestiia* or any party organ followed. Exasperated by such indifference, Antonov-Ovseenko decided to file suit against Sovokin and *Izvestiia*'s editors, but the municipal court only unwillingly registered his complaint and immediately closed the case.[98]

Nevertheless, Anton Antonov-Ovseenko, who had inherited his father's fiery character, was determined to obtain his full rehabilitation. In the biography of Stalin he later published in the West, the historian recounted some of the rebuttals he met from the Party, which demonstrated, in his view, the Soviet leadership's lack of respect toward rehabilitated victims of political repression. He thus recalled the disdainful reaction of a lower-level Party instructor, as he sought redress after being banned from lecturing about his father at the Association for the Blind following "a slanderous accusation" against him for "populariz[ing] a Trotskyist."[99]

Despite the lack of response from the authorities, Antonov-Ovseenko continued to write protests against his father's and other rehabilitated revolutionaries' exclusion from print. He concluded that "now there are two histories of the party—one for those who died in their beds and another for Stalin's victims."[100] In October 1970, he sent two letters to Mikhail Suslov.[101] In the first one, he aired general grievances about the fact that such figures as V. A. Antonov-Ovseenko, V. I. Nevskii, N. V. Krylenko, or P. E. Dybenko were increasingly confined to oblivion. In his second letter, he complained about recent publications for the hundredth anniversary of Lenin's birth, edited by the IML.[102] He bemoaned the poor quality of the work produced, which demonstrated, in his view, how one could turn the "great work of study and propaganda of Lenin's heritage" into "the most blatant hackwork" if one was to regard this as a "lucrative trade."[103] Antonov-Ovseenko, similarly to Snegov and other Old Bolsheviks, set Lenin on a pedestal, endowing him with a status of sanctity, and used the word "profanation" to qualify mistakes committed in biographical accounts of the Soviet leader. This was both a device to prove allegiance to the founding values of the Soviet state and a sign of pious veneration from the son of one of Lenin's disciples. In addition, Anton's indignation was that of a would-be historian, who felt that Party history had been confiscated by a "clique" of professional historians who jealously guarded their sanctuary, managing their trade in an opaque way, away from the eyes of the public. Finally, his frustration also had to do with the Party's immutable official line concerning certain historical figures, who remained personae non gratae in Party history.

Antonov-Ovseenko was also among the signatories of a letter sent to Suslov in December 1970 by a group of Old Bolsheviks, complaining about the alleged falsification of an episode of the history of the Revolution.[104] Many of them had belonged to the armored division Sverdlov, which had greeted Lenin at the Petrograd train station upon his return from Finland in April 1917. Precisely from the top of an armored car from this division, according to the popular version of history, had Lenin made his first call for a socialist revolution. The signatories accused two revolutionaries, Nikolai Podvoiskii and Semen Aralov, of having usurped the achievements of others, among them V. A. Antonov-Ovseenko. In addition, they named fifty-three researchers from the IML and other institutions, whom they accused of being responsible for these falsifications. The signatories concluded with a proposal to create a commission to investigate "a multitude of other instances of falsification of history and of lack of objectivity of some scholars, including amongst the most prominent."[105]

Although this petition and Antonov-Ovseenko's quixotic letters produce in retrospect a painful impression of confusion and unproductively directed energy, they did catch the attention of the Central Committee. However chaotic these epistles were, the prominence of the author and the signatories implied the need to take their grievances seriously. Pavel Fedoseev, from the IML, was therefore asked to examine the complaints and accusations made. Unsurprisingly, he took the defense of his colleagues and dismissed the complaints of both the individual and collective letters.[106] These protests might appear in retrospect as sterile endeavors, but they show that as late as 1972, Anton Antonov-Ovseenko still hoped to obtain justice through official channels. Possibly as a result of this lobbying, Anton obtained the publication of a new augmented edition of his father's biography. It was published by Lenizdat in 1975 under the more explicit title *V.A. Antonov-Ovseenko*.[107]

What these episodes illustrate, most of all, however, is the extent to which Antonov-Ovseenko's later works, in particular his *Portrait of a Tyrant*, were driven by a need for revenge, compensation for the losses and frustration that he had endured, not only in the Stalin era, but also in the post-Stalin years.

The Nekrich Affair

A treacherous attack

The discussion of *June 22, 1941* at the IML constituted a major trigger for what became later known as the "Nekrich Affair." By July 1967, Nekrich had been excluded from the Communist Party—a process analyzed in the fifth chapter. However, reactions of protest came only with the publication of a belated review of Nekrich's book, clearly aimed at justifying ex post facto his exclusion from the Party. Published in September 1967 in *Voprosy istorii KPSS*, the review by G. A. Deborin and B. S. Tel'pukhovskii, two of the participants in the discussion at the IML, was entitled "In ideological captivity of the falsifiers of history."[108]

In considering this review, so strikingly at odds with the authors' more moderate discourse during the IML discussion, it is worth considering the reviewers' previous relationship to party authority. Boris Tel'pukhovskii was among the Institute of History staff who had recognized his guilt after trying to shield the dissident historian Oleg Puzyrev from punishment in 1965.[109] As for Grigorii Deborin, his zeal could similarly be explained as a strategy to make up for his past "mistakes" in the eyes of higher instances. As the son of the philosopher Abram Deborin, who had been branded as "Menshevik idealist" in the Stalin era, the historian had come under attack in 1948 and had been forced into public repentance, according to the testimony of one of Nekrich's colleagues.[110] Moreover, Roy Medvedev writes that, following Nekrich's exclusion from the Party, the PCC had ordered that the personal cases of Boltin, Tel'pukhovskii, and Deborin be examined for their "incorrect" organization of the IML discussion and for their "incorrect" speeches during this event.[111] The historians certainly had grounds to fear reprisals and felt the need to demonstrate their zeal.

The review adopted from the outset a tone of confrontation, inscribing Nekrich's work within a context of ideological conflict between the socialist and capitalist camps. Despite the USSR's successful struggle with "bourgeois falsification of the history of World War II," the publisher "Nauka" had published a book "written in the spirit of bourgeois historiography." The reviewers sententiously declared that Nekrich, "employing an erroneous methodology, has departed from the Communist Party spirit in his research and has shown a lack of scruple in his selection and evaluation of factual material." No wonder his work had been acclaimed by "the most reactionary press" in the West, for it presented a deliberately distorted view of Soviet foreign and domestic policy and denied the inevitability of Soviet victory in the war.[112]

In line with Marxist methodology, the reviewers proposed to research "historical phenomena in their development," placing the emphasis on the ultimate (progressive) results, rather than the (sometimes chaotic) process. Their reasoning converged with Vuchetich's as they declared: "The first months of the Great Patriotic War were not merely a time of serious failures. It already became clear during those months that Hitler's military venture was doomed to failure. June 22, 1941 and May 9, 1945, these two historical dates, are inseparably connected."[113] Nekrich, they claimed, considered the first months of the war in isolation from the victory, which resulted in a lack of objectivity. As a result, the author of *June 22, 1941* concentrated his attention exclusively on "shortcomings, mistakes, and oversights," and he presented in an "extremely tendentious manner" that, which Deborin and Tel'pukhovskii dismissed as mere "difficulties of the growth (*bolezni rosta*) of the Soviet nation."[114]

Deborin and Tel'pukhovskii also found Nekrich at fault in his selection of primary sources: instead of using primarily Soviet sources, "the objectivity of which is undeniable," he chose to rely on a wide range of "reactionary authors."[115] His affinities with bourgeois historiography were also manifest in his failure to describe events from a class perspective, and in his emphasis on personalities. Nekrich's characterization of the war as defensive thus betrayed his fundamentally flawed approach, deemed the reviewers. The war had in fact been a class confrontation between socialism, in support of which the European masses had risen, and "the most monstrous pawn of imperialism, fascism."[116]

Nekrich was also mistaken when he described the Soviet-German pact as a "deft political maneuver" of Hitler. The pact, they argued, had allowed the USSR to avoid a war on two fronts and had broken up the "Munich front" between the Axis powers and France and Britain. Furthermore, Nekrich "whitewashed" the US and British governments, failing to incriminate them for derailing negotiations for an alliance with the USSR.[117] But it was Nekrich's indictment of the Soviet military government that the two authors found most intolerable. The historian accused the military leadership of having failed to identify the threat and to prepare the country for the impending attack. But had this leadership not led the Red Army to victory over the enemy?[118]

The two historians sternly signed the final condemnation of their dissenting peer:

> Thus, A.M. Nekrich, having found himself in the ideological captivity of the bourgeois falsifiers of history has betrayed the scientific principles of Marxist historiography, and therefore historical truth as well. And it is natural that this little book has become a find for the ideologists of imperialism and has been taken by them as a weapon of hostile propaganda against the Soviet Union and of slander against it. The publishing house "Nauka" has displayed irresponsibility in undertaking the publication of this politically harmful book.[119]

By using a rhetoric of class struggle and Cold War confrontation, Deborin and Tel'pukhovskii were appealing to a register well-known to Soviet readers and signaling that their attack had been commissioned from above. According to Moisei Al'perovich, a colleague and friend of Nekrich's, this "unqualified and tendentious concoction (*striapnia*), abounding with crude distortions," was called upon "to convince public opinion of the rightfulness of the party leadership's actions," while the procedure of Nekrich's exclusion remained "shrouded in secrecy."[120] But the reviewers' shrill tone, which was reminiscent of Stalin-era rhetoric, raised indignation among those who actively defended the course of the 20th Party Congress.

The campaign of letters

Nekrich's exclusion from the Party had raised widespread concerns within the liberal intelligentsia, which interpreted the reprisals against anti-Stalinist historians as evidence of an abandonment of de-Stalinization. However, before the publication of Deborin's and Tel'pukhovskii's review, the historian's supporters were at a loss how to defend him. By clearly formulating the act of accusation, the article provided convenient ground for targeted protests, and emotional letters of indignant readers began to flow into the journal's editorial offices.[121]

In October 1967, Nekrich sent his own detailed response to the journal, a copy of which he addressed to Brezhnev. In his letter, the historian complained both about the reviewers' style of critique and about the content of their accusations. They amounted to a covert revision of party resolutions, which Nekrich deemed particularly threatening in the context of a creeping rehabilitation of Stalin. Deborin and Tel'pukhovskii's unconscientious methods of critique, resting upon "the falsification of facts and exaggerations," reminded Nekrich of Stalinist times. The reviewers had put words in his mouth, leveled political accusations at him, and resorted to "unrestrained abuse." Polemics of such a kind, he complained, only "obscure the essence of the question."[122]

But the falsifications were all the more so dangerous as they were politically oriented. After rebuffing all of the reviewers' accusations, the historian concluded that Deborin and Tel'pukhovskii had consciously replaced every critical mention of Stalin in the book by similar statements directed against the Communist Party or the Soviet government. This allowed them to accuse him of disparaging the Party, when he had in fact been solely criticizing Stalin. Moreover, this substitution of words had another goal: by equating Stalin with the Communist Party, the reviewers actually sought to covertly rehabilitate Stalin, by relieving him of any personal guilt for the early setbacks in the war and diffusing this responsibility on the Party as a whole.[123] Since "historical truth" was considered a political notion, Nekrich knew that appealing to the respect of past congress resolutions was a more effective strategy than appeals to scholarly conscientiousness in the handling of facts.

In his memoirs, Nekrich claimed that this response, copies of which he distributed largely around him, was part of a new strategy to refuse to acknowledge his political errors and to fight off every attack against himself.[124] In addition, he could count on the support of many of his colleagues and friends. M. S. Al'perovich and A. G. Tartakovskii thus decided to write a letter of protest providing a detailed critique of the review, revealing the reviewers' "unconscientious devices and methods of polemics," and exposing their "manipulation of facts and gross distortion" of Nekrich's thoughts.[125] This required thorough research in an unfamiliar field, but also a fine balance of firmness and restraint in the tone adopted, to avoid alienating potential signatories, anxious not to go beyond the scholarly debate. Ultimately, they collected nineteen signatures from various institutes of the Academy of Sciences and Moscow State University. While some joined the action without hesitation, a few had misgivings about engaging in collective action and preferred to write individually. They also enlisted the support of several academicians, mostly in the form of individual letters: N. I. Konrad, M. V. Nechkina, N. M. Druzhinin, S. G. Strumilin, and A. A. Guber.[126]

In their letter, Al'perovich and Tartakovskii primarily set out to deconstruct Deborin and Tel'pukhovskii's review, countering their accusations of omission and distortion by providing appropriate quotations from Nekrich's book. On the question of the alleged excessive reliance on foreign primary sources, the authors argued that Nekrich had also used an extensive range of Soviet documents and memoirs. But the study of the question without German sources was impossible, as Deborin and Tel'pukhovskii knew for having used some of these documents in their own works.[127] Moreover, Nekrich's book was "not original scholarly research" but a work of popularization, based mostly on Soviet studies published previously. "Therefore, we were extremely surprised that, qualifying the views presented in A.M. Nekrich's book as unscientific, fallacious and politically harmful, the reviewers omitted to say that we are talking about a *generally-accepted* conception in Soviet [historiography] deriving from party decisions and based on considerable documentary material."[128] Not only had the reviewers themselves expressed similar views in print more than once, but during the discussion of Nekrich's work at the IML, they had given an overall positive evaluation of the book. Finally, Al'perovich and Tartakovskii expressed their dismay regarding the review's tone, "characterized by the sticking of political labels, a flow of abusive epithets in the author's address"—a style of critique which "Soviet public opinion was no longer used to," "restoring the worst traditions of the times of Stalin's personality cult."[129]

In her letter, Academician Nechkina expressed her general agreement with the "letter of the nineteen," judging that Nekrich's book was an "honest, conscientious work of a historian, well-argued on the basis of documents and correct in its basic conception."[130] Academician Druzhinin praised Nekrich's book for its fact-based demonstration of the 20th and 22nd Party Congresses' conclusions on the beginning of the war, guided by "the Leninist precept of learning and teaching others on the basis of mistakes, to avoid repeating them in the future." He and "a large circle of Soviet readers, ha[d] perceived Nekrich's comprehensive book as a truthful, patriotic work, dictated by his concern for the welfare of the Soviet people and the whole humanity."[131] Therefore, Druzhinin expressed his fear, lest Deborin and Tel'pukhovskii's review further alienate an increasingly disaffected youth, confused by the gap between past congress resolutions, which the reviewers had until recently subscribed to, and their current charge against them.[132] As for Academician Strumilin, he expressed his concern that a review, which, "willingly or not, distorts to a point of non-recognition the content [of Nekrich's book]" should have been published in *Voprosy istorii KPSS*. "We cannot accept that the readers of a journal published under the brand of our Party, turning to [this journal] in search of historical truth, should feel even once betrayed on its pages."[133]

The "letter of the nineteen" was sent to *Voprosy istorii KPSS* in early November, with copies to the Presidium of the Academy of Sciences, the publishing house "Nauka," the IML, and the Institute of History. Although Al'perovich and Tartakovskii entertained no hope of its publication, in the absence of any response, they sent further copies of their letter to *Kommunist, Voprosy istorii, Novaia i noveishaia istoriia, Istoriia SSSR, Voenno-istoricheskii zhurnal,* and *Novyi mir*—also to no avail. Nevertheless, Al'perovich judged the campaign successful to a certain extent: he believed that this show of support had convinced the authorities to leave Nekrich in his position at the Institute of History. And when an attempt was made to deprive him of his doctoral degree, in 1969, another show of support made this project fail.[134] This would have constituted a very dangerous precedent, which the historians' community successfully averted. Indeed, their reaction was not simply a show of solidarity for a colleague, but a professional corps's adamant response to a threat from above. For decades, historians had submitted to censorship, painstakingly trimming their works of any subversive formulations and sprinkling them with the required amount of ideological formulas and quotes from the Marxist classics. But if a book approved for publication could be arbitrarily condemned overnight on the basis of circumstances escaping the author's control, then what guarantees did historians have against the regime's interference in their research?

The Grigorenko letter

Another forceful reaction to the review by Deborin and Tel'pukhovskii came from General Petr Grigorenko, a war veteran and well-known dissident.[135] In his letter to the journal *Voprosy istorii KPSS*, Grigorenko not only defended against slander "a valuable, conscientious book," but, based on his wartime experience, he also offered his own historical analysis, going further than Nekrich's on a number of questions. Although Grigorenko hoped to see his letter published in the journal, this long essay soon escaped into samizdat, which provided the editor with an excuse not to publish it.[136]

Grigorenko's essay, entitled "The Concealment of Historical Truth Is a Crime against the People!," argued that, by covering up the causes of the Red Army's defeats in 1941, the reviewers sheltered those guilty of these crimes and thus potentially undermined the country's defense capabilities. The memory of the terrible first days of the war was necessary to avert a repetition of such a tragedy. Therefore, Grigorenko called on Soviet society to acknowledge the real causes of the defeats: "Whoever has either forgotten or does not know this can never understand the greatness of our people's feat. They were able to overcome a terrible blow to their morale and, in less than six months, to hold back and paralyze the mightiest military machine in the world."[137]

How could one explain the lack of preparation of the country and army for the German invasion, in spite of high army spending and the modern technique of the Red Army? Grigorenko denied the superiority of German forces or the existence of a "historical law (*zakonomernost'*)" granting aggressive nations a temporary advantage over their peaceful adversaries, until "permanently operating factors" came into action, as Stalin had claimed. Instead, he insisted on the importance of "subjective factors"—that is, the role of leaders, who supervised the preparation of the country's defense and who were in charge of leading the troops at the time of the invasion.[138] It was precisely in this regard that the Stalin leadership's responsibility was engaged. Extensive purges in the Red Army had deprived it of its most experienced, highly skilled, and authoritative commanders, who constituted at the time the "backbone, the basis of an army of a new type." Stalin replaced them with inexperienced cadres, mostly lacking military education. The Soviet people had paid dearly for these losses in the top-level command, unequaled "in any war, by any army in the world," by millions of unnecessary victims.[139] But Stalin also held responsibility for his refusal to take any decisive action when Hitler's decision to attack became obvious. He thus condemned the army to a desperate show of heroism. This heroism of soldiers who threw themselves on tanks with rifles and Molotov cocktails "will raise not only a feeling of pride for our people, but also hatred towards those who put these people in a position, in which the defense of their native land, of the Soviet people from the enemy could not be guaranteed even by mass self-sacrifice."[140]

Concerning Stalin's foreign policy, Grigorenko went much further than Nekrich had been able to. He denied that Stalin had made an effective use of the time "gained" through the Ribbentrop-Molotov pact. On the contrary, he had only managed to disarm the country, by blowing up the old fortifications along the former Western border, while the new ones had not yet been built. Moreover, instead of "using the contradictions in the capitalist world" in the interest of the Soviet Union, from 1939 to 1941, the Stalin leadership had "willingly tied itself to the military chariot of German fascism and, in the course of two years, submissively trudged this chariot like cattle driven to slaughter."[141]

Grigorenko ended his letter with a call to investigate the personal responsibility of top-level figures in the preparation and conduct of the war. Such a "trial" over the past was necessary in order to denounce the forces guilty of treason in the preparation of the past war, which were still influential. Such an investigation of the causes of the defeats of the beginning of the war would "raise the international prestige of our country and strengthen its defense capability."[142]

In his memoirs, Nekrich tells of his joy, upon receiving a letter by Grigorenko, whom he considered "a symbol of honesty, daring and integrity," along with a copy of his small essay. It read: "No honest person could fail to be indignant about this [review]. . . . I sincerely respect your civic courage and ability, in an accessible and tactful manner, to portray an extremely serious topic."[143] Grigorenko's letter received a very broad circulation and was mentioned by prominent dissidents as an influential text on the history of the war: for Andrei Sakharov, "together with [Nekrich's] book, Grigorenko's article was one of the most authoritative and convincing testimonies on a question, which agitated all people in our country."[144] In his memoirs, Grigorenko claims that he received echoes from readers of his samizdat opus from as far away as Novosibirsk, Alma-Ata, Tashkent, Kiev, or even the subpolar Chukotka region.[145]

The anti-Stalinist protests of the 1960s constituted a transformative moment, both in the life of the Soviet liberal intelligentsia and in the trajectories of dissident researchers. They marked the end of a search for accommodation and docile submission to censorship, and a turn toward civic and political action to try and change the official line. Individual written protests to the Soviet leadership constituted a traditional and legitimate tool of political expression, but the collective actions of the 1960s were marked by greater boldness and an awareness of unity of views. By voicing their grievances in a language both they and their interlocutors deemed legitimate, the *podpisanty* were not simply trying to evade punishment, but staked on the Party's reluctance to renounce its own past commitments. Yet they also interpreted official discourse in original ways, linking political and ethical motives, or even introducing more daring claims, by linking past and present political repression, for instance. Anti-Stalinism also served as a lingua franca, federating broadly within the ranks of the intelligentsia and among Old Bolsheviks. And these protests were not unsuccessful; to what extent they exercised a moderating influence on the Soviet leadership remains unclear, but they did afford some individuals effective protection, as Nekrich's case shows. However, this tactical alliance broke apart toward the end of the decade, following the crushing of the "Prague Spring." Under the impact of increasing repression, a minority continued protesting, generally shifting the emphasis to human rights, while the majority retreated into conformism: thinking differently was one thing, but losing one's position for the sake of expressing one's ideas was quite another.

Dissident researchers had various attitudes toward protest letters. Antonov-Ovseenko was undoubtedly the most prolific author of such epistles, and he repeatedly used his connections in higher spheres to try to obtain satisfaction. His actions, when they concerned specific grievances and did not conflict with the interests of influential figures, were occasionally successful. But they also testified to a bitterness that eventually overshadowed the meager concessions he obtained, convincing him to engage in more radical action. Medvedev considered his work *Let History Judge* as his most potent statement against Stalin's rehabilitation and therefore engaged little in the writing of protest letters. He was keenly aware, however, that the broad support he received from writers, historians, and Old Bolsheviks, particularly in the second half of the 1960s, was closely related to the political context and constituted a hidden form of protest for his supporters. As for Nekrich, we may never know whether he would have engaged in anti-Stalinist protests, had he not himself become the target of repression. He likely would have, but the events led him to assume the role of figurehead of the anti-Stalinist cause, far beyond what he could have expected, as he wrote what was in essence a moderate critique of Stalin's wartime actions. As for Solzhenitsyn, whose case is examined in the next chapter, it was in part through his vocal protests, such as his 1967 Letter to the Fourth Congress of Writers denouncing censorship, that he assumed in those years a role of charismatic leader of the dissident movement. These protests, either by themselves or through the social turmoil they triggered, thus contributed to a further evolution of dissident researchers away from the official sphere and placed them further in opposition to the Party's line.

Eventually, however, it was through their writings that dissident researchers would come into direct confrontation with the authorities. By collecting hundreds of testimonies from Old Bolsheviks and political prisoners, Solzhenitsyn and Medvedev, whose works are examined in the following chapter, opposed a new legitimacy, based on the moral value of collective memory, to the regime's logic of political "expediency." The contribution of this multitude of voices turned dissident histories into collective monuments to the suffering of millions.

4

Writing History through the Voice of the Repressed

Readers of *The Gulag Archipelago* could easily forget that the author of this subversive work had in fact started his career as an acclaimed Soviet author. In a society characterized, in Denis Kozlov's words, by its "literature-centrism," it was precisely in the literary field that the most urgent debates of the post-Stalin era found reflection, in particular, the legacy of Stalinism.[1] Indeed, in the early 1960s, emboldened by the 22nd Party Congress, writers showed a greater degree of audacity than historians and used literature as a tool of historical revisionism. The publication of Aleksandr Solzhenitsyn's novella *One Day in the Life of Ivan Denisovich*, one of the first literary works depicting the life of a *zek* (prisoner) in the Gulag, is therefore usually considered as the high point of de-Stalinization.

The fairytale-like story of *Ivan Denisovich*'s publication is well-known: impressed by the literary talent of this unknown author, Aleksandr Tvardovskii, editor in chief of the liberal literary journal *Novyi mir,* personally convinced Khrushchev to push the publication of this work with the Central Committee, despite opposition from censorship. In the 1960s, Tvardovskii, a peasant-born poet with strong communist convictions and a liberal outlook, turned *Novyi mir* into "the only public embodiment of the intelligentsia's ethos and mentality in post-Stalinist Russia," in Vladislav Zubok's words.[2] The public interest for Solzhenitsyn's novella far surpassed *Novyi mir*'s limited print run, and the eleventh issue of 1962 soon became one of the scarcest goods in the country, with readers waiting for months to get access to the text for a day or two.[3] No less unusual was the flow of responses from fervent admirers or irritated critics, expressed through hundreds of letters to the journal and the author.[4] According to Denis Kozlov, along with other key publications of the time, Solzhenitsyn's work led readers to "reassess the ethical foundations of their existence and, ultimately, of the established sociopolitical order." They began to "view the past through the Prism of Terror," with the year 1937, rather than 1917, increasingly standing out as a fault line.[5]

Solzhenitsyn may never have written *The Gulag Archipelago*, if not for the formidable response he received from Soviet society, with hundreds of letters from former prisoners laying the ground for his history of the Gulag. In this sense, his short-lived "legal" existence as a Soviet writer crucially fertilized his later underground activity. His experience echoed that of another writer who had undertaken work on a documentary historical novel: Sergei Smirnov, the author of *The Brest Fortress*, first published in

1957. Based on testimonies of survivors, this work celebrated the thousands of Soviet soldiers who had heroically defended this fortress on the German border for a whole month, before being made prisoners. The author, who had advertised his call for testimonies in newspapers and radio broadcasts, received up to a million letters, according to Evgenii Dolmatovskii, who remembered that a special group of the Soviet television staff had been assigned the task of managing this gigantic correspondence.[6] The book itself encountered a huge success with the public, and was regularly reedited, with an enlarged version published in 1964. Smirnov received the Lenin Prize in 1965, the year the Brest Fortress was awarded the title of "Heroic Fortress." Solzhenitsyn expressed the regret not to have been able to advertise his call for testimonies the way Smirnov had done.[7] However, Smirnov's work also fell into disgrace in later years. The topic remained politically sensitive: many of the thousands of defenders of the fortress, when they had survived the Nazi concentration camps, had been sent to the Gulag upon their return, and Smirnov's efforts to rehabilitate them remained controversial. In 1975, the 130,000 copies of a new edition of *The Brest Fortress* were destroyed, and in the following years attempts to publish it with significant cuts were unsuccessful. The main hero of Smirnov's story was also arrested on trumped-up charges.[8] This parallel underscores the fluidity of the frontier between the official and unofficial and the influences across this line.

Another testimony to the cross-influences between historical documentary literature and dissident histories was the work of Iurii Trifonov, whose historical novel *Fireglow* (*Otblesk kostra*) was first published in late 1964. Polly Jones uses the expression "mnemonic communities" to describe the networks of witnesses of the past Trifonov relied upon, as he wrote a novel inspired by his father and uncle's revolutionary struggle.[9] Trifonov's writing of *Fireglow* is reminiscent of Antonov-Ovseenko's work on his father's biography: both men sought to rehabilitate their fathers, whose bodies and memories had been devoured by the fire of revolutionary history. Moreover, Trifonov, similarly to Antonov-Ovseenko and Medvedev, developed an extensive network of ties to the community of Old Bolsheviks, who reached out to him following the first journal publication in *Znamia*, allowing him to publish a significantly enlarged version of his work in 1966. Although new editions of the work were precluded in the Brezhnev era, Trifonov continued to interact with his "mnemonic communities" in various ways, contributing to the research of others, including Roy Medvedev, with whom he became friends.

Trifonov was not the only writer to rely extensively on eyewitnesses' accounts: Konstantin Simonov collected countless testimonies about the war and also became one of Medvedev's sources. In the Brezhnev era, even this laureate of six Stalin and one Lenin prizes faced a ban on the publication of his military diaries.[10] Simonov, Trifonov, or Smirnov were no dissidents, yet as writers they sought to cover historical themes that were regarded as politically unsuitable. It was no coincidence that their paths should have crossed that of Medvedev. Nor was it coincidental that the first history of the Gulag camps should have been authored by Solzhenitsyn, the acclaimed author of *Ivan Denisovich*. Because of their place within Soviet society and their relative independence in comparison with historians, writers were best placed to collect testimonies through the letters of their readers.

What is relevant for our analysis is therefore to understand what distinguished dissident researchers from writers who eventually remained within the boundaries of the official sphere. While Nekrich was pushed into dissent by circumstances that partly escaped his grasp, Solzhenitsyn and Medvedev's trajectories reveal a progressive drift, conditioned by the encounters they made, which contributed to a radicalization of their own discourse, and, ultimately, by the loss of perspective of publication in the Soviet Union. Their work over *The Gulag Archipelago* and *Let History Judge* can be considered from two perspectives: as the emergence of a specific genre largely based on oral testimonies, or as part of a process of estrangement from the system. While the former dimension is analyzed in Chapter 7, this chapter concentrates on the impact of witnesses on the formation of narratives which escaped the narrow framework of Khrushchev's de-Stalinization early on and could a fortiori never have passed the test of censorship in the Brezhnev era. Moreover, the networks of witnesses and helpers that the two authors developed, united by a common belief in the need for a denunciation of the Stalin-era terror, threatened the regime's authority, insofar as they affirmed an alternative source of legitimacy, based on the ethical value of the collective testimony that these works constituted. As Alexander Etkind has pointed out, "Under a regime that refused to acknowledge its own violence, mourning its victims was a political act, an important and sometimes dominating mechanism of resistance to this regime."[11]

The Gulag Archipelago

Solzhenitsyn's 227 witnesses

Sentenced at the end of the war for criticizing Stalin in a letter to a fellow frontline officer, Aleksandr Solzhenitsyn emerged from his eight-year Gulag term and three years of exile in Kazakhstan a changed man, in both moral and political terms. Having recovered from cancer in 1954, he believed God had saved him for a reason: "Since then, all the life given back to me has not been mine in the full sense: it is built around a purpose."[12] This purpose would be achieved through writing—an activity to which he devoted himself after his teaching day ended. Once liberated from exile and rehabilitated, Solzhenitsyn became an "underground writer," writing his Gulag-inspired works for "the drawer." The onset of the literary Thaw convinced him that the time had come for him to leave the underground.[13] The need for feedback from readers, and the encouragement given by the speeches of the 22nd Party Congress led him to send a trial balloon. In November 1961, he had his novella sent to *Novyi mir*[14] (see Figure 4.1).

The publication of *One Day in the Life of Ivan Denisovich*, a year later, triggered a flow of hundreds of letters to the author. Readers expressed gratitude and admiration, or sometimes anger and disapproval of his approach to the Gulag theme.[15] Among them were over 200 former Gulag inmates, who wished to share their memories with the author. While they praised Solzhenitsyn's talent and deep understanding of the Gulag world, they also felt frustrated by the novella's shortness and the hero's light fate, in comparison with what they had themselves experienced. Unanimously, they

Figure 4.1 Aleksandr Solzehnitsyn, 1970. Courtesy of Mezhdunarodnyi Memorial Archive, Moscow.

called on the author to write an extensive, all-encompassing novel about life in the Gulag, and often suggested themes, personal stories, or proposed to meet the author to discuss these questions in person. A certain Maksin from the Leningrad region wrote that "having read [the novella] twice, the first thing that one wants to express, is the regret that it is so short and this it is not a novel-trilogy."[16] Chavdarov, from Leningrad, predicted that Solzhenitsyn would be "flooded by letters from comrades of sorrow. Many will tell you about themselves. And there is so much material, so much that has been lived. It would be good to tell everything from the beginning. Arrest, prison, investigation, unfair trial, train journey, camp."[17] Anna Skrypnikova, a Gulag survivor well-known for her activism on behalf of fellow victims,[18] even gave precise instructions as to what the future trilogy she envisioned should contain. She explained that her demands were justified by her belief that Solzhenitsyn would write the great, "tragic," "bitter, even cruel," work on the Gulag that "the whole Soviet people and the whole world" had been calling for. She thought he would "fulfill this order (*zakaz*) from society," as he was endowed "not only with the talent of empathy and reflective observation, but also a Russian's civic courage, honesty and honor!"[19]

These former *zeks* had knocked on the right door: indeed, starting from 1958, Solzhenitsyn had been writing such an all-encompassing research work on the history of the Gulag. At the time, as he recalled, he did not know of any Gulag camp memoirs. Later on, he would come across Varlam Shalamov's *Tales from the Kolyma*, but also Dmitrii Vitkovskii, Evgeniia Ginzburg, and Ol'ga Adamova-Sliozberg's memoirs, which completed his own personal experience.[20] Yet he still doubted the feasibility of his project and realized that his ambitious design would have ideally required a team of several writers: "The chapters should have been shared among people with special knowledge, and we should then have met in editorial conference and helped each other to put the whole in true perspective."[21] He claims he had thought of Shalamov and Vitkovskii as coauthors or editors, but one refused and the other died prematurely.[22] It seems difficult to imagine Solzhenitsyn collaborating with other writers, however, particularly given his disagreements with Shalamov on the meaning of the camp experience.[23] Arguably more suited to his design and character was the form of collaboration that eventually came into being, in which Solzhenitsyn acted as *maître d'oeuvre* conducting a team of volunteers who assisted him in his research.

Yet what made the realization of his project possible was the wealth of testimonies with which he was unexpectedly endowed, following *Ivan Denisovich*'s publication. Moreover, the magnitude of the response meant that he now felt entrusted with a mission.[24] In his preface, Solzhenitsyn writes of 227 witnesses[25] who helped him with their reports, memoirs, and letters.[26] While he could not reveal all their names in 1973, for fear of endangering them, the most recent editions include the complete list. Among them were fellow prisoners Solzhenitsyn had met in prison, camp, *sharashka*,[27] or exile, some of whom had contacted him after reading *Ivan Denisovich*; others were friends, old or new. The scope was further widened by the inclusion of stories he or his witnesses had heard from fellow prisoners in detention.

Among Solzhenitsyn's "Gulag friends" were Iurii Karbe, an engineer he had met at the Ekibastuz camp; Nikolai Zubov, an old gynecologist, and his wife Elena, whom the writer had met in exile in Kok-Terek; or Nikolai Semenov, an engineer and former prisoner of war, Solzhenitsyn's cellmate in the Butyrki prison. All of them had assisted Solzhenitsyn in the past, in particular with the safekeeping of his manuscripts. In the *sharashka*, Solzhenitsyn had also met Lev Kopelev, who served as a model for the character of Lev Rubin in *The First Circle*. As Kopelev was a fellow writer familiar with Moscow circles, Solzhenitsyn initially counted on his assistance when he decided to leave the literary underground.[28] Another friend from Ekibastuz, the young Vladimir Gershuni, was arrested as a student for taking part in an anti-Stalinist group. In the post-Stalin era, his dissenting activities and continued rebelliousness made him a frequent guest of both penal and psychiatric repressive institutions. Gershuni helped Solzhenitsyn by bringing him rare books and works on the Russian revolution. He also introduced him to useful contacts, such as Elena Vertogradskaia, who gave the writer access to forbidden literature at the Party Library where she worked.[29]

Thanks to the publication of *Ivan Denisovich*, Solzhenitsyn was also able to resume his friendship with two Estonians he held in great esteem. In his Lubianka cell, he had met Arnold Susi, a quadrilingual lawyer educated in Petrograd who taught him about the short-lived Estonian experience of democracy in the interwar period.[30] When he contacted Solzhenitsyn, Susi had just been allowed back to Estonia and stayed on a farm in the Tartu countryside, as he was still banned from living in cities. After a first visit in 1963, Solzhenitsyn found Estonia a perfect place to write *The Gulag Archipelago* in peace and spent there the summer of 1964 and several winters in a row. The writer also used Arnold's memoirs for his work, as well as the testimonies of his children about life in internal exile. Solzhenitsyn's other Estonian friend was Georgii Tenno, a naval officer from Saint-Petersburg he had met in the Ekibastuz internal jail, where this "committed jail-breaker" was planning a new camp escape.[31] Upon reading *Ivan Denisovich*, Tenno recognized the author and contacted him. Tenno's testimony occupied a prominent place in *The Gulag Archipelago*, with his account of his spectacular camp escape making up a separate chapter of the third volume.[32] Tenno also repeatedly appeared in Solzhenitsyn's recollections from Ekibastuz's 1952 camp mutiny, in which the Estonian participated before being transferred to a security prison with other unruly prisoners.[33] This mutiny would lead to the famous 1954 Kengir camp uprising, which lasted for forty days and was only crushed by military forces. Solzhenitsyn's was the first account of this large-scale insurrection, which he depicted through the memoirs of one of its participants, Aleksei Makeev.

Most of the former *zeks* who contacted Solzhenitsyn after reading *Ivan Denisovich* were strangers, but the shared camp experience made them brothers in suffering. About these letters, his favorite, Solzhenitsyn said:

> You read it—and feel a warm glow. No, honestly—however many letters you receive, those from zeks stand out unmistakably. Such extraordinary toughness they show! . . . I am proud to belong to this mighty race! We were not a race, but they made us one! They forged bonds between us, which we, in our timid and uncertain twilight, where every man is afraid of every other, could never have forged for ourselves. . . . We no longer need to test each other. We meet, look into each other's eyes, exchange a couple of words—and what need for further explanation?[34]

This simplicity of communication transpired in the letters Solzhenitsyn received. Izmail Pronman, from Moscow, got the impression from reading *Ivan Denisovich* that he had met Solzhenitsyn in the camps. He was eager to share his own experience: "Oh how much I would like to tell, but I have no time. If you want, I would be glad to meet you in person. I have some materials, newspapers left, and, most importantly, what remains is myself, and I remember a lot."[35] Ans Bernshtein was equally ready to help: "If you ever write a book about life in Beria's torture chambers, I will be at your service, for my memory holds material for three volumes on this theme, but I have neither the ability, nor the patience to process it, and my age is already respectable (54). If you are in Leningrad, come over."[36] Nadezhda Surovtseva, who had survived three decades of detention in the Solovki and Kolyma camps, contacted Solzhenitsyn through a common friend. She praised the novella and mentioned she had started writing memoirs[37] about her experience, in which she strove to show how "one can remain a Communist in spite of everything." As Solzhenitsyn was planning on visiting her friend in the Ukraine, she invited the writer to visit her on the way.[38]

All these witnesses yielded unique personal stories, each more moving and astounding than the other. An interesting character who appeared regularly on the pages of *The Gulag Archipelago* was Vasilii Vlasov, accused in the Kady District Case.[39] Arrested for taking the defense of a peasant unjustly accused of Trotskyism, Vlasov then found himself drawn into an imaginary rightist-Bukharinist conspiracy allegedly seeking to overturn Soviet power through wrecking in the Kady District. Buttressed by confessions obtained under torture, the case was considerably weakened by the retractions of the accused during the trial, but Vlasov was nonetheless condemned to death. In the chapter "The Supreme Measure," Solzhenitsyn tells of Vlasov's forty-two days spent expecting execution. Although he refused to petition for pardon, his sentence was eventually commuted to a twenty years' prison term and he lived on to tell the tale.[40]

A particularly endearing letter Solzhenitsyn received was from Natal'ia Milevna Anichkova and her foster daughter Nadezhda (Nadia) Levitskaia, two former *zeks* to whom Solzhenitsyn would later refer to as the "NN." Nadia was the daughter of Grigorii Levitskii, a biologist close to Nikolai Vavilov, repressed as a result of Trofim Lysenko's assault on genetics. The whole Levitskii family was arrested and perished in the camps; only Nadia and her brother survived their camp terms. She was saved by her good fortune and protection from Natal'ia Milevna, then in charge of the camp bakery. The two women became inseparable, and a few years after their rehabilitation, they moved into the same apartment: Anichkova had the precious Moscow registration Nadia lacked, and they had now become like family to each other.[41] Having heard of the forthcoming publication of a novella on the camps, the two women were expecting it "like manna from heaven." The following summer, Anichkova wrote to the author, expressing her admiration and offering to help with translations or small tasks.[42]

As it turned out, Solzhenitsyn was precisely in need of such unconditional assistance for *The Gulag Archipelago* and, having met the "NN" in person, he accepted their offer. However, he imposed his own conditions and strict imperatives of secrecy: during his visits, there would be no idle talk, and no strangers were to be present.[43] Their collaboration was a fruitful one. In the "NN," Solzhenitsyn found selfless helpers, who efficiently fulfilled his requests. They were enthralled to share in his mission. For Nadia, the death of her parents had been the determining event in her life. As soon as she had a chance to "help the man who had opened up the whole horror of that time," she became involved without an afterthought. And in the ninth decade of her life, she still proudly affirmed that not once had she regretted her commitment, despite the risks involved.[44] Nadia helped by translating articles, reviews, and sometimes summarizing foreign books, selecting passages that might be of interest to Solzhenitsyn. But she also frequently served as a courier, bringing documents to Elena Chukovskaia, another of Solzhenitsyn's helpers, or dispatching manuscripts to hiding places. The "NN" stayed with Solzhenitsyn in his small dacha near Obninsk for two summers, in 1966–67, and they lived with him in Mstislav Rostropovich's dacha for two winters, in 1969 and 1971. The small company, also constituted of Solzhenitsyn's second wife Natal'ia Svetlova and Elizaveta Voronianskaia, a devoted typist, was perpetually occupied with such tasks as typing the writer's manuscripts, correcting them, verifying quotes, summarizing books, or going on errands. As for Anichkova, she was particularly helpful in finding the right people for specific purposes, be it Gulag survivors, librarians, typists, a book binder, or volunteers to whom copies of the *Archipelago* could be entrusted for safekeeping. Through her very broad personal network, she could also diffuse samizdat efficiently.[45]

Another former *zek* Solzhenitsyn met was Natal'ia Stoliarova, alias "Eva." She was the daughter of Natal'ia Klimova, a fearless Russian revolutionary who had made an assassination attempt on Petr Stolypin and had successfully escaped from a tsarist penal colony. Although Stoliarova grew up in France, she chose to return to her motherland in 1934, where she was arrested in 1937. Liberated in 1946, she was eventually allowed back to Moscow in 1956, where she became the secretary of Il'ia Ehrenburg, a famous writer. In the spring of 1962, having heard of *Ivan Denisovich*, she obtained the manuscript from *Novyi mir*, under the pretext that Ehrenburg wanted to read it. According to Solzhenitsyn, she made photographic copies and thus launched the book into samizdat. She also contacted the author through their common friend Kopelev and after a first encounter, they became friends.[46]

There were also former prisoners Solzhenitsyn had known before *Ivan Denisovich* was published. In Riazan, where Solzhenitsyn moved after his rehabilitation, he made the acquaintance of two sisters, Anna and Tat'iana Garaseva. The two anarchists had been arrested in 1925 in Leningrad; Anna was liberated three years later, but her sister underwent a second arrest in 1936 and spent years in prison and in the Kolyma camps.[47] Solzhenitsyn not only used the Garaseva sisters' testimony in *The Gulag Archipelago*, but also counted on them to collect material for him, hide his drafts of the book, manuscripts, and magnetic tapes, or to burn documents in their stove.[48] In her memoirs, Anna Garaseva wrote about her encounters with the writer and the personal meaning she gave to her own contribution to his underground work. As she hid Solzhenitsyn's manuscript, she always kept in mind "the sinister Lubianka house, the Solovki islands . . . , the transfer camps, the Higher Urals isolation ward, the distant Kolyma, where [her sister] Tat'iana almost died," and she rejoiced to be able to thus defend the principles to which she had remained faithful since her youth.[49]

Although he was selective in his friendships, Solzhenitsyn did not restrict himself to former prisoners. In a memoir called *Invisible Allies*,[50] he retraces the very broad network of acquaintances and friends who provided logistical assistance, as typists, research assistants, by smuggling microfilms of manuscripts abroad, or by hiding his personal archives. Some of them were also witnesses, while others simply sympathized with his goals. Amid the flood of letters received after the publication of *Ivan Denisovich*, Solzhenitsyn singled out a particularly warm-hearted message from Elizaveta Voronianskaia, the head of a geology library in Leningrad. She wrote, "Let my feeling of love and gratefulness dissolve into this common flow of respect to you. . . . I would really, really like to somehow be useful to you. I am at your disposal as a most honest and devoted friend."⁵¹ In her letter, the writer identified a deep "repentance towards the past, the repentance of a soul that had not known the camps."⁵² After their first acquaintance in 1963, Voronianskaia started collecting information for Solzhenitsyn's novel on the Revolution, *The Red Wheel*, and in 1964, she accompanied him to Estonia to type *The First Circle*. She also typed copies of his shorter pieces for samizdat.

Yet Voronianskaia had a passionate temper and could sometimes act incautiously. Although she lived in an old communal apartment, where every neighbor was a potential informer, she kept a diary in which she mentioned her meetings with Solzhenitsyn and the secret letters they exchanged. In 1967, the writer entrusted her with the responsible task of typing three copies of *The Gulag Archipelago*. Her profound veneration for the book ultimately proved fatal: she mentioned its existence to a few friends and even gave them pages to read. When Solzhenitsyn asked her to burn the intermediary version she had in her possession, she was reluctant to do so. In 1972, she finally announced she had complied with the request, while in reality, she had kept the manuscript hidden at a friend's dacha.⁵³ Her role in the subsequent fate of *The Gulag Archipelago* exemplifies the dangers that were associated with the creation of such broad networks, which were bound to come to the attention of the KGB, regardless of all the conspiracy measures adopted.

Butting heads with the Soviet "Oak"

By 1965, Solzhenitsyn had progressively drifted from the status of publicly acclaimed writer to that of potential dissenter under close scrutiny from the KGB. Nominated for the Lenin Prize in 1964, his failure to earn a well-deserved award did not bode well for the writer's fate. The difficulties *Novyi mir* faced in securing the publication of Solzhenitsyn's novels were equally troubling. Tvardovskii had nothing but praise for *The First Circle* and was intent on publishing it,⁵⁴ but after Khrushchev's overthrow, repeating the feat of *Ivan Denisovich* with a radically anti-Stalinist novel was beyond his forces. Although Tvardovskii had concluded a contract with the author and still intended on fighting this battle, Solzhenitsyn was already exploring other avenues.

Following Khrushchev's ouster, Solzhenitsyn contacted Stoliarova in panic to ask her if she could find a "channel" to send his manuscripts to the West. She introduced him to Vadim Andreyev, son of the famous writer Leonid Andreyev, who lived in Switzerland. On October 31, 1964, he took to the West a capsule containing eighteen years of Solzhenitsyn's writings, including *The First Circle*.⁵⁵ While this was primarily a measure of safety in times of great uncertainty, Solzhenitsyn also felt that Khrushchev's eviction had "liberated [him] from a debt of honor" and obligatory gratitude toward the man who had "elevated" him. The psychological barrier that still prevented him from releasing his works into samizdat and publishing abroad was swiftly eroding, as the perspective of publication in the USSR vanished. Still, he believed better times might come, and, meanwhile, all he longed for was to retreat to the underground, where he would safely write for years in silence, avoiding any public activism.⁵⁶ Securing the time and freedom of action necessary to complete *The Gulag Archipelago* and write the first "knots" of his future novel *The Red Wheel* were his essential objectives.

In the winter of 1964–65, Solzhenitsyn drew up the plan of *The Gulag Archipelago* and began to work on the first and fifth parts: one was mostly historical, while the other was mainly autobiographical, inspired by his experience at the Ekibastuz camp. Over the past year, the writer had been able to collect more material than he could have hoped for. He had contacted his correspondents, asking for details, met some of them, and the circle of secret sympathizers willing to collect material on his behalf had expanded. Through them, Solzhenitsyn could access rare publications, and as a member of the Writers' Union, he was now entitled to use the libraries' special restricted sections.⁵⁷ In his exploration of the history of the Soviet repressive machine, Solzhenitsyn relied extensively on a few works published in the 1920s and 1930s. Particularly useful was the former Chairman of the Revolutionary Tribunal Nikolai Krylenko's *The Last Five years 1918-1922. Indictment Speeches for the Greatest Trials Heard by the Moscow and Supreme Revolutionary Tribunals* (1923), which provided Solzhenitsyn with the template and content for much of chapters 8, 9, and 10 of Part I. Other sources he used were Martyn Latsis's *Two Years of Struggle on the Inner Front: Popular Overview of the Activity of the Cheka* (1920) and Andrei Vyshinskii's *From Prisons to Educative Institutions* (1934).⁵⁸

However, the tranquility Solzhenitsyn hoped to return to was no longer an option, and a strategic faux pas he committed only precipitated the inevitable confrontation with the KGB. Upon returning from his summer holidays, the writer found out about an important ideological conference that had taken place in August 1965. He was particularly distressed by the news that Aleksandr Shelepin, a Politburo member and Central Committee secretary, had advocated an end of de-Stalinization and attacked *Novyi mir*. Having in mind the confiscation by the KGB of Vasilii Grossman's novel *Life and Fate*, Solzhenitsyn took an ill-inspired decision. On September 8, disregarding Tvardovskii's protests, he decided to remove the four copies of *The First Circle* from *Novyi mir*'s safe and to leave three of them in what he believed to be a more secure hiding place, in the apartment of his friends Veniamin and Suzanna Teush, whom he had for years entrusted with a part of his literary archive.⁵⁹ In retrospect, Solzhenitsyn deeply regretted this choice: the old couple lived in a communal apartment, next to a former official of the Ministry of Interior, and more than once demonstrated incaution in their dealings with the writer.⁶⁰ At the time, he was unaware that the KGB knew of their connection and had wiretapped the apartment.⁶¹ On September 12, three days after Andrei Siniavskii's arrest, Solzhenitsyn found out that the KGB had seized the three copies of *The First Circle*. But this was not the end of it: during another search conducted in the apartment of a friend of the Teushes, they had also found part of his literary archive containing *Feast of the Victors*, the most "anti-Soviet" of his works, a play in verse composed in the camps.⁶²

Solzhenitsyn identified his novel's fateful "arrest"—as he would call the incident— as a turning point in his dissident biography. While he had previously merely played with the idea, he attributed his decision to publish his novels abroad to this event, which struck him as a personal tragedy.⁶³ Back in Riazan, Solzhenitsyn burnt his archives, expecting arrest.⁶⁴ Yet repression did not follow, and a new *status quo* seemed to temporarily arise. Although he continued to negotiate with *Novyi mir* over the publication of his less contentious work *The Cancer Ward*, Solzhenitsyn had lost faith in the possibility of an accommodation with the authorities. Yet he knew better than to display his new mindset openly. According to his faithful helper Elena Chukovskaia, Solzhenitsyn's struggle for the publication of his novel was "a kind of smoke screen" concealing his real activities, which revolved around the *Archipelago.*⁶⁵

Elena ("Liusha") was the granddaughter of the famous author of children literature Kornei Chukovskii and the daughter of the dissident writer Lidiia Chukovskaia. Chukovskii was on holiday with Tvardovskii in 1962 when the latter let him read *Ivan Denisovich*. Enthralled by the novella, the writer wrote an enthusiastic review, entitled "A literary miracle," which Tvardovskii then used to persuade Khrushchev to publish Solzhenitsyn's work.⁶⁶ Solzhenitsyn met Chukovskii in person later on, and after his novel's "arrest," the dissident turned to him for assistance. The writer offered to host him at his dacha in Peredelkino and Lidiia Korneevna invited him to stay for a short while in their apartment in the city center, on Tverskaia street, when he needed to go on errands. There Solzhenitsyn made the acquaintance of Elena, a thirty-four-year-old chemist who assisted her grandfather as an informal secretary. Upon hearing that Solzhenitsyn typed his own works, she spontaneously offered: "Let me help you type something."⁶⁷ This marked the beginning of a fruitful collaboration: in Solzhenitsyn's words, from 1965 to 1970, she "stood at the epicenter, at the heart of my intense activity; for all those years, it was towards her that all the lines of action converged, all the communications—questions, answers, messages of documents to be transmitted."⁶⁸ The writer entrusted her with the responsibility of connecting with his various helpers when he was away from Moscow. Equally precious was her advice on strategies of action. Liusha was one of the first to hear about *The Gulag Archipelago*. Not only did she help gather information, but she also dedicated her vacations to help type the manuscript.⁶⁹

Starting from 1966, the writer began to mount repeated offensives, culminating in May 1967 with his famous "Letter to the 4th Congress of the Writers' Union," denouncing censorship in literature and his own exclusion from print.⁷⁰ The publication of his two novels abroad in 1968—*The First Circle* of his own accord, *The Cancer Ward* without his consent—only poured oil on fire. By November 1969, he had been excluded from the Writers' Union and reacted through a fierce letter: "OPENNESS, honest and complete OPENNESS—that is the first condition of health in all societies, including our own. . . . He who does not wish this openness for his fatherland does not want to purify it of its diseases, but only to drive them inwards, there to fester," warned the outcast writer.⁷¹ In the late 1960s, he faced constant attacks and slander in the Soviet media: doubts were shed upon his rehabilitation and quotes from his unpublished play *Feast of the Victors* were used to denounce his "anti-Soviet" views. In 1970, as the Nobel Committee designated him as laureate of the Nobel Prize for Literature, Solzhenitsyn decided against traveling to Stockholm to receive the award, fearing he might not be allowed back into the USSR. He was walking a perilous tightrope, yet he felt the thrill of the struggle, the essence of which he conveyed in the title of his memoirs *Bodalsia Telenok s Dubom* ("The Calf that butted heads with the Oak").

Liusha, unlike her outspoken mother, shied away from the limelight and felt concern for Solzhenitsyn's bold actions, which she feared might trigger the authorities' wrath.[72] Still, she agreed to type over a hundred copies of his "Letter," which he sent to each delegate of the Writers' Congress. Once, he asked her if she was assisting him for the sake of the "Cause," and she answered negatively: her sole ambition was to help him.[73] In fact, her devotion was also fed by the bitter personal experience of losing her stepfather to repression in 1937.[74] However, as Solzhenitsyn's position increasingly diverged from her liberal communist upbringing, Liusha began to question her unconditional commitment.[75]

Although Liusha remained Solzhenitsyn's devoted assistant well into his years of emigration, by the end of the 1960s, their close collaboration was on the wane. Indeed, it was in those years that the writer made the acquaintance of Natal'ia Svetlova, who would become his second wife and the mother of his three sons. They met through Stoliarova in August 1968. "Alia," as he would call her, was a single mother finishing a PhD in mathematics, yet she offered to dedicate two hours daily to help type Solzhenitsyn's works. The writer was struck by her sharp intelligence, deep knowledge of the Soviet past and love for poetry and the Russian language. Soon, Alia demonstrated such efficiency, commitment, and courage that Solzhenitsyn started entrusting her with more responsible tasks, such as archive safekeeping, but also began to see a potential companion in her. In the following years, in the tumult caused by Solzhenitsyn's protracted and painful divorce from his first wife, Natal'ia Reshetovskaia, Alia would prove a most precious source of support and an irreplaceable assistant.[76]

The support from which Solzhenitsyn benefited as he worked on *The Gulag Archipelago* and some of his other works was commensurate with his popularity within the liberal intelligentsia and among former Gulag prisoners. This icon of free thinking appeared as the writer best placed to fulfill "society's order" and publish the first history of the camps. Although he was less widely known, Roy Medvedev also came to be considered as the bearer of a collective truth about the Stalin era.

Let History Judge

Collaborative writing

In the introduction to the first Soviet edition of *Let History Judge*, Medvedev recalled:

> I met and discussed at length with many who had passed through Stalin's labor camps—Old Bolsheviks, including a few surviving adherents of Trotsky, Zinoviev, or Bukharin; former Socialist-Revolutionaries, anarchists, and Mensheviks who had miraculously survived; technical specialists not belonging to any party; former military people, scientists, writers, journalists, party functionaries, and ordinary workers and peasants; people who had been labeled kulaks and those who had "de-kulakized" them; clergymen and lay people; former Chekists (members of the state security police); former Russian emigres who had returned to the USSR; and Russians, Jews, Ukrainians, and Armenians who dreamed of leaving the Soviet Union.[77]

Unlike Solzhenitsyn, who used testimonies from former prisoners primarily to build a collective oral history of the camps, Medvedev mostly used witnesses' accounts as a substitute for archival documents, from which he extracted historical data. These sources were crucial, in Medvedev's view, "because many of Stalin's illegal orders and actions were not recorded in any documents during his lifetime."[78] And although there were potential issues of reliability, the historian pleaded for giving these testimonies the attention they deserved, on ethical grounds:

> Some of the manuscripts I have used report deathbed testimony passed on to Party comrades in Stalinist camps and prisons. In the tortuous journey of such testimony, sometimes measured in decades, distortions and inaccuracies were inevitable. But it would be irreverence to the dead to cast aside their testimonies as unreliable and unobjective, instead of carefully compiling and comparing their various accounts.[79]

He thus affirmed the primacy of the ethical value of the witnesses' words over concerns of accuracy. This tension was central to the works of dissident researchers, as we will see in Chapter 7.

The first Old Bolshevik Medvedev met was Ivan Gavrilov, his father's friend, who had been arrested in 1939 and sent to the Kolyma camps. As he returned home after the war, he met Roy and Zhores and told them about his two encounters with their father in the camp, but also shared the cruder details of his incarceration. He was rearrested in 1948 and released only six years later.[80] Gavrilov became Medvedev's first reader and introduced him to other Old Bolsheviks. These veterans of the Revolution and the Civil War had occupied high positions in the state and party apparatuses under Lenin and Stalin, before falling prey to the purges. A convenient way to step into contact with them was through their unofficial society, an organization that assisted its members with various issues, but also organized cultural activities. As a party member, son of a repressed communist, Medvedev usually elicited trust and sympathy. His work raised interest, and many were eager to assist him or introduce him to others. Over the years, he estimated that he took around 2,000 interviews and read 200 camp memoirs.[81] A letter sent in 1965 by Dora Zorina on behalf of a group of party veterans for the twins' fortieth birthday, testified to the respect and admiration that the Medvedev brothers raised among Old Bolshevik. She praised them for continuing "their fathers' and mothers' revolutionary traditions" and "fearlessly uncover[ing] our mistakes and weaknesses, dig[ging] up the roots of these mistakes, striv[ing] to scientifically analyze party politics and draw[ing] the conclusions from the harsh lesson of history, for which we have all so dearly paid."[82]

One particularly close friendship Medvedev formed was with Suren Gazarian. In 1964, Medvedev heard about the memoirs written by this former NKVD official, who had himself fallen prey to the terror.[83] Gazarian joined the Party in 1919 and participated in the armed insurrection that had led to the installation of Soviet power in Armenia. The Old Bolshevik then started working for the Cheka. By the early 1930s, he had become head of the Economic Section of the NKVD in Transcaucasia and Georgia. Arrested in July 1937, he escaped execution, but was tortured and spent years in solitary confinement. Released in 1947, he was allowed back to Moscow only in 1954, after his rehabilitation. In 1955, Gazarian acted as the main witness of the prosecution in an open trial against former NKVD agents in Georgia, following Beria's arrest. After the 20th Party Congress, he began to write his memoirs, entitled "This must not happen again" (*Èto ne dolzhno povtorit'sia*), but their publication in Armenia was blocked following Khrushchev's ouster. Ironically, his past as an NKVD official also hindered the publication of his work in the West.[84]

Medvedev first met Gazarian in 1964. After a long conversation, they exchanged their manuscripts. Gazarian's were the first memoirs of a former political prisoner to fall into Medvedev's hands, and they produced a very strong impression on him. In 1967, Medvedev shared the manuscript with Tvardovskii, who wrote an enthusiastic letter to the author, expressing both regret not to be able to publish it and the conviction that it would, one day, "see the light of day and serve the cause of communism."[85] This work described the functioning of the NKVD during the 1920s and 1930s, with portraits of some prominent political and public figures from the Caucasus and Azerbaijan. Gazarian let Medvedev use facts and testimonies from his memoirs for his research and met him frequently to discuss specific historical questions. He also became Medvedev's loyal supporter: after the latter's exclusion from the Party, the Old Bolshevik initiated a collective letter of protest.[86]

Another close helper was Lev Portnov, a veteran of the February Revolution, party member since April 1917.[87] He occupied various low-level party positions after the October Revolution, before being arrested in 1937. However, he was released, and his party membership was restored during the short-lived wave of amnesties that followed Beria's nomination to the NKVD's head, in 1938. Appointed director of Moscow's largest commercial center, Portnov developed a vast network of contacts. Following the 20th Party Congress, he joined one of the rehabilitation commissions and during a year he was at work liberating prisoners from the Gulag. He took extensive notes about prisoners and conserved some documents, which he later shared with Medvedev.[88] A committed anti-Stalinist, Portnov decided to help him by any means he could. In a letter dated from September 1964, he expressed his admiration for the historian's "clever work" and offered to convince ten other Old Bolsheviks to present *Let History Judge* for the Lenin Prize.[89] Portnov introduced Medvedev to many useful contacts among Old Bolsheviks, some of whom had worked with the most prominent party figures in the 1920s. From these witnesses, Medvedev received not only precious information, but also documents, memoirs, diaries, and rare books and brochures from the 1920s.[90]

Unsurprisingly, it was Aleksei Snegov who made the greatest contribution to Medvedev's research. They became acquainted in 1964 and met frequently until the late 1960s. Snegov's firsthand knowledge of the Gulag administration made him a particularly valuable source for Medvedev. According to the historian, Snegov was a very gifted orator, a talented propagandist, who had "a colossal knowledge of facts." However, he did not have the synthetic mind of a scholar and could not make sense of this information on his own.[91] His relationship with Medvedev was therefore based on complementarity: while Snegov had attempted in vain to write a book about the origins of Stalinism, Medvedev was a talented mind looking for answers to his queries about the past. They met regularly: in order to stimulate Snegov's memory, the historian would for instance show him other people's memoirs. The Old Bolshevik possessed a huge quantity of documentary material, scattered through his apartment, but he lacked the ability to systematize his own knowledge, according to Medvedev.[92]

According to the American historian Stephen Cohen, in the 1970s, Snegov and Ol'ga Shatunovskaia, another of Medvedev's sources, were "legendary figures among Gulag survivors" he knew and were "referred to as 'Khrushchev's zeks,' both by their admirers and by anti-Khrushchev officials who hated them."[93] Shatunovskaia was, according to her biographer Grigorii Pomerants,

> a living legend of the Baku underground . . . , a party member since 1916 (she was then fifteen years old), in 1918—Shaumian's secretary, condemned by the Turks to be hanged, she survived thanks to a burst of generosity of the newly-appointed Azerbaijani Minister of the Interior. Having contracted typhus while taking care of her sick comrades in Vladikavkaz, which was occupied by the Whites, she was smuggled into Georgia in a bale of carpets and, as soon as she recovered, she returned to underground work in Baku.[94]

As a young woman, she had refused Anastas Mikoian's marriage proposal, but they remained on good terms and in the following years, he would repeatedly come to her assistance. In the 1930s, she worked in the Moscow party organization and became a member of the Moscow Party Committee. Arrested in 1937, she was condemned to eight years of camp and sent to the Kolyma. Liberated thanks to Mikoian's intercession in 1946, she was condemned in 1949 to internal exile for life in the Krasnoiarsk region. After her liberation and rehabilitation in 1954, her party membership was restored. Shatunovskaia was then appointed both to the PCC and to the Central Commission on Rehabilitation. In this position, she relentlessly lobbied the leadership to accelerate the liberations.[95]

In 1960, Khrushchev included Shatunovskaia in the "Shvernik Commission," created to investigate Sergei Kirov's assassination. For two years, the Commission conducted the investigation thoroughly, producing sixty-four volumes of documents and interviewing a thousand people. Shatunovskaia gathered several key witnesses' testimonies about the suspicious circumstances of Kirov's death, pointing to Stalin's responsibility in organizing the assassination. In the archives, she also allegedly found a paper on which Stalin had drawn up a list of members of the two Leningrad and Moscow "terrorist centers," which he claimed were behind the assassination. In addition, she identified a motive for Stalin's actions: during the 17th Party Congress, in 1934, a group of prominent party officials who had gathered in Sergo Ordzhonikidze's apartment supposedly complained about Stalin's "dictatorial style" and concluded that it was necessary to replace him by Kirov as General Secretary. Kirov refused the position, however, fearing for his life. But after the secret ballot at the end of the Congress, the members of the returning board (*shchetnaia kommissiia*) allegedly discovered with horror that 292 votes had been cast against Stalin. Kaganovich ordered them to retain three votes against Stalin—as many as there had been in favor of Kirov—and to burn the 289 other bulletins. The only surviving witness from the returning board,

Vasilii Verkhovykh, agreed to testify about these events.[96] In the name of the Shvernik Commission, Shatunovskaia also obtained from the KGB an official document giving the number of arrests and executions for each semester between 1935 and July 1941.[97] However, according to her memoirists, Shatunovskaia's investigation fell victim to the pressure of more conservative Presidium members, who pushed Khrushchev to postpone the publication of the results for another fifteen years. In 1962, she was forced into retirement and after 1964, she witnessed with dismay the scattering and destruction of the material she had collected.[98]

At least this was the version that Roy Medvedev, but also Anton Antonov-Ovseenko, heard from Shatunovskaia and used in their research. Medvedev noted that she was warier of sharing information with him than Snegov. He explained this by her enduring fear of being watched, followed, or even arrested or killed. On certain topics, such as Kirov's murder, the 17th Party Congress and Stalin's election to the position of General Secretary, or the fates of some Bolsheviks, she agreed to reply to specific questions, but otherwise she remained deliberately evasive.[99]

Shatunovskaia may have been reluctant to speak for another reason. In his study[100] on the Kirov murder based on documents from the Shvernik Commission, Matthew Lenoe points to Shatunovskaia's cavalier accommodation with facts, as she conducted the highly political mission with which she had been entrusted. According to Lenoe, the Khrushchev leadership wished to create a new narrative depicting Kirov as an early opponent of Stalin and tragic victim of his wrath. The testimonies of Old Bolsheviks were central to this project. They were eager to "portray Stalin as the lone devil who had derailed the Communist project," not only to rehabilitate themselves in the public's eyes as Stalin's opponents, rather than his accomplices, but also, on political grounds, to reaffirm Leninism as an unstained doctrine distinct from the distortions of Stalinism. "Unfortunately the evidence gathered for the new story-line was flimsy, and at times downright deceptive."[101] Lenoe claims that Shatunovskaia and her subordinates compiled evidence selectively and "used investigative methods that were bound to distort their informants' accounts."[102] Witnesses suddenly "recalled" after their interview "facts" that had been suggested to them or confirmed the veracity of "evidence" obtained under torture during investigations in 1937–38. Overall, Lenoe concludes that there could not have been 289 votes cast against Stalin at the 17th Congress and that the move to replace Stalin with Kirov at the Party's head was a mere rumor circulating at the time. Nor does he find any corroborating evidence for other elements of Shatunovskaia's narrative, which appear in both Medvedev's and Antonov-Ovseenko's works. According to Lenoe, the closing of the investigation was not a sign of recrudescence of Stalinism, but resulted from the party leadership's doubts concerning the evidence gathered.[103] Still, at the 22nd Party Congress, Khrushchev chose to present many of Shatunovskaia's assertions as facts, in order to accuse his opponents Malenkov, Molotov, and Kaganovich of having obstructed the investigation of Kirov's murder.[104] It follows from Lenoe's research that Medvedev and Antonov-Ovseenko, by taking Shatunovskaia's testimony at face value, lent credence to a Khrushchev-era anti-Stalinist mythologized account of the Kirov murder.

This was obviously one of the pitfalls of the use of oral testimonies, of which Medvedev was aware. Nevertheless, he did trust many of his respondents, including those with dubious pasts, such as the repentant Stalinist Evgenii Frolov. Although Frolov had occupied high positions in the Ideological Department of the Central Committee and in the NKVD, he had escaped repression. During the war, he was recruited for work in the information office of the Soviet counterintelligence services SMERSh.[105] In 1956, as the *partorg* ("party organizer") of the journal *Kommunist*, he was in charge of reading out Khrushchev's Secret Speech to his party cell and secretly copied the text on his typewriter and let Medvedev access it. He had intended to write a book on Stalin based on the Secret Speech. However, he was unable to complete this work and was therefore eager to share his knowledge and his drafts with Medvedev.[106] After he died, in 1966, his relatives gave Medvedev part of Frolov's personal papers.[107]

Evgenii Gnedin was yet another source of information. The son of Alexander Parvus, a famous German Social-Democrat, Gnedin worked in the NKID with Georgii Chicherin in the 1920s. In 1924, when Parvus died, Gnedin traveled to Germany to take possession of his father's inheritance, which he donated in full to the Soviet state. This included a vast archive in Copenhagen, which was passed on to the IML.[108] In 1935, he became First Secretary of the Soviet Embassy in Germany, before being appointed head of the NKID's Press Department in 1937. Just as Litvinov's replacement by Molotov at the helm of the NKID in May 1939 signaled a reversal in Soviet foreign policy, Gnedin was arrested. For two years, he was subjected to torture and interrogations, with the aim of collecting *kompromat* against Litvinov. Yet he obstinately refused to sign any false confession, a circumstance that saved him from execution. He received a ten-year sentence, followed by six years of internal exile. After his rehabilitation and reintegration into the Party, Gnedin tried to become involved again in politics, but remained on the sidelines. When he met Medvedev, he was still restrained by fear, due to his long experience of detention. Over time, however, he gained confidence and began to write his memoirs. He was more inclined to help others by sharing his extensive knowledge of the inner workings of the prewar NKID.[109] Increasingly involved with dissidents, including Sakharov, Gnedin left the Party in protest in 1979.[110]

Among Medvedev's early readers were also official historians, who did not dare to openly break their ties with the system, but nonetheless sympathized with his research and offered their help. In addition to his close friend Norair Ter-Akopian, a Marxist historian, Medvedev received support from Leonid Petrovskii, but also Viktor Danilov, Mikhail Gefter, Aleksandr Nekrich, Iakov Drabkin, from the Institute of History of the Academy of Sciences. Further assistance came from the sociologist Vladimir Iadov and other researchers from the IML or the Institute of the World Workers' Movement. Medvedev noted that "many of these people had much greater possibilities and professional skills than I did to conduct the work that I had begun. But they did not want to do it, although many of them were ready to help me with advice and materials."[111] Medvedev, like Solzhenitsyn, had thus become a torchbearer for all those who had an interest in keeping the history of Stalin's crimes alive. And his reputation soon expanded far beyond party circles.

Besides Old Bolsheviks, Medvedev's closest supporters and helpers were to be found within the creative intelligentsia. In his memoirs, the historian tells of his acquaintance with several prominent writers: Konstantin Simonov, Il'ia Ehrenburg, Aleksandr

Tvardovskii, and Iurii Trifonov. All of them contributed in some way to Medvedev's work and shared their knowledge about the past.

A famous author and former editor in chief of *Novyi mir*, Simonov was the first prominent writer to read the manuscript of *Let History Judge*. Simonov knew Zhores Medvedev and had read his manuscript *Biology and the Personality Cult* in 1963.[112] When he heard about Roy Medvedev's historical research, he expressed the wish to meet him. At the time of Simonov's first invitation, in December 1964 or January 1965, the writer had just published *Soldiers Are Made, Not Born*, a novel in which he represented Stalin in a "very convincing manner," according to Medvedev. As a laureate of six Stalin Prizes, Simonov had met the Soviet leader several times and earned his consideration. He had also played a less than glorious role in the ideological campaigns of the late Stalin era. By the time he met Medvedev, however, the writer was undergoing a profound revision of his earlier views. As he reconsidered Stalin's historical role, including in the Second World War, he became interested in works about this period.[113] A testimony to the evolution of Simonov's views was the text he wrote in April 1965, before the fiftieth anniversary of the Victory, expressing his opposition to Evgenii Vuchetich's pro-Stalinist conceptions on the duty of writers to depict the war in a positive light.[114] Simonov's depiction of Stalin's responsibility for the early Soviet defeats was in line with Nekrich's views. Moreover, as his own works showed, Simonov seemed to possess information historians did not have, and Medvedev was eager to ask him about it.[115]

During their first meeting, Medvedev gave Simonov his manuscript, insisting that he would be working on the subject for another few years. Two weeks later, they met again and the writer expressed "restrained approbation," but without making any specific comments. At first, Medvedev was disappointed to see that his interlocutor was more interested in asking and listening than in sharing his memories about Stalin. However, Simonov suddenly made an unexpected offer: as a famous writer, he often received memoirs and literary works dealing with Stalinist repressions. Although he could not publish them, he did conserve them in his private archive. He would entrust these manuscripts to Medvedev, but on two conditions: the historian would have to read the materials in Simonov's apartment and refrain from taking any notes. The documents could only be cited with their author's authorization. Medvedev gladly took up the offer.[116]

The historian began his work the same day and was invited to come when Simonov was not home, which he did four or five times, overall, in 1965–66. After examining the manuscripts, Medvedev concluded that they fell into three categories. First, there were manuscripts given by their author "until better times come," not intended for samizdat circulation and only for conservation; from these, Medvedev did not take notes, but they helped him understand certain details. Second, some works had been clearly sent to Simonov in the hope of publication; Medvedev would take notes of these manuscripts upon returning home, from memory. Finally, the third category was constituted by transcripts of interviews with military people. Simonov had personally collected these accounts, taken from the whole military hierarchy, from officers to marshals, and used them for his novels on the war. Medvedev received access only to a fraction of these interviews, however.

Although Simonov disagreed with the attempts to rehabilitate Stalin, he was not ready to undertake bold actions of protest. When Medvedev asked him to sign the "Letter of the twenty-five" to the 23rd Party Congress, for which he was collecting signatures, Simonov replied only evasively. He told Medvedev he agreed with the letter but would rather write his own address to the Congress. Medvedev felt embarrassed for him, thinking that he had lied. However, thirty years later, he found out that Simonov had indeed written his own letter.[117]

Medvedev made Il'ia Ehrenburg's acquaintance in late 1965. The historian had begun to join gatherings of former *zeks* and writers in the apartment of Gulag memoirist Evgeniia Ginzburg. It was there that Medvedev met Natal'ia Stoliarova, Ehrenburg's assistant and secretary. She read a preliminary version of *Let History Judge* and decided, with Medvedev's approval, to show the manuscript to Ehrenburg. When they met for the first time, Ehrenburg mentioned that he had read the manuscript entirely, but then refrained from any other comments. Instead, he engaged in what Medvedev qualified as "a long and extremely interesting monologue," recounting such episodes of his life as the show trial of his friend from youth Bukharin, or the short but intensive anti-Semitic campaign in the last months of Stalin's life and the "doctors' plot" of January 1953. A second encounter took place at the beginning of 1966, when Ehrenburg accepted Medvedev's request to sign Ernst Genri's anti-Stalinist petition to the 23rd Party Congress. Finally, the historian visited him a third time, for a dinner with Evgeniia Ginzburg and Nadezhda Mandel'shtam. This time, Ehrenburg spoke about the fate of the Jewish intelligentsia under Stalin and addressed some of the accusations often leveled at him for having remained silent about persecutions of Jewish intellectuals. In this debate, triggered by the publication of Ehrenburg's memoirs *People, Years, Life*,[118] Medvedev adopted a position of comprehension: while he disagreed with Ehrenburg's rather positive attitude toward Stalin, he considered that, given his prominent position in Soviet society, Ehrenburg had no choice but to display at least outward loyalty toward the Soviet leader, if he was to remain alive.[119]

Another early reader of *Let History Judge*, who actively supported Medvedev's endeavor, was Aleksandr Tvardovskii. Tvardovskii was not only a key figure of the literary Thaw in his position as editor in chief of *Novyi mir*, every issue of which Medvedev read avidly, but also an acclaimed poet. As Medvedev began to give his manuscript to read, he came into contact with numerous writers: Vladimir Dudintsev, Aleksandr Bek, Vladimir Tendriakov, Veniamin Kaverin, but also the Gulag camp memoirists Varlam Shalamov and Evgeniia Ginzburg. Many of them were published in *Novyi mir*. However, it was through his brother, who tried at the time to get his manuscript on Lysenko published in this journal, that the editors first heard of Medvedev's historical study and asked to read it.[120] Despite his initial apprehension, the historian responded to their request in the fall of 1966. As Medvedev later found out, his manuscript went through the hands of all editors by turn, until, one day, he received a phone call from Tvardovskii himself, who invited him for a visit.

What the poet liked about the book was not just its serious scholarly tone and systematic presentation of "trustworthy facts," but also "its quiet tone and convincing argumentation." Medvedev's interpretation of Stalinism as a distortion of socialism, rather than a product of it, also held appeal for such a deeply party-minded man as Tvardovskii. The editor also marveled at the wealth of documentary material upon which Medvedev's work was based, including numerous books and articles published during the Thaw, not only in the central press organs, but also in regional newspapers.[121] Tvardovskii's diary testifies to his enthusiasm for *Let History Judge*, expressed in a series of long entries dated from December 1 to December 5, 1966: "What a truly selfless, huge, bold and noble work has one person undertaken, in order to collect everything that is available, and build a comprehensive, convincing, and deeply party-minded account of the history of the Stalin era." This was "a useful book," and the authorities' attempt "to avoid this theme by hiding their heads in the sand" seemed incomprehensible: "One cannot hide from it."[122] Tvardovskii was struck by the fact that Medvedev had been able to complete his work alone, without any support from above. And yet this work had been produced openly, by a party member who did not attack the regime or put into question its ideology. He found that Medvedev's work "strictly sticks to the observance of the authority of the Party," and it was neither nihilistic nor subversive. Still, he feared lest the author "be accused of all of this by the system, which was inherited from the Stalin era."[123]

Medvedev decided to leave his manuscript with Tvardovskii, something he rarely did. After a few more encounters, Tvardovskii began to invite Medvedev to his country house in Pakhra. The historian would bring with him memoirs, novelties from samizdat, or the latest copy of his samizdat journal *Political Diary*.[124] In return, Tvardovskii contributed to the journal by showing Medvedev collections of translated articles from the foreign press, the access to which was strictly restricted in the Soviet Union.[125] He also let him read interesting manuscripts sent to *Novyi mir*, which he could not publish—a crucial assistance for Medvedev's research.[126] They discussed contemporary issues, as well as Medvedev's new book, published later on under the title *On Socialist Democracy*.[127]

In 1969, as Medvedev was threatened with party exclusion, Tvardovskii sent him a demonstrative handwritten congratulation note on May 1—hoping to thus afford him protection.[128] Yet Tvardovskii's own position was on the line, and by February 1970, he had to resign after the authorities dismissed his editorial team. He called Medvedev and gave him three memoirs he did not wish to leave to his successors, among which was Dmitrii Vitkovskii's *Half a life* (*Polzhizni*).[129] In late May 1970, Tvardovskii intervened at Medvedev's request to defend his brother, who had been incarcerated in a psychiatric hospital in punishment for his dissent.[130] By the time Tvardovskii died of cancer, in December 1971, however, the historian was in hiding.[131]

At *Novyi mir*, Medvedev also became very close to the literary critic Vladimir Lakshin, who shared with him his extensive personal archive and his expertise on repressions in the literary field. The two of them saw eye-to-eye on a number of issues, in particular regarding Solzhenitsyn, whom Lakshin had once highly praised in his literary critiques,[132] but who became alienated by the writer's increasingly radical statements and his individualism. After 1969, Roy's hostility toward Solzhenitsyn grew, and in the late 1970s, he helped Lakshin publish abroad an essay directed against Solzhenitsyn's memoirs *The Oak and the Calf*, answering the writer's attacks against *Novyi mir*.[133]

Also important was Medvedev's friendship with Evgeniia Ginzburg. Tvardovskii had rejected for publication the beautifully written Gulag memoirs of this repressed communist on disputable grounds, but she had published them abroad under the title *Into the Whirlwind*, encountering worldwide success. Ginzburg was keen on helping Medvedev with his research, giving him her own materials, and they shared memoirs and other documents they each received from Old Bolsheviks.[134] Moreover, she introduced him to a number of interesting figures. In the 1960s, she gathered around her a circle of dissidents and writers. According to Medvedev, her house was "reminiscent of the salons of the second half of the 19th century." "Here one could meet both famous and little-known writers and poets, but also former 'zeka' of the most varied professions and situations in society."[135]

Through Ginzburg, Medvedev met the writer Boris Iampol'skii, who introduced him to Iurii Trifonov, whose novel *Fireglow* he had read with interest. On their first encounter, Medvedev gave him his manuscript to read, and they formed a close bond of friendship. Born the same year, the two men had both lost their father to the Terror and shared the same political views. Moreover, Trifonov was interested in history, especially of the nineteenth- and twentieth-century revolutionary movements. In the 1970s, he wrote *Impatience*, a novel about the "People's Will," a nineteenth-century revolutionary group. As a fervent bibliophile, he shared with Medvedev his collection of old journals (he had full sets of such rare publications as *Katorga i ssylka* and *Byloe*) and let Medvedev read books from his unique private library. He also shared with him manuscripts and other primary sources, in exchange for samizdat texts Medvedev brought him.[136] In 1976, Trifonov published his most popular novel *The House on the Embankment*, referring to a large building on the Moscow River, across the Kremlin, where prominent state and party *apparatchiks* lived, and which witnessed countless arrests during the Great Terror. The political repressions, however, remained silenced in this novel of childhood friendship, which explains its innocuity in the eyes of censorship.

Thereafter, Medvedev worked on a project suggested by Trifonov on the Don Cossack Filip Mironov. This hero of the Civil War on the Bolsheviks' side was arrested by his own camp and killed in prison in 1921. Medvedev published his historical *Life and Death of Philip Kuzmich Mironov* in 1978, in coauthorship with Sergei Starikov, an old Don Cossack and a veteran of the Civil War himself. Arrested in the 1930s, Starikov had spent the rest of his life gathering documents to rehabilitate Mironov's reputation. As he sought to write a novel on the subject, he contacted Trifonov, who redirected him to Medvedev. They wrote the work in tandem, but the Cossack died before its publication.[137] The same year, Trifonov published a novel also inspired by Mironov, *The Old Man* (*Starik*).

Finally, Medvedev's manuscript also became known among Soviet scientists, and one of its early readers was Academician Andrei Sakharov, coinventor of the Soviet Hydrogen Bomb and future Nobel Peace Prize laureate. In his memoirs, the famous dissident recognized that this book had been "highly interesting" for him and had opened his eyes on many aspects of the history of Stalinism. "Undoubtedly, the concrete information contained in Medvedev's book influenced to a large extent the acceleration of the evolution of my views in these critical years for me."[138] Although, in retrospect, Sakharov insisted that he had always disagreed with Medvedev's views,[139] in his 1968 Memorandum on "Progress, Coexistence and Intellectual Freedom," he mentioned *Let History Judge*—then still unpublished—as "an outstanding work, written from a socialist, Marxist position" offering "a deep analysis of the genesis and manifestations of Stalinism."[140]

Questioning some deeply ingrained taboos

Enthusiastic readers of *Let History Judge* could be found not only among writers, Old Bolsheviks, and dissidents, but even within the Central Committee apparatus. In his memoirs, Georgii Shakhnazarov, a consultant from Iurii Andropov's team in the early 1960s, and later on Gorbachev's adviser, mentions the great impression that Medvedev's historical research produced on him and the closeness of their views. He subscribed to the idea that the historian "was never a hundred-percent dissident, long before Perestroika he presented a wholly reasonable concept of reforms," and he always remained a socialist.[141] Medvedev also claims to have received support and assistance from two other Central Committee consultants: Aleksandr Bovin, who was also Brezhnev's speechwriter, and Iurii Krasin, a sociologist.[142] Bovin mentions one instance in which he was able to help the Medvedev brothers: when Zhores was incarcerated in a psychiatric hospital in 1970, he confronted Brezhnev, who directly called Andropov and obtained the dissident's liberation.[143] On the whole, however, Medvedev's ties were to low-level figures. They could share party documents or publications with him but did not enjoy any influence within the Central Committee, and the party apparatus remained dominated by the conservatives.[144] Still, these connections testify to the extent to which Medvedev's research was considered legitimate, not only by the liberal intelligentsia, but also by part of the Soviet establishment.

How then did he come to be considered a dissident and to be excluded from the Party? As Medvedev recalled, after Khrushchev's ouster, he pursued his work, although the chances of publication became nil, as his line and the Party's increasingly diverged.[145] Under the growing influence of such hardliners as Trapeznikov, the party leadership displayed less tolerance toward independent thought. But Medvedev's views also became more affirmed and his tone sharpened, as he became acquainted with new sources and new witnesses. This evolution is particularly apparent when one compares the successive versions of his manuscript, which he renamed in 1967 *Let History Judge*.

In the version he completed in 1966, Medvedev's tone had become more incisive toward the opponents of de-Stalinization. The historian used the metaphor of the unhealed wound to convey the necessity of facing a painful past. He criticized those who cautioned against "rubbing salt into wounds that are still bleeding." In the process of healing, experiencing pain was unavoidable. Nevertheless, it was necessary to analyze "the causes and the nature of the terrible disease that our Party and our movement have suffered."[146] Addressing the arguments used by his adversaries, Medvedev granted that it was crucial to stick to a certain measure of caution and responsibility in criticizing past crimes. The confusion engendered by the critique of Stalin's personality cult had aroused instances of "political apathy and ideological disaffection, loss of faith and bitterness." However, hoping that these "unhealthy phenomena" could be avoided by "keeping our people and our youth ignorant" was illusory. In a world where various political forces struggled for minds, truth could not remain hidden for long, and the people's loss of faith would be far greater if it learned about Stalin's crimes from another source than the Communist Party.[147] Giving up on this crucial sphere of "ideological struggle" would only make it easier for "bourgeois propagandists to keep speculating on our mistakes and difficulties."[148] Medvedev concluded that Stalinism had dealt a considerable blow to the faith of millions of people in socialism. His task therefore consisted "in returning the idea of socialism to these people," by surmounting the consequences of the personality cult. But this implied first of all overcoming one of its most dangerous effects: "the fear of telling the truth."[149]

The 1966 version of Medvedev's manuscript differed from the 1964 draft in several ways. The focus was no longer exclusively on the 1937 Terror. Such important themes as the collectivization of agriculture and industrialization were now broached in the first part, while a whole chapter was dedicated to wartime and postwar waves of repression. Although Medvedev's treatment of Stalin's struggle with the oppositions remained conservative, with some piques in relation to Trotsky and his personal leadership style, the theme was now given increased attention. Indeed, Medvedev recognized that the question of Stalin's struggle against the "Left" and "Right" oppositions still required "the most serious and objective research," for these years of intraparty struggle corresponded to the rise of Stalin's personal power. Precisely during this period of "unprecedented unity" within the Party had Stalin begun to deviate increasingly from Lenin's norms of party life and understanding of socialism at large. Precisely then had he stepped onto his "path of crime and inflicted such a cowardly stab in the back of Lenin's party, from which it has not yet fully recovered to this day," concluded the historian.[150]

By the spring of 1967, Medvedev had produced a new version of his manuscript. It was now composed of three parts and fourteen chapters. The chronology had been considerably extended: after a first chapter dealing with Stalin's mistakes before and after the Revolution, the author went on to examine in detail Stalin's struggle with the opposition, dedicated a whole chapter to "serious mistakes" committed during collectivization and industrialization, with a new subsection on the repression of "kulaks." Chapter 4 dealt with the first repressions against the technical intelligentsia and the political trials of 1928–31; Kirov's murder now constituted a separate chapter, within which the trials against the opposition were analyzed as a direct consequence of this fateful assassination. In the third part, Medvedev also added a chapter on Stalin's diplomatic and military mistakes and dedicated another one to the consequences of the personality cult in the sciences.

Besides a growing volume of material, this new organization betrayed a fundamental change of perspective, particularly regarding the repression of the oppositions and Stalin's crimes in the pre-1934 period. One explanatory factor of this evolution was Medvedev's encounter with Mikhail Iakubovich, in the summer of 1966. A former Menshevik who had joined the Bolshevik Party after the Revolution, Iakubovich was a civil war veteran and had occupied a high position in the Soviet economic apparatus during the NEP. He was arrested in 1930 and figured prominently in one of the first show political trials, against the "All-Union Bureau of the Mensheviks," in 1931. He then spent twenty-four years in the Gulag, followed by twenty years of internal exile, which he was still serving in a home for invalids in Karaganda, Kazakhstan, at the time of his encounter with Medvedev.[151] Because his condemnation dated back to the years prior to the officially acknowledged period of Stalin's personality cult, he and his codefendants were only rehabilitated posthumously during Perestroika.

In the early 1960s, Iakubovich began writing short historical portraits of political figures he had personally known: Lev Kamenev, Grigorii Zinoviev, Lev Trotsky, and Iosif Stalin. These "Letters to an Unknown Person," as he entitled them, offered a less than orthodox outlook on some of the most vilified leaders of the opposition. In September 1966, the KGB wrote to the Central Committee about the recent circulation of Iakubovich's manuscripts "among a small circle of historians and writers of Moscow." Iakubovich's "letters" on Kamenev and Stalin were attached to the report.[152] Medvedev, who in the late 1970s would publish the letters on Kamenev and Zinoviev in his journal *Twentieth Century*,[153] no doubt read them in 1966, and they clearly influenced his perception of the opposition leaders. Iakubovich was particularly positive in relation to Kamenev: he considered that his merits had been "unjustly forgotten and are either denied or viciously misrepresented and distorted." Admittedly, Kamenev had made mistakes, which Lenin had severely criticized, but why would the Soviet leader have repeatedly entrusted him with the highest party functions, if his behavior had been so objectionable? Why would Lenin have chosen Kamenev to succeed him as head of government during his fatal illness, if he did not trust him? Iakubovich concluded that Stalin's evaluation of Kamenev continued to be dominant, while Lenin's opinion was silenced.[154] The portrait of Stalin in the fourth "letter"—a ninety-page essay spanning the dictator's whole career—was much more negative, depicting him as a crafty, power-thirsty, unprincipled individual apt at outmaneuvering his otherwise more brilliant adversaries by using their weaknesses and psychological flaws.[155] Medvedev quoted from and paraphrased Iakubovich's letters extensively in the first chapter of his 1967 manuscript.[156] His account of Stalin's cunning strategy of exclusion from power of Kamenev and Zinoviev clearly drew inspiration from Iakubovich's letter. Medvedev's opinion of Zinoviev, however, remained mostly negative, although his criticism was more moral than ideological.

Medvedev also offered a more detailed view on the "rightist opposition" of Bukharin, Rykov, and Tomskii. Quite ambiguously, however, he concluded that "the Party's tragedy . . . was that at the head of the opposition were political actors such as Trotsky, Zinoviev and Bukharin, who could not lead our Party back onto the true Leninist path and constitute an acceptable alternative to Stalin's governance."[157] In relation to Bukharin, Medvedev quoted extensively from a 1962 letter to the Central Committee sent by a group of Old Bolsheviks led by Elena Stasova, demanding that Bukharin's condemnation be annulled.[158] Medvedev concluded with a call for an end to the taboo surrounding the opposition, which ridiculed Soviet historical scholarship. Historians could no longer pretend that the 1930s political trials never happened and "that Trotsky, Bukharin, Rykov, Piatakov, Tomskii, Kamenev, Zinoviev and others were never among the brightest leaders of our Party and state." And it was equally absurd that the oppositionists' names should be either absent from Soviet reference works or be ascribed countless sins and mistakes.[159]

As one of the last surviving participants of the show trials of 1928–31, Iakubovich also provided Medvedev with an account of his own case, offering a telling example of the way show trials were fabricated and staged like theater plays. The former Menshevik had refused to sign false confessions and had been subjected to such inhuman torture that he had made a suicide attempt. After being deprived of sleep for twenty days, he finally agreed to sign the interrogation protocol and to play the part that was expected of him at the forthcoming trial. Thereafter, his continuing cooperation was ensured through a mix of persuasion and threat. On the one hand, he was warned that if he failed to play his role, he would be tortured for years. On the other hand, the public prosecutor N. V. Krylenko persuaded him that his participation was in the "higher interest of the Revolution," assuring him that a failure of the trial would deal a huge blow to Soviet power.[160]

This was not the only testimony to enrich the new version of the manuscript. Dozens of witnesses' accounts by Old Bolsheviks, in addition to unpublished memoirs, now gave more depth to what had hitherto been a rather dry overview. Medvedev's account of Kirov's murder and his assassin's trial was now buttressed by several eyewitness accounts. Some informants, quoted anonymously in the 1966 version, were now named, under their full name or initials, testifying to a greater concern for his account's trustworthiness.

The eighth chapter was dedicated to "the use by the NKVD organs of illegal methods of investigation and detention." Showing a prisoner's path through the repressive machine, this chapter covered, in an abridged fashion, the same ground as *The Gulag Archipelago*. Medvedev may have removed it after hearing of the existence of Solzhenitsyn's work, for it disappeared from ulterior versions. It included sections on torture, trials, prison, and the camps, and on the role of NKVD officials. However, Medvedev clearly realized that his short summary could not do justice to a whole universe, which had engulfed three decades of the lives of millions of Soviet citizens, and he implicitly called on historians to fill this gap. Although some literature had appeared on the subject, these were but "a few links of this long chain, that has not yet been created either by our scholarship or literature." He severely condemned those historians, political actors, and writers who participated in perpetuating the "figure of silence" surrounding this difficult theme and failed to find the courage to study this history.[161]

In the field of foreign policy, however, Medvedev betrayed more conservative views. Discussing the Ribbentrop-Molotov pact, he stuck closely to the official version, arguing that the pact was inevitable on security grounds because of the lack of honesty of the French and British governments, who sought to deviate German aggression toward the USSR. Nevertheless, Stalin had been wrong to trust the agreement. Medvedev also justified Western Ukraine and Byelorussia's annexation, arguing that Poland had seized these lands in 1920 and "a significant part of the population" had wished to be reunited to Soviet Ukraine and Byelorussia.[162]

The large use of oral testimonies constituted one of the hallmarks of dissident histories. However, as this chapter has shown, these works were not simply oral histories, they were collective creations which benefited from the input of a very large number of people, who assisted the authors by sharing memoirs, publications, contacts, by providing direct feedback on their manuscripts or by helping them type their works. This assistance was needed due to the very ambitious scope of these histories and the necessity, in a context of underground research, to supplement archival sources. But this collective dimension, by turning these works into written memorials to the victims of political repression, also endowed them with an intrinsic moral value. It can therefore be argued that what made these histories threatening from the point of view of the authorities was not so much their content as the fact that they represented an alternative, moral legitimacy, set in opposition to the regime's policy of silence based on "political expediency."

Saying that the writing of these works played a major catalyzing role in their authors' dissident biographies may seem like stating the obvious, but it is important to emphasize once more that neither Solzhenitsyn nor Medvedev were born dissidents. It was only progressively, as they engaged in the writing of works that were increasingly at odds with official tendencies in the historical field, that they found themselves confronted with the choice of renouncing their projects or leaving the official field. As I show in the following chapter, the drift toward underground practices, from the samizdat diffusion of their writings to the ultimate decision to publish their works in the West, were then triggers that would lead to their expulsion—from the Party, for Medvedev, and from the Soviet Union, for Solzhenitsyn.

5

Exiting the System

From the official field to the underground publishing world

In 1970, in a note to the Central Committee, KGB head Iurii Andropov noted that, in the preceding five years, samizdat had evolved from a channel of circulation primarily oriented toward literature to one focusing on texts of a political-programmatic character. "In the period from 1965, over 400 different research papers and articles on economic, political and philosophical questions have appeared, in which the historical experience of socialist construction in the Soviet Union is criticized from various points of view, various programs of oppositional activity are presented."[1] The type of literature circulated thus increasingly came to mirror censored publications. By the late 1970s, a dissident concurred that samizdat had become "'a state in the state' with its scientists, jurists, politicians, artists, musicians, journalists."[2]

Soviet history was one of the central fields of interest of samizdat readers. In his 1975 overview of historical samizdat, Robert Slusser noted that "the historical problem most passionately debated in dissident intellectual circles in the Soviet Union is the historical role of Stalin," which he explained by the fact that "most members of the democratic opposition identify the repressive system under which they live with Stalin's career and personality."[3] Indeed, historical samizdat was characterized by a strong link between past and present: what interested an increasingly politicized readership was what could shed light on the current political situation. But another important function of historical samizdat, which Slusser failed to mention, was the need to salvage the memory of a painful past, the samizdat text exercising both cathartic and memorial functions. Memoirs and camp literature, in particular, exemplify this function. This could apply for instance to Varlam Shalamov's *Notes from the Kolyma* or Evgeniia Ginzburg's *Into the Whirlwind*, which translated into prose the sheer horror and meaninglessness of the tragedy that had befallen their authors.

Slusser's overview, nevertheless, shows the diversity of expressions of a general thirst for "truthful" knowledge about the past. In a context of defiance toward the censored word in general, and toward Soviet historiography in particular, the value of historical samizdat rested upon readers' conviction that it contained truth. Historical samizdat was part of what Denis Kozlov has called the "historical turn" in late Soviet culture."[4] But while many Soviet citizens only questioned details without putting into question established frameworks of interpretation of the past, historical samizdat raised bold inquiries about taboo themes. It qualified as "forbidden literature," the possession of which might trigger repression.

During the Cold War, Western scholars mostly considered samizdat as a channel of expression of dissident views[5] and used uncensored texts as primary sources for the study of Soviet dissent.[6] H. Gordon Skilling was the first scholar to focus on underground publishing as a social practice. He identified in it an emancipatory potential for the individual, who could, by communicating his or her thoughts through samizdat, "maintain his intellectual integrity and achieve a certain degree of freedom under repressive conditions." It was also "a vehicle of expression which assured the continuity of national culture," as well as "a channel for the expression of political dissent and opposition." Finally, it was "an important source of information, at home and abroad, about the real conditions within a country, countering domestic propaganda and misinformation."[7]

Since the fall of the Soviet Union, many authors have put into question the traditional dualism between official and unofficial realms. As we saw in the third chapter, Sergei Oushakine has criticized samizdat literature's "mimicry" of official discourse and identified "a gradual continuum from underground to official recognition," where dissident discourse, rather than a reversal of official language, was an amplification of it.[8] Ann Komaromi has also insisted on breaking the strict dichotomy between dissident and official spheres, but she argued for the need to "cordon off" a separate field, which she conceptualized anew as "a separate and *autonomous* field of unofficial culture."[9] It encompassed a variety of expressions, ranging from political to artistic samizdat. However, Komaromi insisted that "unofficial culture emerged as an autonomous field from inside Soviet society as a result of its own tensions." Participants in this unofficial culture were born in the Soviet Union; as such, theirs was an experience of ideological crisis of faith from *within* the system.[10] Komaromi's insistence on placing the unofficial field within Soviet society breaks with earlier depictions of samizdat as an attribute of dissident culture, hence outside the system and set in opposition to it. In reality, the official and unofficial fields were closely entangled, not only on a societal, but even on an individual level.

Building on Komaromi's conception, I would argue that samizdat represented an unofficial field, offering a respite from the all-embracing grip of the state and its restrictions, and yet closely intertwined with official discourses and culture. Samizdat offered the possibility to exit partly the obligatory framework of the system into a field liberated from such constraints as censorship, the primacy of ideology and political control. For authors, samizdat served as a laboratory of self-expression and recreated a space of intellectual freedom shielded from the state's interference. For the larger mass of readers, samizdat opened up new horizons of internal freedom, and resulted in the creation of "imagined communities" of protest, fostering emulation. Over time, samizdat became an antechamber of tamizdat, which would offer new possibilities in terms of addressing broad audiences.

Indeed, the emergence of tamizdat in the 1960s and 1970s followed closely the birth of Soviet underground publishing. It came to "mirror the samizdat world in the West,"[11] as works previously circulating in samizdat in the USSR ended up being published abroad. Because the USSR was not party to the Universal Copyright Convention until 1973, Soviet works could be published without their authors' consent—a circumstance which often landed the latter into trouble at home.[12] Particularly reprehensible in the Soviet authorities' view were publications in the Frankfurt-based émigré journals *Posev* and *Grani*, owned by the anti-Soviet group NTS.[13] In order to retain control over their works and to receive royalties, some writers decided to step into direct contact with a Western publisher, but this generally implied renouncing any prospect of publication in the Soviet Union. Never formally forbidden, the practice of publication of uncensored works abroad could nonetheless lead to a prison term, either through a political or a criminal accusation.[14]

Tamizdat was a transnational phenomenon relying on complex networks across the Iron Curtain, involving Soviet dissidents, Russian émigrés, Western and Russian émigré publishers, Western diplomats and cultural attachés in the Soviet Union, Western intellectuals, the KGB, and even European Communist Parties. Although tamizdat could be to a certain extent inward-looking, with authors specifically addressing a Soviet audience, it also contributed to a living dialogue between East and West, and created, according to Friederike Kind-Kovács a "transnational literary community."[15]

The decision to publish in tamizdat, as opposed to samizdat, was influenced by several factors. Only works with a certain commercial potential, of interest not only to Soviet, but also to Western readers, could find a publisher abroad. Yet those authors who managed to make the transition to tamizdat could hope to reach a much broader audience, on both sides of the Iron Curtain, and potentially influence Western discourses about the Soviet Union.[16] Size also mattered: while shorter texts circulated easily in samizdat, larger volumes could not easily be copied on typewriters and their only chance of larger circulation was in tamizdat. In the 1970s, samizdat seemed to decline, as typewritten copies were steadily replaced by copies of tamizdat works smuggled back into the USSR.

This chapter examines two stages of a process of progressive exit from the Soviet system: publication in samizdat often constituted for dissident authors a first step, which could be followed by the more subversive turn toward tamizdat. Ultimately, by drifting away from the official field, these authors exposed themselves to punishment, such as exclusion from the Party or from professional unions, dismissal, administrative sanctions, or even judicial prosecution. Neither *The Gulag Archipelago* nor *Let History Judge* circulated in samizdat before being published abroad. Solzhenitsyn and Medvedev knew the danger they would incur if their works became known before publication in tamizdat afforded them the protection of celebrity.

To illustrate these worlds of historical samizdat and their publics, I will therefore examine two other cases: the underground circulation of a samizdat "bestseller," Abdurakhman Avtorkhanov's *Technology of Power*, a history of the Stalin era, and Roy Medvedev's samizdat journal *Political Diary*. While the former was arguably the most well-known and subversive anti-Stalinist work to circulate in the 1960s, the latter constituted at the time the longest-lived samizdat periodical, with a restricted and yet potentially influential audience. Circulation in samizdat and publication in tamizdat— or the fear thereof—were also central motives in Nekrich and Medvedev's exclusion form the Party and Solzhenitsyn's expulsion from the USSR. In other words, what was punished was not the mere fact of undertaking research, but of sharing it with the "wrong" publics and thus letting it become instrumentalized by "enemy" propaganda.

Avtorkhanov's *Technology of Power*

The success of the political-historical memoir *Tekhnologiia vlasti* ("A study in the technology of power"[17]), written by the Chechen émigré historian Abdurrakhman Avtorkhanov, testifies to the interest that the Stalin era raised among samizdat readers in the 1960s and 1970s. If one believes his memoirs,[18] Avtorkhanov was recruited by the Party in the early 1930s to exercise high functions on the local level in his native Chechnya and in Ingushetia. Allegedly as early as 1927–28, and then in 1934–37, he studied at the Moscow Institute of Red Professors (IKP), an institution of the Central Committee preparing both professors in humanities and the future high cadres of the Party. This experience allowed him to analyze from a unique vantage point the inner mechanisms of the CPSU under Stalin, after he escaped to the West during the war and started publishing works of Sovietology.

Many dark zones remain in the complex biography of this controversial figure, particularly surrounding his defection to the West and wartime activities in Nazi Germany. What is beyond doubt, however, is Avtorkhanov's profound commitment to fight against Communism, which he dates back to his arrest, in 1937, and the simulated execution he claims to have been submitted to as a torture technique.[19] Having escaped the NKVD thanks to the German advance in the Caucasus, he evaded forced repatriation after the war. In 1948, he was recruited by the US Army Russian Institute in Garmisch, Bavaria, where he taught Soviet history and politics until retirement.

In his memoirs, he insists that his motivation was primarily ideological: he had not defected to the West "for a piece of bread," but to fight the Soviet system, which he had seen degenerate into "a totalitarian tyranny" by far surpassing Nazism and fascism, in his view. His vocation, however, was to lead this struggle "not as a political figure, but in the role of a historian of the Soviet Union and analyst of its political system."[20] This determination led him to launch and support several initiatives for the liberation of the Chechen people, and he became a frequent contributor on Radio Liberty.[21] However, it was probably through his books that he managed to gain the greatest influence. Frustrated with the negative reaction of Western Sovietologists to his first study *Staline au pouvoir*[22] and with the petty squabbles of émigré politics, he concluded that his mission should not be to "enlighten" the West as to the real nature of communism, but rather to target directly the peoples of the Soviet Union."[23]

Harassed by the KGB and regarded with suspicion by the FBI, Avtorkhanov set out to write *Tekhnologiia vlasti*, with the aim of documenting the "process of establishment of Stalinist tyranny."[24] Of his own admission, the book's format was "unusual," combining in a single narrative his own recollections and subsequent historical research.[25] While the second part of the book was a political analysis of the rise and fall of Stalinism, the central element of the first part was the author's account of the rise of Bukharinist (rightist) opposition, which he had allegedly closely witnessed during his first year of study at the IKP in 1928–29. However, Michael David-Fox has since cast serious doubts upon the veracity of this testimony. Avtorkhanov's autobiographies, written at the time of his admission to the IKP of History in 1934 and in later years, made no mention of a previous admission at the IKP either in 1927, as mentioned in his memoirs, or in 1928, as he claimed in *Tekhnologiia vlasti*. Instead, he seems to have been in Chechnya at that time.[26] This confirms Roy Medvedev's suspicions, who, based on conversations with former IKP students, denounced Avtorkhanov's work as containing "not only gross distortions, but even conscious inventions."[27]

Published in 1959, *Tekhnologiia vlasti* was introduced in samizdat by General Grigorenko.[28] Having stumbled upon the book in the 1960s, Grigorenko was struck by its content, which was a fundamental revelation for him. He wrote in his memoirs that it was "the most important book" he had ever read, one which could have a decisive impact on its readers' worldviews, and he decided to spread it as widely as he could. As the book's popularity grew, he began to receive a growing number of requests for samizdat copies, despite the significant cost of typewritten reproduction.[29]

However, Avtorkhanov's book was also singled out by the KGB as one of the most subversive items of samizdat. Unverified rumors circulated that the KGB had added a radioactive substance to some photocopies, in order to trace back the book's circulation.[30] In December 1968, three young Leningraders, Iurii Gendler, Lev Kvachevskii, and Anatolii Studenkov, were tried for the reproduction and circulation of literature of "anti-Soviet content," including Avtorkhanov's *Tekhnologiia vlasti*. They received sentences ranging from one and a half to four years of strict regime camp.[31] Following this condemnation, Petr Grigorenko, Il'ia Gabai, Iulii Kim, Petr Iakir, Viktor Krasin, and five other dissidents wrote an open letter of protest, in which they expressed their dismay that the tribunal had recognized the works of Nikolai Berdiaev, Milovan Djilas, and Abdurakhman Avtorkhanov "anti-Soviet."[32] They found this designation "particularly revolting" in relation to *Tekhnologiia vlasti*, which was "for the time being the only one in this field," and whose conceptions no one had yet tried to counter. This, they believed, demonstrated the solidity of the author's arguments, which were buttressed by facts. By equating anti-Stalinism with anti-Sovietism, the court was only justifying the "great leader's" claims.

This was but the first penal case featuring Avtorkhanov's book in the act of accusation. In the following years, the book was seized during house searches in Kiev, Moscow, Odessa, and in Lithuania. In October 1972, Kronid Liubarskii stood accused of copying and circulating samizdat, including *The Technology of Power*. As reported by the samizdat bulletin *Chronicle of Current Events*, the dissident "recognized [these works'] hostility and tendentiousness . . . , but he pointed to the usefulness of reading these books due to the wealth of facts they contain."[33] In his last word, Liubarskii pleaded for the freedom of access to information, so necessary to form an independent opinion. "Information is the bread of scientific workers. The intellect works with it, just as the peasant does with the earth and the [industry] worker with metal."[34] In order to draw lessons from history, it was necessary to study the circumstances of Stalin's accession to power, but Liubarskii could not find a single book on the subject on bookshop shelves, which compelled him to turn to Avtorkhanov's work in samizdat. He asked rhetorically: "Is samizdat a normal phenomenon? No, of course. It is a symptom of illness. In a society with a normal development, all the questions discussed in samizdat should be analyzed in the newspapers. Only in a society with an abnormal development is the discussion of sensitive issues pushed into the underground, thus giving it a shade of illegality."[35]

Avtorkhanov explained the success of his book by the fact that the Soviet authorities singled it out during political trials and designated the author as a Nazi collaborator.[36] Paradoxically, this unexpected fame in the Soviet underground increased American suspicion toward Avtorkhanov and made him a side victim of the détente process. According to Avtorkhanov, after 1970, his new superior in Garmisch prevented him from speaking on "Radio Liberty" and from reediting *Tekhnologiia vlasti*, under threat of dismissal. Nevertheless, the ban on a second edition was lifted in 1974, after a change in the Institute's hierarchy.[37]

Avtorkhanov's *Technology of Power* was one of the first historical works about the Stalin era to find its way into samizdat, at a time when Solzhenitsyn's *Gulag Archipelago* and Medvedev's *Let History Judge* were still unpublished. The success of the book can be explained by the lack of competition on the "samizdat market" at this point, but also by the lively tone in which it was written. The writer Vladimir Voinovich thus remembered: "[Avtorkhanov's] books[38] became samizdat classics. They virtually became a bible of the dissident movement, especially 'The Technology of Power.' With their help, people learned to understand the essence of the Soviet system (*stroi*)."[39] The trials over Avtorkhanov's readers showed the extent to which the Soviet authorities felt threatened by anti-Stalinist samizdat. It also testified to the risk presented by the uncontrolled dissemination of a text, the origin of which could be easily traced back after it had fallen into the wrong hands.

Roy Medvedev's *Political Diary*

Roy Medvedev sought to avoid precisely such an outcome and always carefully controlled all existing copies of his works. Therefore, his journal *Political Diary*, launched in October 1964, in the aftermath of Khrushchev's ouster, can only be conditionally qualified as samizdat.[40] Yet despite its limited readership, it was a unique endeavor in many respects. With around seventy issues spanning the years 1964 to 1971, *Political Diary* was "the first successful effort to establish a regular uncensored periodical or journal," and, for a time, the longest-lived, according to Stephen Cohen.[41] Over time, this monthly historical and political journal grew into a solid publication of up to 100–120 typed pages, with sections covering current politics, history, literature, and economics, featuring samizdat novelties or foreign books' summaries.

Although Medvedev wrote and edited the journal almost single-handedly, he received assistance from many sympathizers, who helped with the collection, discussion, and selection of material, as well as more concrete tasks, such as copying, distributing, and safekeeping of the journal. Among these helpers were numerous Old Bolsheviks, such as Evgenii Frolov,[42] a senior editor of the party journal *Kommunist*, who would provide Medvedev with some exclusive documents that he received access to through his position, until his death, in 1966.[43] Other friends were in charge of reading current issues of Soviet literary and sociopolitical journals, carefully selecting excerpts and cuttings from them, or summarizing recently published books. On this basis, Medvedev produced five copies of the journal and left each one at a friend's place, accessible only to a few dozen readers he could trust and identify. The historian strictly limited the number of copies made and controlled the journal's distribution, which had the effect of drastically limiting the number of readers, but it kept the journal safe from repression. Indeed, unlike the samizdat bulletin *The Chronicle of Current Events*,[44] which for fifteen years (1968–82) informed a wide public about political trials and human rights violations, and whose editorial board was subjected to frequent repression, *Political Diary*'s aim was not only to inform, but "to develop and elaborate various theories and conceptions," according to Medvedev. Had the editor been arrested, the journal could hardly have survived.[45] Nevertheless, some isolated articles occasionally found their way into open samizdat and circulated more broadly. A few of them were even published in Western media.[46]

Medvedev designed *Political Diary* as a liberal Marxist publication and selected his readers accordingly, among "people who themselves wanted to do creative political work and develop Marxist theory, as well as certain writers and other prominent representatives of the intelligentsia."[47] Until 1968, Medvedev's readers were in their overwhelming majority supporters of "socialism with a human face." At the time, Medvedev could still count among his readers not only liberal socialist intellectuals such as Aleksandr Tvardovskii, but also the dissident scientists Valerii Pavlinchuk, Andrei Sakharov, and Valentin Turchin.[48]

In terms of content, *Political Diary* covered a very broad ground. Within the Soviet Union, issues of democracy and freedom, dissidence and political trials, as well as nationalism in the Soviet republics figured prominently on the journal's pages. It reproduced numerous protests of the anti-Stalinist intelligentsia, and summaries or excerpts of the neo-Stalinist publications they were directed against. Medvedev also regularly commented on economic affairs, particularly agriculture. In the international arena, he focused primarily on relations between the Soviet Union and the socialist camp, from Eurocommunism to the Sino-Soviet dispute. In 1968, the Prague Spring filled the pages of *Political Diary* for months, as did the Soviet military intervention. In addition, Medvedev gave much attention to issues of Communist ideology and Marxist philosophy, at a time of ideological crisis for the international communist movement. Medvedev also observed with concern the onslaughts of neo-Stalinists into those fields that were most prone to ideological manipulation: literature and official history. He documented the attacks against *Novyi mir*, which became particularly acute after 1968 and culminated in the eviction of Aleksandr Tvardovskii's progressive editorial team and the editor in chief's own resignation in February 1970. Finally, the historical section constituted a sizeable portion of *Political Diary*'s articles and included summaries of foreign books or samizdat manuscripts, reactions to official historical publications, and short historical and philosophical essays, with a strong focus on the Stalin era, the Revolution, and the memory of political repression.

Medvedev's relation to his journal and his readers was in many ways reminiscent of his work method over *Let History Judge*. In both cases, circles of friends were solicited for material and information, and were, in return, granted the right to read what was perpetually characterized as "work in progress." Characteristically, *Political Diary* was replete with articles that constituted preliminary versions of chapters from his future works *On Socialist Democracy* (1972), *Khrushchev: The Years in Power* (1976), and *Let History Judge* (1971). Medvedev acknowledged this contribution:

> My friends considered the "Political Diary" as a useful and necessary publication and gave me all the help they could. Most of all, however, I found this work useful to myself; it helped me clarify my own views on a wide variety of events, express my thoughts and opinions without looking over my shoulder at any "internal" censor or other editor.[49]

Nevertheless, after publishing the journal for over six years, Medvedev had to interrupt this activity in late 1970. The initially modest publication had grown into a thick samizdat journal that was taking up much of his time and financial resources. Despite considerable financial help from F. F. Korolev, a member of the Presidium of the Academy of Pedagogical Sciences, the journal was still taking up about half of Medvedev's income. Moreover, he had grown tired of a project that he was almost single-handedly managing.[50]

The end of the publication, however, coincided with its new life on the other side of the Iron Curtain. In 1970, Zhores sent microfilmed copies of eleven of the most interesting issues abroad, through *Washington Post* and *The New York Times* correspondents Robert Kaiser and Hedrick Smith.[51] The journalists transmitted the microfilms to a publisher, but also published in their respective newspapers an anonymous selection of articles from *Political Diary*, thus ending the secrecy that had surrounded the journal. The following year, the Amsterdam-based publisher "Alexander Herzen Foundation" released a volume reproducing the eleven selected issues in Russian, still anonymously. In 1975, an additional eight issues were published, this time under Medvedev's name. Finally, Stephen Cohen edited in 1982 an English-language selection of articles from *Political Diary*.[52] By that time, Medvedev had already released several books under his name in the West and felt safe enough to assume authorship of *Political Diary*, all the more so as the KGB seems to have suspected it for a long time.[53]

For Medvedev, *Political Diary* had been a kind of "sandbox," in which he could launch new ideas, experiment with them, and receive direct feedback from his circle of readers, allowing him to clarify his own views and draft new articles and future book chapters. But it was also the necessary "breathing space" for an intellectual who resented the restrictions of censored media and longed for a free exchange of views, characteristic for the ideal democratic socialist society he described in his work *On Socialist Democracy* (1972). Nevertheless, it would be mistaken to regard the journal simply as Medvedev's own playground. As with all samizdat endeavors, readers played a proactive role, either by copying the journal for further diffusion, or by directly contributing to it.

Medvedev, like all dissidents, faced the dilemma of choosing between clandestinity and openness. Remaining in the underground could shield from repression for a time but limited the influence that an author could have. *Political Diary* was not intended to have a broad audience, whereas *Let History Judge* was meant to influence the Communist Party and Soviet society as a whole. The same applied to

The Gulag Archipelago. Only publication in tamizdat could guarantee that these works would reach their public and have an impact. But the price to pay for this leap into the unknown was exposure to repression.

Expulsion as a tool of repression

Leaving the system was not a radical, but an incremental process with numerous stages. As individuals turned to samizdat, or engaged in actions of protests, they progressively burned the bridges still connecting them to the official realm. The reading and circulation of samizdat could sometimes lead to prison, but for many Soviet citizens, this flight into the uncensored world was compatible with a professional and social insertion into the Soviet system. By far not all samizdat readers were human rights activists or dissidents in the traditional sense. For a writer, however, letting one's works circulate in samizdat, or worse, sending one's manuscript to the West for publication, generally meant forsaking any chance of official publication in the Soviet Union.

A further stage in the process of exiting the system was dismissal from one's position or exclusion from official institutions, be it the Communist Party, Komsomol, or professional unions. From the point of view of the authorities, depriving a citizen of membership in organizations that formed the basis of social life constituted a tool of repression, but for dissenters, it could sometimes come with some measure of relief, even as they appealed their sentences of exclusion. Some dissidents, such as Liudmila Alekseeva or Elena Bonner, who had joined the Party in their youth to seek to change it from within, had grown disillusioned but could not freely leave it. Voluntary exit from the Party remained exceptional until Perestroika, as it usually entailed retaliatory sanctions.[54] On the other hand, exclusion from the Party ceased to trigger automatic arrest as it did in the 1930s, although it still meant the revocation of the "safe-conduct" preserving members from judiciary or administrative persecutions.[55] In the post-Stalin era, this sanction could usually be averted by acknowledging one's guilt; conversely, exclusion often resulted from a conscious opposition and a repeated refusal to repent. Moisei Al'perovich, one of Nekrich's close friends and colleagues, thus commented: "I do not think that exclusion from the Party constituted in itself for my friend a strong shock (*potriasenie*) and a great tragedy." Nekrich and his friends "did not feel any particular attachment to a party which had permitted and approved of Stalin's bloody terror, which one could join but not leave without fear." And yet "at the same time exclusion from the CPSU was accompanied by the threat of job dismissal, the impossibility of publication of one's research and other afflictions, that is to say, it virtually placed one outside the law."[56]

Nekrich's party exclusion

Nekrich's exclusion from the CPSU resulted from an evolution of the Party's attitude toward dissent in the historical field, but also from a set of circumstances outside of his control. Although he had not released his works in samizdat or tamizdat, it was the discussion at the IML and the publication of the "short transcript" of this meeting in Western media that triggered the procedure of exclusion. In August 1966, the secretary of the Regional Party Committee of Grodno, in Byelorussia, informed the Central Committee that a samizdat copy of the "short transcript" had been seized at the Soviet-Polish border on a Polish citizen, who had received it from his sister, based in Leningrad.[57] A month later, Major Boltin from the IML reported on the "short transcript," which he had compared with the original stenographic record. He noted that the two texts differed fundamentally: in his view, the author of the short transcript had deliberately overemphasized positive evaluations of Nekrich's book and altogether removed criticisms. To demonstrate that the samizdat text contained distortions and additions, Boltin compared specific passages from the two texts. He concluded that "the goal of this anti-Soviet concoction (*striapnia*) is to stir up the unhealthy moods provoked by the book, to silence criticisms of the author's mistakes and calumniate his opponents. This gives us grounds to assess the 'short transcript' as an anti-party document."[58]

By December 28, news had reached the Central Committee that the "short transcript" and Nekrich's book were the object of a broadcast on the West German station *Deutsche Welle* and an article in the French magazine *Nouvel observateur*.[59] On January 19, 1967, Sergei Trapeznikov and Vladimir Stepakov took the initiative to lobby directly the Central Committee concerning this affair.[60] While Boltin's reports only emphasized the "slanderous" character of the "short transcript," Trapeznikov and Stepakov surreptitiously transferred this label from the transcript to the book. Nekrich's work, they wrote, was based on sources from capitalist countries and "tendentiously selected materials," and it showed "in a distorted way the policy of our Party and state and calumniates the Soviet people's feat in the Great Patriotic War."[61] In the USSR, the book had raised negative reactions from readers, while in the West it was increasingly being used for hostile propaganda purposes, along with the "short transcript." Not only had the discussion at the IML itself gotten out of hand, with "demagogues and irresponsible figures" entirely taking the initiative, but the "transcript" gave an even more subversive image of it. Trapeznikov and Stepakov therefore asked that the KGB investigate the matter of the transmission of the "short transcript" abroad.[62] On March 2, 1967, KGB head Vladimir Semichastnyi reported back to the Central Committee concerning the circulation of the "short transcript" in samizdat and identified Leonid Petrovskii as the author. He recommended conducting a party investigation within the Institute of History, as many party members from among the Institute's staff had attended the IML discussion.[63]

Around the same time, Nekrich was summoned for a talk with the Institute of History's director, V. M. Khvostov. The latter confessed he had refused to take part in a "devastating review" of Nekrich's book and warned him that a case had been initiated against him. The best course of action was to write to the Central Committee without delay to acknowledge the faults and errors in his book and express regret. This dialogue, however friendly and well-intentioned on Khvostov's part, certainly brought up reminiscences from Nekrich's two bitter experiences of "public repentance" during the Stalin era. A few days later, he was shown a draft of Deborin and Tel'pukhovskii's review, which was under preparation at the IML. Yet he decided against the course advised by Khvostov: this time he would not confess to imaginary political mistakes.[64]

Nekrich believed that what had "tipped the scales" of his fate was the publication in the West German magazine *Der Spiegel*, on March 20, of the short transcript of the IML discussion, preceded by an insert stating that Brezhnev had intended on rehabilitating Stalin at the 23rd Party Congress, but that this attempt had been opposed by "intellectuals, scientists, young officers."[65] Trapeznikov allegedly showed Brezhnev the article, causing him to fly into a rage over the idea that he had sought to rehabilitate Stalin.[66] Whether the story is authentic may never be known, but the timing speaks for it: two days later, the Central Committee Secretary issued a resolution entrusting the PCC with the party investigation relating to the discussion of Nekrich's book and the transmission of the short transcript abroad.[67]

In preparation for the examination of Nekrich's case, the PCC requested reviews of *June 22, 1941* from two Soviet Marshals, veterans of the Second World War: Marshal I. S. Konev and F. I. Golikov.[68] The latter's position was particularly delicate: as one of Nekrich's key sources, he bore his share of responsibility for the book's content; moreover, he had expressed a positive opinion of *June 22, 1941* in a letter to the author, in November 1965. In early June 1967, at the Central Committee's request, Golikov wrote a new, thirty-two-page review. He denied that the book was "politically ill-intentioned" and stated that Nekrich had made a positive impression on him, that of "a Soviet [i.e. communist] person and a scholar with honest and serious intentions." Nevertheless, Golikov regretted the author's "incompetence on a series of important questions," his biased approach to some of them, his reliance "on various kinds of personal statements and impressions (often by memory)" and a "penchant towards the clamorous (*kriklivost'*) and the sensational." Moreover, the author lacked the necessary "ideological-political maturity" and had taken upon himself a task well beyond the capacity of a single researcher.[69]

As for Marshal Konev, who was well-known for his Stalinist sympathies,[70] he zealously fulfilled the task he had been entrusted with, writing a scathing review of Nekrich's book. He found it "superficially and tendentiously" written, "intentionally sensational," lacking evidence to buttress the author's claims. "All historical facts are selected and aligned in such a way that they constitute an act of accusation for inaction against the TsK, the government, Stalin personally and the Ministry of Defense."[71] Nekrich, he concluded, had written his study "in an accusatory tone," which made everything appear "gloomy."[72] In addition, the PCC appended to Nekrich's file an unpublished article by Marshal K. S. Moskalenko, then vice-minister of Defense. Intended for *Izvestiia*, this piece on the beginning of the war contained a short paragraph denouncing Nekrich's views.[73]

On May 22, 1967, Nekrich was summoned to the PCC. Two officials were in charge of the investigation: S. I. Sdobnov and I. N. Gladnev. During the first meeting, the discussion revolved around the book, its conception and Nekrich's motivations. The party investigators, Nekrich later realized, tried to determine whether he had intentionally sought to inflict harm on the Communist Party and state's interests.[74] The historian remained deliberately evasive concerning his responsibility for the turn taken by the IML discussion. However, when prompted to answer whether he found "political expediency or historical truth" more important, he was forced to clarify his position. The question was no longer about the book's accuracy, Nekrich reasoned, but rather how "politically appropriate" it was to raise such historical questions at the time.[75] The historian still tried to maneuver: why should the two notions be necessarily incompatible? Ultimately, "historical truth was in keeping with political expediency," as experience had shown.

> "Still, which for you is more important?" asked Sdobnov again. "Historical truth or political expediency?"
> "Historical truth," I replied.[76]

During the two following meetings, Nekrich was required to comment on his book, the IML discussion and Western reactions. He insisted that *June 22, 1941* had successfully passed censorship and received positive evaluations, both during the IML discussion and in the foreign communist press. The latter "considered the book to be a weapon against the bourgeois reactionary press," demonstrating that rumors of a rehabilitation of Stalin were mistaken. As for the hostile reactions in Western media, he could not be held accountable for them. He had protested in writing against *Deutsche Welle*'s "slanderous broadcasts," but he disingenuously observed that most Western publications concerned not his book as such, but the transcript of the IML discussion. Informed of the accusations leveled at him, Nekrich claimed he refused to comment the charges or to step into negotiations that might lead to a public repentance.[77]

Did he still hope to avert exclusion at this stage or was he consciously renouncing the prospect of reintegration? One of his colleagues believed that Nekrich had not foreseen his exclusion, even after being summoned by the PCC. "He considered, and rightly so, that he did not do anything reprehensible."[78] Indeed, Nekrich was only one actor among several, connected by a chain of responsibility for what had become the "Nekrich Affair." He may have written a flawed book according to shifting ideological standards, but others published it, and yet others advertised it abroad. Nevertheless, by refusing to acknowledge his fault, Nekrich sent a clear signal that he no longer accepted the rules of the game: ultimately, his actual guilt mattered little, as long as he acknowledged the Party's primacy. The historian could not ignore this simple tacit rule.

On June 28, Nekrich attended a final meeting presided by Arvid Pel'she, head of the PCC and Politburo member. The accusations leveled against him related to his interpretation of historical events, but also the use of his book by "hostile [Western] propaganda." In his statement, the historian recognized that his work was not beyond reproach from a scholarly point of view, but he rejected the political accusations built up on alleged scholarly critique. Inscribing his action within the framework of the Party's policies, he concluded the following: "I thought it my duty as an historian to participate as much as I could in the party's struggle to overcome the mistakes of the Personality cult period and help draw the necessary lessons from it."[79]

Also on the dock were Aleksandr Samsonov, head of the publishing house "Nauka," and Leonid Petrovskii. Samsonov duly acknowledged that publishing *June 22, 1941* had been a mistake—a confession of guilt welcomed by the Committee. Petrovskii, however, held fast. Ahead of the meeting, he had circulated an open letter praising Nekrich's book and warning against the risk of restoration of Stalinism in the Soviet Union.[80] During the hearing, he behaved provocatively, openly confronting the investigators. He denied the anti-Soviet nature of his speech at the IML and rejected accusations of authorship of the "short transcript," but also insolently repeated his praise of *June 22, 1941*.[81]

The floor was then given to Petr Pospelov, head of the IML, and Grigorii Deborin. Both sought to make up for their serious oversight during the discussion at the IML by a particular zeal in denouncing both the book and its author. Finally, the Committee members unanimously condemned Nekrich in their final speeches for having lost his "party spirit" and called for his expulsion. Dumbfounded by this outpouring of hatred, Nekrich then heard Pel'she's final sentence: he was to be expelled from the Party "for the deliberate distortion in the book *June 22, 1941* of the politics of the Communist Party and Soviet government on the eve and at the beginning of the Great Patriotic War, which was used by foreign reactionary propaganda for anti-Soviet purposes."[82] As Nekrich later realized, the use of the word "deliberate" was justified by his refusal to repent, which deepened his guilt in the eyes of the Party.[83]

The PCC resolution also provided for the punishment of Nekrich's "accomplices": Samsonov received an official reprimand and, ultimately, was dismissed from the publishing house "Nauka"; Tel'pukhovskii and Boltin were blamed for the faulty organization of the IML discussion; shortcomings in the work of the Institute of History party organization were to be addressed through the creation of a commission of verification; finally, the conduct of some communists who had participated in the IML discussion was to be examined.[84] Several of them received a severe reprimand from the PCC[85] and many had to confess their guilt to avoid further reprisals. Such was the case of Evgenii Gnedin: this former *zek* who had spent seventeen years in the Gulag yielded to party pressure and acknowledged his faults: he had not read Nekrich's book, and had he known "that the book would be recognized as defective (*porochnaia*)," he would not have spoken up.[86] As for Snegov, he was hospitalized at the time. Medvedev considered that the Old Bolshevik's exclusion from the Party had been planned at the time, but it was temporarily postponed.[87] Finally, punishment was meted out to the book itself: a decree of Glavlit dated August 20, 1967, ordered its removal from all libraries that did not have a special section (*spetskhran*) and its destruction.[88]

Nekrich did not remain silent after his exclusion. Already on July 4, he sent an appeal to the Politburo for the reconsideration of his case. When he received the official notification of expulsion, on July 15, he sent another letter, addressed to Brezhnev personally. However, in November 1967, his appeal was rejected. As would be repeatedly hinted to him in the following years, the conditions for a reintegration into the Party were clear: he had to repent.[89] Lev Slezkin, Nekrich's friend and colleague, wrote that they later on realized that the PCC's "only goal" was to obtain a confession of guilt from the accused, whether heartfelt or just "to save one's skin." This repentance would have achieved several goals: confirm the Party's "strength and righteousness," reinforce its line, further discredit the book through the condemnation of its erstwhile defenders, and, finally, throw discredit upon Nekrich himself, who would not only lose his status of "public and scientific authority," but would also renounce active opposition, out of shame for his own conduct.[90]

This was not the only determining factor, however. Despite refusing to repent, Nekrich was not dismissed from his position. This can be explained by his fame in the West and the large support that he received from the Soviet academic community, but also by the very moderate degree of his guilt: Nekrich was no active dissident, he had not been directly responsible for what had grown out of proportion into the "Nekrich Affair," and his book had, after all, been officially approved for publication. The authorities could now expect him to toe the line, and this is largely what he did. But Nekrich had now become the figurehead of a dangerous anti-Stalinist movement within the Institute of History, and the next move was to crush the hotbed of rebellion represented by Danilov's Party Committee. Many of Nekrich's former colleagues considered that his exclusion had been aimed at dealing a blow at the *partkom* and the Institute of History as a whole, and threats of dividing the Institute of History had been hanging in the air since early 1967.[91] In his notes on the Nekrich Affair, Roy Medvedev wrote that Nekrich's exclusion may have been aimed at providing "an ideological basis" for the division of the Institute, which Trapeznikov and his peers so resented.[92]

On July 12, 1967, Danilov was officially notified of Nekrich's exclusion and the *partkom* adopted a resolution through which it "took notice" (but did not approve) of this expulsion. Initially, Danilov intended to support Nekrich's petition for party rehabilitation through a *partkom* resolution. However, he received word from "above" that such a step would lead to reprisals and decided that his priority was to shield the Institute from repression.[93] Nevertheless, the *partkom* requested from the PCC an explanation for Nekrich's exclusion, expressing concern, both for the severity of the punishment and the accusation of "deliberate distortion of the party and government's policies." They feared lest the PCC's resolution lead to an "infringement of the rights and duties of the scholar . . . to speak up and defend his point of view," and, ultimately, to "a revival of the ideology and atmosphere of the era of the 'personality cult.'"[94]

Meanwhile, the Commission of investigation set out to collect evidence, summoning historians for interrogation and gathering complaints. The Commission's conclusions revealed that Nekrich had enjoyed widespread support within the Institute and the *partkom*. In addition to Danilov's refusal to adopt a resolution approving of Nekrich's exclusion, several colleagues also defended the historian during interrogation and attacked Deborin and Telpukhovskii's review, which they considered as revisionist and spurious.[95] Thus doing, they delegitimized the decision of the PCC. On December 27, the *partkom* adopted a "note of response," rejecting the investigation's conclusions, which, they argued, were based on "tendentiously selected testimonies and interpreted in a hardly conscientious manner."

This open affront did not lead to immediate reprisals, but, in the aftermath of the invasion of Czechoslovakia, in August 1968, the expected division of the Institute of History into an "Institute of History of the USSR" and an "Institute of General History" took place.[96] Through this partition, the authorities could "divide like-minded people, suborn the new administrators, and through the recruitment process eliminate 'trouble-makers,'" according to Slezkin. Nevertheless, both he and Nekrich were granted positions in the new Institute of History of the USSR: as *June 22, 1941* received praise in the socialist countries where translations were being published, the authorities did not wish to attract accusations of persecution of the author of a legally published book.[97]

While Nekrich had been excluded from the Party for a book legally published in the Soviet Union, Medvedev was about to undergo the same treatment for his authorship of an unpublished manuscript, which the authorities feared could circulate in samizdat or be published abroad.

Medvedev's party exclusion

In September 1967, the PCC contacted Roy Medvedev to request a copy of his manuscript *Pered sudom istorii* (*Before the Tribunal of History*).[98] As the historian later found out, on August 26, his manuscript had been seized in Leningrad during a house search in the apartment of his university classmate Igor' Nikolaev, who had copies of some of the historian's works for safekeeping. Nikolaev, who was an assistant professor (*dotsent*) of philosophy, used Medvedev's manuscript and other samizdat historical works, such as the "short transcript" of the IML discussion, for home seminars with students. Following a denunciation by some of them, he was arrested and locked in a psychiatric hospital for three months.[99] Thereafter, he was dismissed from his institute and excluded from the Party. As he appealed the exclusion sentence, he argued that he used Medvedev's work and others for his own research on Lenin and the personality cult.[100]

On September 19, Medvedev was summoned by Party Investigator Gladnev, who asked him whether he was the author of the manuscript circulating in Moscow and Leningrad. Medvedev confirmed his authorship but denied that his work was circulating in an uncontrolled way: he had produced a limited number of copies, which he gave to read to those who could help with advice or material. However, he refused to submit a copy of his work to Gladnev, whom he did not consider "competent in theoretical problems of history and theory of Marxism." He would only answer such a request if it came from the Central Committee's Ideological Department or the direction of the IML. Moreover, Medvedev justified his refusal to submit his work to Gladnev's judgment based on the investigator's "extremely tendentious and mistaken" handling of the Nekrich case.[101] But Medvedev also contested the Party's prerogative to control his work. He believed that a communist should act based on his own convictions and conscience, rather than blindly conform to party discipline. Gladnev disagreed with him on this point: "The notions of party discipline and party conscience are inseparable in our country." Medvedev retorted: "Unfortunately, it is far from always being the case, and I, as a historian, can provide you with a thousand examples of divergence of these notions."[102]

Instead of leaving his manuscript with Gladnev, Medvedev decided to submit it to the Central Committee. He wrote to Mikhail Suslov to request a meeting to discuss his research, attaching a table of contents of his book to the letter.[103] Vladimir Stepakov, head of the Department of Agitation and Propaganda, was mandated to report on this matter. On October 13, his deputy F. F. Makarov received Medvedev. The historian explained that his manuscript was not ready for publication, but he asked the Party to support his research, particularly in terms of access to archives and restricted library sections. A similar request he had made three years earlier had been ignored, and he entertained little hope that the situation would change. But if the Central Committee refused to assist him in his work, he argued, then he was entitled to refuse the Party's control. He added: "Those abnormalities that are taking place in [the manuscript]'s discussion and diffusion are due in the first place to the abnormal conditions in which this work is being conducted." He left the first half of his manuscript and reiterated his request for assistance in his research, which he deemed of primary importance for the Party.[104]

On November 14, Stepakov submitted to Suslov his report on Medvedev, which condemned the historian's work unequivocally. His analysis of the table of content and first eight chapters had shown that Medvedev's research was "utterly negative from beginning to end." The author seemed to relish in the description of "monstrous crimes," mistakes, and tragedies. Although the designated culprit was Stalin, behind this, one could not "help seeing an accusation against the whole Party and its leadership."[105] What Stepakov found especially objectionable was Medvedev's mild stance on the political opposition, but also his negative evaluation of collectivization, dekulakization, and even industrialization—Stalin-era processes that were counted among the Soviet state's greatest achievements. In Stepakov's view, Medvedev's "tendentious, subjectivist" conclusions contradicted "historical truth," and the work as a whole was "politically damaging."[106] A major ground for concern was Medvedev's determination to deepen by any means possible his study, on which he was prepared to work for another four years. Moreover, some sections of the book were already circulating underground, raising discussions, particularly in Leningrad. Stepakov therefore recommended that the Moscow City Party Committee inquire into Medvedev's activity, "in order to avert the circulation of this mistaken and damaging research" and to examine the question of Medvedev's "party spirit."[107]

On November 30, Medvedev was summoned to the PCC again. His notes of the meeting reflect the historian's exasperation with the Party's yoke. He refused again to submit a copy of his work, both in protest for Nekrich's exclusion from the Party and because he had already submitted one to the Central Committee. As for the reasons that had prompted him to undertake his research, they were clear: "If those who are in charge of establishing historical truth by their profession do not do so," then private research such as his would "inevitably see the life of day." The IML should be dealing with such research, but instead, its recent publications in the field of Party history had shown that it "continues to deal in falsifications (*zanimat'sia fal'tsifikatsiei*)."[108]

On December 28, Medvedev had to face yet another party body: he was called to the Education Department of the Moscow City Committee (*gorkom*), in the office of G. Ia. Perova, who was now mandated to handle his case. She acquainted him with an official review of his work, but refused to name its author, and confessed that she had not read the manuscript herself. The historian protested that the evaluation was "tendentious and incorrect," distorted his views, and lacked any concrete quotes from the manuscript. He concluded that he could not answer an anonymous review read by an intermediary unacquainted with his work and expressed the regret not to have been invited to discuss it with the Department of Agitation and Propaganda. As for the Education Department of the Moscow *gorkom*, he did not deem it an appropriate organ to deal with his scholarly research.[109]

As Medvedev called Makarov a few hours later to express his surprise and reaffirm that he did not acknowledge the Education Department's competence to deal with his case, Stepakov's deputy replied acerbically:

> You, comrade Medvedev, work at the Academy of Pedagogical Sciences, you are a pedagogue. Nevertheless, you consider yourself a specialist in Party history and write on this theme large works. Why do you think that the *gorkom* Education Department staff is less competent than you for this kind of work? We know better than you do who is competent in which field.[110]

In a letter Medvedev submitted to Perova the next day, he repeated that he had expected Suslov himself to read his research and was prepared to wait, if the latter was currently unavailable. If the *gorkom* insisted on evaluating his work, then they should consider that "any more or less objective evaluation of this work, which is based on testimonies and materials from several dozens of Old Bolsheviks and specialists-historians, cannot be given by one or another employee of the TsK apparatus or the Party *gorkom*, but only by a group of wholly competent comrades." He went on to name a few people who could serve as experts for such an evaluation, including his friend Nikolaev.[111]

In January 1968, Medvedev transmitted the second part of his manuscript to Perova and notified her that he had decided to interrupt his work on the topic for a year "to reflect more fundamentally on some of the theses and conclusions of the research." Therefore, it did not make sense to discuss his manuscript in official instances during this time. Nevertheless, should the *gorkom* insist on conducting such a discussion, Medvedev proposed a new list of "competent, objective and principled" historians to invite. He objected against the transmission of his manuscript to the IML, which he accused of silencing Stalin's crimes in its recent publications.[112]

The Party *gorkom* seems to have renounced inquiring further into Medvedev's case in the course of 1968. However, the KGB kept him on a close watch, and the tense political situation in the context of the Prague Spring meant that Medvedev's reformist socialist views raised increasing suspicions. On August 4, 1968, Iurii Andropov wrote a report on Medvedev, after a new version of his manuscript had fallen into his hands. The head of the KGB deplored Medvedev's new friendship with Andrei Sakharov, who had provided him with information about Stalin-era repression of physicists for his study. Andropov noted the historian's hostility toward the prospect of a Soviet military intervention in Czechoslovakia and stated that Medvedev intended to turn to the analysis of the current international situation after he finished his historical research. Not only had Medvedev read Sakharov's samizdat article "Reflections on Progress, Peaceful Coexistence and Intellectual Freedom," but he had set out to reproduce and circulate it with Leonid Petrovskii's help.[113] The head of the KGB also warned: "Medvedev's book, once it is finished, will undoubtedly be circulated, and it will raise a multitude of undesirable interpretations, as it is based on tendentiously selected, but authentic data, fitted with a skillful commentary and catchy demagogical conclusions." Andropov recommended summoning Medvedev to the Central Committee Department of Propaganda for a discussion, before deciding on further measures to "prevent the appearance of this book." Remarkably, Andropov judged that one of the ways to neutralize Medvedev would be to invite him to write a book "on the period of the life of our state of interest to him under appropriate party control."[114] However, the Ideological Department of the Central Committee rejected this proposal and settled for a more radical course of action.[115]

A February 1969 report by Trapeznikov, Stepakov, and Vassilii Shauro underlined the "clearly expressed anti-Soviet character" of Medvedev's work.[116] The historian's goal was the "denunciation of I.V. Stalin as a historical personality." He described Stalin's struggle against the oppositions as an "unprincipled intra-party squabble, the fault for which lay with I.V. Stalin, who strove . . . to remain in power at all cost." Moreover, the historian did not conceal his sympathies for Trotsky, Kamenev, Zinoviev, and others. His views on industrialization, collectivization, and dekulakization were also unorthodox: he blamed party organizations for the escalation of class struggle in the countryside in the early 1930s. Medvedev accused Stalin, "without a shred of evidence," of assassinating Frunze, Kirov, Ordzhonikidze, and others. Furthermore, "the author writes that Stalin conducted the organized and planned destruction of the main cadres of the Bolshevik Party, that he is 'spattered with the blood of millions of innocent Soviet people,' that 'obviously it would be ridiculous to note . . . any "merits" of Stalin before the Soviet people.'"[117] Equally nihilistic were Medvedev's views on questions of foreign policy. Basing himself primarily on Nekrich's book *June 22, 1941* to evaluate the Soviet government's action on the eve of the war, he described the whole history of the Great Patriotic War "as a series of mistakes and stupidities committed by the Supreme Commandment." As for Stalin's postwar politics concerning Eastern Europe, he described them as "socialist cesarism"—that is, imperialism—and such episodes as the Berlin crisis or the Korean War as "consequences of the Soviet Union's aggressive politics."[118] The report also accused Medvedev of opposing the one-party system and "calumniously" ascribing this position to Lenin. Equally slanderous was Medvedev's affirmation that Stalin created a "cult of the Russian people" and instated state anti-Semitism. The authors added: "[Medvedev's] elementary ignorance and his extreme viciousness (*ozloblennost'*) appear particularly vividly in his conclusion that it is still early to talk about the victory of socialism in our country, that under the guise of socialism, what one can find [in the USSR] is state-capitalistic, semi-feudal and even state-slaveholding relations."[119] The authors of the report therefore advised "taking all measures to impede the expedition of this calumnious manuscript abroad." There was no point in meeting the author, since this was "no isolated incident in the biography of R.A. Medvedev" and showed that he had not changed his pernicious views.[120] Therefore, the question of his party membership should be examined.[121]

Around the same time, the *Chronicle of Current Events* noted that *Pered sudom istorii* had just begun to circulate broadly in samizdat.[122] In April 1969, Grigorii Deborin was mandated to review the third part of Medvedev's manuscript on behalf of the IML and produced a devastating report. He considered meaningless to step into polemics with the author of this "spiteful pamphlet." "Under the guise of a criticism of Stalin's personality cult," Medvedev aimed at "heaping a maximum of calumny upon the Communist Party and Soviet society, to blacken and belittle socialism."[123] Deborin concluded his review with a note on the author's sources. Apart from his reliance on bourgeois historiography, Medvedev proved to be "surprisingly well-acquainted" with letters sent to "Western newspapers and journals" by "some representatives of Soviet intelligentsia striving for personal glory, and at the instigation of bourgeois journalists." He also used "articles and books condemned by Soviet press, but also various transcripts containing inventions from some writers, not intended for publication." This clearly referred to Nekrich's book and the transcript of the IML discussion. Deborin concluded that "wittingly or not, R.A. Medvedev became the mouthpiece of this muddy wave, which for a time rose up (*vzmetnulas'*) in some social strata (encompassing not hundreds, not dozens, but precious few individuals), but which was liquidated in a timely manner through the efforts of party organizations." Therefore, the manuscript deserved "the harshest condemnation."[124]

On May 26, 1969, Perova summoned Medvedev and showed him Deborin's review, along with that of another IML researcher. She made it clear that Medvedev was threatened with exclusion. After this talk, Medvedev sent Perova a copy of his open letter of protest to the journal *Kommunist* against Stalin's rehabilitation,[125] presenting it as a summary of his views, as exposed in his book. He harshly criticized the two reviews, which only dealt with a few pages of his study, without touching upon its fundamentals, and contained obvious distortions of his words. Concerning Deborin, Medvedev expressed his astonishment that a historian who had actively participated "in a series of shameful political actions in the recent past" had been selected as a reviewer. He considered him "unworthy of the title of party member and of the status of historian," and refused to comment on his review.[126] Furthermore, Medvedev insisted that his work was still in progress, that he had twice fundamentally reworked it since submitting the manuscript eighteen months earlier, and that he had already benefited from remarks made during previous discussions at the *gorkom*. Finally, the historian reaffirmed his communist credentials, arguing that he had always followed the line of the 20th and 22nd Party Congresses in his work. Therefore, he considered the threats of exclusion proffered against him "inacceptable," and announced he would write a letter of protest to the Politburo.[127]

Upon returning from his summer holiday in early August 1969, Roy Medvedev was summoned by the Lenin District Committee (*raikom*). After the *raikom* secretary communicated him orally an official evaluation of his work, he sent a letter to refute it, in which he rejected most of the accusations leveled at his research. He also addressed the charge that he had let his manuscript circulate: it was not in an author's interest to "lose control over an unfinished work." However, such a research could not be conducted in isolation. And interest for his work had considerably increased in the past year due to a widespread desire to protest the ongoing campaign for Stalin's rehabilitation.[128]

On August 7, the *raikom* examined the "Medvedev case." The session lasted for a mere twenty minutes, after which the Committee Secretary stated that Medvedev, having refused to acknowledge his mistakes, would be expelled for "convictions incompatible with membership in the Party" and "calumny on the Soviet social and state system."[129] According to Medvedev, the party procedures had clearly been violated, as his exclusion should have been debated in his basic party organization—that is, his workplace. However, the fear that the historian might benefit from his colleagues' support, which would in turn "compromise the ultimate verdict" probably dictated the choice of an alternative instance for the decision of exclusion.[130]

On September 22, Medvedev lodged an appeal with the Party Commission of the Moscow City Committee. He obtained the removal of the accusation of calumny against the Soviet regime, which could open the way to judicial prosecution, but the verdict remained otherwise unchanged. A collective letter of protest written by a group of Old Bolsheviks to the Committee simply went ignored. Medvedev's appeal to the supreme instance, the Central Committee's PCC, was treated more seriously. During several hearings of a few hours each, Medvedev was interrogated by two party investigators acquainted with his work, who produced a new report, read during a meeting presided by Arvid Pel'she. Nevertheless, the previous sentence was upheld.[131]

Despite his exclusion from the Party, Medvedev remained employed at the Academy of Sciences. The historian claims that the director of his research institute was summoned to the Central Committee and was ordered to "overload him" with work. As a result, Medvedev was entrusted with larger and more time-consuming responsibilities, so that he would have less time to dedicate to independent research.[132] As in Nekrich's case, this mild sanction seems to have been dictated by the belief that Medvedev would now learn his lesson and concentrate solely on his research in the pedagogical field. The KGB's logic was not purely repressive, it was "educational": "prophylactic warnings" and other sanctions on the lower end of the repressive scale were meant to convince Soviet citizens who had strayed from the "correct" path to toe the line.

A first warning that publication in the West would constitute a red line for the authorities had come in February 1969, when Zhores Medvedev was dismissed from his position as a biologist in Obninsk. What he was incriminated was his correspondence with Western publishers regarding the edition of his book on Lysenko, but also prospective contacts for the publication of *Let History Judge*. In retrospect, the scientist judged that the latter question was paramount, since the Brezhnev leadership had long denounced Lysenkoism.[133] A further warning came in late 1969, when a professional contact with obvious connections to "higher instances" secretly informed Roy Medvedev that his career would not suffer if he renounced publication in the West. Although Medvedev had been threatened with arrest during an appeal of his party exclusion, his interlocutor reassured him: "City committees do not arrest [people]."

The historian, however, considered that tamizdat publication would on the contrary afford him protection.[134] In early 1969, he had sent the microfilm of his manuscript to the West, through Elisabeth Markstein. As the daughter of Johann Koplenig, General Secretary of the Austrian Communist Party for twenty years, she had grown up in the USSR and regularly traveled back and forth. Medvedev had met her through the Old Bolshevik Wilhelmina Slavutskaia, a former Komintern worker with extensive links to the Austrian and German communist parties.[135] Through Lev Kopelev, Markstein had also met Solzhenitsyn, whom she assisted by translating *The Gulag Archipelago* into German.[136] In the West, Markstein transmitted the manuscript to Medvedev's representatives, the socialist historian Georges Haupt in France, and David Joravsky in the United States, a historian of Soviet science and friend of Zhores's, who spoke Russian and could competently edit the book.[137] In the fall of 1969, Medvedev sent signals to the West that he wished to publish his book, and by the end of the year Joravsky had signed a contract with the publisher Alfred Knopf on his behalf.[138]

Solzhenitsyn's expulsion from the USSR

A year earlier, in June 1968, Solzhenitsyn had also sent a microfilmed copy of *The Gulag Archipelago* to the West through the grandson of Leonid Andreyev, a Russian émigré writer.[139] Arrangements were made with Olga Andreyev-Carlisle, Andreyev's granddaughter, to supervise and edit the English translation of *The Gulag Archipelago*. This collaboration would eventually end in mutual acrimony, due to the Carlisles' failure to deliver the edited translation in time.[140] Initially, however, Solzhenitsyn intended on delaying the publication for as long as possible, until he had gathered enough material for *The Red Wheel*, his master work on the Revolution. Yet, once again, the KGB caught him by surprise and forced him to play his trump card ahead of time.

The Soviet authorities were growing ever wearier of the dissident's provocations. In March 1972, following a report by Andropov on Soviet dissent, the Politburo members unanimously condemned Solzhenitsyn and called for his expulsion from Moscow. However, the question of the sentence remained open. Should he be sent into internal exile or expulsed from the USSR? Fears that "bourgeois propaganda" would use whatever sentence was pronounced were a great concern to the Soviet leaders, particularly in the context of détente with the West. For the time being, they decided to postpone the decision.[141]

By July 1973, reports were growing more alarming. Andropov warned the Central Committee about *The Gulag Archipelago*, which Solzhenitsyn called in a private conversation "a killer work, a real knockout blow." All of this proved, in Andropov's view, that Solzhenitsyn was "a dedicated opponent of the Soviet state" who had harnessed the "Western propaganda machinery" in his "anti-Soviet struggle." Andropov concluded that the KGB was in the process of documenting Solzhenitsyn's activities "with the goal of *pressing criminal charges*" against him.[142] Among the evidence collected was Elizaveta Voronianskaia's diary. The old lady wrote of the overwhelming, life-changing impact of *Gulag* on her life and that of others. She concluded: "I cannot find the right words to describe this book, which recites the most gruesome and bloody tragedy of our two-hundred-million-strong people in the many centuries of its existence."[143] The diary of Voronianskaia's friend Nina Pakhtusova, seized in August 1973, concurred:

> No book like this has ever been written in the entire history of humankind . . . . This is the Gospel of the twentieth century! And this Gospel was created by a Prometheus, it is a political time bomb, and if by some miracle the entire people were able to read it without hindrance, it would lead to a revolt and barricades![144]

Pakhtusova also noted with concern that Solzhenitsyn had decided to publish *Gulag*, although he had always said that it would be published only after his death. "And I can understand that—if it were published in his lifetime, it would kill him at once," she reasoned.[145]

In August 1973, Elizaveta Voronianskaia was arrested upon returning from a vacation in Crimea. After five days of interrogation, the ailing old lady confessed where she had hidden the unburned copy of *The Gulag Archipelago*. After her release, she could not endure the burden of her betrayal and committed suicide.[146] Through a complex chain of communication, Solzhenitsyn found out about her death and on September 5, he sent word to the West for the publication of *The Gulag Archipelago*, to be announced through a public news release.[147] The same day, he sent to Brezhnev his "Letter to the Soviet Leaders."[148] According to Michael Scammel, should Brezhnev have responded favorably to this bargaining plea, the writer might have withheld the publication of the last part of *Gulag*, which dealt with the post-1956 history of the camps.[149] However, he received no answer, except for an offer, transmitted through his ex-wife, to abstain from releasing new works for twenty years, in exchange for the publication of old ones in the USSR, starting with *Cancer Ward*.[150] Meanwhile, Andropov repeatedly urged the Politburo to initiate criminal proceedings against Solzhenitsyn, or, as a more moderate alternative, to ask a Western European government to grant him political asylum.[151]

On December 28, 1973, the Paris-based publisher YMCA-Press released the first volume of *Gulag* in Russian. This was the last straw for the Soviet leadership. In a January 2 report, Andropov noted that "foreign reactionary centers in different countries are simultaneously attempting to organize a widescale anti-Soviet campaign around Solzhenitsyn's book to discredit our country and Soviet foreign policy," and he reiterated his earlier proposals.[152] Five days later, realizing that radical action could no longer be postponed, the Politburo convened to discuss the treatment to be meted out to the dissident. Brezhnev declared: "Under our law, we have every reason to sentence Solzhenitsyn to jail because he has encroached on everything that is most sacred: Lenin, our Soviet system, the Soviet government, everything that is dear to us."[153] Yet the unavoidable negative reactions that this would trigger in the West also had to be factored in. Andropov raised the alarm concerning the danger that the dissident posed but privileged a solution that would overrule the risk of excessive exploitation of the "Solzhenitsyn Affair" by "bourgeois propaganda."

> Comrades, since 1965, I have been raising the issue of Solzhenitsyn. Today he has gone to a new, higher stage in his hostile activities. He tries to create an organization within the Soviet Union made up of former convicts.[154] He opposes Lenin, the October Revolution, and the socialist system. His *Gulag Archipelago* is not a work of fiction; it is a political document. This is dangerous. . . . On the whole, there are hundreds and thousands of people among whom Solzhenitsyn will find support. . . . He exploits the humane attitude of the Soviet government and carries out hostile activities with perfect impunity. Therefore, we should take all the measures that I wrote about to the Central Committee, i.e., deport him from the country.[155]

Andropov's solution eventually prevailed over hardliners' calls to try and imprison the writer. This solution, however, depended on a Western government's willingness to accept Solzhenitsyn. Only with the German Federal Republic's cooperation could the soft line be implemented.

In order to prepare the Soviet public for the writer's expulsion, Mikhail Suslov orchestrated a preliminary propaganda campaign against the "literary Vlasovets."[156] One author, writing in *Pravda*, thus wrote that Solzhenitsyn, "choking with pathological hatred" for his country and the Soviet system, attempted "to fool and deceive gullible people with all kinds of inventions on the Soviet Union."[157]

Solzhenitsyn writes in his memoirs that he was now prepared to face any outcome, including attacks against his children. In an interview with *The New York Times*, on January 19, he displayed confidence: "I have fulfilled my duty to the dead, and this gives me relief and calmness. Once the truth seemed doomed to die. It was beaten. It was drowned. It had turned to ashes. But now the truth has come alive. No one will be able to destroy it."[158]

On February 12, the Nobel laureate was arrested. The smear campaign and arrest triggered a wave of protests. Liberal intellectuals and dissidents expressed concern over the fate of a writer who had dared to "break through the blockade of silence"[159] and had conveyed to the world the sheer scale, but also the individual dimension, and the broader meaning of events long consigned to oblivion by the regime. At the Lefortovo prison, Solzhenitsyn was informed that he faced an accusation of "treason to the motherland," which could trigger anything from a fifteen-year term to a death sentence.[160] The next day, however, he was flown to Frankfurt-am-Main. Exiled for life.

As I argued in the preceding chapters, the confrontation between dissident researchers and the Soviet authorities was a self-reinforcing dynamic: the progressive exclusion of anti-Stalinist narratives from the official sphere led to protests, to the radicalization of dissident histories away from a compromise with censorship and, eventually, to the displacement of these works into the unofficial sphere and their publication abroad, which in turn triggered a repressive response. I argued that this response was conditioned not so much by the content of the works themselves, as by their publication in tamizdat, uncontrolled dissemination in samizdat, or instrumentalization in Western media broadcasts. While anti-Stalinist narratives as such were not condemnable as long as they stuck to the letter of the Secret Speech's discourse, Solzhenitsyn and Medvedev's works were perceived as overstepping the limits, one for establishing a continuity between Lenin and Stalin, the other for justifying the intraparty oppositions to Stalin and criticizing the conduct of collectivization and industrialization. What worried the Soviet leaders was the subversive interpretations that would be given to these works if they fell into the hands of the Soviet public, as well as their use by Western propaganda. Interestingly, the opposition between pro-Stalinists and moderate conservatives within the leadership did reflect on the treatment of dissident researchers. Exclusion from the Party could be pronounced based on reports from the heads of Central Committee departments Trapeznikov and Stepakov, two pro-Stalinist historians. But when it came to more repressive measures, only Politburo members had a say in the fate of such a famous dissident as Solzhenitsyn. As KGB chief and Politburo member, Andropov had a crucial influence in this regard. His advocacy of the "soft" option of Solzhenitsyn's deportation from the country as a way to neutralize Western propaganda, and his recommendation that the Party "co-opt" Medvedev rather than repress him, testify to his more tactical and less repressive approach to the question.

The "prophylactic" methods that the KGB generalized in those years obeyed a similar logic. Repression against dissidents came in stages, offering space for retreat to those who seized the second chance they were granted. The aim of "prophylactic warnings," dismissals, exclusion, or even psychiatric incarceration was not so much to punish as to "reeducate," to force those who "thought differently" into submission. Judicial prosecution was only a last resort, used in relation to those who proved "unreformable." Increasingly, however, emigration provided a convenient alternative. Nonconformist authors like Nekrich embraced exile as a road to intellectual freedom. And in a context of international détente, the Soviet authorities increasingly put pressure on their political opponents to emigrate, in order to avoid the bad press associated with an arrest. In the 1970s, dissidents who refused to conform thus faced two avenues: inner emigration or exile, the former associated with the threat of arrest, and the latter, with the prospect of eternally parting with one's homeland.

6

From "Inner Emigration" to Exile

In his work of political philosophy *On Socialist Democracy* published in 1972, Roy Medvedev wrote that the Soviet people was still deprived of two fundamental liberties: the right to choose one's place of residence and to travel abroad. Unlike Soviet authorities, who were considering generalizing exile as a repressive measure against dissidents, Medvedev believed that freedom of emigration for all would have a favorable impact on life within the country, "because fear of a 'brain drain' would force state and party bodies to take much more seriously all the democratic rights and freedoms that are formally proclaimed as belonging to all Soviet citizens."[1] Yet a more prominent advocate of the right to emigration was Andrei Sakharov. In 1973, he incurred the Soviet leadership's wrath for advocating the adoption of the Jackson and Vanik amendment, an amendment to a Soviet-American trade bill that made the granting of Most Favored Nation status to the USSR conditional on the adoption of specific targets in terms of Jewish emigration.[2]

The reason emigration became a prominent topic on the agenda of Soviet dissidents in the 1970s was a widespread loss of faith in the possibility of reforming the system from within. The protests of the 1960s had yielded only limited results and the failure of the "Prague Spring" had a disheartening effect on those who believed in "communism with a human face." Moreover, repression peaked in the aftermath of the invasion of Czechoslovakia. Already in 1967, a "fifth division" was created within the KGB to deal with dissidents, with KGB cells implanted at the local level, including in research institutions.[3] On August 25, 1968, eight dissidents organized a demonstration of protest on Red Square, holding out banners proclaiming solidarity with the Czechoslovak people, but within minutes they were arrested. By 1969, repression in the form of dismissal or exclusion from the Party and professional unions intensified, confronting dissenters with the alternative of submission or reprisals. At this stage, erstwhile allies in a common struggle, fellow *podpisanty*, petition signatories, parted ways, as the majority retreated into conformism, while a few activists persisted in their struggle.

After exclusion from official organs and after losing official employment, Soviet dissidents found themselves in a highly precarious situation. Under intense KGB scrutiny, they were often pressured into collaborating with the State Security organs, under threat of prosecution. Moreover, the loss of a stable livelihood exposed them to poverty and administrative sanctions against "parasitism." Life in "inner emigration"[4] was therefore frequently an antechamber to arrest. In the late 1970s, dissidents who had burned all bridges with the regime were sooner or later confronted with a stark ultimatum: exile or prison. In this regard, Roy Medvedev's life as an "inner émigré," which is examined in this chapter, is somewhat of an exception, yet it also demonstrates the countless difficulties and permanent harassment that dissidents who refused to emigrate faced.

Aleksandr Nekrich's path into exile, on the other hand, shows emigration as a way out for intellectuals who had lost any prospect of work in the Soviet Union. Following the Six-Day War, in 1967, an increasing number of Soviet citizens of Jewish nationality were allowed to emigrate to Israel.[5] While only 4,000 had left between 1960 and 1970, the numbers grew steadily from 13,000 in 1970 to 51,300 in 1979, for a total of 291,000 over the decade, with 57 percent of emigrants settling in Israel.[6] In addition to Jews, another group that benefited from the opening up of emigration were ethnic Germans, who had originally settled in the Volga region before their deportation to Siberia and Kazakhstan during the war. In the context of the German Federal Republic's *Ostpolitik* in the 1970s, the number of ethnic Germans allowed to emigrate jumped from 1,145 in 1970 to 9,704 in 1977, decreasing again thereafter to reach 1,958 in 1982.[7]

However, both groups also faced significant restrictions in this right to emigrate. Many applicants were denied an exit visa on various grounds, be it for their alleged exposition to state secrets in their professional activity, or because of their obligation to support elderly parents. The case of Anatolii Shcharanskii, a famous Jewish activist advocating the right to emigration, exemplifies the plight of "refuseniks." Denied an exit visa in 1973, he was arrested in 1977 for alleged espionage activities but was eventually released to the West in an exchange of spies between the two blocs in 1979.[8] As for those Soviet citizens who were granted the permission to leave, they were usually dismissed from their job from the moment they applied for emigration and had to face harassment from their colleagues and hierarchy.[9]

The relative liberalization of Jewish emigration resulted partly from the action of refuseniks, who organized protests within the USSR, and on whose behalf demonstrations were staged in the West. However, these protests were effective primarily because they took place in the context of détente, a policy of relaxation of international tensions which led to a relative opening of the Soviet Union to the West. The high tide of détente came with the Helsinki Accords, signed by the states party to the Conference on Security and Cooperation in Europe (CSCE) in 1975. The so-called third basket on cooperation in the humanitarian, cultural, and educational fields provided for the respect of freedom of information and the press. Considered merely as a token commitment by the Soviets, it nevertheless proved to be a "foot in the door," allowing Soviet dissidents to set up Helsinki monitoring groups in Moscow, Kiev, and other cities, and to receive support from a whole network of international and nongovernmental organizations, from the CSCE to Helsinki Watch.[10]

The rise of human rights in international politics constituted the backdrop of these developments on the international stage. Samuel Moyn has argued that human rights constituted the "last utopia" of the twentieth century and came to replace the utopia of socialism, discredited after the 1968 invasion of Czechoslovakia. Soviet dissidents, he argues, came to adopt this strategy of action as part of a global ideological shift, mirroring similar developments in Latin America.[11] Benjamin Nathans, however, has shown that the dissidents' defense of human rights had its roots in Esenin-Vol'pin's "legalist strategy," and did not entail any radical break with socialism, but rather resulted from a progressive disenchantment with it, starting from 1956.[12] I would argue that it was the convergence of local and global developments that made the cause of Soviet dissidents so prominent on the international stage. In isolation, human rights activists only had a limited impact on the Soviet leadership, but when their calls were echoed in Western media and in international fora, they acquired added strength. The election of Jimmy Carter to US presidency in 1976, and his insistence on the observance of human rights in the Soviet bloc, was an important watershed. Yet beyond state actors, a primary role in enforcing Soviet compliance with its own constitution, the Universal declaration of human rights, and the Helsinki Accords belonged to interconnected networks of activists in the USSR and in the West.[13]

Whether they chose inner emigration or exile, Soviet dissidents were closely inserted in these networks across the Iron Curtain, which involved journalists, NGOs, Western politicians, publishers, and other activists. For those who remained in the USSR, like Roy Medvedev, these "dangerous liaisons" with the West constituted both an incriminating factor in the eyes of the Soviet authorities and a precious source of support affording protection from potential arrest. For Soviet émigrés, like Nekrich, resuming their activism in the West was a way of maintaining a spiritual connection to their homeland and contributing to the enlightenment of the Soviet people.

Living in "Inner Emigration": Medvedev's fragile compromise with the authorities

The Soviet authorities' failure to arrest Roy Medvedev has often been taken as an indication of his connivance with the regime or even as proof of his collaboration with the KGB.[14] However, to put Medvedev's case in perspective, it is necessary to take a larger view of late Soviet repressive policies. The treatment of famous dissidents shows that celebrity did shield certain well-known figures from repression—until they crossed a certain limit. Solzhenitsyn was allowed to publish two of his anti-Stalinist novels abroad, whereas Daniel' and Siniavskii had been sent to the camps for such an act. And it was only after the author of *Gulag* dealt a major blow to the regime that the Soviet leaders decided, not to imprison him, but to expel him from the USSR. Andrei Sakharov thrived as an outspoken dissident for a decade before being sent to Gorkii in internal exile in 1980 for his critique of the invasion of Afghanistan. Such "mild" reactions contrast starkly with the harsh treatment meted out to less famous figures. Therefore, in order to understand Roy Medvedev's trajectory, it is essential to differentiate two periods: before and after the publication of *Let History Judge*, which turned him into a popular icon of Western media. While Medvedev's arrest was a real possibility in 1971, it became unlikely after this date, both because of his fame, and his awareness of the limits he should not overstep.

Feeling the wind of arrest

In April 1969, Roy Medvedev wrote an open letter to the journal *Kommunist* protesting against recent pro-Stalinist publications.[15] He sent a copy to Brezhnev, Suslov, and Demichev, urging them to disown the article.[16] After circulating in samizdat, the letter crossed the Iron Curtain and was soon published without Medvedev's consent. It first appeared in the Russian émigré journal *Posev*, then as a separate brochure in Paris and was finally broadcast on Radio Liberty.[17] This publication in *Posev*, a journal considered as anti-Soviet by the regime, coincided with Medvedev's exclusion from the Party, and some Western observers wrongly assumed the two events to be connected.[18]

Medvedev knew that exclusion from the Party could be a prelude to arrest. Therefore, when he heard in December 1969 that *Posev* would soon publish an article by "R. Medvedev from Moscow" entitled "Truth about the present day," the historian suspected the KGB's hand. Radio Liberty broadcast the text of this article, describing it as a "programmatic document" by the historian R. Medvedev. Meanwhile, Medvedev received access to the journal and read the article, which he found "very strange, full of various lies and fantastic assertions, in a far-leftist style, similar to Maoism," and containing open calls to overthrow the Soviet regime.[19] Medvedev released an official statement to the Soviet Press Agency "Novosti" denying his authorship of the piece, but also wrote a harsh open letter of protest to the journal, which he distributed to Soviet and Western newspapers.[20]

Calculated risk was Roy Medvedev's trademark, and he knew when he could afford to expose himself. In March 1970, he signed a common memorandum written by Sakharov and Valentin Turchin, addressed to the Soviet leaders and calling for a progressive democratization of the regime. Having received no response, the authors released the text into samizdat.[21] However, the following months showed that the Soviet authorities could go to great lengths to suppress dissent. After his dismissal for his contacts with foreign publishers, Zhores Medvedev had completed two other manuscripts: *Secrecy of Correspondence Is Guaranteed by Law* and *International Cooperation of Scientists and National Frontiers*, which he jointly published in July 1971 under the title *The Medvedev Papers*.[22] The first work attacked the KGB's practice of confiscating correspondence as a form of postal censorship, and the second called for more transparency and freedom of cooperation between Soviet scientists and their colleagues abroad. It was obvious that the biologist had not heeded the KGB's "friendly advice" to concentrate on his scientific research. In May–June 1970, he was incarcerated in a mental hospital in Kaluga, where he was diagnosed with a form of "latent schizophrenia," expressed in his tendency to combine scientific work with publicistic activities. However, he was released three weeks later, thanks to international publicity and the active support of prominent scientists, including Sakharov, Petr Kapitsa, and Boris Astaurov. Although he could not mention it at the time, Roy's friends in the Central Committee, particularly Aleksandr Bovin, had played a crucial role in Zhores's liberation.[23] Far from being intimidated by this first experience of repression, the two brothers published in 1971 a detailed account of these events, under the title *A Question of Madness*.

In the summer of 1971, Roy Medvedev had reasons to experience fear: he was expecting the release of four of his books in the West: *Let History Judge, On Socialist*

Democracy, A Question of Madness, and the first volume of *Political Diary*. In August and September 1971, first excerpts from the samizdat journal appeared in American newspapers. According to Medvedev, although the publication was anonymous, analysis of the content could easily betray his authorship. As he found out two decades later, the decision to arrest him was taken around this time.²⁴ When the police knocked on his door on October 12, 1971, his fate seemed to be sealed. The official warrant for a house search pretexted the theft of library books by a work colleague, Sh., some of which might be in Medvedev's possession. However, after five hours, the police and KGB officials had filled seven bags with a total of forty items, among them manuscripts of the two brothers, foreign and Soviet historical books, samizdat, including some of Solzhenitsyn's unpublished works, and, most importantly, whole files containing work material, none of which had any relation to the theft of library books.²⁵

The day after, the historian was summoned by phone to the Public Prosecutor of the USSR's Office. Unlike a written court summons, a phone call left no documental trace and was therefore not legally binding. Medvedev decided to disregard it and vanish for a while.²⁶ Zhores Medvedev's account of the successful escape shows how closely his brother avoided arrest. As he swiftly left his house, Roy soon noticed the black "Volga" following his bus. To cover his tracks, he entered a twelve-floor building where several of his Old Bolshevik friends lived. Having found refuge with Suren Gazarian, Roy observed that a constant surveillance had now been put in place near the building's entrance and on two floors. However, Gazarian's daughter-in-law, who worked at a theater, appealed to a professional actor of her acquaintance to disguise Medvedev with a wig and fake beard. When he exited the house the next day, dressed up as a bent old man, the KGB agents failed to recognize him. Medvedev bought a ticket to Odessa and stayed in the south for a few months, before traveling to Leningrad.²⁷

Meanwhile, on the basis of the house search's official protocol, which the historian had left on the table before leaving, his brother sent a series of letters to the Public Prosecutor, protesting against violations of official procedures by the police.²⁸ On October 14, the biologist complained that the officials conducting the house search, who had found no library books stolen by Sh., "decided, in the process, to conduct a study of R.A. Medvedev's personal archives and the confiscation of manuscript material."²⁹ He further demanded that the materials that belonged to him personally be returned and that the people responsible for these illegal actions be punished. When the authorities denied that any violation of legal procedure had taken place, Zhores Medvedev sent another protest on November 3, pointing out a number of irregularities. Two weeks later, losing patience, the dissident threatened to turn to the Western media and concluded: "Why [let] this scandalous situation spread further?"³⁰ He noted sarcastically that his manuscripts confiscated during the search denounced precisely such violations of Soviet legality as had taken place. Although he assured his interlocutor that he had "listened to the advice of friends and official instances" and had concentrated for the past year on his scientific work, the Prosecutor's "strange position" forced him once again to address legal issues. Should this discussion become public, he felt certain that public opinion would stand on his side.³¹

In January 1972, as Roy Medvedev was still in hiding, an official summons was sent to his home address to attend the trial of Sh. as a witness. Also involved in this affair were the historian Viktor Danilov and literary critic Vladimir Lakshin. Sh. had convinced Medvedev that she could freely obtain books earmarked for disposal by the Lenin library, and he had in turn invited Danilov and Lakshin to select items of use for their research and professional libraries.[32] Proving that Sh. had misled them and that they had acted on good faith was not easy, and Medvedev may well have been inculpated as Sh.'s accomplice. However, according to Zhores, pressure from the KGB on the judge, a young woman of independent views, "proved counterproductive": instead of incriminating Medvedev, she expressly cleared him of all charges and condemned Sh. to six years of camp imprisonment.[33] Nevertheless, in an article published after the trial, the historian and his friends were accused of "facilitating" Sh.'s "criminal actions."[34]

Roy Medvedev returned from hiding shortly after the publication of *Let History Judge*. The publicity surrounding the Medvedev brothers' actions and publications in the past years had brought them celebrity in the West. This proved the "best defense against new repression."[35]

Establishing a modus vivendi with the regime

The New York Times correspondent Hedrick Smith described Roy Medvedev as "the most meticulous, the most organized Russian" he had encountered. His files were so well-sorted that the KGB had no pains in clearing his whole work archive in a few hours in 1971, but the historian had taken the precaution of duplicating his documents and had hidden a set of copies separately.[36]

> This unruffled equanimity was Roy's trademark. It was of a piece with the careful calibration of his protest, his calculated tactic of refraining from extremes that would make the authorities feel compelled to garrote him. Unlike Sakharov and Solzhenitsyn, he pointed out to me, he had not been attacked in the Soviet press. Moreover, he said he had let officialdom know his basic lines of research. . . . Even when writing about contemporary Soviet life, Roy has avoided attacking the Party head-on but has criticized neo-Stalinist "deformations" and conservative dogmatism. In short, Roy Medvedev is an unusual phenomenon among dissidents. He constitutes the loyal opposition.[37]

From 1971 to 1985, Roy Medvedev benefited from a unique position among dissidents: he became, in his own words, a "free scholar,"[38] whose activities of independent research and tamizdat publication on historical and political themes were de facto tolerated by the regime. Yet this position was not one of unrestrained freedom: he remained at all times under close watch from the KGB and knew the boundaries he could not afford to cross—if he did, he was sure to be reminded of them. The term of "inner emigration" seems adequate to describe his situation: like an émigré, his whole professional activity was oriented toward the West and he was known mostly on the other side of the Iron Curtain. After his brother's deprivation of Soviet citizenship, in 1973, he could count on the services of a devoted personal agent, official representative, coauthor, and editor based in London, and he lived on foreign royalties from his books. Despite continuous

KGB harassment, Medvedev seemed to have reached a kind of tacit modus vivendi with the regime.

At a time when international phone calls were both pricey and monitored by the KGB, the twins' written correspondence constituted a precious lifeline, fulfilling both personal and professional communicative functions. They exchanged letters almost daily, discussing publishing projects, commenting on the life of Soviet émigrés and dissidents, and crafting strategies in relation to their opponents, on both sides of the Iron Curtain. The study of their correspondence yields a detailed picture of their activities and testifies to the security measures they adopted and the constraints they faced. The logistics of these exchanges were sophisticated. The two brothers carefully avoided giving away any compromising information in their open correspondence or they "coded" some elements. Foreign correspondents and embassies also played a crucial role in sustaining this contact: resorting to newspapers' special postal channels and diplomatic pouches was essential for sensitive questions and to send parcels with books or microfilmed manuscripts. Confidential letters were, for example, sent to Peter Osnos, a *Washington Post* correspondent, who could use the American diplomatic mail channel through Helsinki. Through the intermediary of correspondents, Roy received history books and subscribed to Russian émigré journals, forwarded by Zhores. Acquaintances traveling to the Soviet Union could also occasionally carry mail or parcels (a practice called *okaziia*). Parcels containing stationary also arrived on a weekly basis, sometimes accompanied by coffee table books, which could be sold in the Soviet Union for a good price, supplementing Roy's income.[39]

Letters sent through regular mail were registered and numbered, to ensure they all reached their destination, and important documents were duplicated for safety. And although some got lost, most of them were eventually delivered. Indeed, Zhores was an expert in this field: he had written a book on the secrecy of correspondence and was used to claiming his rights when a registered letter had been "lost" by Soviet mail.[40] Nevertheless, in 1978, the KGB sought to demonstrate that it could effectively cut this vital communication line between the Medvedev brothers. In early October, a parcel containing materials for Medvedev's book on Bukharin, sent by Stephen Cohen from the United States through a newspaper correspondent, was allegedly "found" on the street and opened by the Ministry of Foreign Affairs.[41] The historian interpreted this as an attempt to intimidate his correspondents.[42] As he was simultaneously subjected to a blockade of his regular mail, Roy demonstratively warned his "secret readers" in a letter to Zhores: if his letters no longer arrived, he would start sending four to five registered letters with duplicates daily, and would file complaints or a lawsuit. After all, the law guaranteed all citizens equal access to postal services, with restrictions applying only to convicts.[43] The two brothers had successfully applied this method during a temporary "mail blockade" in early 1978. Letters from abroad, but also domestic ones, had ceased to reach Roy. In reaction, Zhores and other friends began to send numerous registered letters, but also parcels containing items they overevaluated: in case of disappearance, the country responsible for the loss was obliged by international conventions to pay a compensation. After a month and twenty letters lost, the historian wrote an official protest to the Universal Postal Union and the Soviet Ministry of Communications. Through this show of determination, he wished to demonstrate that he could turn the affair into an unpleasant scandal. Moreover, the confiscated letters made it clear that the blockade had failed to interrupt the connection between the Medvedev brothers.[44]

The safe delivery of letters was essential precisely because it was central to the historian's professional activity. As he went into hiding in late 1971, Medvedev sent his resignation through his wife to the Academy of Pedagogical Sciences.[45] From then on, he devoted himself entirely to historical research. In three decades, besides numerous articles on Soviet politics and history, he published over twenty books. He pursued his research on Stalinism with two augmented editions of *Let History Judge* (1974 in Russian; 1989 in English) and an additional volume on this theme (*On Stalin and Stalinism*, 1979), and also biographies of Stalin's contemporaries (*All Stalin's Men*, 1983; *Nikolai Bukharin: The Last Years*, 1980). He studied the history of the Revolution (*La révolution d'octobre était-elle inéluctable?*, 1976; *The October Revolution*, 1979) and the Civil War (*Philip Mironov and the Russian Civil War*, 1978). He delved into a delicate affair in the field of literary politics with a study on Sholokhov's (non-)authorship of *Quiet Flows the Don* (*Problems in the Literary Biography of Mikhail Sholokhov*, 1975). He wrote biographies of Soviet leaders of the post-Stalin era (*Khrushchev: The Years in Power*, 1975, coauthored with Zhores Medvedev; *Khrushchev*, 1982[46]; *Political Portrait of L.I. Brezhnev*, 1991 (untranslated)—to be followed in the 1990s by two biographies of Iurii Andropov). In the field of Soviet and international politics, in addition to *On Socialist Democracy* (1972) and *Political Diary* (1972–75), he edited his journal *Twentieth Century* (1977–78) and published *Leninism and Western Socialism* (1982); several volumes of conversations with Italian journalists on Soviet politics and dissent (in English: *On Soviet Dissent*, 1980 and *Time of change: an insider's view of Russia's transformation*, 1989); and *China and the superpowers* (1987). Most of these works were translated into several languages.

Zhores Medvedev played a pivotal role as an external relay for all negotiations concerning his brother's publications, translations, contracts, and financial questions. He acted as his representative, signing contracts in his name, but also giving him valuable advice concerning Western audiences and publishers' expectations. Although he had a full-time research position at the London National Institute for Medical Research, the geneticist engaged in a range of political and public activities. He was also in charge of managing Roy's book royalties, which constituted the historian's sole source of income. Before his brother's emigration in 1973, Roy Medvedev had to rely on the assistance of foreign visitors: it was Heinrich Böll who had brought him his first 1,000-dollar advance royalty check for *Let History Judge*.[47] Financial transactions across the Iron Curtain were allowed through "Vneshposyltorg," an organ of the Soviet Foreign Trade Ministry in charge of trade with capitalist states. Foreign currency wired to Soviet citizens (usually by relatives who were state employees on service abroad) was converted into "certificates," to be used in special restricted-access "Berezka" shops. As Anna Ivanova has observed, one of the paradoxes of the USSR's foreign currency policy at the time was that dissenting authors who countered censorship were given the privilege to access elite stores inaccessible to the majority of Soviet citizens.[48] Roy Medvedev recalls that he received about 500 dollars a month for his living expenses from his brother.[49] However, in 1976, the Soviet authorities put an end to this absurd situation: from then on, "gift transfers" to Soviet citizens could be paid only in rubles and were subjected to a 30 percent tax, with an exemption for Western royalties received by Soviet authors published legally through the All-Union Agency on Copyright (VAAP).[50] As a result, the two brothers had to resort to alternative channels—for example, the sending of parcels containing books or valuable items that could be sold for profit in the Soviet Union. Medvedev also asked foreign correspondents to shop for him in Berezka stores as a payment for articles he had written for their newspaper.

Nevertheless, the historian's situation was precarious: he knew he remained at all times at the KGB's mercy. On August 31, 1973, as Zhores had just been deprived of his Soviet citizenship, the trial against Petr Iakir and Viktor Krasin and a smear campaign against Sakharov in the media seemed to signal a general clampdown on dissent. A new wave of house searches had begun and Medvedev's name seemed to be discussed in higher spheres. An acquaintance reported being told during an interrogation: "Roy M. has gone over to the other side of the barricade, he doesn't work and doesn't want to work, lives on royalties sent from abroad." To avoid being accused of "parasitism," the historian sent a job application to the Academy of Pedagogical Sciences.[51] This was a pure formality, as he knew he would get no reply, but it was a necessary protection measure. A few times, a police lieutenant visited Medvedev to inquire why he had no official work. He answered that he was refused a position in his field of specialization: with a PhD in pedagogics, he could work either in schools, publishing houses, or research institutes, but all his job applications remained unanswered. This made the accusation of "parasitism" void.[52]

In early 1975, Medvedev had just completed his book questioning Mikhail Sholokhov's authorship of *Quiet Flows the Don*.[53] This attack on the nemesis of Soviet dissidents,[54] ten years after he had received the Nobel Prize for his novel, seemed calculated to provoke the authorities' wrath. Moreover, the historian had started editing a new samizdat journal, *Twentieth Century*. Clearly, he had not abandoned his "anti-Soviet activities." On March 14, he was summoned for a five-hour discussion by the Public Prosecutor. In a letter to his brother, Medvedev judged the conversation "quite pacific for a start, without threats or warnings," but he believed that "other steps may follow."[55] On April 7, he expressed renewed concerns: he had heard that the Ministry of Health was discussing the possibility of psychiatric hospitalization as a repressive measure against him. He commented:

> All these are just conversations, but it is important to take them into account. I have of course consciously begun editing the journal precisely now (after the book on Sholokhov) and have also assumed the authorship of Political Diary. In for a penny, in for a pound. All of this immediately raises the stakes in this political game that I have to play, and if I win, then it will be very important for everyone. But I might also lose, and I am also prepared for this.[56]

This time, however, he would not go into hiding as he had done in 1971. He understood that he had better constantly remain "in the limelight." As he planned on going to the North Caucasus on a vacation, Medvedev warned his brother that an interruption in their daily correspondence would indicate that something had happened to him.[57] Ten days later, he affirmed with greater calm that he had concluded that the authorities would not have him arrested. Rather than betraying panic and going into hiding, as they expected him to do, he believed he should appear quiet and self-assured.[58]

When the police appeared on his doorstep for a house search, sometime later, Medvedev says he reacted cold-bloodedly. He made it clear that he would not allow them to seize whole files of newspaper and journal clippings, as they had done in 1971, pointing out that these were excerpts from *Pravda* and *Izvestiia*, not "forbidden literature." The law obliged them to list every single item separately, and if they contravened this law, he was determined to oppose physical resistance and they would have to arrest him. But his arrest was not planned, and a phone call convinced the police not to waste time listing individual items and they just seized tamizdat books. He believed the authorities expected him to protest the search, but for his journal's sake, he decided to keep a low profile.[59]

In the following years, the pressure exercised on him was often indirect, through his family members. In October 1976, Roy wrote that in the spring, an acquaintance had informed him that a range of measures were being discussed in higher spheres: his son would be prevented from entering university, his family would not be granted a cooperative apartment and his wife would not be able to defend her doctoral dissertation. "And all of this is being considered as a first warning," added the secret informer, the ultimate goal being to force Medvedev to emigrate.[60] Forewarned, the historian took his son's university entrance exams under control and closely averted what was clearly a plan to fail him. However, it became clear that the warning also held true as far as the cooperative apartment was concerned. The plan had been to enter a housing cooperative, which was building new houses in the southern district of Novye Cheremushki, closer to the city center, in exchange for their old apartment in the northern Khovrino neighborhood. His wife had bought a share and been attributed an apartment in the future building, but the District Executive Committee had rejected her application for registration.[61] In November, Roy confirmed that all members of the cooperative had been registered, except for his wife. "All of this is important as a symptom of relations," he judged. Pressure, not only on him personally, but also on his family and friends, seemed to continue "despite the *modus vivendi* (*vzaimootnosheniia*) that had taken shape."[62] In the following months, his wife's attempts to file a complaint or even a lawsuit remained unsuccessful, and she eventually gave up on the cooperative apartment. In addition, as planned, she was also prevented from defending her doctoral dissertation.

Intimidation tactics of the same kind continued throughout the years. In summer 1978, Medvedev's family and close friends began to repeatedly receive letters containing obscene verses featuring him and various women of his acquaintance. The KGB's goal seemed to be to isolate him, by convincing his supporters that "acquaintance with Roy Medvedev is not such a safe thing." And indeed, intimidated by this "moral terror," some former colleagues did turn away from him.[63]

However, it was only after Brezhnev died, in 1982, that repression seemed to take a more serious turn. Andropov was now at the Party's helm, but he no longer had direct control over the KGB and his successors did not show the same tolerance toward Medvedev's activities. On January 19, 1983, Medvedev was summoned to the Public Prosecutor's Office, where Deputy Prosecutor O. V. Soroka presented him with a written "warning" demanding that he cease his "anti-Soviet activities, which are harmful to the interests of the Soviet state." In response, he immediately convened a press conference in his apartment and issued a declaration of protest rejecting this demand.

> In a country like the Soviet Union, an honest historian must not only be a researcher but an investigator and a judge as well, making political and moral judgments, regardless of whether those in power like them or not. I am little troubled by the evaluation of my work by the prosecutor and by the KGB. Any honorable and independent historian should care only about one thing—the search for truth. The prospect of punishment does not frighten me, so it is pointless to issue me warnings or make threats.[64]

In an article, Mikhail Agursky, a friend of Medvedev who had emigrated to Israel, attributed this warning to power struggles at the top of the Soviet leadership. While Medvedev had "always enjoyed Andropov's protection," according to Agursky, the Public Prosecutor Aleksandr Rekunkov, who was one of Andropov's political opponents, had acted without KGB approval to sabotage the Soviet leader's relations with the West.[65] It was certainly true that struggles of power were taking place within higher spheres after Brezhnev's death, yet Agursky was mistaken in thinking that the KGB was unconnected with the warning. On April 8, 1983, a memorandum to the Central Committee signed by Rekunkov and KGB head Viktor Chebrikov recommended more radical measures against the dissident.[66] Medvedev was described as "a convinced opponent of the Soviet state and social regime," whose "hostile activity" consisted in "publish[ing] works in the West, which are constantly used for goals hostile to the Soviet Union." Interestingly, the report underscored Medvedev's peculiar position, by claiming that the historian sought to cover up his activities "by collaborating with publishing houses of some Western Communist parties" in Italy, Spain, France, and England. But he also had regular contacts with foreign correspondents and diplomats, through whom he "equipped Western mass propaganda organs with insinuations concerning domestic political events in the country, spread anti-Soviet inventions and biased evaluations of the USSR's position on various international problems." Therefore, the report recommended instituting criminal proceedings against Medvedev and preventing him from leaving Moscow. Then, if international protests arose and a Western government offered to take him, he should be allowed to emigrate. If not, then a sentence of internal exile should be pronounced.[67]

Around that time, Austrian Chancellor Bruno Kreisky, following a request from Ken Coates, from the Bertrand Russell Peace Foundation, intervened on Medvedev's behalf with the Soviet authorities. They replied that, should the Austrian government support Medvedev's application for emigration, this request would be positively settled.[68] However, Medvedev would probably not have left the Soviet Union of his own accord, and the authorities were not prepared to expel him as they had done for Solzhenitsyn. In a 1983 interview, the historian thus declared: "I don't think the authorities would forcibly expel me, and I will never voluntarily leave for abroad. . . . I would rather spend some years in prison than leave the Soviet Union."[69] While an arrest was unlikely at this stage, Medvedev may well have shared Andrei Sakharov's fate. However, for repressive measures to be implemented, the KGB needed Andropov's approval, which the General Secretary refused to grant.[70]

In his biographies of Andropov, Medvedev writes about the strange favor that he seems to have enjoyed with the Soviet leader, dating back to his first and only direct contact with him, in 1964. In 1989, after being elected People's Deputy, Medvedev met Ivan Abramov, who once worked in the fifth division of the KGB, in charge of dissidents. "We wanted to arrest you, but Andropov was against," confessed Abramov.[71] Andropov was certainly a contradictory figure: as the KGB's longtime chief (1967–82) he was responsible for repression against dissidents, yet he increasingly resorted to administrative measures and forced emigration rather than judicial prosecution.[72] He seems to have held more liberal views than many of his Politburo colleagues and, unlike hardliners, he could distinguish between Medvedev's "loyal opposition" and Solzhenitsyn's truly anti-Soviet views. While his concern for the preservation of détente certainly influenced his treatment of dissidents in the 1970s, it could no longer play a primary role in the colder international climate of the 1980s.

After Andropov died, in February 1984, the threat of arrest reappeared. In a letter sent through confidential channels, the historian wrote that on February 20, he had received a strict warning from the KGB, accusing him of being "a paid informer of Western correspondents and secret services."[73] After he rejected these accusations, a surveillance post of two to three policemen was installed on his staircase, keeping foreign visitors from entering. A car stood by the building entrance and shadowed him wherever he went. Expecting arrest, Medvedev gave his brother instructions for the publication of his biography of Brezhnev and an expanded edition of *Let History Judge*. He hoped to have enough material for two or three years and to be able to finish his current projects if sent into exile. Nevertheless, he had decided not to tell journalists about his situation and not to protest openly. He had already resorted to this strategy one year earlier and could not afford to repeat himself.

The same day, he wrote another letter to his brother through open mail, demonstratively addressing his invisible "curators": he announced he would not file any protest, since he was not subjected to a house arrest. As for the visit of foreign correspondents, he would gladly do without them, since they only inconvenienced him, "asking for [his] 'opinion,' but always refusing to help [him]," even with simple requests.[74] A month later, he wrote with his "invisible readers" in mind that, although the situation remained unchanged, he was not worried. While he had feared arrest in 1971, he had now published his main works. The authorities would do well, he suggested, to offer him "an official position at an institute of history, or even better, philosophy. I would gladly spend 6-7 years of my life studying purely philosophical questions that I have had on my mind since my student years."[75] This suggestion, which was in line with the proposal Andropov had made in his KGB report on Medvedev's activities in 1968,[76] would have required a turn toward a strategy of cooptation of less radical dissidents—a perspective hardly conceivable under Chernenko. It would take Gorbachev's accession to power for such an evolution to take place.

Although Medvedev could still see foreigners outside his apartment, he mostly remained at home, leaving his guards idle. This intensive and demonstrative surveillance, which lasted until May 1985, occupied up to thirty people, according to the historian's estimate. He believed that this very costly apparatus aimed primarily at intimidating him.[77] If the goal was, as he suspected, to convince him to emigrate, then the move was unsuccessful: Medvedev would rather remain in this precarious state of inner emigration. In this he differed from dissidents who chose the road to exile, like Nekrich.

Exile as the ultimate form of exit

Nine years in Limbo

In his memoirs, Nekrich described his agonizing situation during the nine years between his exclusion from the Party and his emigration in these terms:

> Time went by, and my concerns, my uneasy feelings about my professional degradation, took ever greater hold on me. A historian, like a writer, needs to have his reading public. If he doesn't have it, then he gradually fades, and he loses his professional skills. I worked, I wrote, and then I put away in a desk drawer whatever I had written. Things could not go on that way forever.[78]

From 1967 to 1976, he faced "an unspoken quota" on publishing of one publication per year.[79] Over the next decade, he was able to publish a few articles in the Institute's annual yearly review and in *Novyi mir*, while Tvardovskii still stood at the journal's helm. As for his books, they were simply banned from print. In late 1969, he submitted for publication a study entitled *British Policy in Europe 1941-1945*. Despite approval by two institutes of the Academy of Sciences, the Editorial Publications Council refused to publish it without special instruction from the Central Committee of the CPSU. Nekrich's attempt to protest the decision in a letter to the president of the Academy of Sciences yielded no results.[80] Moreover, the historian increasingly experienced frustration in his professional work. Traveling abroad for archival research, a rare privilege, was now precluded, and his freedom to take part in academic events was also drastically curtailed. In 1970, as the World Congress of Historians gathered in Moscow, Nekrich was instructed by his Institute superiors not to attend the conference. Nekrich protested this decision through a letter to the chairman of the Congress, but also informed some of his Western colleagues. Eventually, he received a guest pass, but was kept under close watch throughout the event.[81]

Although he retained his position of senior researcher at what was now the Institute of World History, Nekrich felt that the ideological climate of the institution had become more conservative after the invasion of Czechoslovakia. Danilov's anti-Stalinist *partkom* had been dissolved in the aftermath of the Nekrich Affair, and the division of the Institute of History had shuffled the cards further. The pro-Stalinists seemed to have decisively benefited from these changes, and they multiplied their attacks against revisionist scholars. Mikhail Gefter's Section of Methodology was disbanded and other liberal historians were either harassed or driven to resignation.[82] In 1970, the replacement of the Russophile archaeologist Boris Rybakov as director of the Institute of History of the USSR with the historian Pavel Volobuev seemed to signal the onset of a more liberal course. However, after launching a few attacks against orthodox historians, Volobuev drew upon himself Pospelov and Trapeznikov's wrath and had to publicly repent and resign from his position in March 1973.[83]

In these circumstances, Nekrich's position was not simply stagnant, it was becoming increasingly precarious. In the fall of 1969, an attempt to strip him of his degree of "doctor of historical sciences," earned in 1963, was only averted thanks to a considerable show of support from fellow historians, but also from the president of the Academy of Sciences.[84] Two months later, Evgenii Zhukov, Secretary of the Department of Historical Sciences, summoned Nekrich to his office and explained that the authorities regarded his continued employment by the Institute as undesirable. His refusal to "recognize his mistakes," but also the publication of *June 22, 1941* in Western Europe, sometimes under provocative titles, added to their irritation. In order to placate such hostile moods, Zhukov asked Nekrich to write a statement to the effect that the foreign translations of his book had appeared without his consent, and that he condemned "any attempts to distort the thrust or content of [his] book by way of tendentious changes in its title, through format, footnotes, distortion, or isolated quotation from the text."[85]

One may ask why Nekrich chose to endure such repeated vexations and did not become an independent historian the way Medvedev did. Many factors made this outcome unlikely, starting from the natural reluctance to forsake a privileged position: in a society where the state had a monopoly over employment, dismissal could lead to a definite loss of income. In order to live off Western royalties as Medvedev did, Nekrich should have been an equally prolific writer, focusing on themes of interest to the Western public. This implied a switch from his primary field of research, British foreign policy, to Soviet history. Only after 1972 did he shift his research focus, as he began collecting material for his future book *The Punished Peoples*. Yet he never took the risk of publishing in tamizdat and waited until his emigration to publish his work abroad. As in the Stalin era, the historian was reluctant to directly step into opposition with the regime. In his memoirs, published after his emigration, Nekrich conspicuously sought to demonstrate his "dissident status" and distance himself from his erstwhile communist convictions. He wrote that his faith in communism, shaken by his exclusion from the Party, had suffered fatal wounds on August 21, 1968. At the same time, the crushing of the Prague Spring had initiated a process of spiritual rebirth within the intelligentsia and had led him to take "the firm decision to do battle with conformism everywhere and always, not shrinking from confrontations, regardless of the consequences."[86] Despite these declarations, it seems that for a long time, the hope of regaining his lost status was actually stronger than the urge to speak up, if only out of sheer lack of alternative perspectives.

As the 1970s wore on, the cautious opening of emigration to Soviet Jews increasingly appeared as the solution to his conundrum. Yet this eternal parting with one's past, relatives, and friends could only seem a viable option at the last stage of a protracted process of maturation. Gradually, he wrote, he began to make changes in his life "in accordance with [his] moral convictions."[87] One of these changes was his work on *The Punished Peoples*, the first study he wrote specifically for a Western audience, without any prospect of publication in the USSR. Inspired by his wartime experience in Crimea, Nekrich's research focused on Stalin's deportation of ethnic groups from the Caucasus and Crimea, in reprisal for their alleged collaboration with the Germans. The historian also examined the sensitive question of their rehabilitation and return to their homeland. This commitment eventually led him to support the struggle of Mustafa Dzhemilev, the leader of the Crimean Tatars, who reclaimed the right for his people to resettle in the peninsula, from which they had been collectively deported in 1944. Nekrich's work drew largely on doctoral theses defended during the Thaw by historians from the deported minorities: many of them by party secretaries who had benefited from the opening of local archives. He acknowledged the contribution of their research in a special note on his sources.[88] One author, Refik Muzafarov, not only had written a manuscript entitled *Far from the Crimean Mountains: Anatomy of a Deportation*, but had also sent it to the Central Committee, hoping for a decision allowing the return of his people to their ancestral land. Local newspapers and some Soviet works and encyclopedias also provided valuable information. Finally, Nekrich had been able to use several Western monographs based on German archives, by Alexander Dallin, Robert Conquest, and others.[89] In the summer of 1975, with the prospect of emigration in mind, the historian sent his manuscript to the West.

A few months earlier, Nekrich had decided to clarify his situation by exhausting all possibilities of legal recourse. Following the usual procedures, he tried to take action through his union. Without any real expectations, he aired his grievances, complaining about the discrimination he suffered from. Ignoring renewed calls to acknowledge his mistakes, the historian stated that he considered "redirecting [his] entire life so that the final years remaining to [him] for creative work would not be for nothing, as have been the past seven years."[90] Yet the specific demands he made remained unanswered and he realized that things could only take a turn for the worse, "such as being dismissed during a regular cutback in staff or perhaps just giving in."[91] Years later, Nekrich remembered fantasies he had at the time about his funeral: his colleagues from the Institute of History would ask to organize a commemoration, but, following a call from "above," it would be decided to simply send a representative from the local Party Committee to the graveyard. Yet, ultimately, what Nekrich cared about was not so much his death as what remained of his life and his scholarly potential, which was going wasted. "In fact, I was condemned to a slow death. And I decided to leave."[92]

In his memoirs, Nekrich explained that his decision to emigrate meant his rejection of two alternative paths: remaining quietly in his position until retirement or joining the dissidence. While the former seemed morally inacceptable, the latter raised several reservations. Although he had begun taking part in some dissident actions, he did not find any positive program he could join, and he preferred to "remain under [his] own banner." Moreover, he doubted that the people, in whose name dissidents claimed to be acting, really needed him to defend them. Overall, he thought he could make a greater contribution to the democratic movement through his research.[93]

It seems that Nekrich was in contact with the British Second World War specialist John Ericson as early as 1973 and expected to secure a scientific invitation that would have allowed him to emigrate.⁹⁴ However, these contacts remained without effect, and Nekrich resigned himself to resort to the "Israeli channel" of emigration. In the summer of 1975, he contacted a cousin who lived in Israel to request an official invitation. His mother died in August, leaving this divorced and childless man of fifty-five free of any family ties. After submitting his application and notifying Zhukov of his departure, the historian had to endure the humiliating treatment future emigrants were usually subjected to. During a meeting convened for this purpose, Zhukov announced Nekrich's decision and opened the floor for statements of reprobation. Finally, the attendees adopted a resolution condemning Nekrich's "treason" and calling for further party meetings to be convened. Nekrich ignored the summons and failed to attend any of them. Ultimately, he was informed of the final resolution, urging him to request to be released of his functions at the Institute. However, Nekrich claimed that he refused to submit to this diktat and urged the Institute instead to arrange for his visa procedure to be expedited.⁹⁵

In preparation for his future life in the West, Nekrich made microfilms of his research notes for *The Punished Peoples*, but also of documents he intended to use for future studies, in particular on the "anti-cosmopolitan" campaign at Moscow State University in 1949.⁹⁶ He also made use of his newly acquired internal freedom—and simultaneously prepared the ground for his reception in the West. In April, he heard that after Mustafa Dzhemilev had been condemned by a court in Omsk, clashes had occurred between the police and Andrei Sakharov, who was attending the trial. The historian wrote a declaration of protest, calling on historians to rise up to defend Dzhemilev and other prisoners of conscience incarcerated in the USSR. He concluded: "It is our duty—both human and professional. Let us put an end to our shameful silence."⁹⁷ He transmitted this call to the Reuters Agency and the British Communist newspaper *Morning Star*. The day after receiving the authorization to emigrate, on May 25, 1976, Nekrich attended the appeal of Dzhemilev's trial in Moscow, in Sakharov's company.⁹⁸

Roy Medvedev took a cynical view of Nekrich's call to historians in a letter to his brother. He considered that after the Nekrich Affair, "he, for one, 'shamefully kept silent' for almost ten years. He never protested against anything. He had some impulses, wanted to write something, asked me to find some materials for him (I spent a lot of time doing this), but he did not even start anything."⁹⁹ Several times he had promised to write articles for Medvedev's journal *Twentieth Century* but had backed down. Nekrich's bolder protest after filing for emigration contrasted with his careful restraint in earlier years. Medvedev interpreted this as "a clear and immoral calculation." On the one hand, it sent the authorities a strong signal: if they delayed granting Nekrich a visa, he would also become a "dissident." On the other hand, once he received the authorization to leave, he could always pretend to have been threatened with incarceration and forced into exile. "And he will arrive abroad crowned with the glory, not of one who has remained silent for ten years, but of a 'dissident.'"¹⁰⁰

The final date of Nekrich's departure was set for June 7, giving him just under two weeks to pack an entire life. For Soviet exiles, emigration was an irreversible leap into the unknown, akin to a new birth. The new life awaiting Nekrich would be radically different.

"Uncle Sam's new clothes"

Nekrich followed a path many Soviet-Jewish emigrants had trodden before him. After spending three weeks in Vienna, where he was handed a *Fremdenpass*, an alien passport allowing a stateless person to travel freely for a year, he pursued his journey westwards, instead of proceeding to Israel. The historian temporarily relocated to Rome, where he began exploring avenues for an academic position. As a specialist of British foreign policy, Nekrich initially hoped to secure a position in England. However, his aspirations failed to materialize. He therefore reluctantly accepted a ten-month fellowship offered by Edward Keenan, director of the Harvard Russian Research Center, but he asked to delay for two months the beginning of his fellowship, in order to travel for a few months. He went to Israel, France, and Britain, where he gave two talks, in London and Scotland.[101]

Nevertheless, upon applying for an immigrant visa to the United States, an unpleasant incident occurred, which would prove fateful. Nekrich spoke with the American consul, Wagner, who asked him about his past membership in the Communist Party, and whether he had entered the Party of his own will. The historian gave an honest response: he had joined the Party by conviction during the war. At the time, party membership "carried only the privilege of being killed earlier than the other combatants."[102] He further elaborated on his differences with the Party and his exclusion in 1967. Wagner seemed to consider Nekrich's a "satisfactory explanation" and asked him to consign it to paper. However, the historian still felt uneasy about bureaucratic intrusions into his personal life.

> I denied his, or anyone's right to demand an explanation of my life in the Soviet Union as it had no connection with the United States, her politics or laws, and further stated that American law nowhere demands such a written explanation. I added that in my opinion the anti-Communist law, which was written during the Cold War, was out-of-date, and ought to be abolished. Mr. Wagner informed me that if I refused, I would be denied an immigrant visa. I replied that if this was indeed US policy, I no longer desired to have the resident visa, but asked instead for a Visitor's visa, which would allow me ten months' time at Harvard.[103]

With Edward Keenan's assistance he was eventually allowed into the United States for the duration of his Harvard fellowship on a tourist visa. Nekrich soon realized that this incident could jeopardize his situation: although he was too principled to ever lie about his past, providing a written explanation would have been a lesser evil. "If I had not left the USSR so recently, my reaction might have been quite different. But under the circumstances I sensed from the conversation that I was dealing with a familiar mentality, and I began to reconsider my choice of America as a new home."[104]

Nekrich arrived in Cambridge, Massachusetts, on October 28, 1976. Although the Russian Research Center welcomed him with open arms and facilitated his installation, the first months were difficult, partly because of his limited English skills.[105] In a letter to his Russian émigré friend Michel Heller, he commented: "The situation is a bit frugal, so much so that they will pay the first [installment of] my stipend only on November 30."[106]

Although he received financial assistance from the Jewish community, he regretted having spent all of his savings during his travels. Three months later, he had settled into a new apartment, but still vastly exceeded his 650-dollar monthly stipend. His friends Stephen Cohen and Robert Tucker helped him make ends meet, but also gave him advice concerning the publication of *The Punished Peoples*.[107] He received additional financial and professional assistance from the Program for Soviet émigré scholars.[108]

Now determined to remain in the United States and more familiar with the realities of academic life in the Western world, the historian explored possible sources of funding for his research. He privileged research fellowships over university professorships, partly because he had no teaching experience, but also because of the lack of stable academic positions available to foreign specialists. He complained that the offers he received were short-term and "in the province."[109] "Americans, especially young ones, are more or less used to this kind of perturbations. But what about a Russian who is used to working in the same position for years, if not decades?"[110] Moreover, after almost a decade of academic ostracism and as he approached retirement age, he wished to devote most of his time to a few research projects he had in mind.[111]

As his Harvard fellowship had expired, he was awarded a two-year $20,000 grant from the National Endowment for the Humanities and a $11,000 grant from the Ford Foundation, on the basis of a new project, entitled "Twilight of the Stalin Era," spanning the postwar period and the early 1950s.[112] In addition to small stipends from Brandeis University (MA), where he lectured in 1977, and from the Washington, D.C. Kennan Institute, where he was a fellow in May 1978, these grants gave Nekrich greater financial security.[113] He also devoted part of his time to revising his memoirs, entitled *Forsake Fear*. The full manuscript was ready for publication by the spring of 1978. However, his expectations concerning the publishing potential of his works proved overblown. While *The Punished Peoples* was indeed published in several European languages in 1978, the royalties remained modest. As for *Forsake Fear*, it appeared only in Russian (1979) and in German (1983), with a very delayed English edition (1991). Only *Utopia in Power* (1982), his voluminous history of the Soviet Union, coauthored by Michel Heller, would bring him the success he longed for.

However, the greatest challenge Nekrich faced during his first years in the West was the instability of his situation. In January 1977, concerned about the renewal of his visa, Nekrich contacted Robert Gordon, from the organization Action for Soviet Jewry. Gordon then wrote to Massachusetts Congressman Robert Drinan to ask him to sponsor a private bill that would allow Nekrich to get a permanent immigration visa, despite his past membership in the Communist Party.[114] However, Drinan advised Nekrich to deny that he had joined the Party voluntarily, which the historian refused to do. He replied indignantly that he had no "intention to buy the status of permanent resident of the United States at the price of a lie."[115] Drinan then encouraged him to seek legal advice from an immigrant law attorney.[116]

With the assistance of his lawyer, Joseph O'Neill, Nekrich then proceeded to apply for political asylum. His application, however, was rejected on October 31 on the grounds of his possession of a valid Austrian *Fremdenpass*, which entitled him to return to that country. Unless he reapplied for asylum, he would be subjected to deportation.[117] Judging the grounds for asylum denial spurious, Nekrich set out to mobilize supporters to his cause. On December 1, 1977, a group of Harvard and Boston academics (Abram Bergson, Adam Ulam, Sanford Lieberman, David Powell, and Daniel Yergin) wrote a collective letter to Congressman Thomas O'Neill expressing their support for Nekrich's "effort to remain within this country and secure US citizenship." They warned that Nekrich's expulsion would elicit strong protests, not only in the United States, but also abroad. "Perhaps more important, it would damage America's image as a defender of political freedom and would undercut our efforts (through the Helsinki Accords and President Carter's policies) to promote human rights," argued the signatories.[118]

Meanwhile, an informal meeting with the Immigration Services yielded an important finding: although the McCarran Internal Security Act precluded admission into the United States of former Communist Party members, a waiver could be granted "if proof of five years of active opposition to communism is provided"—a provision that clearly applied to Nekrich.[119] The deportation hearing, initially scheduled for February 1978, was postponed to May 22 due to weather conditions. In April, following Abram Bergson's advice, Nekrich wrote to Marshall D. Shulman, special adviser to the Secretary of State on Soviet Affairs.[120] He was also offered assistance by Dimitri Simes, from the Union of Councils for Soviet Jews, who claimed that his organization had "both considerable resources and experience in dealing with cases like [his]." He proposed to lobby for Nekrich's case through Congress, State Department, the White House, and the CSCE, and, if necessary, through a public campaign.[121]

For unclear reasons, the May 22 hearing was canceled, and by July, Nekrich was notifying his lawyer that his *Fremdenpass* had now expired, which could potentially simplify his situation, if he reapplied for asylum. As his attorney failed to give him a straight answer, Nekrich grew nervous: "I would like to stress that time is of fundamental importance to me. I am not a young man anymore and I need the most of it for establishing myself in a new country. The fact that I am not a permanent resident of the USA reflects negatively on my professional career here."[122] Not only had he been obliged to refuse participation in two international conferences in Europe, but his project funded by the National Endowment for Humanities required research in British and German archives. Settling the question of his status was essential to allow him to travel abroad.[123]

As Nekrich filed a new application for asylum, the Immigration Services notified him that "in view of the current situation in the USSR," the officer had approved his application, which would be reviewed within a year. Meanwhile, he could apply for permanent residency.[124] On August 31, Nekrich performed a "Sworn Statement," a short interview procedure confirming his defection from the Party and opposition to the Soviet regime. The interview ran smoothly and he filed the application for permanent residency, being under the impression that his case had been definitely solved. By November, he was assured he would soon receive a "Green Card."[125]

However, he was in for a new disappointment. In early January, the district director of the Immigration Services declared that there was "insufficient evidence" as yet that Nekrich qualified for defector status. He feared "that Nekrich may remain a communist in principle although he rejects the Soviet system in practice." A day-long interview was therefore necessary, and the burden of proof to establish defector status would lie on Nekrich.[126] This declaration enraged Nekrich's supporter Donald Carlisle, a Boston

University professor, who complained to Marshall Shulman and Zbigniew Brzezinski, then National Security Adviser. "The Immigration service's hostile attitude towards [Nekrich] is shameful and degrading.... It is my belief, although I cannot prove it, that Nekrich continues to be singled out because his earlier indiscretion in Rome affronted the Immigration Service."[127]

Meanwhile, Nekrich was summoned for an appointment with Immigration Officer Joel Dorfman and was required to mail in advance of the meeting affidavits of people who had known him in the Soviet Union, along with a written statement concerning his past Communist Party membership, his opposition to Communism since his expulsion, but also about his beliefs "concerning the type of political and economic system that [he] would advocate for the US and for the world."[128] Nekrich sent three affidavits from Soviet émigrés: Aleksandr Kazhdan, his former colleague from the Institute of World History; Dina Simis-Kaminskaia, lawyer of famous dissidents, and her husband, both of whom had known Nekrich since the 1930s; and Iurii Tuvin, a Soviet dissident. The latter insisted that "membership in the CPSU (former or present) does not reveal the nature of people in the USSR," as numerous dissidents had once been party members. He affirmed that Nekrich had taken an active part in the dissident movement and would have incurred repression if he had remained in the USSR.[129]

On January 25, 1979, Nekrich met Dorfman for a long interview.[130] The range of questions was very broad, touching upon Nekrich's, but also his relatives' relation to the Party, his election to the Institute's Party Committee, his trade-union membership, experience of anti-Semitism, his attitude toward particular leaders, the doctrine of Marxism-Leninism, or capitalism. However, Nekrich was on slippery ground when Dorfman asked him to prove his opposition to the regime. Why, given his change of views and what he had endured, had he waited for so long before emigrating? Nekrich replied: "Because I wanted to fulfill my duties to the USSR as a citizen, as a historian, because I felt that I have a duty for my people to assist and to tell them the truth, and I did it until the moment when I felt it is impossible." And although he did oppose communism, "a totalitarian system which oppressed the natural feelings of human beings," his had been a slow realization. "This is not easy to understand if you didn't live in the USSR, because understanding comes gradually. Your vision of the world enlarged, you know. There is a process. This is not like suddenly you open your eyes."[131]

In May 1979, Nekrich finally obtained a "green card" and could thus travel more freely: he took on visiting professorships at Tübingen University, Germany (1980 and 1981), in Canberra, Australia (1981), and at Hokkaido University, Japan (1983). In April 1985, he received American citizenship.

The struggle must go on

It was in these circumstances that Nekrich completed what was perhaps the most significant work of his career. His coauthor Michel Heller (Mikhail Geller of his Russian name) was a historian and literary scholar who had studied with Nekrich in Moscow. After his liberation from the Gulag, in 1956, Heller left the Soviet Union. Thanks to his wife's Polish nationality, he emigrated first to Poland, then to France, in 1968, where he taught at the Sorbonne.[132] In late 1976, Nekrich discussed with Leopold Labedz a new project of a History of the Soviet Union, specifically aimed at the Soviet reader: "My idea consisted in giving *our fellow countrymen* a quiet, dispassionate book, in which they could read about their history. I assumed that in the center of our attention would be the same people for whom we write—*homo sovieticus*."[133] Although Labedz warned him that Americans would buy the book only if it was oriented toward a Western audience, Nekrich decided to submit his idea to Heller. By October 1977, Labedz had renounced participating in the project, but Nekrich and Heller were discussing a division of chapters and periods among themselves.[134] Nekrich took charge of the Second World War and the postwar era, while Heller wrote about earlier Soviet history.

This long-distance collaboration was a fruitful one, only impeded by Nekrich's visa issues. Nekrich began working on his part in the fall of 1978. In September 1979, he could finally travel to Paris to spend a few weeks with Heller jointly revising the manuscript for publication, to ensure that these were not "two books under one cover," as his coauthor put it.[135] Still, the two historians' different life experiences and political opinions did transpire in the course of their work. In retrospect, Heller judged that, although they had received the same education, their views had long differed: Nekrich had joined the Party during the war and had worked for twenty years within the Academy of Sciences, whereas he had never been employed by official Soviet institutions. But in exile, both of them changed, and this was particularly true for Nekrich, so that, Heller concluded, "in the end we developed a common point of view on history."[136]

A clear expression of this convergence of viewpoints was Nekrich's willingness to deal with the most controversial issues in Soviet history: he had decided to "write about events that have been kept secret by Soviet historiography as fully as possible," on the basis of "concrete facts." These included the 1939 Ribentropp-Molotov pact, Katyn, the Finno-Soviet war, the Vlasov movement, the treatment of Soviet prisoners of war, the deportation of "punished peoples," or wartime losses.[137] Significantly, Heller expressed his satisfaction precisely with Nekrich's treatment of those most delicate issues.[138] Moreover, they converged in their ambition to write a comprehensive work encompassing, not simply the history of the Soviet people, but also of their Russian compatriots who had emigrated following the Revolution or after the war. Their own experience obviously justified this interest, but it also stemmed from a desire to enlighten their potential Soviet readers about a culture they had been radically cut off from by the Iron Curtain. Nekrich argued that such a perspective would allow for "an organic inclusion of Russia abroad in the common history of the country" for the first time.[139]

Nevertheless, minor divergences in approaches also emerged. When Heller insisted on placing an emphasis on popular resistance to the regime, Nekrich expressed fears about the lack of available material, but was also wary not to distort reality. He insisted on the progressive evolution of the people, from enthusiasm for socialism to disenchantment. "Concerning resistance to the authorities—that's very good. And we should write about it.... [But] apart from resistance, there was also *enthusiasm*."[140] On the other hand, he approved of Heller's decision to write only briefly about intraparty struggles. In the center of their attention should be the people: "How the people lived, how it built a new state, which enslaved it [the people], and how [the people] itself changed, without even noticing it—in the sense of psychology, etc. And what the result was."[141] Nekrich probably had his own experience in mind, which contrasted with Heller's trajectory through the Gulag.

Still, overall, the coauthors converged in their harsh critique of the Soviet regime. The purpose of their work was to counter the monopoly exercised by the authorities over Soviet history. Rejecting attempts by some Soviet historians to trace the roots of the communist regime back to medieval times, Heller and Nekrich drew a sharp line between the Russian and Soviet eras. They agreed with Solzhenitsyn's view that the October Revolution operated a transition that "was not a continuation of the spinal column, but a disastrous fracture that very nearly caused the nation's total destruction."[142] By taking total control over "all spheres of existence on a scale never before known," the Party had "distorted the normal processes at work in contemporary societies and ha[d] resulted in the emergence of a historically unprecedented society and state."[143] Yet the people did not remain passive:

> The history of the Soviet Union is one of a society and state subjugated to a party, that of a state which has enslaved society, and that of a party which seized state power in order to create a human type that would allow it to keep power forever. It is also, however, a history of eloquent human resistance to that enslavement.[144]

Nekrich's initial idea of writing for the Soviet reader was based on the belief that enlightenment about the past was essential to reveal the regime's true nature. Citing Orwell in their introduction, the authors stated: "Memory makes us human. Without it people are turned into a formless mass that can be shaped into anything the controllers of the past desire."[145] However, this orientation progressively retreated to the background—probably because publishers required a focus on a Western audience. Nevertheless, Nekrich seems to have stuck to his early intention of smuggling the book into the Soviet Union. When negotiating contracts, he insisted that the agreement state that the royalties should depend on the number of copies, but not on the number of copies sold, since in the Soviet Union, the book would not be sold.[146] *Utopia in Power* was written in 1978-79 and first published in France in 1982, with subsequent editions in Russian, German, Italian, English, and Polish.

In a dissident trajectory, inner emigration—often followed by arrest—or exile constituted the ultimate stages of a process of estrangement from the system. This process had been punctuated by regular "prophylactic" warnings, which discouraged the majority of *inakomysliashchie* from persevering in their dissenting activities. Only the most determined persisted. The KGB's strategy of encouraging the emigration of dissidents in the 1970s was a clever move: it offered a way out for those who, like Nekrich, had grown tired of living with a mask, or who were on the verge of being arrested for their activities; those who would not leave of their own initiative could be presented with an ultimatum to emigrate; and sometimes, prominent dissidents could be exchanged with Soviet spies or political prisoners from the Western bloc. This emigration policy, which was welcomed and encouraged by the West, was compatible with détente and a good substitute for judicial prosecution. It did not signify the end of activism, however: as the example of Nekrich or Zhores Medvedev shows, despite a personal situation that was often precarious, emigration often allowed dissidents to pursue their activism in new forms. Nekrich even felt emboldened by his new freedom, after having been dominated by fear for so long, as the title of his memoirs *Forsaking Fear* shows.

A minority of dissidents, however, could not conceive of life in exile and refused all ultimatums to emigrate. For little-known dissenters, it usually meant accepting judicial prosecution, but for famous figures such as Roy Medvedev, whose arrest or deportation within the country or abroad would have caused considerable international outcry, inner emigration could be a lasting option, provided they did not cross a red line. Both Solzhenitsyn and Sakharov eventually crossed this line: their moral considerations outweighed any fear they may have had for their own fate. Medvedev, by contrast, considered the possibility to pursue his work unimpeded of greater importance than the urge to get across a particular viewpoint. His caution and unwillingness to provoke the authorities, coupled with the moderation of his stance, caused accusations of collusion, which I find, however, to be unjustified.

None of the researchers examined in this study were sentenced to imprisonment in the post-Stalin era. Beyond the factor of celebrity and the support they enjoyed within the intelligentsia, which contributed to protect all of them, another factor that may arguably be pointed to was the enduring legitimacy of anti-Stalinist narratives. What had once been allowed into the open could hardly be wholly shoved under the carpet. The 22nd Party Congress's resolutions had never been repealed, and anti-Stalinism represented a less threatening language than that of human rights. Only narratives equating Leninism with Stalinism were fundamentally anti-Soviet. This distinction would be important when these dissident researchers' works would be published in the Soviet Union during Perestroika.

These differences in emphasis, justified by various political views and interpretations of the meaning of the Stalin era in Soviet history, also provided for conflicts among dissident researchers. Indeed, although all claimed to be restoring historical truth, there were not one, but several, sometimes antagonistic renditions of this "truth." For these authors wrote with various moral, political, and personal motives, sometimes with an inner self-censorship, and with varying concern for factual accuracy.

7

Diverging Truths

As she reviewed one of Solzhenitsyn's works, the Russian writer Tat'iana Tolstaia acerbically noted: "As is well-known, Aleksandr Solzhenitsyn supposes that there is a single truth, that the truth is one. The combined evidence of his work, especially his polemical articles, suggests also that he believes it is known to him alone."[1] This belief in a single truth, concealed by the Soviet regime and ready to be uncovered, was certainly a powerful driving force for dissident researchers. In his February 1974 pamphlet "Live not by lies," Solzhenitsyn called on each and every one to refuse partaking in the general lie imposed by the regime.[2] This motive was also central to his 1970 Nobel Prize Lecture. In his call "One word of truth shall outweigh the whole world," addressed to writers worldwide, he expressed his conviction that artists bore a particular responsibility for mankind's moral development. "But writers and artists can achieve more: they can CONQUER FALSEHOOD! . . . And no sooner will falsehood be dispersed than the nakedness of violence will be revealed in all its ugliness—and violence, decrepit, will fall."[3] Solzhenitsyn's stark binaries of truth and falsehood, good and evil, stood in contrast with the murky morals and daily compromises with one's conscience characteristic of Soviet life, but also with the "political expediency" that dictated the relevance of historical themes in the Soviet Union. An uncompromising moral stance and a thirst for justice are everywhere the propelling forces of dissent, but the primary moral function of dissident histories was also in tension with their value as documents claiming to record the past "truthfully."

The Gulag Archipelago opened with the statement: "In this book there are no fictitious persons, nor fictitious events. . . . It all took place just as it is here described."[4] Nevertheless, Solzhenitsyn's concern for veracity varied. The accuracy of individual accounts seemed irrelevant for "anthropological" chapters describing a prisoner's path: what mattered was not the truth of the detail, but the broader truth of the picture, which emerged from the sheer volume of testimonies. One person's words could be contested, but the voices of hundreds could hardly be denied value. However, when Solzhenitsyn resorted to oral testimonies for historical sections, his literary verve sometimes conflicted with historical accuracy. Nevertheless, he believed in the inherent ethical value of Gulag survivors' testimonies. He set modest boundaries to his role as author: "I would not be so bold as to try to write the history of the Archipelago. I have never had the chance to read the documents. And, in fact, will anyone ever have the chance to read them?" What he did have was a firsthand experience of that world, as well as testimonies, documents, and letters he had received.⁵ More than a privilege, Solzhenitsyn considered these testimonies entrusted to him as a responsibility: he had become the "accredited chronicler of camp life, to whom people brought the whole truth."⁶ It was therefore this sense of a moral mission that was paramount for dissident authors and explains the dangers to which they willingly exposed themselves for the sake of sharing their works with the Soviet people.

In the late 1960s, the notion of "restoration of historical truth" had become a common trope in samizdat. What the authors sought to restore was *pravda*, truth as justice: Stalin's crimes had cost the lives of millions, and present generations had the duty to honor their memory and expose perpetrators. Transparency (*glasnost'*), set in opposition to censorship, was the precondition for the revelation of historical truth, just as active dissimulation of the past was the accomplice of crime. Roy Medvedev thus wrote in *Let History Judge*: "We now know that Stalin's crimes were so great that it would be a crime to remain silent about them."⁷

From the realization of a collective responsibility before the victims' memory to the individual vocation to "restore historical truth," whatever the cost might be, there was but one step that dissident researchers crossed with a sentiment of righteousness. Antonov-Ovseenko thus described his moral mission in the introduction to his 1980 biography of Stalin: "It is the duty of every honest person to write the truth about Stalin. A duty to those who died at his hands, to those who survived that dark night, to those who will come after us.⁸ This language of ethical duty hardly fitted Western representations about scholarly commitment to objectivity and impartiality. Yet, Antonov-Ovseenko embraced subjectivity as a necessary by-product of personal experience. He had lost both of his parents to political repression and had spent his youth in the camps. After belatedly realizing "Stalin's true place in history and in the life of our society," he felt the need to speak out. "I understood that to remain silent about Stalin today is to betray. And I resolved to do my duty as a human being."⁹

However, these embattled researchers struggled not only against the regime's lies, but also, increasingly, against each other. As Tolstaya's quote emphasized, Solzhenitsyn's messianic stance of the prophet who brings truth to the world, so attuned to Cold War thinking, also caused the author to step into frequent polemics with bearers of alternative truths. Indeed, beyond the moral motives that animated their authors, dissident histories also followed a political agenda. For Medvedev, public knowledge about past crimes was needed, "not only because the ashes of our tortured fathers and brothers continue to burn in our hearts," but also to prevent a repetition of past abuses and to allow the Party to "move forward in the necessary direction."¹⁰ No less pervasive was the political subtext of *The Gulag Archipelago*. Therefore, the two closely intertwined moral and political dimensions of dissident historical works explain Western historians' criticism, but also internecine feuds among their authors. The "truth" they revealed was bound to be subjective, one-sided, partial, and deeply political. Solzhenitsyn's "anti-Communist truth" about the Soviet repressive system could not but contradict Medvedev's "liberal Marxist truth" about Stalinism. And the authors' occasional cavalier treatment of facts could not but undermine their claim to be restoring "historical truth."

This chapter will examine the conflicts that arose among dissident researchers on factual and political grounds. In addition to the largely political opposition between Medvedev and Solzhenitsyn, which took a number of forms, I will consider the conflict between Anton Antonov-Ovseenko and a group of young dissident researchers who criticized his work for its factual inaccuracies. Finally, I will make the case for considering dissident histories as a specific genre distinct from both literature and professional historiography, and therefore obeying different imperatives.

Two truths about the Soviet past

Medvedev's Liberal Marxist truth

Medvedev concluded his introduction to *Let History Judge* by reaffirming "that it is communists who should be the strictest judges of their own history." To "restore the unity, moral purity, and strength of this great movement" had been "the prime motive of [his] work, which in all respects has been far from easy."[11] The book's subtitle, "The Origins and Consequences of Stalinism," clearly circumscribed the study, but also showed that the author considered Stalinism as a phenomenon taking roots in previous developments.

In his preface to the English edition of the book, David Joravsky recognized that "the Soviet audience for which this book was written would take for granted many things that may puzzle or annoy outsiders," in particular Medvedev's sharp distinction between Stalinism and Communism.[12] Medvedev's emphasis on Stalin's criminal intent in the rise of terror was justified by his belief that a deterministic approach focusing on long-term historical trends would amount to "a denial of Stalin's responsibility." American readers, recognized Joravsky, may find this to be a "simpleminded confusion of historical causation and moral responsibility." Yet, the historian's nuanced approach to scales of responsibility along the political hierarchy showed the reproach to be unfair.[13]

Western reviewers of *Let History Judge*, while unanimously praising the quality of Medvedev's research, have invariably pointed out his political bias.[14] Marshall Shatz criticized the dissident for his "glorification" of the October Revolution, and his tendency to consider "historically necessary and justifiable" anything that contributed to its success. Medvedev failed to see that the Revolution had accustomed people to violence and led to "a cheapening of human life by justifying its sacrifices in the name of ideological principles."[15] Robert Slusser also acknowledged that Medvedev's communist convictions had a "pervasive influence in the book."[16] Yet he implicitly recognized that American historians themselves wore political blinkers. Their critique of Medvedev for failing to understand the allegedly obvious connection between Lenin's policies and Stalinism betrayed their own incapacity to interrogate the historical roots of Stalinism, a question they deemed solved once and for all. And despite his tendency to absolve Lenin of any responsibility for subsequent developments, Medvedev did trace the roots of Stalinism back to the first years of the regime and gave "the fullest and most searching analysis of this problem yet provided by any scholar." Slusser therefore hoped that his treatment of the question would "lead to a profound rethinking of it" in the West.[17]

The first two parts of *Let History Judge* dealt with the origins and causes of Stalinism. In part one, he retraced the dictator's ascent to power, the development of his cult, and his increasing use of political repression, starting from his struggle with the opposition and his conduct of collectivization and industrialization, down to Kirov's assassination and the Great Terror. Part two examined the question of Stalin's responsibility and conditions that had facilitated his "usurpation of power." In the third part, finally, Medvedev analyzed the long-term impact of Stalinism: its consequences for the conduct of the Second World War; its impact on domestic policies in the field of agriculture, industry, nationality politics, arts and sciences; and, finally, on the functioning of the Party and state.

Echoing official rhetoric, Medvedev used the metaphor of an illness to describe the relation of Stalinism to socialism. The exposure of Stalin's cult had been the first step toward recovery, but "the process of purifying the communist movement, of washing out all the layers of Stalinist filth" was by no means over and had to "be carried out through to the end."[18] By defining Stalinism as a disease, Medvedev accomplished two goals. First, he escaped the accusation of creating a "new personality cult in reverse" by attributing the blame for Stalin-era crimes to a sole figure. This allowed for an examination of the whole command chain that had underpinned the system of terror. The historian thus recognized that "Stalin involved millions of people in his crimes. Not only the punitive organs but the entire Party and government *apparat* participated actively in the campaigns of the 1930s." And all levels of the hierarchy were concerned, down to "millions of ordinary people [who] took part in meetings and demonstrations demanding severe reprisals against 'enemies.'"[19] Stalin's personality cult explained in part such collective hysteria, but Medvedev also examined other factors that had facilitated his ascent to power, many of which preexisted the cult, such as the Party's centralization, the notion of "party discipline," or the role of punitive organs created in the wake of the Revolution. Although Medvedev insisted that Stalinism could have been avoided, he identified "hereditary factors" that provided a "favorable terrain" for the disease, implicitly inculpating Lenin and the Party as a whole.

Second, the metaphor of the illness implied both the possibility and the necessity of a cure. The system had not been fatally wounded, it could recover, but this would demand serious measures for the restoration of party democracy and socialist legality. Although Khrushchev's reforms had shown the way, a lot remained to be done. In this regard, *Let History Judge* should be considered in conjunction with Medvedev's work of political philosophy *On Socialist Democracy*,[20] which appeared shortly thereafter and drew a political program for the democratization of the Soviet system. The Stalin era had been, in Medvedev's conception, a period characterized "not only [by] the struggle between socialism and capitalism in their open manifestations but also [by] the struggle between socialism and barrack pseudosocialism."[21] Medvedev's position thus stood in opposition to two currents of thought, which both considered the Stalin era as an intrinsic part of the communist experience: the anti-Communist current, which threw the baby of socialism out with the bath of Stalinism; and the neo-Stalinist current, which glorified Stalinism as the apogee of socialist construction.

Medvedev's representation of Lenin in *Let History Judge* directly derived from his conception of Stalinism. Just as nations need a usable past for their identity construction, ideology-based regimes need positive ideological references. In the post-Stalin era, filling the gap left by the denunciation of Stalin's cult, Lenin achieved in Soviet ideology a godly status: he had become a distant, semi-mythical figure whose word was sacred and whose image inspired veneration.[22] Characteristically, *Let History Judge* opened with four epigraphs on the need for truth and self-critique, by Alexander Herzen, Rosa Luxemburg and two by Lenin, thus anchoring Medvedev's words in references to the classics of Marxist-Leninist thought. In the first chapter, describing Stalin's ascension to power in the Party, the historian repeatedly emphasized Stalin's disagreements with Lenin, and in particular Lenin's "Testament," in which the Soviet leader called on the Party to remove Stalin from the position of General Secretary. On the whole, Medvedev remained very close to the "faithful Leninist" critique of Stalinism, such as was found among student revisionist Marxist circles of the 1950s or among Old Bolsheviks. In later years, he would slightly sharpen his critique of Lenin,[23] but in *Let History Judge*, his main task was to denounce Stalin.

An interesting critique of *Let History Judge* was given by Boris Souvarine,[24] a prominent French communist who had spent a few years in Moscow in the early 1920s, before being expelled from the French Communist Party for his opposition to its "bolshevization." In 1935, he had authored the first critical biography of Stalin and subsequently spent his life denouncing Stalinism. His appraisal of Medvedev's work was nuanced: although he harshly criticized the author's style and bias, he recognized that "his ideological position gives added weight to his work and the series of testimonies he brings up." Despite closely following "in Khruschev's footsteps" and remaining "faithful to the Party's theses," Medvedev went far beyond the authorized boundaries, producing a "staggering document." Admittedly, the historian's deference toward the Party and self-censorship made for a disconcerting "Dzhugashvilesque" style.[25] "Some phrases thus seem to have been written as a counterweight to others, to defend the author against inevitable accusations and give him the possibility of pushing through an even more serious critique and more naked truth."[26] Nor could Medvedev wholly detach himself from the spirit of Marxism-Leninism in which he had been formed, "despite his sincere wish to to bring his contribution to the search for historical truth, which lies beyond the ideas he [can] receive."[27] The pervasive influence of ingrained dogmas was particularly visible in his unreflective use of such ideological stamps as "personality cult," "repressions,"—to qualify reprisals against innocents—or "petty bourgeois"—in relation to Stalin. According to Souvarine, the only cult had been "the cult of the party created by Lenin," which had transformed the "dictatorship of the proletariat" into a "dictatorship of the Central Committee," and, in the final instance, of Stalin. Medvedev heavily criticized Trotsky, Zinoviev, Bukharin, Kamenev, and others, while Lenin remained exempt from any serious critique.[28]

Nevertheless, Souvarine insisted that the unprecedented wealth of hitherto unknown documentation and testimonies collected outweighed any possible criticism. Although the theme of the book was not new, and Souvarine himself had explored it, "for obvious reasons, Medvedev leaves behind all previously existing documentary compilations."[29] The reviewer emphatically concluded:

Medvedev thus widely transcends his Marxism-Leninism, having compiled and presented a truly apocalyptic document. Animated by his moral impulses, uncompromising and unconditional, he, by his own words, will stand in front of the tribunal of History, "as an unforgetting prosecution witness." Thousands of books written about the Soviet Union will disappear and be forgotten, but his testimony will remain forever.[30]

Western critiques of *Let History Judge* betrayed the fundamental discrepancy between the intended audience of the book, the Soviet public, and the actual Western and Russian émigré readership Medvedev reached by resorting to tamizdat publication. For understandable reasons, after opting for publication abroad, he had not rewritten his book to make his argument fit a Western historiography he was very poorly acquainted with at this stage. Nor could he abandon his central political conception, which he had adopted not on opportunistic grounds, but as a result of deeply held socialist views he would retain throughout his life. Nevertheless, like other dissident researchers, he did convince a large public, less by his interpretation than by the moral strength of his statement.

Solzhenitsyn's anti-Communist truth

Solzhenitsyn's "truth" about the Soviet past contrasted markedly with Medvedev's. The writer ostensibly shunned the term "Stalinism" and did not emphasize Lenin and Stalin as historical figures, depicting instead the Terror as a product of the Soviet system, rather than the result of individuals' will. It was the communist regime, be it in its most extreme embodiment under Stalin's iron grip, or in its milder Brezhnevite form, and foremost its ideology, that was the source of *evil*.

The Gulag Archipelago was also fundamentally original in its construction. Within a general chronological framework charting the history of the Gulag, the author inserted chapters retracing an individual's path to and within the camps. The reader followed each stage of the journey, from arrest to sentencing, from transfer to the camps to liberation. The alternation of narrative and historical chapters created an illusion of continuity and uniformity, as individual testimonies from the 1920s to the 1950s merged into a common collective experience. The writer used metaphors from geography, but also from natural sciences to describe processes seemingly escaping human grasp. The Gulag, this "small zone" of confinement, was an "archipelago," both separate and intimately connected to the "greater zone" of unfreedom on the "continent." But it did not have the fixity of geographical features: it grew and metastasized as the cancerous tumor Solzhenitsyn had developed in detention.[31] And just as the tumor "exuded poisons and infected the whole body," "our whole country was infected by the poisons of the Archipelago."[32] Yet Solzhenitsyn's use of the metaphor of illness fundamentally differed from Medvedev's: he saw this disease not as a distortion, but a product of socialism; and the only cure was excision of the tumor from Russia's body.

In contrast to the official chronology of Stalin-era terror, peaking in 1937, Solzhenitsyn identified countless "waves" or "flows" of repressions. These streams and rivers of varying width all led to a common "sewage disposal system."[33] In this "natural" order, personalities played only a limited role: Stalin, the continuator, stood in the shadow of Lenin, the initiator. Solzhenitsyn pushed Stalin's symbolical dethronement to the utmost, mockingly referring to him as "Great Leader," "the Wise Teacher," guided by the "One-and-only-true" Teaching, Marxism-Leninism. Lenin, on the other hand, appeared determined, cruel, and pitiless. Already in December 1917, he was reflecting on new forms of punishment. "And even while sitting peacefully among the fragrant hay mowings of Razliv and listening to the buzzing bumblebees, Lenin could not help but ponder the future penal system."[34]

Solzhenitsyn openly contested official justifications of past crimes. More than paltry admissions to the commission of "certain errors," what was required was the courage to point to the Party's, and not just Stalin's, responsibility. "If Stalin committed all these errors—where were you at the time, you ruling millions?" asked the writer provocatively.[35] Recalling his own tendency to abuse power during his short officer's career, Solzhenitsyn recognized that evil people as such did not exist, only the ideas that guided them were at fault. While the system tended to pervert men, and turn them into informers or hangmen, an inner path to freedom and enlightenment was open to those who experienced prison. Intoxicated by his early successes, he had acted cruelly, covering his actions with a veneer of ideology. Only in the camps had he experienced "the first stirrings of good." "Gradually it was disclosed to me that the line separating good and evil passes not through states, nor between classes, nor between political parties either—but right through every human heart—and through all human hearts."[36] Evil could not be entirely expelled from the world, as revolutions tried to do in vain, it could only be "constricted" within each human being through moral rectitude.[37] Religion, then, was a fundamental positive reference point standing in opposition to the Soviet system's force of evil. Another positive reference was tsarist Russia, whose excessively "mild," "humane" penal regime Solzhenitsyn set in contrast with the Soviet Gulag. This leitmotif aimed at drawing a sharp historical boundary in 1917 and pointed to a suitable political alternative to the communist regime.[38]

Martin Malia, who reviewed the three volumes of *Gulag* in 1977, observed that Soviet readers had been divided in their reactions. Although they were "virtually unanimous in their satisfaction that something approximating the full story of Soviet terror has at last been recorded," they were more ambivalent about Solzhenitsyn's political message. Only a minority accepted it unequivocally, while the majority found Solzhenitsyn's "debatable or even obnoxious" ideological observations secondary, given his work's moral importance, and only a small minority rejected *Gulag* outright for being politically harmful.[39] In the West, however, the book's reception had been undermined by the polemics surrounding Solzhenitsyn's public pronouncements in exile.

For Malia, *The Gulag Archipelago* was a fundamentally political work, albeit in a characteristically Russian manner. Its primary function was truth-telling, as a prerequisite for justice:

> Only once this Truth has been told will it be possible to break the spell of the Lie which holds the nation in thrall; for Soviet power rests on the mute complicity of an entire society in pretending to believe what everyone knows is false (II, 632-636).

The Gulag is thus first of all history as exorcism, exorcism of all the unavowed demons of the Soviet past, which, until they have been named and branded, will continue to corrupt the whole of national life.[40]

Solzhenitsyn had broken the silence forever for the world to judge and turned his work "into a surrogate for a Nuremberg Trial of Stalinism, both before the Soviet public and before the West."[41] Those who claimed that he had hardly revealed any new information were mistaken. The power of the book lay in the writer's truer-than-life rendition of each stage of a prisoner's experience. And his very lack of psychological objectivity, expressed in the "gallows humor that accompanies the revelation of each new horror," only added to the work's credibility.[42]

Gulag offered the most comprehensive and searching overview of the camps' history to date. But the influence of the author's ideological position was too paramount to be ignored. Three main lines of interpretation emerged: the equation of communism and fascism; the discontinuity between the Tsarist and Soviet eras; and the "monolithic character of the Soviet phenomenon" from the Revolution to the present day. Malia agreed with Solzhenitsyn's claim that "the ideological and institutional framework that made the mass psychosis, the epic holocaust of Stalinism possible, and indeed easy" originated with Lenin. Hence the impossibility of reforming communism, which had "entrenched itself on a mountain of unavowed and unexpiated crimes during the reign of Stalin."[43]

Although the writer's designation of ideology as the source of evil was based on an oversimplified "caricature" of Marxism-Leninism, it was precisely in this form that it had been applied, not only in the USSR, but in other socialist states. And Marx's or Lenin's original motives, however "humanistic" they may have been, eventually mattered little to Solzhenitsyn.[44] But by emphasizing the role of ideology, Solzhenitsyn could also symbolically absolve Russia for generating this evil, which originated in European thought. Therefore, the Western Left was rightly ambivalent about *Gulag*: although the author pleaded "the cause of the oppressed," and addressed other traditional values of the Left, his plea was voiced in terms "directly antithetical to most programmatic positions of the Left." Solzhenitsyn had thus failed in his crusade against ideology. Nevertheless, Malia concluded, no one could deny him "the rank of the foremost Russian writer-prophet of the Soviet era."[45]

While Western reviewers were ambivalent about the political message of dissident histories but did not feel they had the moral legitimacy to criticize these works, dissident researchers showed much less restraint in the polemics they engaged in against each other, and this was particularly visible in the conflicts between Medvedev and Solzhenitsyn.

Skirmishes on the historical battlefield

That the authors of two works indicting the history of Soviet political repression should have come into conflict was in no way predetermined, although their ideological differences made this a likely outcome. In the 1960s, Zhores Medvedev and Solzhenitsyn had developed what Zhores called in retrospect "a business-oriented friendship of two *samizdat* authors, who strove to unite their various forces and possibilities for a common goal."[46] As Zhores recounts in his memoirs and in several books,[47] he first met the writer in September 1964. The geneticist was then facing potential repression for his manuscript on Lysenko, and Solzhenitsyn contacted him to express his support. In 1970, he protested Medvedev's psychiatric incarceration. In 1972, Zhores devoted a memoir to their friendship, entitled *Ten Years after Ivan Denisovich*.[48] However, after Zhores's forced emigration, in 1973, their relationship began to deteriorate. When Solzhenitsyn was arrested, Roy Medvedev made an official declaration in his support, calling on the authorities to release him.[49] In March, Zhores offered to visit the writer in Zurich, but Solzhenitsyn met this proposal with a rebuttal, judging that such a friendship "confused Europeans, blurred all boundaries."[50]

Reasons for this conflict were not simply personal, but largely political. Starting from the fall of 1973, the Medvedev brothers took publicly position in favor of détente, in opposition to Sakharov and Solzhenitsyn's positions.[51] The dissident community perceived the Medvedevs' stance as pro-regime, and it earned them many enemies, on both sides of the Iron Curtain. By December 1973, they were the object of violent attacks in the Russian émigré press. The writer Vladimir Maksimov thus reproached them with attacking "selflessly spirited people of our time, Russia's moral pride, the academician Sakharov and Aleksandr Solzhenitsyn," precisely when their lives were at risk.[52] In the following years, Solzhenitsyn repeatedly attacked the Medvedev brothers in the press.

Medvedev's review of *The Gulag Archipelago*

A clear reflection of the divergences between Solzhenitsyn and Medvedev are the historian's reviews of the three volumes of *The Gulag Archipelago*. Admittedly, each text must be considered within the context of its writing. In January 1974, Medvedev received the first volume of *Gulag* and wrote a review for the American press. This first appraisal by a Soviet reader also circulated in samizdat.[53] Out of solidarity for a fellow dissident who was the object of a smear campaign in the Soviet media and might be arrested at any moment, but also under the strong impression produced by the book, Medvedev initially adopted a conciliatory tone. The two other reviews, however, appeared at a time when Solzhenitsyn and Zhores Medvedev engaged in open warfare in the Western media.

As he reviewed the first volume, Medvedev took pains to defend Solzhenitsyn against the allegations of Soviet propaganda. Solzhenitsyn's facts were not "unreliable fancies of a morbid imagination or cynical falsifications," as *Pravda* claimed.[54] And if there were a few inaccuracies, inevitable in the conditions of secrecy in which Solzhenitsyn wrote, "the number of errors [was] very small in a work of such weight."[55] Nor was *Literaturnaia gazeta* justified in saying that *Gulag* "contained nothing new." "Although I have been studying Stalinism for over a decade, the book told me a great deal I had not known before. With the exception of former inmates of the camps, Soviet readers . . . know hardly one tenth of the facts recounted by Solzhenitsyn."[56]

Nevertheless, Medvedev disagreed with Solzhenitsyn's interpretation of Lenin and Stalin's respective roles. Recognizing that the delineation between the Stalin era and the revolutionary period was artificial, Medvedev pleaded for considering minor political turning points, such as 1937, 1934, 1929, 1924, or 1922. Stalinism was "a genuine counter-revolution," he claimed, and future research would show that Stalin had taken "sharp turns and fundamental reversals" in relation to "Leninist norms."[57] Still, he recognized the need to analyze Lenin's role in the early revolutionary period with utmost scrutiny. Although he deemed some degree of violence during the Revolution and Civil War inevitable, he could not deny "that already in the first years of Soviet power the reasonable limits of such violence were frequently overstepped." Yet, he remained "convinced that the overall balance sheet of Lenin's activity was positive."[58] Despite Solzhenitsyn's refutation of the term "Stalinism," Medvedev concluded that *Gulag* had inflicted neo-Stalinism the heaviest blow ever.[59]

In his review of the second volume, the historian still praised *Gulag* but stated more openly his disagreement on some crucial questions.[60] While acknowledging that Lenin created concentration camps in 1918, Medvedev insisted that it would be a mistake to compare these early camps to the Stalin-era Gulag and pleaded for taking into account the context of the Civil War. More importantly, he disagreed with Solzhenitsyn's judgment that the repression of communist leaders was justified by their previous crimes. Among the victims were leaders with very diverse personal qualities, who also differed in their degree of responsibility for the "lawlessness" of previous years. Alongside some "deeply depraved" leaders, there were others who were simply "misguided," blinded by "the cult of party discipline" or well-intentioned but confused by official propaganda.[61] Overall, Medvedev judged the death of most revolutionary Bolsheviks "one of the most terrible tragedies in the history of our country." "One should clearly state that no man deserved the terrible fate that befell the leaders arrested in 1937-38. And it is impossible to relish the thought of their humiliations and sufferings, even if one does know that many of them deserved the penalty of death."[62]

Medvedev also opposed Solzhenitsyn's views on redemption through religion. Not only religious people were capable of moral judgment, as the writer seemed to imply. Socialism, even though it had hitherto failed to elaborate "a fully satisfactory solution of ethical and moral problems" could become "the basis of a truly humanist morality."[63] Conversely, religion, just as any ideology, could easily be "distorted and turned against man and humanity," instances of such "obscurantism" abounded in the past, including in the history of the Orthodox Church.[64]

The third review was written in a more belligerent tone. Although Medvedev reiterated that *Gulag* was "one of the greatest books of the twentieth century,"[65] he vehemently attacked several key conceptions underpinning the third volume. In contrast to the first volumes, the last part had met with little sensation in the West. The reason, Medvedev claimed, was that Solzhenitsyn had alienated the traditionally liberal audience, which read the most, by advancing "many reactionary and utopian ideas and . . . some obviously absurd theories, revealing his lack of knowledge of the elementary facts of both Russian and world history."[66] Increasingly, the question of veracity arose, since Solzhenitsyn had begun resorting to "flagrant distortion, juggling of the facts, deliberate omission or . . . smear techniques against people he does not agree with."⁶⁷ These methods had created doubts about the trustworthiness of his work. Therefore, Medvedev felt obliged to confirm "that all of the basic facts about the Gulag Archipelago presented in the third volume do correspond to the truth."⁶⁸ Nevertheless, he asserted that

> if one were to follow the formula used in the American court system.... "Do you swear to tell the truth, the whole truth, and nothing but the truth?" Solzhenitsyn would not be able to assent to the last two parts of this formula. For the terrible truth the great artist has revealed to the world in his book bears within it a layer of untrue and tendentious argument that, though not great in size, is rather obtrusive in substance.⁶⁹

The historian particularly disagreed with Solzhenitsyn's apology for Russian collaboration with Nazi Germany during the Second World War. He also criticized Solzhenitsyn's double standards in judging the positive or negative actions of communists and non-party members. Moreover, he deplored the writer's ridiculing of "the supposed 'savagery' of the Russian Tsars" and his expressed regret that tsarist repression against socialists had been too mild, failing to prevent their ascent to power.⁷⁰ Finally, he denounced Solzhenitsyn's claim that he and other camp prisoners had hoped for a Third World War to rescue them from their ordeal. Medvedev severely concluded that Solzhenitsyn was a victim of the Stalin era, and besides "firmness and courage,... extraordinary persistence and stubbornness," these sufferings had fostered in him "bitter intransigence bordering on fanaticism, fierce attachment to a single, narrow idea," intolerance for other people's convictions, a Manichean outlook and a firm belief that the end justifies the means. Indeed, the techniques he used to combat socialism were only "too reminiscent of everything he justly denounces" in *The Gulag Archipelago*.⁷¹

Solzhenitsyn replied to these reviews fiercely. In the press conference he gave in Stockholm following his Nobel Prize lecture, in December 1974, he commented on Medvedev's first review. The historian's goal, he claimed, had been to "neutralize" his book through an essentially negative review, published before *Gulag* was available in translation in the West. Moreover, Medvedev had come to the defense of Lenin, the idea of communism, and "those very Old Bolsheviks who until the last day before arrest helped the grinding machine destroy others." Medvedev himself, Solzhenitsyn warned, was no dissident: "Nothing threatens him personally, because he, generally speaking, defends the regime in the best way—more cleverly and flexibly than the official press can."⁷²

These confrontations may have been justified by the two authors' diverging views, but by sorely dividing the dissident community, they resulted in Medvedev's growing isolation. This was aggravated by his defense of an Old Menshevik who had every reason to resent Solzhenitsyn.

Mikhail Iakubovich against "Vetrov"

In January 1975, as Roy Medvedev founded a samizdat and tamizdat journal of socialist orientation entitled *Twentieth Century* (*XX vek*), he opened his pages to Mikhail

Iakubovich, whose account of the trial of the "All-Union Bureau of Mensheviks" he had reproduced in *Let History Judge*.[73] Through Medvedev's journal, the old *zek* was able to regain a public credibility which he felt *The Gulag Archipelago* had undermined. Solzhenitsyn had used Iakubovich's testimony in his work to demonstrate how show trials of the 1930s were organized, how the accused were led to confess to the most absurd crimes. The writer thus described Iakubovich's interrogation by Prosecutor General Nikolai Krylenko:

> It turned out that they knew one another very well. . . . And here is what Krylenko now said:
> Mikhail Petrovich, I am going to talk to you frankly: I consider you a Communist! [His words encouraged Yakubovich and raised his spirits greatly.] I have no doubt of your innocence. But it is our Party duty, yours and mine, to carry out this trial. [Krylenko had gotten his orders from Stalin, and Yakubovich was all atremble for the sake of the cause, like a zealous horse rushing into the horse collar.] I beg you to help me in every possible way, and to assist the interrogation. And in case of unforeseen difficulties during the trial, at the most difficult moments, I will ask the chairman of the court to give you the floor.
> !!!!
> And Yakubovich promised. Conscious of his duty, he promised. Indeed, the Soviet government had never before given him such a responsible assignment. And thus there was not the slightest need even to touch Yakubovich during the interrogation. But that was too subtle for the GPU. Like everyone else, Yakubovich was handed over to the butcher-interrogators, and they gave him the full treatment—the freezing punishment cell, the hot box, beating his genitals. They tortured him so intensively that Yakubovich and his fellow defendant Abram Ginzburg opened their veins in desperation. . . .
> And at the trial Yakubovich not only repeated obediently all the gray mass of lies which constituted the upper limit of Stalin's imagination . . . . But he also played out his inspired role, as he had promised Krylenko.[74]

In Solzhenitsyn's account, the sequence of events defied all logic: why torture Yakubovich if he had already agreed to play the part expected from him? The question was not trivial. Through Iakubovich's example, Solzhenitsyn sought to establish a model applicable to all 1936–38 show trials. "And I find that it is altogether as though Bukharin or Rykov were explaining the reasons for their own mysterious submissiveness at their trials. Theirs were the same sincerity and honesty, the same devotion to the Party, the same human weakness, the same lack of the moral strength needed to fight back, because they had no individual position."[75] While the writer had skillfully used individual testimonies to depict the collective experience of the Gulag, he was on weaker ground when he sought to build sweeping historical generalizations on the basis of a single testimony.[76]

In contrast, Medvedev's version of Iakubovich's story in *Let History Judge* was the exact rendition of the witness's words, as he reproduced *in extenso* Iakubovich's account of his trial in his petition for rehabilitation, sent to the Public Prosecutor of the

Soviet Union in May 1967.[77] Solzhenitsyn had received a copy of this document shortly thereafter.[78] The tone was radically different: after describing the inhuman tortures that had led him to sign false confessions and his suicide attempt, Iakubovich expressed the moral dilemma he faced: "I was beside myself. How should I behave at the trial? Deny the depositions I had made during the investigation? Create a worldwide scandal? Whom would that help? Wouldn't it be a stab in the back of the Soviet regime and the Communist Party?" Moreover, Iakubovich feared the reprisals that awaited him if he revoked his previous deposition. "If it were only death. I wanted death. I sought, I tried to die. But they wouldn't let me die; they would slowly torture me, torture for an infinitely long time." It was in such a state of mind that he had been summoned to Krylenko's office. In reply to Krylenko's request that Iakubovich cooperate at the trial, the latter "mumbled something indistinctly, but to the effect that [he] had promised to do [his] duty," with tears in his eyes.[79]

The old Menshevik was indignant about Solzhenitsyn's distortion of his words, and he considered *Gulag* "a political manifesto," which gave the author "the possibility of identifying the practice of the 'Archipelago' with the idea of socialism and the idea of any revolution in general."[80] The Soviet authorities grasped the potential of this "betrayed voice" for anti-Solzhenitsyn propaganda early on. In December 1974, the eighty-four-year-old man told Medvedev that two journalists from the Soviet news agency APN had flown from Moscow to visit him in his home for invalids in Karaganda, Kazakhstan. They had interviewed him about *The Gulag Archipelago* and had "ordered" an article from him. Iakubovich had not read the second volume of *Gulag* yet, but had heard from his acquaintances that Solzhenitsyn confessed in it of having been "recruited" as an informer in the Gulag under the alias of "Vetrov." "I would not have believed this piece of information, if it had not come from Solzhenitsyn himself. But, having become 'Vetrov,' he could not fail to take further steps, despite his assertion to the contrary."[81] The APN seemed satisfied with Iakubovich's anti-Solzhenitsyn's stance, for they came back with a television team and shot an interview, which they promised to broadcast.[82]

In January 1975, Roy Medvedev sent Iakubovich several of his reviews of Solzhenitsyn's work. Justifying the somewhat moderate tone of his critique, he explained that he had to take into account "the relationship to [Solzhenitsyn] of the Moscow liberal intelligentsia, which considers him a victim and is only beginning to 'see the light' now." Moreover, Medvedev published in the Western media, not in the Soviet Union, which imposed certain limits on him. Yet he intended on "intensifying the criticism." "At the moment in the West, disappointment and irritation with Solzhenitsyn are growing, and the left-wing intelligentsia is already breaking ties with him." Nevertheless, Medvedev said there were some issues in *Gulag* he felt he had no legitimacy to discuss, particularly the question of Solzhenitsyn's recruitment as an informer: "For moral reasons, only veterans of the 'Archipelago' can raise this kind of question, but on this point the opinion of many of them converges with yours."[83]

In April, Iakubovich sent the historian an article entitled "Solzhenitsyn and Roy Medvedev," which he had written on request from the APN. They had summoned him in Moscow and asked whether he would agree to speak in front of a foreign correspondent to defend Medvedev against Solzhenitsyn's allegations at the Stockholm press conference concerning the historian's review of *Gulag*. Although the APN apparently approved of his article, the interview did not take place. Iakubovich observed that "competent instances" had apparently judged it "undesirable."[84] Indeed, Iakubovich remained unrehabilitated and this permanent stain on his political biography seems to have made him a less than ideal candidate for instrumentalization in the anti-Solzhenitsyn campaign.

Whether or not the interview was broadcast on television remains unclear, but at any rate both the Russian émigré community and the Moscow intelligentsia were apprised of Iakubovich's attacks against Solzhenitsyn, and former acquaintances had begun to shun him.[85] But Medvedev was intent on supporting Iakubovich, and when the old man requested that a rectification of Solzhenitsyn's version of his trial be published in *XX vek*, the historian wrote a ten-page essay on this theme. However, his brother, who was in charge of the edition in London, was more cautious and refrained from publishing it; instead, he chose to act through legal channels.[86] Nevertheless, the second volume of *Samizdat Register*, the English-language tamizdat version of *XX vek*, did feature Iakubovich's two essays on Kamenev and Zinoviev with an introduction by Zhores Medvedev exposing Solzhenitsyn's distortion of Iakubovich's testimony. "One can easily compare the full text of [Iakubovich's deposition for rehabilitation] ... with Solzhenitsyn's distorted version of the same document ... to realise that for Solzhenitsyn the historical truth did not mean too much when it contradicted his explanation of the tragedy of Stalin's terror."[87]

In parallel, Zhores Medvedev, who had become Iakubovich's editor and representative in the West, contacted Solzhenitsyn's British publisher Collins&Harvill to demonstrate the distortion of Iakubovich's testimony and request that appropriate changes be made in future editions of *The Gulag Archipelago*, short of which the publishing house could be sued for libel. Insisting that Iakubovich was still alive and providing his address, Medvedev assured the publisher that he would not make the matter public, but advised him to apologize to Iakubovich and offer a small financial compensation, preferably taken from Solzhenitsyn's royalties.[88] As the matter was referred back to Harper&Row's in New York, Zhores was informed that Solzhenitsyn denied having had access to Iakubovich's Letter to the Prosecutor and had based his account on his sole oral testimony. Meanwhile, Iakubovich suffered a heart attack and could not be reached, leaving the matter pending for the rest of 1977.

In 1978, Roy Medvedev received a new letter from the old Menshevik. He mentioned that the APN had ordered the third part of his essay "From the History of Ideas" and had invited him to stay in a sanatorium to complete the task. Iakubovich ended with words of disenchantment and hostility toward Solzhenitsyn: "My case is shown in the light of the enemy, who has crept to me under the disguise of a 'friend.'"[89] Zhores decided to send a copy of this letter directly to the British publisher. From it, they could infer that "the case could take a different turn. If, instead of Zhores and Roy Medvedev, they were confronted by those 'nice people from the APN' who were sending Iakubovich to the 'Miners' Sanatorium.'" Although this might not be clear to Western publishers, "Solzhenitsyn, if he was sent a copy, undoubtedly understood."[90] Indeed, the writer eventually agreed to rewrite the section concerning Iakubovich, and new editions of *Gulag* appeared with the corrected version.[91] In his memoirs, however,

Solzhenitsyn described Medvedev as being solely motivated by financial reasons, and deceivingly concluded: "Zhores gave up. There was no trial against the *Archipelago*." He failed to admit that he did modify the book's text under pressure.[92]

Yet, Iakubovich's thirst for revenge was not quenched, and his resentment soon found a new outlet. In November 1975, Roy wrote to Zhores that the old man had received documents signed "Vetrov" from a Baltic lawyer, who had allegedly found them while working on rehabilitations in the camp where Solzhenitsyn had been imprisoned. Roy advised him not to speak publicly about it, as he had "no convincing version of how he had found these documents."[93] Nevertheless, in March 1980, Iakubovich wrote that he had received a copy of Tomáš Řezáč's *Solzhenitsyn's Spiral of Treason*,[94] a libelous biography of Solzhenitsyn sponsored by the APN, with an acknowledgment from Řezáč to his "coauthor," Iakubovich. The latter denied having met Řezáč and suspected that the Czech journalist had obtained his materials from the APN. Still, he judged that Řezáč had reproduced his opinion "correctly" and, generally, the APN had been "entirely loyal" toward him.[95] In another letter, he claimed he assumed "moral and political responsibility" for Řezáč's conclusions. "At the basis of the *Spiral* is precisely my thought that [Solzhenitsyn] was a camp snitch and ended up in the 'sharashka' described in the novel [*The First Circle*] as an 'informer.'"[96]

The last years of Iakubovich's life were filled with a multitude of physical ills. Perhaps more biting was the disappointment caused by the APN's loss of interest in him, as Solzhenitsyn had ceased to be a sensation in the West. Not only had the broadcast of his interview never taken place in the USSR, but his essay in three parts "From the History of Ideas," for which the APN had paid him advance royalties, had not been published. He complained: "Generally speaking, the ban on my name remains in place, and, clearly, I will remain 'classified' until the end of my life."[97] Roy Medvedev was inclined to judge the old man with indulgence and did not consider that Iakubovich had been "recruited" by the KGB. The APN had simply used him the same way they had used Solzhenitsyn's elderly aunt, whose interview with the West German weekly *Stern* had thrown discredit on the writer.[98]

> We cannot judge an eighty-five-year-old man, who has been his whole life tormented with unfair accusations, and whom Solzhenitsyn has also presented in a totally false light, for having used the possibility that the APN gave him to defend his reputation. Just as we cannot judge those people and writers who, having failed to find a publisher at home, turn to foreign publishers if they consider that the content of their works is more important than who publishes it and where. If one has two or several options, one must choose the best. But sometimes one has no other option.[99]

Iakubovich died in October 1980, still unrehabilitated. As for his accusations against Solzhenitsyn, they would be revived during Perestroika, at a time when no past or present idol was immune from attacks.[100] Yet Solzhenitsyn was not alone in mishandling facts or testimonies. A number of reasons, from the difficulty of accessing sources to the need to "produce an effect" on readers, could explain small and large deviations from "truth" in works of dissident researchers.

Between history and folklore

Antonov-Ovseenko's *Portrait of a Tyrant*

In his preface to *The Time of Stalin: Portrait of a Tyranny*, Anton Antonov-Ovseenko assured his readers: "I have striven for truthfulness, and not only from a historian's sense of responsibility. There are no fabrications in this book. What would be the need? The truth is horrendous enough."[101] The fabrications, the author made clear, were on the side of the authorities, who continued, three decades after Stalin's death, to conceal the dark pages of the Soviet past. As for himself, his task had only consisted in exposing "Stalin's criminal essence, to reveal the gangster and hoodlum that he was."[102]

Understanding what led the former *zek* to publish at age sixty a tamizdat biography of Stalin, with all the risks involved, requires taking into account both his fiery character and his numerous, yet largely unsuccessful, lobbying actions in the 1960s. We are reduced to conjectures concerning the slow maturing of this decision, but the very late timing of the book shows the author's qualms about exiting a system his father had contributed to building. His first priority had been to write his father's biography, but he also admitted that his conception of Stalin had taken a long time to mature. After his father's arrest, he did not blame the Soviet leader. For the teenager that he was, "Stalin's name was sacred." It took his own arrest, years of camp, and many encounters with more enlightened "enemies of the people" for him to come to the realization of Stalin's place in history. "What an ocean of suffering I had to go through before I saw clearly," he bitterly concluded.[103]

After his rehabilitation and return to Moscow, he made new acquaintances and received access to a few works by Western historians. One of them was Harrison Salisbury's *The 900 days: The Siege of Leningrad* (1969), which he discovered through the oral translation of a friend. Later on, he read Robert Tucker; Robert Conquest's *The Great Terror* (a Russian translation of which appeared in 1974), and also Roy Medvedev's *Let History Judge*, published in Russian the same year.[104] Combined with the frustration of years of essentially fruitless lobbying of the authorities to further his father's rehabilitation, these eye-opening readings probably tilted the writer toward dissent.

As he worked on his father's biography, Antonov-Ovseenko began to think about a new project of biography of Stalin, and by the end of the 1960s, he had begun to gather material and testimonies. His very impaired eyesight was a serious hindrance on his work capacity, yet he made up for this handicap by remarkable obstinacy, as well as privileged access to many Old Bolsheviks, who readily entrusted their comrade's son with their testimonies about the Stalin era. One of them was Aleksei Snegov, who had contributed to Anton's "enlightenment" in the 1960s. They lived close to each other and met frequently. Just as he had helped Medvedev, Snegov was ready to assist Antonov-Ovseenko in his research.[105] Among Antonov-Ovseenko's witnesses were also Ol'ga Shatunovskaia, along with one of her key sources, Vassilii Mefod'evich Verkhovykh. The latter had been part of the returning board at the 17th Party Congress, in 1934, and had allegedly observed the destruction, on Kaganovich's order, of 289 ballots cast against Stalin.[106] After spending seventeen years in a camp, Verkhovykh reappeared to testify in front of the Commission investigating the circumstances of Kirov's murder, after the 20th Party Congress. Still wary of possible backlash, Verkhovykh reluctantly agreed to testify in front of the Central Committee and to provide a written statement.[107]

Antonov-Ovseenko also had access to witnesses who did not belong to Medvedev's circle of Old Bolsheviks. Probably thanks to his father's fame, he seems to have been able to talk to more orthodox party members. Among them was an Old Bolshevik who had remained a faithful Stalinist throughout his sixteen years of camp: Ivan Mikhailovich Gronskii. This longtime editor of *Izvestiia* (1925–34) and the literary journals *Krasnaia niva* and *Novyi mir* (1931–37) was close to Stalin, whom he could freely call and visit in the 1930s.[108] He occasionally used this privileged position to intercede in favor of writers. When he tried to do the same in relation to Marshall Tukhachevskii, however, he hit a wall, and by July 1938, he had himself been arrested.[109] Antonov-Ovseenko recalled that he had extensively used his interviews with Gronskii for his research. Perhaps more than facts, the historian borrowed from him his representation of Stalin as an actor (*litsedei*), who could "change his face as a kaleidoscope."[110] In his memoirs, Gronskii thus commented:

> Stalin was a brilliant artist. His talent of instantaneous transformation truly reached the scale of [Fedor] Shaliapin's. For instance, Stalin is talking with someone. [He is] affectionate, tender. Both his smile and his eyes—everything is sincere.... He walks him out. And already in a few seconds, a completely different facial expression. He says: "What a bastard!"—"Comrade Stalin, but you just said the opposite."—"I had to encourage him, so that he would work."[111]

Antonov-Ovseenko concurred, on the basis of additional testimonies: "Stalin entered into each part so thoroughly that he sincerely began to believe it. Nature blessed him with this unusual capacity to assume many roles."[112]

Among Antonov-Ovseenko's witnesses was also Margarita Vasil'evna Fofanova (1883–1976), a friend of Nadezhda Krupskaia's, Lenin's wife, and a party member since April 1917. Lenin hid in her apartment in July and October 1917.[113] Retired in 1934, she somehow escaped repression. As a former intimate friend of the Lenin-Krupskaia couple, Fofanova was privy to many of their reflections and suspicions regarding Stalin's behavior. Deeply resenting Krupskaia's ostracism after Lenin's death, Fofanova eagerly believed her friend had been poisoned, when the old lady suddenly died of "abdominal embolism" after the banquet given for her seventieth birthday.[114] Fofanova shared her impressions with Anton, who was keen on ascribing to Stalin the worst possible intentions and avidly collected information on "suspicious deaths" that seemed to involve Stalin.

Elena Dmitrievna Stasova (1873–1966) had an impressive party record and, having escaped repression, she remained a highly respected party veteran, decorated in 1960 with the Order of Socialist Labor. She had known Vladimir Antonov-Ovseenko during years of fierce struggle; as a Central Committee Secretary after the Revolution, she sent him on missions to various cities and admired his dedication to the Party and his courage.[115] As she was already over ninety-year-old and severely ill, Anton regularly visited this "living memory of the Central Committee."[116]

Among Antonov-Ovseenko's friends were also sons and daughters of repressed communists: Leonid Petrovskii, Iurii Tomskii, Nadezhda Ioffe, Iurii Larin (Bukharin's son), and others. Although many of them had been too young to remember the events leading up to the execution of their parents, a few could contribute testimonies. Iurii Tomskii, for instance, shared with Anton information he had about Kirov's murder.[117] He was the son of Mikhail Tomskii, who had belonged to Bukharin's "rightist" block and had committed suicide in 1936. Iurii's whole family died during the Great Terror and he was himself imprisoned, sharing a cell with Anton's father at some point.

Anton Antonov-Ovseenko's good fortune was that he only came under suspicion belatedly. In the 1960s, as he worked on his father's biography, he could still access archives, but also libraries' restricted sections (*spetskhran*), where he read forbidden literature, including Trotsky's works.[118] However, he also had to overcome countless difficulties. His near blindness was arguably the main challenge he faced. Yet other factors also came into play. Despite his talent for collecting testimonies, Antonov-Ovseenko conducted his project in isolation and kept it secret: probably for security reasons, he preferred not to share his manuscript with others. In retrospect, it was this solitude he emphasized: "I worked alone, without archives, without anything."[119] Medvedev also underlined this significant difference between their works: although he considered Antonov-Ovseenko's book "good, useful," he deplored that "it contained many inaccuracies." He explained this by the fact that Antonov-Ovseenko had not subjected his work to the "peer review" mechanism that was characteristic for Medvedev's work method. *Let History Judge* had gone "through hundreds of hands" before publication. "And if there were inaccuracies, then they were corrected. But Antonov-Ovseenko, no, he worked alone."[120] Nevertheless, Anton did receive some technical assistance. He recalled that his third wife had edited his manuscript, before their divorce.[121] In 1978, he also hired a typist, Inna Levitan. This young housewife and mother of three readily accepted this dangerous mission. She felt admiration for Anton: he was "determined, a fighter, passionate, he had a striving for truth. There were no such people around me. He wasn't afraid of anything."[122]

A crucial intermediary for the tamizdat publication was Stephen Cohen. Starting from 1976, the historian spent long periods of time in Moscow. As the author of a biography on Bukharin, he was a frequent guest in the Larin family, with Bukharin's widow and son. As he wished to undertake research on Gulag camp returnees, Cohen turned to Anna Larina for contacts, but also to Roy Medvedev and Antonov-Ovseenko, with whom he became friends.[123] In his memoirs on this period, Cohen describes Anton as "nearly blind, but wiry and determined, ... capable of boundless research and writing." "Like another former zek, Solzhenitsyn, he was embattled, willful, and overly confident in his Gulag-acquired cunning. As our friendship developed, his frequent requests for my assistance in exposing 'Stalin's hangmen,' past and present, sometimes worried me."[124] This friendship led Cohen to take Antonov-Ovseenko's manuscript out of the country for publication in the West, at personal risk. *Portrait of a Tyranny* appeared in Russian in 1980 at Valerii Chalidze's New York-based "Khronika Press" and in translation in 1982. The same year, as the KGB performed a house search in Anton's apartment, they found his correspondence with Cohen, and the latter faced a visa ban from the USSR for years.[125]

A secret note of the KGB signed by Iurii Andropov stated that over fifty "anti-Soviet" publications had been seized in Antonov-Ovseenko's apartment, along with a typescript of his new research on Lavrentii Beria.[126] This work, the report noted, mostly repeated previous Soviet and Western research on the subject, but also contained "anti-Soviet and slanderous inventions." The author thus tackled such delicate subjects as "the forced Sovietization of Georgia," condemned the collectivization of Soviet agriculture and the "reunion" of Western Ukraine and Byelorussia to the USSR. He spoke of the "annexation" of the Baltic states and "resurrect[ed] the 'Katyn Affair.'" Finally, Antonov-Ovseenko spoke of the "degeneration" of the Soviet state and called Trotsky "Lenin's 'closest companion.'"[127] Although these counts of indictment fully justified criminal prosecution, Andropov concluded that, "taking into account his belonging to the family of a famous revolutionary, Antonov-Ovseenko's unjustified past arrest, but also his health condition (weak eyesight), we consider it possible to restrict ourselves to a cautionary discussion at the [KGB]."[128] In November 1984, following a new house search, the Western media reported on Antonov-Ovseenko's arrest, probably mistakenly.[129]

In his work over Stalin, Antonov-Ovseenko pursued an agenda in which the personal and the political were tightly interwoven. He had rushed his book into print, hoping to get it published in time for Stalin's hundredth anniversary, in December 1979. "I wanted my work to be a warning to all those who continued to see a hero in him."[130] In retrospect, he admitted that he should have acted without precipitation, taking the time to correct mistakes.[131] Yet this tendency to rush was probably a legacy of his tragic personal experience. Over two decades after the 20th Party Congress, Stalin remained an object of admiration for many, while his victims progressively retreated from the stage. New generations were growing up in a state of amnesia. The introduction conveyed this sense of urgency:

The name of the butchers, the informers, the pogromists must be known *today, now*. ... Telling the truth about those who died should not be put off until later. The children and grandchildren do not have the right to turn their backs on the truth, because the fate of those who perished is their own fate. They have an obligation to know who is to blame. And to know it *now*.[132]

Stalin's heritage was not a thing of the past; it persisted "in the habits, behavior and thoughts of the living." In a rhetoric reminiscent of Medvedev's, the author declared that silence was not the cure for what remained an open wound: only through a thorough investigation and public condemnation of the past could society move forward: "Revelation of the truth about Stalin is an act of simple justice, which must be carried out first of all in Stalin's own country."[133]

Despite using sources that partly overlapped with Medvedev's, Antonov-Ovseenko differed in his approach to the Stalin question. He was certainly not indifferent to Medvedev's work. The 1974 Russian copy of *Let History Judge* that the old historian kept in his library when I visited him in 2012 lacked a cover and several chapters, showing clear signs of having been repeatedly read, with pencil annotations on numerous pages. Yet when asked about it, he stressed his fundamental disagreements with the author. "For me there is no Stalinism. For me there is only *stalinshchina*, as a variety of state banditry."[134] Although he never defined clearly the word, he seemed to equate *stalinshchina* with the reign of one individual's arbitrariness, a realm of submission to the tyrant's despotic grip. Unlike Solzhenitsyn, who attacked the Soviet regime as a whole and downplayed the role of personalities, Antonov-Ovseenko focused solely on Stalin's personality, to whom he ascribed all of the regime's faults. Symptomatic of this was the Russian title of his book: "Portrait of a Tyrant."

It would be vain to try to translate Antonov-Ovseenko's position in political terms, however. His fundamental reference points did not belong to the political, but, in line with his Gulag experience, were inscribed in the interpersonal realm, with a strong use of criminal vocabulary. The feisty temperament that had helped Antonov-Ovseenko survive in the Gulag transpired in his analysis of the Stalin era. Just as he denounced Stalin's gang (*shaika*), he identified with the adverse "gang" of Old Bolsheviks who, along with his father, had honestly fought for the establishment of a just world, and had perished or been repressed along with him. Out of loyalty for this milieu, rather than to the Party, to which he had never belonged, Antonov-Ovseenko adopted the Old Bolsheviks' rhetoric, denouncing Stalin's dictatorship as "an anti-socialist phenomenon." His discussions with those who had known Stalin had shown all too clearly that "Stalin is a careerist who introduced himself (*pronik*) into the sphere of intelligent comrades, of idealistic fighters."[135] This personal allegiance to the Old Bolsheviks as a fundamental positive reference, transcending politics, showed his lasting attachment to the revolutionary legacy of his father. Moreover, this identification with Stalin's victims allowed Antonov-Ovseenko to draw the lines of a personal confrontation with his archenemy and his contemporary heirs, who sought to rehabilitate him. More than a political pamphlet, *Portrait of a Tyranny* was indeed an "act of vendetta," where personal feelings of hatred dominated over political reflections.

However, Antonov-Ovseenko's loyalty to his father's comrades was not devoid of ambiguity either. By the time *Portret Tirana* was published in New York, many of his witnesses had passed away and could no longer react to the publication. But the reaction of Aleksei Snegov, who had been the fieriest anti-Stalinist advocate among Old Bolsheviks and had only narrowly escaped party exclusion, was probably symptomatic of the gap that existed between two generations of anti-Stalinist activists. Antonov-Ovseenko recalled: "Our friendship came to an abrupt end after the publication of my book in New York 'Portrait of a Tyrant.' Fearing wiretapping—starting from 1980, the author of this book was assimilated to dissidents—Snegov went out with me, and in a quiet alleyway, with the voice of a party orator (*tribun*), he condemned my anti-Soviet conduct."[136] The authenticity of this episode remains open to doubt, but the Old Bolshevik may well have felt betrayed by the publication of Anton's book. The fact that he took the precaution to speak out of witnesses' ears showed that he expressed heartfelt indignation and was not demonstratively "dissociating himself" from Anton. Having assumed that Antonov-Ovseenko was "party-minded" by right of birth, he found in his work none of the genuflections before the Party's authority that *Let History Judge* had contained. Moreover, the mere fact of publication abroad was assimilated in party circles to betrayal, as the *Doctor Zhivago* Affair and the trial over the writers Iulii Daniel' and Andrei Siniavskii had shown. By adopting the methods of the dissidents without cloaking his words in communist rhetoric, Antonov-Ovseenko had thus betrayed the fundamental values of this Old Bolshevik milieu which had once actively supported him.

An unreliable account

From the point of view of professional scholarship, however, a fundamental critique that could be addressed to Antonov-Ovseenko's work was his excessive faith in the witnesses' words. This could be explained both by his tendency to ascribe Stalin the worst possible intentions and by his loyalty toward his witnesses, which kept him from questioning some of their affirmations. As we saw in regard to Shatunovskaia's testimony, many anti-Stalinist "myths" were accepted uncritically by this group, which had suffered from Stalin's terror and had felt betrayed by the "thermidorian" turn of their Revolution.

The fourth issue of the tamizdat historical collection *Pamiat'*, published in 1981, featured a review of Antonov-Ovseenko's *Portrait of a Tyranny*, published under the pseudonym of M. Dovner.[137] This particularly scathing critique did not spare any of the work's weaknesses. One was entitled to expect from a new work on Stalin not only the introduction of new sources, but also an analysis of the extensive material now at the disposal of researchers of this period. All the more since Antonov-Ovseenko was nearly an insider himself and had access to "witnesses from almost the epicenter of events."[138] However, *Portrait of a Tyranny* did not live up to these expectations. The reviewer found the author's psychological portrait of Stalin, which reduced him to the image of a common "criminal," unconvincing. As for Antonov-Ovseenko's historical conception, it was "simplistic": failing to discuss the question of the historical roots of Stalinism, the historian simply described Stalin's rise to power as a series of criminal actions, which his weak opponents, perpetually divided, had failed to counteract.

"Dovner" recognized that Antonov-Ovseenko could also have restricted himself to the role of a "chronicler," who performs the "great, difficult and responsible work" of collecting and comparing material, evaluating the veracity of the facts related.[139] Yet, although the historian had indeed collected a vast quantity of new testimonies, he had treated them with little discernment. While claiming that there were "no fabrications" in his book, Antonov-Ovseenko had to recognize that "many facts are undocumented and cannot be verified." Moreover, of his own admission, "for obvious reasons," he could not name "all the witnesses and actors of the events, authors of unpublished memoirs, oral testimonies"[140] "Dovner" understood the limitations that the historian faced; nevertheless, he considered that the author should have given at least some indirect clues as to the witnesses' position in relation to the events, whether the information was received from first or second hand, as well as the time of its collection. Was it "in the thirties, when he could hear something from his father's friends, in the camps, or after the 20th Congress, when memoirs of Old Bolsheviks took on a distinctive anti-Stalinist character, or after Solzhenitsyn's *Gulag Archipelago*, which gave a new impulse, already of a different kind, to the writing of memoirs"?[141] Failing to give the reader any information in this respect, the author could not expect to inspire trust.

Moreover, Antonov-Ovseenko showed, more than once, "an uncritical attitude towards facts," for instance by presenting as fact a testimony about Stalin's murder of his wife, while failing to mention the widely acknowledged version about her suicide.[142] The reviewer cited a series of contradictions in the text and doubtful interpretations of testimonies or documents, but also errors in the dates and chronology. "Dovner" concluded pessimistically:

> The book contains a number of new, sometimes unique facts. It is the author's merit to have found them and introduced them to scholars and readers. But in light of what we have exposed, knowing the mistakes the author has committed in relation to commonly-known facts, easily verifiable, can we consider with trust new facts, in particular those which we are not yet in a position to confirm or infirm, due to the lack of sources? No, I suppose.
> ... And still, this book has a certain value, if only because it reflects, to a large extent, folkloric representations of Stalin; folkloric in the broadest sense, from "rank-and-file" citizens up to the highest party nomenklatura.[143]

Although personal disagreements might have fueled this review,[144] the consternation of *Pamiat*'s editorial team was real. "It is hard to tell where the typos end and where the mistakes begin"—exclaimed one of the editors during the discussion of Antonov-Ovseenko's book.[145] This point of view was shared by another anonymous samizdat reviewer. He considered that Antonov-Ovseenko "took his revenge on Stalin, without caring about historical objectivity and without even laying a claim to impartiality." And although the "information collected personally by the author, stories and rumors from the spheres close to the TsK," presented interest for the reader, "some of them do not refer to any verifiable source" and the reliability of the book was therefore "open to doubt."[146]

Western historians expressed similar uneasiness. Admittedly, Stephen Cohen gave a positive evaluation to the book in his preface to the English-language edition.[147] But other historians were more critical: in particular, Leo Van Rossum devoted a short note to the question of the reliability of Antonov-Ovseenko's work, based on *Pamiat*'s review.[148] For Western scholars, the mix of genres and the lack of distance toward one's subject of study were disconcerting at best. Teddy J. Uldriks judged it "a fascinating, complex but ultimately unsatisfying work."

> It is at one and the same time a fiery political tract, an anguished memoir and an attempt at a comprehensive, scholarly analysis of the Stalin era. . . . Above all, *The Time of Stalin* is a bitter indictment of the dictator and his henchmen. The author is emotionally too close to his subject to render a balanced judgement.[149]

Antonov-Ovseenko's work was not a novel, it purported to be a history of Stalin's reign, yet it failed to abide by the rules of classical historiography. The same could be said of *The Gulag Archipelago* and perhaps to some extent of *Let History Judge*. This was not coincidental, for dissident authors felt the need to adapt the form of their works to match their objectives, disregarding traditional formats. This arguably entitles us to speak of dissident histories as a specific genre.

Dissident histories as ethical manifestos

Western critiques of dissident histories have been divided between, on the one hand, admiration for the authors' courage and moral stance and, on the other, criticism of their inadequacies from a scholarly viewpoint.[150] However, both approaches failed to grasp the essence of dissident histories. As a rule, nonprofessional dissident researchers neither sought to replicate professional scholarship, nor felt unconditionally bound by its established norms of validity. Antonov-Ovseenko thus remained bitter about the fierce review of his work in *Pamiat'*. Not only had the reviewers ignored the fair play rules of dissident solidarity, but they had harshly criticized a work which he felt should have been standing above pretty criticism. "How can you, when I am publishing a book against Stalin, organize such a devastating critique? On the whole, it is truthful (*pravdivaia*), although in the details, of course, I could make mistakes."[151] In the logic of the author, his work was thus inherently "truthful" and just, by virtue of the fact that it was produced in opposition to official lies and dissimulation.

Moreover, the format of dissident works had to be adapted to best convey the author's message and produce the intended effect on readers. Solzhenitsyn's "Experiment in Literary Investigation" famously escaped any straightforward categorization. The author subsequently defined the genre as follows: "An artistic investigation draws upon real-life, factual material (untransmuted, that is) but also employs all the resources available to the artist in uniting these individual facts and fragments, such that the overall design emerges with conclusiveness no wit less complete and compelling than that of a piece of scientific research."[152] The necessity of creating a new literary genre not only derived from a need to weave oral testimonies into a historical canvass, but also resulted from the book's twin functions. On the one hand, Solzhenitsyn wished to provide an overview of the history of the Gulag as a penal institution, with the successive "flows" of political repressions that justified its continued existence. On the other, he sought to convey to the readers the world of the Gulag as a life experience, through its various stages. While the first objective could be fulfilled within the framework of a traditional historical study, the second was best accomplished through literary means.

Evgeniia Ivanova argues that the context in which Solzhenitsyn wrote *Gulag* led him to simultaneously endorse three roles traditionally taken on by different persons at different times: that of a chronicler, collecting "legends" (*predanie*); that of a historian, weighing evidence and analyzing sources; and that of the publicist and writer, conveying this material to the larger public.

> The time and the exceptional historical mission of this book allowed it to unite various genres, which usually exist independently, into a new literary genre, which we would call a historical testimony, an indictment in front of the tribunal of history, and a publicistic address *urbi et orbi* in the name of victims who have silently come to their grave. And although the isolated parts of meaning of this narrative belong to various genres, all of them taken together convey a unique truth: the truth of the testimony.[153]

For Solzhenitsyn, testimonies served as illustrations, samples of a myriad of lives, united into a common narrative of suffering, survival, and heroism. By revealing the names and the fates of a few hundreds, Solzhenitsyn symbolically gave a voice to the silent multitude that had suffered side by side with him. However, the limit to what Solzhenitsyn could show in his work was the boundary of his own personal experience, and hence his capacity to convey the unspeakable, the unfathomable to the world. Those who had suffered most in the camps had not survived to share their testimonies, so that "no one now can ever tell us the most important thing about these camps." As for the author, he realized that "the whole scope of this story and of this truth is beyond the capabilities of one lonely pen. All I had was a peephole into the Archipelago, not the view from a tower."[154] Nevertheless, his literary talent and his anthropological-historical approach arguably allowed him to convey the "truth" of this world much more successfully than a traditional historical study would have allowed for.

Antonov-Ovseenko also recognized that his book was a hybrid creation, combining lively (reconstituted) dialogues with quotes from primary sources, abounding with literary devices and biting irony. His "strange, sometimes unscientific approach" to the study of the Stalin system might not have been to everyone's liking, but his goal had been "to penetrate the criminal nature of the imposter Leader (*Vozhd'*) and through him recreate the portrait of the era."[155] He had not strived "to produce an especially scientific research," nor did he reflect upon the genre of his work as he wrote it. "Some call the book a political pamphlet, others, an attempt to draw Stalin's political portrait, a documentary novel. Some consider it a perfectly serious scholarly biography of Stalin."[156] These categorizations eventually mattered little to the author. And he did not take umbrage at the critics who reproached him for his lack of objectivity. As a survivor of the terror, he admitted that he might not have "sufficiently restrained [his] personal feelings"[157] and this reflected on his work. "All of this went through my soul, was born from the pain of life itself."[158] But objectivity was not an option: "I am not an outside observer of my people's tragedy. I address not only my reader's mind, but also his heart," he explained.[159] Nor did he consider impartiality as a desirable end.

> I disagree on many points with authors who call for a balanced evaluation of Stalin. On which scales can we balance out his actions: on one side, you put dozens of millions of victims of repression, and on the other, the Generalissimo's uniform with golden buttons, the brilliance of which continues to this day to obscure the eyes of many.[160]

Many orphans of the Terror shared this view: Iakir, Kim, and Gabai thus observed that "an objective relation towards a perpetrator is also a fact of moral pathology."[161]

Even the format of Medvedev's *Let History Judge* was in some ways nontraditional, with its interdisciplinary approach to a question of political philosophy. Nevertheless, unlike Solzhenitsyn and Antonov-Ovseenko, Medvedev did strive for maximal reliability and did perceive himself as a historian, rather than just as a publicist. Still, he made no mystery of his political commitment.

Dissident histories were therefore hybrid works combining the most various genres: historical scholarship, autobiography, documentary or historical novel, and political pamphlet, to cite but the most common. But their defining feature was certainly the moral and political commitment of their authors. Certainly, this peculiar genre is not unique to the Soviet historical context. In his World Guide on *Censorship of Historical Thought*,[162] Antoon de Baets covers the persecution of both historians and "non-historians." Explaining this methodological choice, de Baets emphasizes that censorship targets indiscriminately professional and nonprofessional historians. "Indeed, popular history is as much a target of censorship as is academic history, probably even more so. In addition, nonprofessional historians are often the first to explore taboos or break the silence."[163]

The dissident researchers' motives for writing, the form of these histories, and the authors' fate were three closely connected dimensions. Their primary motivation was ethical, and this influenced in turn the format of these works, which was built around the purpose of "truth-telling." Moreover, because dissident researchers were animated by a moral purpose, which went far beyond the simple desire to recover and share knowledge, they were prepared to incur repression for the sake of bringing their works to the public. I have argued that dissident histories represented a specific genre, and I understand this genre in a broad sense, not only as being characterized by a specific form and work methods, but also serving a common function, in this case fulfilling a moral purpose.

The natural corollary of this moral impulse, however, was the belief in the superiority of one's truth, not only over official lies, but also over alternative truths. While Western reviewers were perplexed by dissident histories, they perceived their moral value, and mostly refrained from any sharp criticism. Dissident researchers, on the other hand, had no such qualms about attacking each other and feistily defended their own works against the seemingly petty attacks of contradictors. These conflicts, in turn, provided Soviet propaganda with munition in its attacks against dissidents. Yet these disagreements also showed the different degrees to which dissident authors had emancipated themselves from Soviet official anti-Stalinist discourse. Medvedev and Antonov-Ovseenko remained loyal to the Party and to the Old Bolsheviks whose testimonies had constituted the basis for their research, and restricted their critique to the figure of Stalin, whereas Solzhenitsyn had willfully broken with the official interpretation of the terror and affirmed his own anti-communist narrative.

The fate of dissident researchers, as could be expected, was correlated to the radicality of their works and the degree to which they departed from official discourse. By leaving Medvedev and Antonov-Ovseenko free, the Soviet authorities were not simply showing leniency, but also preserving alternative, more moderate voices that had the moral legitimacy to contradict Solzhenitsyn's views. While in the Brezhnev era, this potential was used only for Western audiences, during Perestroika, Medvedev's loyal anti-Stalinism would receive particular prominence for the same reasons.

8

Unleashing the Past

The Soviet authorities' ambivalent relationship toward de-Stalinization evolved with the onset of Perestroika and the launching of a much more thorough denunciation of Stalin's crimes. In this new context, dissident researchers had a role to play, and although they were belatedly allowed back into the official sphere, they benefited from a moral capital which gave them particular authority in contrast to the discredited guild of professional historians. They did not benefit from an immunity from critique, however, and the approximations in their works, which came to the fore with the multiplication of publications on the Stalin era, were the subject of heated discussion and sometimes fierce critique. Medvedev and Antonov-Ovseenko, who had remained in the Soviet Union and whose works stuck most closely to the new official anti-Stalinist discourse, were in a position to reap the benefits of years of opposition to the regime. Medvedev, in particular, managed to convert his moral capital into a political one and to launch what could have been a brilliant political career, if not for the fall of the Soviet Union. Solzhenitsyn and Nekrich, on the other hand, participated less actively in these debates, not only because they still lived in exile, but also because the radicality of their anti-communist histories did not fit the needs of Perestroika.

This chapter concludes this research by showing the reintegration of dissident histories into mainstream Soviet historiography and the public's reaction to these works. Dissident authors had always written primarily for a Soviet audience, and the legalization of their writings signified for them a vindication of their moral claims, but also the opportunity to have a political impact. Yet in the chaos of the last Soviet years, their voices were drowned in a din of competing narratives.

Perestroika and the resurgence of history

As Gorbachev came to power, in March 1985, he represented a new generation of Soviet leaders formed in the postwar period. Yet no one suspected the scale of the reforms he would undertake, which would ultimately lead to the fall of the Soviet Union. Many authors have analyzed Gorbachev's turn to the policy of "Glasnost" (*transparency*) as a strategy to garner support among liberals in counterweight to the conservative wing of the Party, which felt threatened by his economic reforms. For Vladimir Shlapentokh, Gorbachev, unlike his predecessors, relied heavily on intellectuals, both to elaborate and support his reforms. Through their critique of the Brezhnev regime and Stalinist model, they legitimized Gorbachev's reforms, which conflicted with the basic tenets of Soviet ideology. The Soviet leader thus believed that intellectuals "would be his most faithful allies," as the main beneficiaries of his liberalization measures in the political and cultural fields.[1]

The turning point came at the Central Committee Plenum in January 1987. In his speech, Gorbachev emphasized the link between democratization and economic reform. Attacking "scholastic theorizing" in the social sciences and "administrative, unfounded intrusion" which had impeded the creative process in the arts, Gorbachev called for a furthering of Glasnost as a "mighty lever of improvement of work on all our construction segments, an effective form of nationwide control." He called on the media to pursue their effort of "criticism and self-criticism" and insisted that "in Soviet society, there should be no zones closed to criticism."[2] Shortly thereafter, the General Secretary held a meeting with editors and media figures, in which he called for an end to "blank pages" in the historical and literary fields.[3] He advocated a balanced evaluation of the past: all seventy years of the country's history had to be valued, but its difficult pages should not be presented "through rose-coloured spectacles." Balancing between "joy and bitterness," history had to be presented "as it is." "There was everything; there were mistakes, it was hard, but the country moved forward."[4]

These official statements coincided with the onset of an anti-Stalinist wave in the artistic field, starting with the film *Repentance* by Tengiz Abuladze, watched by 2.5 million viewers in Moscow alone in January–February 1987.[5] Throughout the year, literary "thick journals" began to publish previously banned works, written for the most part during and after the Thaw. Among them were *The White Robes* by Vladimir Dudintsev and *The Bison* by Daniil Granin about the repressions against Soviet biologists; *The Inseparable Twins* (*Nochevala tuchka zolotaia*) by Anatolii Pristavkin about the deportation of Chechens and Ingushes in 1944; *By Right of Memory*, a poem by Tvardovskii about the deportation of his family, or Anna Akhmatova's *Requiem*. Most successful of all, however, was Anatolii Rybakov's novel *Children of the Arbat*, the first literary work published in the USSR to offer a portrait of Stalin as a central figure.[6] By mid-1987, works from the 1920s and 1930s, such as Andrei Platonov's novels, and even émigré authors, such as Ivan Bunin, made their way into print. Ironically, the delay in publishing these works had turned them into "historical novels" for the contemporary Soviet reader.[7] The wave of publications intensified in 1988 with the release of *Doctor Zhivago* by Boris Pasternak, Evgeniia Ginzburg's *Into the Whirlwind*, Vassilii Grossman's *Life and Fate*, which drew a parallel between Nazism and Stalinism, or Varlam Shalamov's *Kolyma Tales*. The playwright Mikhail Shatrov had published in 1986 *The Dictatorship of Consciousness*, in which he staged a trial over Socialism. In his 1988 play *Further, further, further...* he questioned the October Revolution's *raison d'être* and showed Lenin apologizing for initiating a process that had ultimately led to Stalinism.[8]

During Perestroika as during the Thaw, literature was at the forefront of historical revelations and "played the role of humanities, from political science to sociology, from history to philosophy."[9] However, historical publications also filled the generalist press, from *Ogonek* to *Moskovskie novosti*, from *Znamia* to *Druzhba narodov*. The Soviet people was seized by a passion for history, which was reflected in the huge print runs of popular newspapers and journals of liberal orientation, while the conservative and party press attracted ever fewer readers. *Argumenty i fakty* thus increased its print run from 3 to 9 million and *Novyi mir* jumped from 500,000 to 1.5 million subscribers.[10] In 1987–88, the Soviet public faced a landslide of revelations about the past: new names of Stalin's victims, but also of perpetrators, came to light every day. New themes opened up for discussion, from the conduct of collectivization and industrialization to the end of NEP.[11] In 1988, *Oktiabr'* published *Triumph and Tragedy*, a portrait of Stalin by Dmitrii Volkogonov, director of the Institute of Military History, who had been able to access numerous hitherto unknown archival documents.[12]

On the whole, however, professional historians remained on the sidelines of this flow of publications. As noted by William Husband, "Glasnost caught professional historians unprepared. To their embarrassment, historians possessed no significant reservoir of previously suppressed works comparable to those in literary and film circles."[13] Even those historians who had been inclined toward revisionism seemed wary of a possible ideological reversal as had taken place after the Thaw. Therefore, they turned to the reform of their professional institutions instead of reinterpreting the past.[14] Nevertheless, they were also keenly aware of their inability to satisfy society's thirst for "historical truth" and they fundamentally questioned their societal role in light of the current tasks set by Perestroika. Donald Raleigh emphasized the historians' dilemma in relation to publicists, who had been able to raise critical historical questions "with amazing dispatch, and with greater autonomy from the Party leadership" than them.[15] Not only had they deprived professional researchers of their audience, but they had also "discredited them in the eyes of the public." Nevertheless, historians were also "in the publicists' and writers' debt for keeping the public's interest in history alive" and many of them perceived this challenge as a stimulus to revise their conceptions of the past.[16]

The first to challenge openly the whole profession was Iurii Afanas'ev, who had just been appointed head of the Moscow State Institute of Historian-Archivists. In his inauguration speech, published in January 1987 in *Moskovskie novosti*, he used the word "stagnant" to characterize past Soviet historical scholarship, which he accused of "lagging behind world level." In the 1960s, Afanas'ev recalled, some historians had started showing that "world history was much more complicated, diversified, and variegated than it was customarily presented" in Soviet textbooks. However, these discussions were silenced. From then on, "history began to turn into a servant of the lopsided 'propaganda of success,' into apology for whatever had already been achieved."[17] Afanas'ev's speech was soon echoed by Aleksandr Iakovlev, Politburo member and close supporter of Gorbachev, who criticized historians for adopting a defensive position in relation to "bourgeois historiography" and failing to innovate, for breaching the rules of historical scholarship and for their "colorless writing."[18]

Many historians responded to these challenges by engaging in discussions on their profession's goals and place in Soviet society. Countless roundtables and public meetings on historical topics took place throughout 1987 and 1988, the proceedings of which were regularly published in the press.[19] During the first roundtable organized with both Soviet and American historians, in January 1989, Pavel Volobuev declared:

It is only in recent years that our science, including historical scholarship, has come out of a long period of stagnation. In essence, it is still in a state of crisis—a methodological and theoretical crisis, a crisis over the problems to be dealt with, a crisis of historical source material. Recognizing this, of course, is painful; and talking about it is even more painful.[20]

Viktor Danilov, however, took a more optimist view of the situation. "I believe that this explosion in both nonprofessional interest and unprofessional (so to speak) research has a positive significance in one respect—as a form of pressure on the historical profession." Moreover, he saw an "observable improvement in scholarly research" in connection with two external factors: the rehabilitation of historical figures of the opposition and opening of archives from the Soviet period.[21]

Gorbachev had resumed the process of rehabilitation of victims of Stalinism initiated by Khrushchev in the 1950s with the creation of a commission dedicated to this question. It inherited from its Thaw-era predecessor hundreds of volumes of documents and possessed similar extended investigation prerogatives, but no judicial powers. The commission reexamined dozens of famous trials, many victims of which had already been rehabilitated under Khrushchev. However, the commission's power to report on its conclusions in the media meant that the public was now informed of these rehabilitations. After a year of work, it became clear that the only way to proceed swiftly and efficiently was to annul all sentences pronounced by extrajudicial organs under Stalin. This was made possible through the January 16, 1989 law, which foresaw, however, an exclusion clause for the crimes committed during the war, on Nazi-occupied and recently annexed territories, to be examined individually. While only 13,500 rehabilitations had been pronounced in 1988, in 1989, the number swelled to 838,500. Moreover, in contrast to the Khrushchev era, a real effort was made to rehabilitate victims socially and restore their reputation. This process, necessarily public, could only be conducted in conditions of Glasnost.[22]

These rehabilitations had momentous implications for historians as well, by expanding the realm of what could be discussed. The rehabilitation in July 1987 of prominent Soviet economists condemned in 1931, 1932, and 1935 trials against "specialists" opened the way to a reexamination of their ideas.[23] By February 1988, the "rightist" oppositionists Nikolai Bukharin and Aleksei Rykov had been rehabilitated, soon followed by Grigorii Zinoviev and Lev Kamenev, and a flow of articles about these and other famous Bolsheviks appeared in the press. A balanced portrait of Trotsky, the erstwhile most vilified leader, even appeared in print in May 1988.[24] These rehabilitations opened for historians the question of possible alternatives to Stalinism after the Revolution.[25] Professional historical journals also began to publish archival documents and texts by rehabilitated oppositionists, thus raising the public's interest and increasing their own print runs.[26]

The other positive change mentioned by Danilov, the opening of archives, was a more protracted process. Calls for a law, which would set rules comparable to those regulating Western archives, increasingly sounded within Soviet society. As Maria Ferretti noted, the "battle for archives" was "an ethical battle for the right to remembrance, a memory that became a moral duty towards the victims of Stalinist repression."²⁷ As safekeepers of the "social memory of the collectivity," archives had to be returned to Soviet society and should remain fully accessible."²⁸ A testimony to the wealth of information that could be extracted from archives was the card index of 128,000 names of victims of repression, compiled by twenty-two-year-old Dmitrii Iurasov in several state archives over a period of ten years.²⁹ Civil society initiatives such as the "Memorial" archive or the "People's Archive," collecting personal documents and salvaging the "social memory," which state institutions were uninterested in preserving, lay the foundations for the creation of a "counter-memory."³⁰ However, state archives remained closed to non-historians and had an opaque functioning with numerous restrictions, even for professional researchers.³¹ In 1987, it was announced that 767,000 out of 1,109,000 restricted-access items from central state archives would be made available to researchers.³² In 1989, the publication of *Izvestiia TsK KPSS*, a journal publishing archival documents, was resumed after a sixteen-year interruption.³³ Still, the drafting of new rules, which would be neither too restrictive, nor too permissive, was longer in the making. Only in August 1991 were the first laws of reorganization of state archives enacted.³⁴

For the Soviet population, however, these waves of rehabilitations and revelations had a destabilizing effect. Roy Medvedev recalled that "the former picture of the history of the whole 20ᵗʰ century that people were used to was crumbling in front of their eyes," yet no one could yet provide them with any new conception. To many people, this came as a shock.³⁵ On June 10, 1988, secondary school history examinations were canceled until new textbooks could be made available. Afanas'ev approved of the measure, claiming it was "immoral" for students to take an exam based on a textbook that did not contain "a single page without a falsification."³⁶ During the following year, history teachers were allowed a great degree of latitude, which they used to discuss previously taboo topics or to cling to old narratives. Materials recommended by the Ministry of Education ranged from Lenin and Gorbachev's writings to articles by Roy Medvedev.³⁷ By September 1989, an interim textbook had appeared, but a more stable version could only be produced after the pace of revelations had slowed down. Two years later, textbook writers were still "caught between the possibility of being criticized as overly negative and sensationalist, on one hand, and censure for failing to incorporate new material and reflect the state of contemporary historical discourse, on the other."³⁸

Soviet history teachers were not the only ones confused by the new course: the Soviet regime's authority as an ideological state rested on a unity of views enforced from the top. But as previous dogmas were declared void, without any new incontrovertible narrative to replace them, opposition to Gorbachev's course began to mount.³⁹ Shlapentokh observed that Glasnost had allowed "intellectuals to choose between various ideological trends in a much freer manner than had been possible in the 1970s." The opposition between liberals and Russophiles, which emerged in the Brezhnev era, now became a major ideological dividing line. While the former now enjoyed the regime's backing, the latter felt emboldened by Glasnost and realized the support they could gain from Gorbachev's rivals in the Politburo.⁴⁰

This line of fracture, which partly overlapped with the 1960s' divide between anti-Stalinists and pro-Stalinists, was not restricted to the intelligentsia. A strong warning sign was sent by the publication of Nina Andreeva's article "I Cannot Forsake My Principles" in *Sovetskaia Rossiia*, on March 13, 1988. This "manifesto of anti-Perestroika forces," planned and broadly publicized by Egor Ligachev, a conservative Politburo member, was presented as a letter to the editor by a Leningrad chemistry teacher.[41] Andreeva protested against the deleterious effects of Glasnost on her students, particularly the discussions regarding the Stalin era. She complained that the term "personality cult" now included the history of "industrialization, collectivization and cultural revolution, which have carried our country forward among the great world powers." Although she condemned the mass repressions of the 1930s and 1940s, she protested against the "monochrome" depiction of "contradictory events, which has now begun to dominate in some press organs."[42] She went on to offer her own, positive portrait of Stalin. Andreeva's letter was officially rebuffed on April 5 in *Pravda*, following a stormy Politburo meeting. The article attacked Andreeva's "essentially fatalistic understanding of history" based on the conception that "when you chop woods, chips fly."[43] The Party had "restored Truth (*Pravda*) to its rights" but this truth was bitter, and many were tempted to "whitewash the past." "To silence the sensitive questions of our history means to dismiss truth, to treat disrespectfully the memory of those who became innocent victims of lawlessness and arbitrary. There is only one truth. We need full clarity, precision and consistency, a moral orientation towards the future."[44]

The divide between Russophiles and liberals was also a significant feature of the emerging civil society—the former often forming tactical alliances with the Stalinists. In the broad landscape of clubs and organizations of the Perestroika, two groups symbolized the divide between anti-Stalinist and national memories: Memorial and Pamiat'.[45] Memorial was an organization born from a petition to the Soviet leadership to erect a monument to the victims of political repression. By 1989, hundreds of local branches had sprouted up throughout the country and Memorial struggled for official registration, with an agenda combining human rights defense with historical research and commemoration of Stalin's victims. The emergence of Memorial was symptomatic of a new era when "citizens not only began to talk openly about the past but to publicize the status of victims, to challenge historians' competences, and to demand compensation for past injustices."[46] Pamiat', by contrast, was a nationalist, anti-Semitic movement born from the Pan-Russian Society of Safeguard of Historical Monuments and Culture. These two movements were characterized by a different relationship between past and present. While anti-Stalinist memory called for "mastering the past" in the name of the future, national memory focused on the past as a "given, a system of values."[47] Both memories, however, were selective. Memorial focused primarily on the 1930s, leaving the Revolution and early 1920s untouched, whereas Pamiat' privileged an ancient, mythicized Russian past, the legitimacy and continuity of which was negated by the Revolution. The Russophiles refused to single out the victims of the 1930s and preferred to refer to the victims of 1917 writ large, including the Civil War and collectivization, which had decimated the countryside. Ultimately, this debate merged with the nineteenth-century discussion opposing Slavophiles and Westernizers, as anti-Stalinists saw integration with the West as the best remedy to both Russian backwardness and the Stalinist heritage.[48]

Eventually, however, Gorbachev's Glasnost proved destructive for the system it was called upon to legitimize and renovate. Although it had initially fostered hope among the intelligentsia, most authors agree that, in the long run, "the impact of glasnost was to erode fatally the sustaining myths of the Soviet regime and to destroy what legitimacy remained to it."[49] For Robert Strayer, "attacks on Stalin turned into criticism of Marx, Lenin and the revolution itself, discrediting the entire Soviet experience." It became clear that "the historical foundations of Soviet socialism were built on violence and criminality of monstrous proportions."[50] Paul Hollander concurred: Gorbachev "opened the floodgates of criticism on the assumption that unfettered public discussion would infuse Soviet society with new vitality." However, this only "increased the popular awareness of everything that was wrong with the system and further eroded its legitimacy."[51] Thomas Sherlock has examined how historical Glasnost escaped the regime's control, and unleashed and legitimized "insurgent narratives," which threatened Soviet core myths. This proved particularly destructive in the non-Russian peripheries, where the "public expression of ethnic myths and memories strengthened the cohesion and sense of grievance of these groups and worked to revive or create separatist agendas."[52]

This interpretation, which explains the crumbling of the ideological edifice under the combined weight of insurgent ideological narratives, certainly makes more sense than attributing a key role to the publication of a single work, be it as potent as *The Gulag Archipelago*. Yet dissident histories did play a role in this process as well: their belated return to the Soviet public at a key moment in Soviet history allowed them to have an impact, albeit diminished by the concurrence that they now faced.

The belated return of dissident histories to the Soviet public

Roy Medvedev: The return of the prodigal son

By the time Perestroika started, Medvedev had turned sixty. In March 1986, he wrote: "I have only 5-6 years of active work left. Life in the USSR will become quieter, I think, there will still be reforms, but no dramatic events. Starting from next year, I will start working more on my memoirs."[53] His peaceful retirement plans, however, were soon to be upset. A few months later, he began to write long overviews of the changes in Soviet cultural life for Western newspapers and was increasingly solicited for interviews and articles about ongoing political changes. He observed with fascination the publication of long-banned works and resumed his contacts with such past acquaintances as Anatolii Rybakov, author of *Children of the Arbat*.[54] Historical journals, however, remained unaffected by Glasnost, and historians found themselves in a "sad situation," Medvedev noted. Revisionist historians from the 1960s were now too old to launch new projects. As for the younger generation, "they had been forced to falsify history consciously and honest people had gone into adjacent fields." But they now faced increased pressure to react. As for prominent historians, they simply waited for the "anti-Stalinist wave to recede."[55]

In December 1986, Sakharov was allowed to return to Moscow from internal exile and most political prisoners were amnestied in the following months. In March 1987, Medvedev was contacted by two Soviet journals with offers of publications. However, he noted that they had acted of "their own initiative" and although they claimed they would fight for publication, he remained doubtful that any of his works could appear in the Soviet press.[56] In May, the historian wrote about the flourishing of independent societal clubs. Although they had invited him to their meetings, he had declined the offer. He found the participants too young, inexperienced, and disdainful of his generation's experience. Moreover, it was not "timely" for him to speak publicly, he would rather work quietly at home. Still, he keenly gave them advice and generally welcomed their activism.[57]

In early 1988, he received requests for publication of his books from Poland, Hungary, the GDR, and Yugoslavia. In February, he reluctantly agreed to an interview with *Sobesednik*, a supplement of *Komsomol'skaia pravda* with a 1.5 million print run, although he deemed this a "loss of time."[58] Unexpectedly, however, the publication was authorized by Iakovlev himself, in the context of ideological struggle at the top triggered by the publication of Nina Andreeva's letter.[59] The interview appeared in late April 1988, officially "legalizing" Medvedev after two decades of dissent. The journalist expressed the wish that Medvedev's books be soon published in the Soviet Union: "Poignant, polemical, provoking debate and appealing to the voice of conscience in every one of us, astonishingly truthful and honest. The [current] times call for these books."[60] The interview focused on possible alternative developments of Soviet history—a theme of particular interest to Soviet readers at the time. Medvedev underscored the publication's symbolic meaning: now that Gorbachev had appropriated the dissidents' call for the restoration of historical truth, no one could ignore "private research" such as his.[61] However, he complained about the unconscientious editing of his words. "I said, for example, that we must finally have an honest and truthful history, and the text mentions 'an honest and truthful Leninist (*po-leninski*) history.'"[62]

Roy Medvedev's position now changed radically, and his influence began to grow. "I understood that my personality, my pen, my works are already becoming necessary to Gorbachev, to his politics."[63] Two months later, he had found publishers for several of his works. In July 1988, during Ronald Reagan's visit for the Moscow Summit, Medvedev was added to a list of Soviet intellectuals invited for a meeting with the US president at the House of Writers.[64] From October to December, he published around twenty articles and interviews, not only in the central press, but also in the provinces, in the Ukraine and Byelorussia.[65] He was invited to discuss his position on Stalinism with professional or independent historians at roundtables and in newspapers publications.[66] Although he mostly denounced Stalin-era crimes, Medvedev's posture as a former dissident also allowed him to throw discredit on the Brezhnev regime, which Gorbachev dismissed as an era of "stagnation." Medvedev's article on the scandalous life of Brezhnev's daughter thus enjoyed great success among Soviet readers, and excerpts from his biography of the Soviet leader contributed to further tarnishing the latter's reputation.[67] In the fall, he began receiving invitations to public conferences in Leningrad and Moscow from academic and cultural institutions, universities, ministries. By January, he was giving several conferences a week, with audiences ranging from 500 to 1,500 people, and hundreds of written questions sent every time. He would usually read excerpts from one of his works for forty to fifty minutes and then answer questions from the public for around two hours.[68]

In November–December 1988, Medvedev also gave a dozen lectures to history teachers, on request from the publisher Prosveshchenie, which planned to publish the transcripts as a textbook.[69] As a former schoolteacher and specialist in pedagogics, but also thanks to his renown as an independent historian, Medvedev appeared well-placed to give orientations in a time of crisis of faith in discredited textbooks. His lectures did not cover precise historical topics, but broad philosophical and methodological questions such as "What history teaches and to what it educates"; "History as a part of national or the people's life"; "Falsifications of history"; or "On the alternative paths of development of history." Medvedev's idea was to provide his interlocutors with the critical tools to reflect upon historical events independently, instead of feeding them ready-made interpretations to replace discredited dogmas. However, he faced disoriented audiences, whose questions betrayed a lack of basic factual knowledge about history and great concern for the political implications of ongoing changes. One person thus asked whether Marxism-Leninism was a utopia; another inquired about the successes of social-democracy and which kind of regime was preferable; a third asked whether rule of law could be established in the USSR and how. Others wanted to know if Stalin was a Menshevik, Beria a foreign agent, or if Kosygin or Mikoian were positive historical figures. Their thirst for precise and objective evaluations about key events or historical characters betrayed a naïve faith in Medvedev as a new incontrovertible authority. The textbook based on these lectures, however, was never published, despite positive editorial reviews. Perhaps was it too open-ended to satisfy the needs of the time or it may simply have been that the events unfolded too rapidly for a textbook to reflect the new state of historical scholarship adequately.

In January 1989, *Znamia* began the publication of chapters of *Let History Judge* under the title *On Stalin and Stalinism*. However, the confrontation between Russophiles and anti-Stalinists was raging, and the nationalist press began to launch attacks against Medvedev for having published his works abroad. The editor in chief of *Znamia* wanted to end the publication after three issues, instead of four, but Medvedev threatened to turn it into a public scandal.[70] Meanwhile, *Iunost'* began in March to serialize *All Stalin's Men*, and *Druzhba Narodov* published *Khrushchev* over the summer. And this was only the tip of a larger iceberg, with more publications planned in the provincial and republican press and in book format. In May, Medvedev observed that he would probably be the most published Soviet author in 1989 and 1990, without even having to solicit publishers and journals.[71]

In January 1989, the official congress of foundation of "Memorial" took place. Medvedev had been elected to the organization's "social council," constituted of famous public figures. However, he refused to attend the conference, both because of his exhaustion and his exasperation with "scholastic debates about who should be considered a victim of Stalinism and who should not, and should one speak of victims of Leninism." Moreover, he disliked Memorial's strict structure, which reminded him of a party. Rather than "an organization with membership cards," he would prefer to see it become "a social movement," which "any old widow who comes from the countryside" who sympathized with the movement could freely join, without having to attend any meeting.[72] This was in fact what Memorial was about, but the old historian cherished his independence too much to join an organization he had played no role in founding.

Medvedev also began to professionalize, hiring assistants to collect oral history, or initiating collaborations with younger historians to coauthor monographs or publish revised editions of his books.[73] However, he was forced to turn down numerous invitations from abroad for conferences and lectures, as he became immersed in politics, after his election to the Congress of People's Deputies, the first freely elected Soviet parliament, in April 1989. Nevertheless, in the following year, he published several of his books in the USSR, starting with *The Life and Death of Philip Kuzmich Mironov*, followed by *On Stalin and Stalinism* and his biography of Khrushchev.[74] In March 1990, he finally traveled to the West for the first time, for the Congress of the Italian Communist Party. And by 1991, as the foundations of the Soviet Union were shaking, he published the political biography of Leonid Brezhnev he had been working on for years.[75]

Antonov-Ovseenko: The comeback of an embattled *zek*

For Anton Antonov-Ovseenko, public recognition in his homeland also came belatedly, as he was approaching the eighth decade of his life. As could be expected, it was with a publication on his father, in August 1988, that he first returned into print.[76] But the publication was more revolutionary than it seemed: for the first time, he was able to give an objective account of his father's support to the "declaration of the 46," which had earned him the label of Trotskyite. He reaffirmed, once again, that Vladimir Antonov-Ovseenko was not "an enemy of the Party and that all those labels—Trotskyite and enemy of the people" had only been stuck by Stalin, who wished to destroy his enemies.[77] This article's content was also incorporated into an augmented edition of Antonov-Ovseenko's biography of his father, published in 1989.[78] The new edition insisted on V. A. Antonov-Ovseenko's alleged attempt to "defend legality" in his position of Public Prosecutor of the RSFSR in 1934–36 and shed light on his last days, based on the *Novyi mir* publication of 1964.[79] On the seventy-first anniversary of the Revolution, on November 7, 1988, *Moskovskaia pravda* published an interview with the historian entitled "The Father, the Son and the Truth of History."[80]

By then, the gates of Glasnost had been widely opened, and the most subversive of Antonov-Ovseenko's works could now be published. In September 1988, the journal *Zvezda* began to serialize his biography of Beria.[81] After the manuscript's confiscation during a house search, the historian had had to rewrite it from scratch. However, this interruption forced him to reconsider previously overlooked sources, such as Caucasian periodicals, which added up to his numerous interviews with widows of executed Chekists.[82] His works on Stalin and Beria were closely connected: they shared, in his view, the same criminal nature, and he liked to call them by their Caucasian nicknames "the Little Pope" and the "Great Pope."[83] "Beria was the closest [to Stalin] in spirit. Kindred natures, they mirrored each other, the Great Pope and the Little Pope. For thirty years they walked side by side, knee-deep in blood, [trampling underfoot] the living and the dead," wrote the historian.[84] While "hundreds of books" had been written about Stalin, "no serious monograph" had been written about his "minion," and Antonov-Ovseenko wished to fill this gap.[85] *Iunost'* and *Kommunist Tatarii* published chapters of *Beria*, and the book was released in 1991.[86] A revised edition of *Portrait of a Tyranny* also appeared in 1990 under the title *Stalin unmasked*, after its serialization in *Voprosy istorii* in 1989.[87]

In numerous interviews in the following years, Antonov-Ovseenko recalled his father's fate and unveiled his conception of Stalin and *Stalinshchina*. Using a rhetoric reminiscent of Solzhenitsyn's, the historian spoke of his duty, as a "living receptacle of memories," to share these with the public, rather than privilege the preservation of his health and peace of mind.[88] His "greatest joy, for the sake of which one works," was to get his books into the Soviet readers' hands.[89] He considered that "both historians and journalists must write about what happened." They had to reveal the names of those who accomplished Stalin's deeds. Journalists had a "huge responsibility": "The fewer speculations appear in print, the more will people believe us, the more convincing will [our] writings become."[90] Although the work of historians and publicists was complementary, he denounced "the unconscientiousness of professional researchers, the shallowness of some of our publicists," including Volkogonov. "The frivolous, irresponsible approach to such an important theme discredits our Glasnost not only in the eyes of opponents of this process, but also in the eyes of those readers who honestly wish to assert their new historical consciousness."[91] However, he also faced criticism for factual mistakes himself. In March 1989, he thus apologized to the readers of *Iunost'*, promising to use their corrections for his book and justifying his errors by his necessary reliance on oral history. "Here mistakes and imprecisions are inevitable, and the historian's duty is to limit them to the minimum."[92]

Solzhenitsyn: Return in print of the regime's "number one enemy"

The most expected return, in literary terms, was Aleksandr Solzhenitsyn's, but it was also the most problematic from the regime's point of view. As all the names once forbidden made their way into print, from Grossman to Shalamov, and from Pasternak to Ginzburg, the road seemed clear for the Nobel laureate. Admittedly, due to his long absence and the smear campaigns against him, the Soviet public was left with a hazy representation of a subversive writer who, for unclear reasons, had "either left the USSR himself, or been expelled,"[93] but whose works remained unknown to the vast majority. Yet the curiosity surrounding this forbidden fruit grew, and in May and July 1988, Sergei Zalygin, the editor in chief of *Novyi mir*, tried to contact Solzhenitsyn with an offer to publish *The Cancer Ward* and *The First Circle*. For the writer, however, this was too little, too late. He made clear that his first work published in the USSR would have to be *The Gulag Archipelago*, which had caused his expulsion. "One cannot act as if the *Archipelago* had not been, and step over it. The duty towards the dead does not allow it. And through their suffering, our living compatriots have earned the right to read it," explained the writer.[94] Solzhenitsyn expected his bold demand to be rejected, but, unexpectedly, *Novyi mir*'s editorial team voted in favor of publishing *Gulag*, starting from January 1989. Predictably, however, it took longer to obtain the authorization from "above": in October 1988, the Politburo vetoed an announcement of the forthcoming publication and the journal's cover had to be reprinted. For Gorbachev, it was still too early; for the conservatives, the publication of an "enemy," who attacked Lenin, was unacceptable.[95]

However, public opinion now played a prominent role in Soviet society. In August 1988, Lev Voskresenskii wrote in *Moskovskie novosti* about his rediscovery of *Ivan Denisovich*, calling the novella "one of the greatest, milestone achievements of [our] national literature."[96] The same month, Elena Chukovskaia launched an appeal in *Knizhnoe obozrenie* to restore Solzhenitsyn's Soviet citizenship. Although this was not a precondition for the publication of his works, it would be a symbolical gesture and the redress of a historical injustice. She recalled the painful path of abuse Solzhenitsyn had trodden, leading up to his expulsion from the country. His homeland now obligingly consented to publish his more innocuous works, "using up the results of his labor, the fruits of his trampled life," expecting gratefulness in return. But was it not elementary justice to first annul "the unfair sentence accusing him of betrayal of his motherland"? "Only after this will the publication of his books and their critical analysis on the pages of our journals and newspapers become appropriate."[97] If any justification was needed, then Solzhenitsyn's bitter and courageous fate, from the frontline, where he defended his fatherland against Nazi Germany, through the Gulag, where his anti-Stalinist critique led him, and on to the struggle for glasnost in the 1960s, were sufficient proof of his merit.

This publication raised a flow of hundreds of readers' letters, mostly in support of the writer. *Knizhnoe obozrenie* published an overview of these reactions. Many readers recalled that Solzhenitsyn had been deprived of his citizenship precisely for his struggle for the values which now underlay Perestroika: anti-Stalinism, glasnost, and human rights. Some had read all of his banned works; others remembered with fondness his early publications; whereas a few did not need to read him to know that he was an "*antisovetchik*." For Viacheslav Kondrat'ev, Solzhenitsyn had become an "ally," whose words were now sorely needed. "Because no one will tell about our past with such power, such degree of artistry. We do not have any writer in Russia on this level."[98] Igor' Shafarevich called for the restoration of Solzhenitsyn's Writers' Union's membership. Father Aleksandr Men' placed him on a par with Tolstoi, Dostoevsky, and Gogol and recalled that "many Russian classics who fought for truth were accused of anti-patriotism." A few discordant voices resonated as well: I. Kriukov, a war veteran, thus wrote: "Let him remain where he is well paid by his CIA curators."[99] Boris Kagarlitskii, a left-wing dissident, also stood out from the chorus of praise. Having read most of Solzhenitsyn's works, he could not condone the writer's opposition to democracy and socialism and accused him of being an "inverted Stalinist." Still, he considered that his works, just like Trotsky's, should be published, so that readers may see both "his literary talent and his anti-socialist political philosophy."[100]

Throughout the following year, civil society's campaign to obtain the publication of Solzhenitsyn's works intensified. In December, for the writer's seventieth birthday, numerous commemorative events were planned by the artistic unions, and prominent figures of the intelligentsia wrote collective letters in his support. "Memorial" asked the writer to join its "social council," but he declined: he had already fulfilled his duty toward Gulag victims and, from exile, he could not take part in his homeland's social life.[101] In June 1989, from the tribune of the Congress of People's Deputies, the writer Iurii Kariakin called for the restoration of "Russian citizenship to the man who dared first tell the truth about *stalinshchina*, who was the first to call upon himself and ourselves not to lie—to the great writer of the Russian land, to the great humanist Solzhenitsyn."[102] Meanwhile, a few early publications appeared: in October 1988, *Rabochee slovo*, a Kyiv newspaper, published *To live not by lies* and in January *Neva* published the *Letter to the Fourth Congress of the Writers' Union*. In July 1989, finally, Sergei Zalygin announced that the Secretariat of the Writers' Union had unanimously approved the publication of *Gulag*, and the July issue of *Novyi mir* featured his Nobel Prize lecture.[103] The editor in chief had put pressure on the Soviet leadership and Gorbachev had finally given in; the Writers' Union could only rubberstamp this decision and reintegrate Solzhenitsyn into its ranks.[104]

In August 1989, the first chapters of *The Gulag Archipelago* finally appeared in *Novyi mir*, preceded by a foreword by Zalygin. Describing Solzhenitsyn as a "clever, honest opponent" of the regime, he conceded that one may not agree with everything he wrote. Still, "we have neither the moral, nor the intellectual right not to know and listen to him." And his new readers were no longer the Soviet people he had once appealed to. "Being different, having learned, understood and lived through much, we will read him differently as well, quite possibly not even the way he would have wanted us to." But this was "this long-awaited freedom—the freedom of the written word and the freedom of its interpretation," which was the essential condition for a full-blown literary life.[105] The four issues of *Novyi mir* featured a selection of chapters—about a third from the 1,800-pages work. This publication was certainly a huge symbol, but it came late, after two years of historical revelations, which partly attenuated its effect on readers. Still, the demand for *Gulag* far exceeded the journal's 1.6 million print run, and although several Soviet journals began to publish it, only with the book version could the readers' thirst be quenched.[106]

Following the publication, a flow of readers' letters, unparalleled since the publication of *Ivan Denisovich*, began to reach *Novyi mir*.[107] "*The Gulag Archipelago* is not a libel against Soviet reality, as the defenders of perpetrators are depicting it, but the pain and anger of a citizen loyal to his motherland," wrote M. S. Kovalenko already in November 1988, demanding *Gulag*'s publication. Many readers asked for the book to be read out on television. As in 1962, former camp inmates responded keenly and offered their testimonies on specific episodes or figures mentioned. "We are not among those who did not know anything. We are among those who lived through this in one form or another," wrote the daughter of an "enemy of the people" and granddaughter of a "kulak."[108] Unaware that *Novyi mir* had published only a fraction of the book, some regretted the omission of certain elements. G. S. Klimovich thus called upon Solzhenitsyn to write more extensively on the subject. "The facts presented in 'The Gulag Archipelago' warrant explanation. And it would be bad if the one commenting on these facts were the historian Roy Medvedev, who does not know the taste of the camps' *gorbushka* [bread ration], and without this knowledge, it is impossible to restore truth."[109] In December 1989, as the last chapters of *Gulag* appeared in print, *Pravda* had republished Medvedev's 1974 review of the first volume, and many letter writers contrasted the two dissidents' vision.[110] A. B. Diachkov regretted *Novyi mir*'s choice to publish only "opponents" of socialism and recommended publishing Roy Medvedev's works, in which he polemicized with Solzhenitsyn. V. V. Bryl', on the contrary, reproached Medvedev with "attempt[ing] to refute 'scientifically' the main thoughts and conclusions written with the blood of tens of millions of victims."[111] Both Solzhenitsyn's opponents and his supporters, however, agreed that the work dealt a heavy blow to the regime. S. Dudko, a thirty-seven-year-old Siberian doctor, wrote that the book had had a great influence on her worldview. If the people had been able to read Solzhenitsyn's works earlier, "I am sure that life would have been very different, people would have been different, one cannot help changing, having read *The Gulag Archipelago.*"[112] V. A. Baltiitsev, a young worker, implicitly equated Solzhenitsyn's works with a Trojan horse, containing anti-communist views under the guise of historical truth.[113] However, some readers also shared E. V. Kiseleva's heartfelt indignation: "What are you doing? Why are you publishing this Christ-seller [*sic*] Solzhenitsyn? . . . What right does he have to spit on our world, our history? . . . It is painful, when what was holy for us is scorned."[114]

In 1990, *Novyi mir* continued the publication of Solzhenitsyn's works with *The First Circle* (no 1–5) and *The Cancer Ward* (no 6–8). In mid-August, his Soviet citizenship was restored, but he declined an official invitation to visit his homeland: he refused to return as a simple guest.[115] In December 1990, he was awarded the RSFSR state award for *The Gulag Archipelago*, but, again, declined it. He argued that the book remained unavailable to many former prisoners and that the phenomenon of the Gulag had still not been overcome in the USSR, "either morally or judicially."[116] Finally, in September 1991, the charges of high treason leveled against him were dropped.[117] Solzhenitsyn remained closely involved in his homeland's fate, publishing in 1990 an essay entitled *Rebuilding Russia*. In 1993, he finally returned from exile and settled back in Moscow.

Nekrich: A guest in his homeland

By the late 1980s, Nekrich had been living in the West for over a decade and was engrossed in the life of the Soviet émigré community. An active contributor to Russian-language media, the historian edited for four years *Obozrenie*, a bimonthly supplement to the Paris-based weekly *Russkaia mysl'*. However, the publication ended after the twenty-first issue in October 1986 for financial reasons.[118] But with the onset of Perestroika, Nekrich observed with fascination the return of a long-repressed history in his homeland. In October 1989, he was interviewed by *Moskovskie novosti*. To balance Nekrich's subversive views, the weekly included comments by two Soviet historians, Vladlen Loginov and Al'bert Nenarokov, and the economist Egor Gaidar, who contested his views on current political and economic reforms and the continuity between the Lenin and Stalin eras.[119] A few weeks later, Nekrich visited Moscow for the first time since his emigration, on an exchange of the Harvard Russian Research Center with the Historical-Archival Institute. During his visit, he gave a series of lectures on Perestroika in history, a topic he had been studying for some time.[120]

In an interview given to *Sobesednik* during his visit, Nekrich complained that *Utopia in Power*, despite having undergone thirteen editions in the West, and despite the acute need for a new historical narrative in the USSR, remained unpublished there. The historian called on Soviet editors to publish his work but entertained few illusions in this regard.[121] In Poland, meanwhile, the book had aroused "great interest," according to its Polish underground editor, who wrote to the author in August 1987. The book had sold out despite its high price (1,800 zl. for two volumes), and requests for more copies had been flowing from all over the country. Historians from the Department of Russian Philology at Wroclaw University had even assigned the book to their students. The editor concluded the following: "Believe me it is not so common to have a thick underground book being read 'from cover to cover,' and I know many people, who, having read it all, are encouraging their friends to its careful study."[122]

There would never be any Soviet edition of *Utopia in Power*, however, and the book would only be published in Russia in 1995, two years after Nekrich's death. According to Leonid Heller, his father, who was very critical of Gorbachev's Perestroika, would have strongly objected to a publication in the Soviet Union.[123] But it is likely that the book's radical critique of the Soviet experiment was also at fault. As for *June 22, 1941*, Nekrich received offers from Soviet publishers for its reedition in 1989, but he realized that, three decades after the first publication, the book needed to be updated with newly available archival documents. The new edition came out in 1995, with primary sources relating to the history of the book and the text of the Ribbentrop-Molotov pact.[124] And although there was talk of publishing *The Punished* Peoples and *Forsake Fear*, none of these projects seems to have yielded results.[125] Besides the author's anti-Communist tone, his émigré status—a label still tainted with opprobrium—may have undermined his publishing potential. Moreover, Nekrich remained largely cut off from Soviet debates, observing them as he did from a distance.

Nevertheless, Perestroika also meant the possibility for Nekrich to resume his archival research in the USSR for his new project on Soviet-German relations from the 1920s to the 1940s. In 1989–91, he was thus granted access to several state archives.[126] The Soviet Army State Archive, however, remained closed to him, despite official announcements about its opening to the public.[127] Nekrich's topic of particular interest, the Soviet-German pact, was one of the most sensitive questions of Soviet history. The existence of the Soviet protocols providing for the annexation of the Baltic states was only officially acknowledged in 1993.[128] Nekrich's monograph, *Pariahs, Partners, Predators: Soviet-German Relations 1922-1941*, would appear posthumously in 1997.[129] The historian died in exile in 1993.[130]

Questioning dissident histories' factual accuracy

How many . . . ?

In February 1989, a reader of *Argumenty i Fakty* wrote: "As I am preparing a material on Stalin-era repression, I come across huge numbers of victims. I ask myself: 'Is this really true?' Maybe AiF could name the exact figure of those repressed under Stalin?"[131] To answer this question, which preoccupied many readers, the weekly interviewed Roy Medvedev. The historian began with a note of caution: "It is a difficult question and one cannot answer it exactly." Nevertheless, he attempted to give a rough estimate, by category: ten to twelve million deported as "kulaks"; six to seven million deaths from the 1932–33 famine; 1.5 to 2 million peasants arrested for stealing grain (law of the "three spikelets"); one million deported from large cities as "class alien" elements; five to seven million arrested in 1937–38, including one million executed and one million rehabilitated in 1939; wartime deportation of two million ethnic Germans and three million Muslims from small nations; two to three million condemned to Gulag terms for tardiness at work; ten to twelve million former POWs or inhabitants of occupied territories condemned for collaboration after the war; 1 to 1.5 million political arrests in the postwar period. Medvedev therefore estimated the total number of victims of Stalinism to about forty million.[132]

Although Medvedev was very cautious in his formulations, the figure named in the article's headline produced a strong impression on readers. Translated into an estimate of twenty million dead in a *New York Times* report on the article, the number did not appear far-fetched when compared to similar figures named by Robert Conquest.[133] However, according to Evgenii Krinko and Sergei Kropachev, estimates based on archival documents have since proved these figures to be overblown. Arsenii Roginskii has estimated that about 4.5 million were condemned to various sentences and about seven million deported between 1921 and 1953.[134] Yet, it should be noted that Medvedev counted not only the dead, but the repressed, and took a large view of this notion, including not only those deported without judgment, but also those condemned under nonpolitical repressive laws. Moreover, his could only be rough estimates, since he had had no access to archival documents. Nevertheless, some Western historians bring up similar numbers: the introduction to Stéphane Courtois's *Livre noir du communisme* states that the Soviet regime caused the death of twenty million people—a calculation which includes summary executions during the Civil War, deaths from the 1921–22 and 1932–33 famines (respectively five and six millions) and deportations of kulaks and national groups, while executions during the Great Terror alone amount to 690,000 victims.[135]

Medvedev's article triggered a large wave of letters from readers, predominantly negative.[136] Many readers regretted that a newspaper intended for propagandists published such "muddy statistics," not buttressed by any document, instead of "incontrovertible facts." V. I. Zaguliaev was shocked to see "with what ease com[rade] Medvedev plays with (*razbrasyvaetsia*) millions of human lives, how he can simply . . . throw, according to his imagination, assumption, or some calculation, *around ten million* human lives onto our regime's conscience, our Party's conscience."[137] In the spirit of the Nina Andreeva letter, many accused Glasnost of shattering patriotic myths, such as that of Pavlik Morozov, the young boy who had denounced his father. "Yes, Glasnost has opened in front of us the hitherto invisible possibility of democratization, has thrown light upon many negative phenomena, misuses, mistakes of the past. But Glasnost does not mean laissez-faire (*vsedozvolennost'*), [the right] for each to interpret in his own way the road our people has travelled," wrote Vladislav Lygan. Only "truth" was needed, and those who wrote about the past had to be guided by "love for the motherland." It was inacceptable to "instigate hostility" between fathers and sons, to present his generation as one which had only written denunciations, built prisons and sat in them.[138] For Ivan Kuravshov, the press only sought to "dig up" sensational news, mostly negative. Instead, he called on newspapers to contribute to an improvement of the situation by "heightening work discipline" and helping liquidate such shortages as that of soap and washing powder.[139]

Some readers contested specific numbers and came up with alternative calculations, based for instance on the number of deported kulak families in their own village, providing estimates up to forty times lower or three times higher. Others denied that certain categories could be considered as victims. For Lygan, it was "immoral" to consider as victims deported ethnic Germans or those who had lived on occupied territory. Despite living under occupation, he had not been arrested, only those who had collaborated had been repressed. Among them were "supporters of Makhno, White Guards, kulaks and all kinds of criminals who went to serve the fascists in faith and truth."[140] A war veteran from Lviv who had joined a kolkhoz during collectivization recalled that in 1931–32 "there was ubiquitous sabotage, especially in the Ukraine," but "as soon as repression began, the situation of peasants improved," and starting from 1934, no one died of starvation. He could not believe the number of forty million: during his seventy-three years of life, he had not known anyone repressed, "except for deserters, traitors to the Motherland, bandits, thieves, speculators and other malefactors (*zloumyshlenniki*)."[141] A few readers, however, found Medvedev's calculation too conservative. G. M. Bugai proposed to replace the word "repression" by "genocide" and hoped that "soon our statistics will give a more accurate number of victims of this misanthropist-sadist, Soviet Hitler (Stalin)—65 million, i.e. the figure that the radio station 'Voice of America' named decades ago already."[142]

In April 1991, Antonov-Ovseenko joined the debate on the number of victims of Stalinism. In his *Portrait of a Tyranny*, he had brought up the number of a hundred million arrests and deaths from the Revolution to 1953. He commented: "Not all those arrested in the repressive campaigns perished, and not all those who perished were on Stalin's 'conscience.' But nearly all. Nearly all."[143] In an article on Shatunovskaia's investigation of the Kirov murder published in *Literaturnaia gazeta*,[144] he named the figure of 19,840,000 victims of repression from 1935 to 1941, seven million of whom had died the year following their arrest, mentioned in an official document Shatunovskaia claimed to have seen. Based on other sources, Antonov-Ovseenko estimated to sixteen million the postwar Gulag population. He also attacked V. N. Zemskov, a historian who had recently published in *Argumenty i fakty* lower numbers.[145] According to archival documents Zemskov had consulted, as of January 1, 1940, the Gulag system counted 1,344,408 prisoners, and in 1937–38 its population fluctuated from about 820,000 to one million. For Antonov-Ovseenko, such numbers were incompatible with what he had himself witnessed; therefore, they had to be false.

Zemskov did not let the accusation of fraud go unanswered. He replied in the journal *Istoriia SSSR* that, while forging a single document was possible, his calculations were based on a whole archival fond, containing thousands of files with numerous primary sources. And the combined data contained in these documents coincided with the numbers cited in statistical documents of the GULAG administration, as communicated in reports to the NKVD chiefs and to Stalin himself. This proved that the numbers were exact. Moreover, there was no ground to suspect the GULAG or NKVD authorities of deliberately underestimating the number of prisoners, since this might have led them into trouble for "insufficient activity."[146] Antonov-Ovseenko's figures, Zemskov claimed, were based on unreliable testimonies. A clear example was the number of sixteen million prisoners in the postwar period, based on the number of food rations distributed. Zemskov knew this document, but Antonov-Ovseenko's name was not on the users' list. Therefore, the latter must have received the information from second hand, which would explain why he had failed to see the dot: 1.6 million instead of 16.[147] However, Krinko and Kropachev noted that Zemskov's figures, far from the tens of millions estimates of dissident historians, raised mistrust among readers, who were quick to accuse him of falsifying official statistics.[148] After decades of falsifications of official history, the burden of proof was on professional historians, while former dissidents enjoyed public trust, based on their acquired moral capital.

How truthful?

In 1991, Nikita Petrov, vice-head of the Council of "Memorial," published an article entitled "Roy Medvedev as a Historian-Dissident."[149] Examining the case of the man who had turned so suddenly from a famous opponent of the regime into one of its allies, Petrov denied the applicability to him both of the terms "dissident" and "historian." Medvedev's had been "the most innocuous criticism," and the fact that he could receive royalties from abroad proved that he had never been a dissident. Moreover, the mistakes in Medvedev's works, deriving from his "false conception," proved that he was no more a "historian" than a dissident. At fault was Medvedev's use of oral sources. Petrov characterized *Let History Judge* as "a kind of oral creation by repressed party members," which should have been published as a collection of primary sources but not "pass[ed] off as scholarly work." The credibility of these testimonies could be explained chiefly by the lies of official historiography, the reference to which seemed to exempt Medvedev "from the study of the bibliography and generally from any research of primary sources." Petrov concluded that Medvedev's "literary (*belletricheskie*) speculations" were no valid alternative to discredited "falsifications of Soviet pseudo-specialists."[150]

This critique was radical, but not wholly isolated. Letters that Medvedev received following the publication of *On Stalin and Stalinism* show that Perestroika readers turned a critical eye toward historical publications and did not blindly accept what they read. Most of the letters, nevertheless, expressed gratefulness for Medvedev's work, calling it a "civil feat" and "a contribution to the struggle for historical truth." B. N. Tikhomirov wrote that, while he considered Medvedev's work to be of enormous significance "for the establishment of our historical self-consciousness," it was crucial that he avoid any approximation when dealing with the "ghastly statistics" of the Terror. "For behind all of this are lost human lives." Vladimir Alpatov, a linguist from the Institute of Eastern Studies, filled thirteen pages of remarks and corrections, apologizing for his "dilettantism."[151] Eduard Beltov was less charitable: in a five-page letter, he listed all the mistakes he had uncovered, expressing the regret that the author had not removed them before publishing his work in the USSR. He praised Medvedev's research for uncovering "a huge quantity of facts of illegal Stalin-era repression." However, he regretted, "the inaccuracies and mistakes listed above lower to a certain extent its value and this is, to say the truth, highly regrettable."[152] In a letter published in *Molodoi kommunist*, a student in history also pointed out numerous mistakes in recent publications by Medvedev and Antonov-Ovseenko.[153]

However, many relatives of the repressed also wrote with new information about individual fates. One letter came from Lemara Abdullaevna Rozybakieva, daughter of one of the founders of Soviet Kazakhstan, who expressed gratefulness for the mention of her father's fate.[154] Iia Smirnova wrote that she was seventeen in 1938:

> My father died in this meat-grinder. I knew many of those you wrote about. We lived in the same building as some of them, we went on holidays with some, Dad went to school and worked with others. . . . I am writing all of this for you to understand that I am not indifferent to what you write.[155]

Other relatives of victims mentioned in Medvedev's essay asked for details concerning their fate, often assuming that the historian had access to archives. Some offered testimonies or asked for help in getting research about lost family members published. A. F. Kovalev, from Minsk, wrote: "On page 221 my name is mentioned among the deceased leaders of Byelorussia, but as you see, I am alive and writing to you. My last name is misspelt . . . . I was indeed on the verge of dying. I endured the most sophisticated sufferings of the prison hell." Kovalev had written his tale of woe and published it in a journal but asked for Medvedev's help in getting it published as a book. Medvedev replied that the misspelling was the editor's mistake and offered to act as a reviewer for the publisher.[156]

In his letters to his brother, Medvedev repeatedly complained about the insufficient copyediting of his work by *Znamia*. But although the typos and factual mistakes in the journal version may have lowered the value of his work in the eyes of a few educated readers, the letters the author received were also part of a new feedback mechanism Medvedev had elaborated. He had always counted on reviewers to contribute to the improvement of successive versions of his manuscript and he now relied on a pool of thousands of readers to point out errors in his work but also offer additional information. In 1989, he began publishing early versions of his historical essays and monographs in the regional press, expanding his works thanks to the material thus collected. He could also reach a wider audience: some of the local newspapers had print runs of several hundred thousand copies and people read them with interest, unlike books, which often remained unread on the buyer's shelf, in his view.[157] In 1990, he thus wrote that he planned on publishing individual chapters of his book on Brezhnev in the provincial and youth press, which had short publishing cycles and large print runs.[158]

But the critiques aimed at Medvedev were not simply caused by mistakes in his works, which were probably inevitable in those times of publishing bustle. They also derived more largely from his actions as a public figure and in the political field, which raised some controversy.

From the underground to the Central Committee

In a quote reproduced on one of Roy Medvedev's 1989 electoral posters, Andrei Karaulov, editor of the journal *Teatral'naia zhizn'*, commented on the ironic twist of fate that had turned the dissident overnight into "one of the most popular and respected people in our artistic intelligentsia's circles."[159] This comment reflected a radical shift in the dissident's career, which had been made possible partly by co-option from above, partly by genuine popular support. In his struggle with his conservative opponents, Gorbachev was looking for new liberal allies. Roy Medvedev was ideally suited for this role: neither a radical, nor a conservative, he was known for his socialist convictions, and enjoyed popularity within Western left-wing circles.[160] Nevertheless, it was through the popular vote that Medvedev initially entered politics.

In December 1988, a new electoral law was adopted, which foresaw the competitive election of a Congress constituted of 2,250 People's Deputies. While one-third of the seats were reserved for representatives from political and social organizations and professional unions, the other two-thirds were disputed within territorial and national-territorial constituencies. In each electoral district, work collectives and voters' meetings of over 500 citizens were entitled to nominate potential candidates and a "constituency meeting" would select suitable candidates among the nominees who had confirmed their candidacy. When Roy Medvedev was unexpectedly nominated in three territorial constituencies, one in the northern city of Syktyvkar, and two in Moscow, he entertained little hope of being selected as a candidate, expecting little from the recent electoral reforms. He confirmed his candidacy in the two Moscow districts, but did not postpone his planned conference tour to Leningrad. Despite failing to attend the constituency meetings, however, his candidacy was eventually confirmed, along with those of five other nominees, in the 6th Voroshilov constituency. Although the standard practice was to select only two candidates, in practice it proved difficult to make a selection among equally qualified nominees, and some districts chose to approve all confirmed candidacies.[161]

Medvedev's views were far from radical by the measure of the time, yet he could play on his image of dissident excluded from the Party for his fight for "historical truth," at a time when his opponents had remained silent. During the electoral campaign, the historian spoke in public two or three times a day and, despite lacking support from any official structure, he seemed to enjoy the public's favor.[162] The organization Memorial issued a leaflet calling to vote for the man "whose voice will be heard and who has always fought for perestroika."[163] His electoral program combined support for socialism with the struggle for glasnost and democracy. He insisted on the thirty-year struggle for the "reconstruction (*perestroika*) of Soviet society" he had led "as a pedagogue, a historian, and a philosopher, but also as a citizen." "I spoke up not only for the restoration of historical truth and against falsifications of history, but also for the development of internal party democracy, the development of a new system of economic management, the broadening of glasnost, freedom of information and human rights." He "had never been afraid of criticizing openly the negative phenomena of Soviet social and political life" and, if elected, would continue doing so in office. He promised he would never "mechanically vote for any law and decree." He saw as his function to monitor the activity of the executive branch and struggle against any abuse of power.[164]

On March 25, 1989, Medvedev led the first round of the election, with 35 percent of the vote, and faced in the run-off Kseniia Razumova, a professor of the Kurchatov Institute of Atomic Energy. Despite claiming official support from the very popular

Boris Yeltsin and relying on a large campaign budget, Razumova lost the electoral battle, and Medvedev was elected with 52.33 percent of the vote on April 9. The historian noted: "It turns out that my supporters were people of conviction and I think that many of them are my readers."[165] He estimated that he had been one of around fifty independent candidates elected throughout the country.[166] Shortly thereafter, he was reinstated in the Party and his archive, confiscated in 1975, was returned. His reintegration, he felt, was necessary primarily for the Soviet leadership, at a time when many people were leaving the Party.[167]

The First Congress of People's Deputies opened on May 25, 1989. It was a moment of inspiration and hope for millions of Soviet citizens who regained faith in the democratization of the Soviet system. The Congress sessions were broadcast live on TV and literally the whole country watched them with fascination until late at night.[168] This first democratic experiment was not entirely conclusive and underwent many hiccups, but it did give a prominent tribune to liberal democratic deputies, who formed the opposition Interregional Deputies' Group. The most striking voice was that of Andrei Sakharov, who had returned from seven years of exile in Gor'kii with the aura of a martyr for freedom and was determined to stand for his ideas in this new democratic forum.

In contrast, Roy Medvedev decided against joining the Interregional Deputies' Group, whose political program he mostly approved of, but whose methods he found too radical.[169] As a deputy, he displayed unfailing loyalty toward Gorbachev, despite growing doubts concerning his politics. During the first Congress, the historian intervened impromptu several times, seeking to solve crisis situations, or to bring his political weight to bear on a decision. When the Congress discussed the creation of a commission on the Ribbentrop-Molotov Pact, Medvedev thus insisted that the Baltic states had been annexed and called on Minister of Foreign Affairs Eduard Shevarnadze to chair the commission.[170]

His interventions did not go unnoticed, nor his loyalty unrewarded: during the first Congress, he was elected to the Supreme Soviet, the Congress's working body, and placed at the head of a commission in charge of examining the activity of the prosecution group headed by Tel'man Gdlian. Gdlian and his deputy Nikolai Ivanov had been leading a vast prosecutorial operation against corruption in Central Asia since the early 1980s and now stood accused of using illegal methods of investigation, such as torture, blackmail, and arrest of relatives. This was a delicate affair, as Gdlian and Ivanov had both been elected deputies and enjoyed great popularity, particularly after they denounced alleged acts of corruption in higher party circles, involving Politburo member Egor Ligachev himself. Medvedev had accepted this heavy responsibility upon request from Anatolii Lukianov, First Deputy Chairman of the Supreme Soviet, and noted that many had refused the job. Involvement with this affair proved costly for Medvedev's image within liberal circles, largely favorable to Gdlian, and unfairly earned him the reputation of a compliant, if not opportunistic, politician.[171] However, by the time the commission presented its preliminary results in front of the Second Congress, in December 1989, the criticism, but also interest in the Congress itself, had abated.

Medvedev was once more rewarded for his loyalty in July 1990, when he was elected to the Central Committee of the CPSU. Yet by that time, this ruling organ had lost much of its power and control over an increasingly volatile situation. The historian held Gorbachev responsible for the dire fate of Perestroika. "I saw an obvious paralysis of power but could not understand its reasons. One had the impression that the country had no leader, that is, there lacked what M. Gorbachev himself then called a strong political will."[172] By the spring of 1990, Medvedev no longer wore his People's Deputy badge on the street for fear of aggressions. Soon, the regime he had sought to reform would crumble and his country would fall apart. He concluded bitterly: "The illnesses, which Gorbachev set out to cure in our social and state system, had been neglected for too long. One should have started healing them in the fifties, and there is no ground whatsoever to praise Gorbachev as a reformer."[173]

The publication of dissident histories in the Soviet Union was a long-awaited coda for several decades of repression of independent historical narratives. They were returned to their intended audience, the Soviet public, as part of a very broad movement of rehabilitation of previously banned works, and as such, they raised enormous public interest. The thirst for knowledge about the past expressed by Perestroika readers would remain unequaled in the following decades. Yet dissident histories, once hailed as lonely voices of truth piercing the wall of Soviet censorship, were now drowned in a sea of equally or more radical accounts. Those who craved for reliable facts criticized their approximations, due to a heavy reliance on oral testimonies. And those who merely wished to learn about past repressions had many alternative accounts to choose from. Nevertheless, as dissidents, their authors enjoyed an aura of moral authority, which was arguably unequaled.

From the point of view of the regime, however, all of the dissident histories were not equal. On the one hand, Medvedev and Antonov-Ovseenko's anti-Stalinist narratives fitted very nicely with the new official line on the Stalin question, and their moral capital as dissidents could be instrumentalized to reinforce the regime's legitimacy. On the other hand, Solzhenitsyn's more radical anti-communist narrative and Nekrich's works from exile still had no place in Gorbachev's ideological plan. It was only under public pressure, as the Soviet leadership was increasingly losing control over the Glasnost it had unleashed, that *The Gulag Archipelago* was finally returned to the Soviet public.

Conclusion

Larisa Bogoraz and Sergei Kovalev, prominent representatives of the human rights movement, wrote in 1991 that the usual delineations between the "Thaw," "Stagnation," and "Perestroika" was artificial, for each of these periods "bore within itself the seeds of the following." Within the "swamp rot of stagnation," some "viable sprouts proved resistant to this decay and bloomed in our days."[1] Certainly, the example of the dissident researchers we have examined testifies to the persistence throughout the Brezhev era of an independent intellectual life taking its roots in the Thaw, and which eventually blossomed during Perestroika. Yet these seemingly lonely voices were never isolated, as Western observers assumed, and as the Soviet authorities asserted. They enjoyed the support of many intellectuals who "thought differently" but had no vocation to join the dissidence, many party members who dared not openly disagree with the official line, and many anonymous Soviet citizens who avidly read and typed samizdat but otherwise led conformist lives. These "communities of dissent" gathered very different profiles, who shared in the hope that had been triggered by Khrushchev's Secret Speech, in 1956, and occasionally raised their voice to defend the cause of anti-Stalinism. It was their testimonies, their silent assistance that allowed for the writing of *The Gulag Archipelago*, *Let History Judge*, or *Portrait of a Tyranny*. It was open support from these intellectuals and old party members that turned the "Nekrich Affair" into a case of academic rebellion.

The traditional dichotomous categories of dissent versus conformism fail, in my view, to do justice to the complexity of the phenomenon. Dissent was not a personal characteristic or even a state, it was a type of behavior. One could speak out repeatedly according to one's convictions and face dismissal or other sanctions, or one could sign a protest once and then retreat into conformism. A historian could seek to expand the scope of what could be discussed in official scholarship, defend his colleagues from attacks, and yet later recant to avoid exclusion from the Party. The researchers examined here and those who supported them represent various nuances of this broad spectrum from conformity to dissent, and I have sought to underline what united them, in terms of their values, convictions, and aspirations, rather than what differentiated them in terms of their individual choices.

Although for the sake of simplicity I used the word "dissident" to qualify the authors examined in this research, I have sought to transcend this static category by retracing the complex trajectories that led these individuals into dissent. I argued that these researchers progressively exited the official sphere as a result of a self-reinforcing dynamic, in which both dissenters and the regime played a role. After initially seeking to work within an official framework and submitting to censorship, the change of political atmosphere led them to radicalize their discourse and participate in protests against Stalin's rehabilitation. This radicalization, coupled with their exit from the official realm into samizdat and tamizdat, provoked in turn a more forceful reaction from the authorities, leading to such "prophylactic" sanctions as dismissal, exclusion from the Party or from creative unions. While many dissenters preferred to retreat into conformity at this stage, those who persisted were increasingly ostracized and, ultimately, faced a difficult choice between exile and inner emigration. If they opted for the latter and persisted in their activities, the next stage was usually judicial prosecution.

The different fates examined in this research testify to the various strategies that dissidents adopted, but they cannot lay claim to representativity: because these subjects were selected from amongst the most famous figures in their field, they benefited from greater immunity from judicial prosecution than less well-known activists. Publicity in the West, combined with support from the intelligentsia, played a crucial role in shielding individuals from repression, especially in the context of international détente. But other factors than celebrity also came into play: repressive measures were generally proportional to one's degree of guilt, loyalty, and willingness to repent. If there were so few open dissidents, it was due to the successful operation of a system of dissuasion, which forced into repentance many independent spirits who had once "strayed" from the right path but could be persuaded not to ruin their careers for the sake of their convictions.

Despite my focus on the anti-Stalinist struggle as a cause that united the liberal intelligentsia in the late 1960s, I have attempted to go beyond the traditional opposition between Soviet society and an oppressive regime. I downplayed Brezhnev's role in initiating the ideological shift of 1965-66 on the Stalin question, emphasizing instead the struggles of influence within the leadership and debates within society. The outcome was a compromise position between the reactionary demands of pro-Stalinists and the calls of liberals to further de-Stalinization. Moreover, in spite of the progressive exclusion of anti-Stalinist narratives from print, I argued that the anti-Stalinist cause continued to benefit from some degree of legitimacy after 1964, due to Brezhnev's decision not to repeal the resolutions of the 20th and 22nd Party Congresses. This circumstance allowed anti-Stalinist activists to appeal to these resolutions to legitimize their cause.

Furthermore, this study underscored the affinities of views between some liberal elements in the lower echelons of the Central Committee of the CPSU and such a "loyal dissident" as Roy Medvedev. This circumstance could explain the relative protection from which the dissident benefited from Iurii Andropov during his career as KGB chief and General Secretary. This example shows that some degree of opposition to the Soviet leadership could be tolerated in some circumstances. Although this remains a speculation, it could also be that Andropov perceived Medvedev as an objective ally in the Soviet regime's struggle against Solzhenitsyn, after the two dissidents stepped up their confrontation in the Western media in the 1970s. Medvedev's anti-Stalinist narrative, which constituted a more radical critique than Khrushchev's Secret Speech but remained inscribed within the same paradigm, was a more efficient weapon against Solzhenitsyn's anti-communist views than the primitive Soviet propaganda. The same line of demarcation between anti-Stalinist and anti-communist narratives would inform the official approach toward dissident histories during Perestroika.

During the 1960s, however, under the influence of pro-Stalinist elements within the leadership, such as Sergei Trapeznikov, a harder line initially prevailed. From their perspective, publication in tamizdat represented the ultimate "anti-Soviet crime," a symbol of disloyalty and treachery, an objective alliance with "bourgeois propaganda" against the Soviet Union. The actual content of dissident works mattered less than the very act of countering censorship, subverting the wall that protected Soviet citizens from the enemy's disinformation. Yet one did not have to publish in tamizdat to be accused of treason: it sufficed to let one's work escape into samizdat and be published without the author's consent in an anti-Soviet journal, or simply to have one's work "instrumentalized" by Western propaganda, as happened to Nekrich. The refusal of dissident authors to submit to censorship, I argued, was thus more important than the content of their works.

The four researchers examined here were not selected by chance: all of them acquired fame in the West for their writings, but also their moral stance and resistance to the regime. But they were not the only individuals to do independent historical research in the Soviet Union. Many others wrote "for the drawer" or circulated short texts in samizdat, without seeking out a publisher in the West. The young Armenian Georgii Khomizuri was thus condemned to six years of camp in 1982 for reproducing samizdat and for writing a review of Avtorkhanov's book and an annually updated "History the Leadership of the CPSU" listing all Politburo members since 1917.[2] More prominently, a team of young amateur historians in Moscow and Leningrad released five volumes of the historical collection *Pamiat'*, published in New York and Paris, before the arrest of the editor in chief, Arsenii Roginskii. Their project, however, contrasted with the dissident histories examined here in their refusal of ideologized "grand narratives" and striving to publish objectively commented documents representing a large spectrum of viewpoints.[3] There were many faces to the underground resistance to a discredited Soviet historiography and this research does not lay claim to exhaustiveness.

The three main works examined in this study, however, differ from most other anti-Stalinist and historical samizdat and tamizdat publications of the time in so far as they constitute sophisticated documentary accounts, buttressed by hundreds of testimonies and written sources. A crucial characteristic of historical research produced underground was indeed the use of nontraditional primary sources, in particular oral testimonies, as a substitute for unavailable archival documents. Reliance on witnesses' accounts provided dissident histories with great moral authority, as their authors could claim to speak in the name of many. These sources were of great interest to Western Sovietologists, as they offered otherwise inaccessible information, but they also presented challenges in terms of reliability. Judged by Western scholarly standards, dissident histories did not fare well: the political engagement and subjective approach of their authors, but also, sometimes, their insufficiently critical acceptance of dubious narratives or distortions of witnesses' words make these works prone to criticism. Yet these critiques, I argued, fail to take into account the specific function of these histories, which differed from that of professional historiography. As Medvedev emphasized, although he felt less competent than professional historians for the task, he and other dissident researchers were the only ones willing to write on these subjects. Out of moral considerations, they endorsed a role they felt was vital for their society:

a role of chronicler of their people's tragedy, fulfilling at the same time a function of commemoration of victims and indictment of the perpetrators in the "court of history." These ethical and political functions outweighed any scholarly considerations and justified the use of nontraditional forms, best adapted to the authors' goals. Still, the authors' strong normative rhetoric, through calls for the "restoration of historical truth," and appeals to counter official lies, could conflict with their works' occasionally pervasive political subtext and subjectivity. When interpretations of the same events diverged, or witnesses' words were put to a disputable use, conflicts between bearers of alternative truths could arise.

Dissident researchers defined themselves in opposition to official historians, whom they collectively held in low esteem, despite their connections to some nonconformist scholars. This somewhat unfair judgment did not dissipate during Perestroika. As the cards were reshuffled, nonprofessional researchers and publicists proved more capable than professional historians of adapting to the new political context and of providing historical "fodder" for an avid readership. In the midst of a new, more thorough de-Stalinization, those dissident narratives that had remained closest to the line of the 20th Party Congress were also allowed back into the official realm earlier, as Gorbachev hoped to harness the moral legitimacy of these histories for his own political aims. The same did not go for Solzhenitsyn's works, which remained ostracized longer and were only published under public pressure.

Finally, a question which may legitimately be asked is that of the connection between dissident histories and the fall of the Soviet regime. Jonathan Bolton has rightly argued against this kind of questioning in relation to Czech dissent. "Rating different dissident practices according to which were most 'effective' or most useful in the post-1989 transitions, it treats dissent as a proto-political party with particular goals and strategies, rather than as a form of culture, a set of common stories, a style of political behavior, or a collection of practices that had meaning in and of themselves."[4] Dissident researchers pursued not only moral, but also political goals, and their works, despite dealing with past events, were bound to have an effect on current politics. Soviet leaders believed that revealing the whole truth about Stalin-era repression would undermine the regime's legitimacy, and they were not mistaken. During Perestroika, the combined weight of historical revelations did contribute to a weakening of the Communist Party's leadership. However, in this flow of publications, dissident histories lost their significance as sources of information, and their belated release into print diminished their impact on readers. Ultimately, their moral legitimacy, which the Gorbachev leadership sought to harness or counter, proved of greater significance than the facts they revealed.

As a rule, dissidents were no politicians. They did not aspire to constitute a political opposition but defined themselves as a moral movement. According to Roy Medvedev, "The dissident movement did not aim at removing the CPSU from power, in the 1960s-1970s, this task seemed to us all unlikely."[5] Still, he considered that if Perestroika had happened in 1975, dissidents might have played a greater role in it. A decade later, the movement had been bled white by emigration and repression, and many famous dissidents had gone to their grave or left public life. As a result, in the 1980s, the main role was played by specialists in the humanities who had already risen to prominent positions by the time Perestroika started, and who were best placed to influence its course. Medvedev explained this by the fact that those moral qualities which allowed dissidents to step up and fill a void in the 1960s did not necessarily go along with professional excellency in their fields of specialization. By the 1980s, as courage ceased to be a decisive factor, the field was open to all, and competition was fierce. The dissident researchers' small adjustments with truth and their amateur methods came under increased scrutiny, undermining their hitherto uncontested claim to be restoring "historical truth."

Questioning the role of dissident histories in the fall of the Soviet Union also requires considering the role of Western support to dissident historical research. In the context of the Cold War, Western, and particularly American assistance was a double-edged sword: while Western recognition could afford protection, it could also cause repression. And while tamizdat publication constituted both an indirect means of reaching out to a Soviet audience, and a potential source of income for dissidents, it could also damage a reputation or trigger judicial prosecution. The Nekrich Affair may well have never been, if not for the "scandal" raised by Western publications of the short transcript of the discussion at the IML. As Soviet dissident Gabriel' Superfin noted in an interview, in the early 1980s, dissidents remaining in the Soviet Union had become so demoralized, that as he emigrated to the West, they asked him to ensure that their names were mentioned on Radio Liberty less often. "We have to live here."[6] Accusations of instrumentalization by the adverse camp were rife, and sometimes justified. Newly emigrated Soviet dissidents were only too happy to find employment with Western organs of anti-Communist propaganda, and the United States often used the struggle for human rights as a political weapon against the Soviet Union. Nevertheless, Roy Medvedev's career as an independent historian would have been unthinkable without the financial autonomy procured by Western royalties, or without the international recognition of Western media, which he was able to convert into lasting protection from arrest. This circumstance was paradoxical for an author who professed loyalty to the Soviet project, and yet such paradoxes testify to a greater degree of ideological complexity than traditional narratives account for. Medvedev's success thus speaks against the idea that the West promoted only anti-communist narratives: although it was marginal, the "third way" of Eurocommunism did forge its way in tamizdat, between the Soviet hammer and the capitalist anvil.

Notes

Acknowledgments

1 Barbara Martin and Anton Sveshnikov, eds., *Istoricheskii sbornik Pamiat': Issledovaniia i materialy.* (Moscow: Novoe Literaturnoe Obozrenie, 2017); Barbara Martin and Anton Sveshnikov, "Between Scholarship and Dissidence: The Dissident Historical Collection Pamiat' (1975-1982)", *Slavic Review* 76, no. 4 (Winter 2017): 1003-26.

Introduction

1 "Solzhenitsyn's Counterattack," *Time* 103, no. 4 (January 1974): 42.
2 On the "legalist strategy," see Benjamin Nathans, "The Dictatorship of Reason: Aleksandr Vol'pin and the Idea of Rights under 'Developed Socialism,'" *Slavic Review* 66, no. 4 (December 1, 2007): 630–63.
3 Roger D. Markwick, *Rewriting History in Soviet Russia: The Politics of Revisionist Historiography, 1956-1974* (Basingstoke: Palgrave, 2001).
4 See, for example, Paul Goldberg, *The Final Act: The Dramatic, Revealing Story of the Moscow Helsinki Watch Group* (New York: Morrow, 1988); Sarah B. Snyder, *Human Rights Activism and the End of the Cold War: A Transnational History of the Helsinki Network*, Human Rights in History (Cambridge: Cambridge University Press, 2011); Mark Hurst, *British Human Rights Organizations and Soviet Dissent, 1965-1985* (London: Bloomsbury Academic, 2016).
5 On the problematic use of the word, see Jonathan Bolton, *Worlds of Dissent: Charter 77, the Plastic People of the Universe and Czech Culture under Communism* (Cambridge, MA: Harvard University Press, 2012), 2–3.
6 This definition is inspired by one proposed (among others) by Aleksandr Daniel' and Larisa Bogoraz: "Any conscious act in opposition to the regime and violating certain (open to some degree of variation, depending on the place, time and circumstances) 'given' limits of social behavior. The criterion here is the possibility of repressive (in the broadest sense of this word) reaction on the part of the authorities." (Aleksandr Daniel' and Larisa Bogoraz, "V poiskakh nesushchestvuiushchei nauki (Dissidentstvo kak istoricheskaia problema)," *Problemy Vostochonoi Evropy*, no. 37–38 (1993): 147.)
7 Detlef Pollack, ed., *Dissent and Opposition in Communist Eastern Europe: Origins of Civil Society and Democratic Transition* (Aldershot: Ashgate, 2004), xiii.
8 See Dietrich Beyrau, "Arcane and Public Spheres in the Soviet Union," in *Underground Publishing and the Public Sphere: Transnational Perspectives*, ed. Jan C. Behrends and Thomas Lindenberger (Wien: Lit, 2014), 99–142.
9 Roger D. Markwick, "Catalyst of Historiography, Marxism and Dissidence: The Sector of Methodology of the Institute of History, Soviet Academy of Sciences, 1964-68," *Europe-Asia Studies* 46, no. 4 (January 1, 1994): 579. Emphasis in the original.

10 Marshall S. Shatz, *Soviet Dissent in Historical Perspective* (Cambridge; London: Cambridge University Press, 1980), 13.
11 Martin Malia, "What Is the Intelligentsia?," in *The Russian Intelligentsia*, ed. Richard Pipes (New York: Columbia University Press, 1961), 3; Inna Kochetkova, *The Myth of the Russian Intelligentsia: Old Intellectuals in the New Russia* (London: Routledge, 2010), 17.
12 Vladimir Shlapentokh, *Soviet Intellectuals and Political Power: The Post-Stalin Era* (London; New York: I.B. Tauris, 1990), 3.
13 Kochetkova, *The Myth of the Russian Intelligentsia*, 12.
14 Leopold Labedz, "The Structure of the Soviet Intelligentsia," in *The Russian Intelligentsia*, ed. Richard Pipes (New York: Columbia University Press, 1961), 64.
15 Roi Medvedev and Zhores Medvedev, *1925-2010. Iz vospominanii*. (Moscow: Izd. "Prava cheloveka," 2010); Roi Medvedev and Zhores Medvedev, *V poiskakh zdravogo smysla*, OKhDLSM F. 333, sd. op. 14, u.d. 13 (also sd. op. 1, u.d. 30); Zhores Medvedev's memoirs have been serialized in the online weekly *Ezhedel'nik 2000* and should be published as a book in the coming years. Aleksandr Nekrich, *Forsake Fear: Memoirs of an Historian* (Boston; London: Unwin Hyman, 1991); M.S. Al'perovich, ed., *Otreshivshiisia ot strakha: Pamiati A.M. Nekricha. Vospominaniia, stat'i, dokumenty*. (Moscow: Institut Vseobshchei Istorii RAN, 1996).
16 Michael Scammell and Catherine A. Fitzpatrick, eds., *The Solzhenitsyn Files: Secret Soviet Documents Reveal One Man's Fight against the Monolith* (Chicago: Edition Q, 1995); Galina Andreevna Tiurina, ed., *"Dorogoi Ivan Denisovich!..": Pis'ma chitatelei 1962-1964* (Moskva: Russkii put', 2012).
17 I refer to Aleksandr Isaevich Solzhenitsyn, *The Oak and the Calf* (Collins/Fontana, 1980); Alexandre Soljénitsyne, *Les Invisibles* (Paris: Fayard, 1992); Aleksandr Isaevitch Soljenitsyne, *Le grain tombé entre les meules: Esquisses d'exil. Première partie* (Paris: Fayard, 1998).
18 Soljénitsyne, *Les Invisibles*.

Chapter 1

1 According to Robert Hornsby's estimates, one in six Soviet citizens attended meetings where the Secret Speech was read out, so that a large part of the population would have heard about it. (Robert Hornsby, *Protest, Reform and Repression in Khrushchev's Soviet Union* (Cambridge: Cambridge University Press, 2013), 31–32.)
2 OKhDLSM, F. 333, s.d. 1, u.d. 74.
3 Markwick, *Rewriting History in Soviet Russia*. Emphasis in the original.
4 Nikita Sergeevich Khrushchev, *The Crimes of the Stalin Era: Special Report to the 20th Congress of the Communist Party of the Soviet Union* (New York: The New Leader, 1956), 65; Arup Banerji, *Writing History in the Soviet Union: Making the Past Work* (Berghahn Books, 2008), 146.
5 Nancy Whittier Heer, *Politics and History in the Soviet Union* (Cambridge, MA: The MIT Press, 1973), 64–66.
6 Miriam Dobson, *Khrushchev's Cold Summer: Gulag Returnees, Crime, and the Fate of Reform after Stalin* (Ithaca, NY: Cornell University Press, 2011).
7 "Zakliuchitel'noe slovo pervogo sekretaria TsK KPSS tovarishcha N.S. Khrushcheva," *Pravda*, October 29, 1961: 2. Quoted in Heer, *Politics and History in the Soviet Union*, 121.

8   *XX s"ezd Kommunisticheskoi Partii Sovetskogo Soiuza. 14-25 fevralia 1956 goda. Stenograficheskii otchet*, vol. I (Moscow: Gosudarstvennoe izdatel'stvo politicheskoi literatury, 1956), 362.
9   Heer, *Politics and History in the Soviet Union*, 147.
10 O.Iu. Shmidt, ed., "Antonov-Ovseenko," *Bol'shaia Sovetskaia Entsiklopediia*, 1926, cols. 96–97.
11 According to Stéphane Courtois, the rebellion was crushed with the use of mass hostage-taking, executions, deportation of entire villages (Stéphane Courtois, ed., *Le Livre Noir du Communisme: Crimes, Terreur, Répression* (Paris: R. Laffont, 1998), 136–37.)
12 Vladimir Antonov-Ovseenko, *V semnadtstom godu*, 1st ed. (Moscow: Gosudarstvennoe izdatel'stvo khudozhestvennoi literatury, 1933), 3–4.
13 Ronald Radosh, Mary R. Habeck, and Grigorij Nikolaevič Sevosťânov, *Spain Betrayed: The Soviet Union in the Spanish Civil War* (Yale University Press, 2001), 70; Francisco J. Romero Salvadó, *Historical Dictionary of the Spanish Civil War* (Lanham, MD: Rowman & Littlefield, 2013), 50–51.
14 Copy of V.A. Antonov-Ovseenko's personal rehabilitation file, Personal papers of Anton Vladimirovich Antonov-Ovseenko; "Poedinok so vremenem," *Vecherniaia Moskva*, July 1, 1989.
15 Anton Rakitin, ed., "On bral Zimnii," *Novyi Mir* 11 (November 1964): 212.
16 According to Valentina Tikhanova, Vladimir Antonov-Ovseenko's stepdaughter, Anton's mother was schizophrenic and her erratic behavior bordering on political dissent had led to her arrest. (Interview of V. Tikhanova, October 25, 2014.) Galina, Anton's elder sister, described her mother as a Trotskyite who often argued with her husband and was imprisoned after attempting to defect abroad. (Sergei Noril'skii, "Vlast' idei i uzi krovi," in *Kniga pamiati zhertv politicheskoi repressii Tul'skoi oblasti. 1917-1987*, ed. S.L. Shcheglov, vol. 3 (Tula: Grif i K, n.d.), 20.)
17 Anton Antonov-Ovseenko, *Vragi naroda* (Moscow: Intellekt, 1996), 29.
18 In his autobiographical account *Enemies of the people*, Antonov-Ovseenko remains very vague about this case: "I was arrested with two friends. They worked at a construction office, performed operations with materials in deficit, dressed up stylishly, went to the 'Metropol' [hotel], where they met foreigners" (Antonov-Ovseenko, 30). In an interview, he explained that his roommate Sergei Fukel'man, an NKVD informer since 1938, brought him into contact with his friends from Baku, who had some "shady affairs." At the trial, they failed to mention that Anton was unaware of their dealings. (Interview of A.V. Antonov-Ovseenko, June 29, 2012.) Anton's foster sister, Valentina Tikhanova, claims that Anton was arrested for engaging in small trade in the countryside, a private business that was illegal under Soviet law. (Interview of V. Tikhanova.)
19 Antonov-Ovseenko, *Vragi naroda*, 30–33.
20 Antonov-Ovseenko, 67.
21 Antonov-Ovseenko, 72–80; A.V. Antonov-Ovseenko, Interview. Antonov-Ovseenko's personal papers contained copies of his rehabilitation file, which includes protocols of Fukel'man and Spirkin's depositions.
22 Liudmila Fomina, "Teatr vremen ottsa narodov," *Moskovskaia pravda*, May 15, 1995; Anton Antonov-Ovseenko, *Teatr Iosifa Stalina* (Moskva: Gregorii Peidzh, 1995).
23 Interview of A.V. Antonov-Ovseenko.
24 This was a public rehabilitation, insofar as Mikoian defended Antonov-Ovseenko against some unfair political accusations by Russian historians. It preceded and probably

accelerated the official rehabilitation that ensued. (*XX s"ezd Kommunisticheskoi Partii Sovetskogo Soiuza*, I:326.)
25 Anton Antonov-Ovseenko, *The Time of Stalin. Portrait of a Tyranny* (New York: Harper and Row, 1981), 336.
26 Anton Antonovich claims that at the time of his birth, his father was not allowed to live in large cities and that he remained in exile in Tambov until his rehabilitation in 1963. (Interview of A.A. Antonov-Ovseenko, September 22, 2017.) However, the lack of a Moscow registration seems like a more compelling explanation for his presence.
27 Interview of V. Tikhanova; Interview of A.V. Antonov-Ovseenko.
28 Interview of A.A. Antonov-Ovseenko.
29 RGANI, F. 5, op. 55, d. 2, l. 48.
30 Ibid., l. 45–46.
31 Letter of A.V. Antonov-Ovseenko to A.I. Mikoian, April 5, 1963. Personal Papers of A.V. A-O.
32 Letter of P. Kudriashov to A.V. Antonov-Ovseenko, March 15, 1963. Personal Papers of A.V. A-O.
33 Letters from the Personal Papers of A.V. A-O.
34 Letter of S. Trapeznikov and V. Stepakov to the Central Committee of the CPSU, August 24, 1965. RGANI, F. 5, op. 35, d. 111, l. 133–135.
35 RGANI, F. 5, op. 35, d. 211, l. 96. Interestingly, Anton Antonov-Ovseenko identified Likholat as the historian whom Mikoian had criticized at the 20th Party Congress for his critique of V.A. Antonov-Ovseenko. (Antonov-Ovseenko, *The Time of Stalin*, 329.)
36 RGANI, F. 5, op. 35, d. 211, l. 87.
37 Letter of A.V. Antonov-Ovseenko to V.P. Danilov, April 27, 1966. Personal Papers of A.V. A-O.
38 Letter of A.V. Antonov-Ovseenko to A.I. Mikoian, February 25, 1965. Personal Papers of A.V. A-O.
39 This is a reference to the famous poem published by the Soviet poet Evgenii Evtushenko in 1961.
40 Letter by A. Ianin to A.V. Antonov-Ovseenko, October 22, 1964. Personal Papers of A.V. A-O.
41 "Poedinok so Vremenem," *Vecherniaia Moskva*, July 1, 1989. A request for TsGAOR documents, dated from 1973, also remains in the Personal Papers of A.V. A-O.
42 Letter of A.M. Chekotillo to A.V. Antonov-Ovseenko, n.d., Personal Papers of A.V. A-O.
43 Letter of A.V. Antonov-Ovseenko to the Secretary of the City Party Committee of Kraslava, June 29, 1964. Response of G. Kirilov, July 27, 1964. Personal Papers of A.V. A-O.
44 Letter of I.I. Iakovlev to A.V. Antonov-Ovseenko, July 9, 1964. Personal Papers of A.V. A-O.
45 Letter of B. Dal'nii to A.V. Antonov-Ovseenko, May 22, 1963; Text by A.V. Antonov-Ovseenko "Work on the book about the life and activity of V.A. Antonov-Ovseenko," 1965. Personal Papers of A.V. A-O.
46 "Imenem Revoliutsii," *Tambovskaia Pravda*, November 7, 1963.
47 "Poedinok so Vremenem."
48 Rakitin, "On bral Zimnii."
49 Interview of A.V. Antonov-Ovseenko.
50 Polly Jones, "The Fire Burns On? The 'Fiery Revolutionaries' Biographical Series and the Rethinking of Propaganda in the Brezhnev Era," *Slavic Review* 74, no. 1 (Spring 2015): 32–56.

51 Jones, 41.
52 "Transcript of the discussion of the manuscript of A. Rakitin 'In the name of the Revolution' at the historical section of the Main Editorial Committee," November 20, 1964. RGASPI, F. 623 (Fond Politizdat), op. 1, d. 293.
53 "Transcript of the discussion…"
54 "Transcript of the discussion…"
55 "Transcript of the discussion…"
56 "Transcript of the discussion…"
57 "Transcript of the discussion…"
58 "Transcript of the discussion…"
59 Interview of A.V. Antonov-Ovseenko.
60 Interview of A.V. Antonov-Ovseenko.
61 "Poedinok so vremenem."
62 V. Pogudin, "Review: Anton Rakitin. Imenem Revoliutsii… (Ocherk o V.A. Antonove-Ovseenko. M., Poliizdat, 1965. 191 Str.," *Kommunist*, no. 12 (August 1965): 125–26.
63 Pogudin, 126.
64 Interview of A.V. Antonov-Ovseenko.
65 Letter from T.P. Pimenova to A.V. Antonov-Ovseenko, October 24, 1967. Personal papers of A.V. A-O.
66 "Soldat oktiabr'skogo shturma," *Druzhba narodov*, no. 11, (1966); "Memuary V.A. Antonova-Ovseenko kak istochnik po istorii revoliutsionnykh sobytii 1917 goda," *Trudy MGIAI* 24, no.2 (1966); "Odin iz pervykh (u istokov sovetskoi diplomatii)," *Novoe vremia*, no. 32 (1967); *Gvardeitsy revoliutsii (Ocherk – upolnomochennyi Lenina)*, Voronezh, 1967; *Geroi oktiabria (biografiia V.A. Antonova-Ovseenko)*, vol. 1, Leningrad, 1967.
67 Medvedev and Medvedev, *1925-2010. Iz vospominanii.*, 11.
68 Medvedev and Medvedev, 18–22.
69 Medvedev and Medvedev, 28.
70 OKhDLSM, F. 333, sd.op. 1, u.d. 74.
71 Roy Medvedev had already attempted to join the Party during his studies in university, but despite good recommendations, his application had been rejected. (Interview of R. Medvedev (1), June 19, 2012.)
72 Interview of R. Medvedev (1).
73 Interview of R. Medvedev (1).
74 Roy Medvedev, *On Soviet Dissent* (Columbia University Press, 1980), 29–30. This is a slightly stylistically reworked version of the dialogue which Medvedev consigned to paper directly after his interrogation in 1967. See original in OKhDLSM, F. 333, sd.op. 14, u.d. 31.
75 OKhDLSM, F. 333, sd.op. 1, u.d. 74.
76 Interview of R. Medvedev (1).
77 It might not have been the first version, but it was the first one that was conserved and shown to higher instances. (Roy Medvedev, *Pered sudom istorii,* 1964. OKhDLSM, F. 333, sd.op. 9, u.d. 1.)
78 Medvedev, 1.
79 Medvedev, 4.
80 Medvedev, 16.
81 Medvedev, 47.
82 Medvedev, 47.
83 Medvedev, 51.
84 Medvedev, 61.

85 Medvedev, 118.
86 Medvedev, 241.
87 Medvedev, 205.
88 Medvedev, 225.
89 Medvedev, 226.
90 Medvedev, 274.
91 Medvedev, 265.
92 Medvedev, 309.
93 Medvedev, 311.
94 Medvedev, 315.
95 Medvedev, 316.
96 Communication of Zhores Medvedev, November 20, 2015.
97 Interview of R. Medvedev (1).
98 Interview of R. Medvedev (1).
99 Interview of Z. Medvedev (1), May 29, 2014.
100 Interview of R. Medvedev (1).
101 "Conclusion on the manuscript of R.A. Medvedev 'Pered sudom istorii,'" A. Kotelenets, OKhDLSM, F. 333, sd.op. 14, u.d. 31.
102 "Conclusion on the manuscript of R.A. Medvedev…," 1.
103 See Chapter 2.
104 "Conclusion on the manuscript of R.A. Medvedev…," 3.
105 Nekrich, *Forsake Fear*, 152–53.
106 Nekrich, 1.
107 Nekrich, 39.
108 Nekrich, 66.
109 HIA, Nekrich (Aleksandr Moiseevich) Papers 1940–1996, Box 62, Microfilm 1.
110 Former ambassador to Britain, associated with Maxim Litvinov's policies, Ivan M. Maiskii (1884–1975) escaped the 1937 purges, only to be arrested in February 1953, on the eve of Stalin's death. Brought to trial in 1955, he was released shortly thereafter.
111 Nekrich, *Forsake Fear*, 70.
112 Nekrich, 72–73.
113 Nekrich, 80.
114 Nekrich, 88–89.
115 Leonid Petrovich Petrovskii, "Delo Nekricha," *Vestnik RAN* t. 65, no. 6 (1995): 528.
116 Nekrich, *Forsake Fear*, 102.
117 L.Iu. Slezkin, "Pamiati druga," in *Otreshivshiisia ot strakha. Pam'iati A.M. Nekricha: Vospominaniia, stat'i, dokumenty*, ed. M.S. Al'perovich (Moscow: Institut Vseobshchei Istorii RAN, 1996), 23.
118 Nekrich, *Forsake Fear*, 102–03.
119 See Chapter 2.
120 Aleksandr Nekrich, *June 22, 1941: Soviet Historians and the German Invasion*, ed. Vladimir Petrov (Columbia, SC: University of South Carolina Press, 1968), 33.
121 Nekrich, 33.
122 Petrovskii, "Delo Nekricha," 1995, 529.
123 Nekrich, *Forsake Fear*, 142.
124 Nekrich, 144.
125 Nekrich, *Soviet Historians and the German Invasion*, 140.
126 Nekrich, 146.

127 Nekrich, 139.
128 Nekrich, 94–95.
129 Nekrich, 226.
130 Nekrich, *Forsake Fear*, 146.
131 Nekrich, 149.
132 Nekrich, 150–51.
133 Nekrich, 153.
134 Nekrich, 154.
135 For the translation of this article, published in *Novyi mir* (n°1, 1966), see G. Fedorov, "A Measure of Responsibility," in *June 22, 1941: Soviet Historians and the German Invasion*, ed. Vladimir Petrov (Columbia, SC: University of South Carolina Press, 1968), 264–70. The other review appeared in *Komsomolets Tadzhikistana* ("Facing the truth" by A. Vakhrameev).
136 Fedorov, 269.

Chapter 2

1 On the reasons behind Khrushchev's ouster, see Susanne Schattenberg, *Leonid Breschnew: Staatsmann und Schauspieler im Schatten Stalins. Eine Biographie* (Köln: Böhlau Verlag, 2017), 269–75.
2 Edwin Bacon, "Reconsidering Brezhnev," in *Brezhnev Reconsidered*, ed. Edwin Bacon and Mark Sandle (Houndmills, Basingstoke: Palgrave Macmillan, 2002), 16.
3 On the oligarchic nature of Brezhnev's rule, see Franklyn Griffiths and Harold Gordon Skilling, *Interest groups in Soviet Politics* (Princeton, NJ: University Press, 1971); John P. Willerton, "Patronage Networks and Coalition Building in the Brezhnev Era," *Soviet Studies* 39, no. 2 (1987): 175–204; T. H. Rigby, "The Soviet Leadership: Towards a Self-Stabilizing Oligarchy?," *Soviet Studies* 22, no. 2 (1970): 167–91.
4 Georgii Arbatov, "Iz nedavnego proshlogo," in *L.I. Breznev. Materialy k biografii*, ed. Iurii Aksiutin (Moscow: Politizdat, 1991), 63.
5 Willerton, "Patronage Networks and Coalition Building in the Brezhnev Era," 176.
6 Schattenberg, *Leonid Breschnew*, 420–21.
7 For examples of reactions to the Secret Speech, see Kathleen E. Smith, *Moscow 1956. The Silenced Spring* (Cambridge, MA; London: Harvard University Press, 2017), Chapter 3.
8 See Susanne Schattenberg, "'Democracy or Despotism?' How the Secret Speech Was Translated into Everyday Life," in *The Dilemmas of De-Stalinization: Negotiating Cultural and Social Change in the Khrushchev Era*, ed. Polly Jones (London: Routledge, 2009), 66; Dobson, *Khrushchev's Cold Summer*; Vladimir Kozlov, Sheila Fitzpatrick, and Sergei Mironenko, eds., *Sedition: Everyday Resistance in the Soviet Union under Khrushchev and Brezhnev*, Annals of Communism (New Haven: Yale University Press, 2011); Hornsby, *Protest, Reform and Repression*, Chapter 1.
9 Hornsby, *Protest, Reform and Repression*, 40–41.
10 Polly Jones, *Myth, Memory, Trauma: Rethinking the Stalinist Past in the Soviet Union (1953-1970)* (New Haven; London: Yale University Press, 2013), 50–52; Markwick, *Rewriting History in Soviet Russia*, 48.
11 Jones, *Myth, Memory, Trauma*, 57; Smith, *Moscow 1956*, 308–09.
12 Markwick, *Rewriting History in Soviet Russia*, 51–62; Heer, *Politics and History in the Soviet Union*, 84–88.

13 Jones, *Myth, Memory, Trauma*, 90–91; Hornsby, *Protest, Reform and Repression*, 105–7. Lev Krasnopevtsev was a graduate student of Party history at Moscow State University who formed an underground Marxist circle in 1956–57. He and the eight history students and professors in his circle were condemned to various sentences of imprisonment for circulating an anti-Soviet leaflet demanding that Stalin's henchmen be tried. On Marxist revisionism as a reaction of Soviet students to the confusion engendered by the Secret Speech, see Benjamin Tromly, *Making the Soviet Intelligentsia: Universities and Intellectual Life under Stalin and Khrushchev* (Cambridge; New York: Cambridge University Press, 2014), Chapter 5.
14 Heer, *Politics and History in the Soviet Union*, 124–27.
15 Stephen F. Cohen, "The Stalin Question since Stalin," in *An End to Silence: Uncensored Opinion in the Soviet Union, from Roy Medvedev's Underground Magazine Political Diary*, ed. Stephen F. Cohen (New York: W. W. Norton & Co Inc, 1984), 41.
16 Scammell and Fitzpatrick, *The Solzhenitsyn Files*, 3.
17 Stephen F. Cohen, "The Friends and Foes of Change: Reformism and Conservatism in the Soviet Union," in *The Soviet Union since Stalin*, ed. Stephen Cohen, Alexander Rabinowitch, and Robert Sharlet (Bloomington, IN: Indiana University Press, 1980), 11–31.
18 Cohen, 17.
19 Roy Medvedev, *On Socialist Democracy* (London [etc.]: MacMillan, 1975), 53–56.
20 Iurii Aksiutin, ed., *L.I. Breznev. Materialy k biografii* (Moscow: Politizdat, 1991); Aleksandr Bovin, *XX vek kak zhizn'* (Moscow: Zakharov, 2003).
21 Wolfgang Leonhard, "Politics and Ideology in the Post-Khrushchev Era," in *Soviet Politics since Khrushchev*, ed. Alexander Dallin (Englewood Cliffs, NJ: Prentice-Hall, 1968), 44.
22 Fedor Burlatskii, "Brezhnev i krushenie 'ottepeli,'" in *L.I. Breznev. Materialy k biografii*, ed. Iurii Aksiutin (Moscow: Politizdat, 1991), 107–08.
23 Burlatskii, 112.
24 "Velikaia pobeda Sovetskogo naroda. Doklad tovarishcha L.I. Brezhneva," *Pravda*, May 10, 1965.
25 Arbatov, "Iz nedavnego proshlogo," 64–65.
26 Roi Medvedev, *Lichnost' i èpokha. Politicheskii portret L.I. Brezhneva.* (Moscow: Izd. "Novosti," 1991), 64; 143–45. Trapeznikov only became "corresponding member" of the Academy in 1976.
27 V.S. Aleksandrov, Session on Party History, June 21, 1965, RGANI, F. 5, op. 35, d. 211, l. 87.
28 V.M. Khvostov, Session on History of the USSR, June 23, 1965. RGANI, F. 5, op. 35, d. 212, l. 139–40.
29 Ibid.
30 V.S. Aleksandrov, Session on Party History, June 21, 1965, RGANI, F. 5, op. 35, d. 211, l. 88.
31 K.K. Dubina, Session on History of the USSR, June 23, 1965. RGANI, F. 5, op. 35, d. 212, l. 116.
32 Trapeznikov, Session on Party History, June 21, 1965. RGANI, F. 5, op. 35, d. 211, l. 124.
33 E.M. Zhukov, Meeting of the Ideological Commission, November 15–18, 1965, RGANI, F. 5, op. 35, d. 210, l. 65.
34 Ibid., l. 67.
35 Trapeznikov, Meeting of the Ideological Commission, November 15–18, 1965. Ibid, l. 75.

36 Ibid., l. 89.
37 In his memoirs, Nekrich identifies Iudin as a "close ideological supporter of Stalin" in the 1930s and denounces his role in the political ostracization of his mentor, the philosopher Abram Deborin, for failing to recognize Stalin's supremacy in the philosophical field. (Nekrich, *Forsake Fear*, 6.)
38 Speech of Pavel Iudin, Meeting of the Ideological Commission, November 15–18, 1965. RGANI, F. 5, op. 35, d. 210, l. 127.
39 Ibid., l. 128.
40 Konstantin Ostroviatinov, Meeting of the Ideological Commission, November 15–18, 1965. Ibid., l. 167–69.
41 "Kuchkin, Andrei Pavlovich," *Bol'shaia Sovetskaia Entsiklopediia* (Moscow: Sovetskaia Entsiklopediia, 1978), dic.academic.ru.
42 Andrei Kuchkin, Meeting of the Ideological Commission, November 15–18, 1965. RGANI, F. 5, op. 35, d. 210, l. 178–79.
43 Ibid.
44 E. Zhukov, V. Trukhanovskii, and V. Shchunkov, "Vysokaia otvetstvennost' istorikov," *Pravda*, January 30, 1966.
45 Nekrich, *Forsake Fear*, 175.
46 Zhukov, Trukhanovskii, and Shchunkov, "Vysokaia otvetstvennost' istorikov."
47 Zhukov, Trukhanovskii, and Shchunkov.
48 RGANI, F. 5, op. 35, d. 223, l. 53–56.
49 Ibid., l. 54. Emphasis in the original.
50 Ibid., l. 58.
51 Nekrich, *Forsake Fear*, 175.
52 Nekrich, *Forsake Fear*, 175.
53 Nekrich, 155.
54 Cited by Nekrich. Coincides with archival document: RGASPI, F. 629 (Pospelov P.N.), op. 1, d. 80, l. 19.
55 Nekrich, *Forsake Fear*, 156.
56 For Moisei Al'perovich, the Central Committee had decided to organize a "public *prorabotka*" [Stalin era-style criticism] of the book "in order to bring back to order the undisciplined intelligentsia and all the adversaries of totalitarianism." (M.S. Al'perovich, "Knigi imeiut svoiu sud'bu," in *Otreshivshiisia ot strakha. Pam'iati A.M. Nekricha: vospominaniia, stat'i, dokumenty*, ed. M.S. Al'perovich (Moscow: Institut Vseobshchei Istorii RAN, 1996), 81.) See also Petrovskii, "Delo Nekricha," 1995, 531; Evgenii Gnedin, *Vykhod iz labirinta* (Moscow: Memorial, 1994), 131.
57 Nekrich, *Forsake Fear*, 155–56.
58 RGASPI, F. 629 (Pospelov P.N.), op. 1, d. 80.
59 Ibid.
60 Nekrich, *Forsake Fear*, 157.
61 See for instance Roger Markwick's account of the discussion (*Rewriting History in Soviet Russia*, 210.)
62 For instance, in the English and French editions: Vladimir Petrov, ed., "A Meeting of the Division of History of the Great Patriotic War of the Institute of Marxism-Leninism of the CC CPSU, February 16, 1966," in *June 22, 1941: Soviet Historians and the German Invasion* (Columbia, SC: University of South Carolina Press, 1968), 246–61; Aleksandr Nekrich, *L'armée Rouge Assassinée: 22 Juin 1941* (Paris: B. Grasset, 1968).
63 See Leonid Petrovich Petrovskii, "Delo Nekricha," *Vechernii Klub*, December 17, 1994; Petrovskii, "Delo Nekricha," 1995.

64 Aleksandr Nekrich, ed., "Obsuzhdenie knigi A.M. Nekricha '1941, 22 iunia' v Institute Marksizma-Leninizma pri TsK KPSS (Stenogramma)," in *1941, 22 Iunia* (Moscow: Pamiatniki istoricheskoi mysli, 1995), 279–333.
65 Nekrich says there were "over two hundred participants," (Nekrich, *Forsake Fear*, 157) while the samizdat minutes give the number of 130. (Petrov, "A Meeting of the Division...," 248.) Gnedin mentions 300 participants (Gnedin, *Vykhod iz labirinta*, 131.)
66 Nekrich, "Obsuzhdenie knigi A.M. Nekricha," 281–82.
67 Nekrich, 296. Born 1925, Colonel Viacheslav Ivanovich Dashichev was an expert on the Second World War.
68 Nekrich, 299. Daniil Efimovich Melamid (1916–1993) was a prominent expert on German fascism and international relations. According to the samizdat transcript, he was affiliated with the Institute of History.
69 Nekrich, 317. Boris S. Tel'pukhovskii was not only a military historian but also a colonel. He is known for a monograph on Peter the Great's Northern War (*Severnaia Voina 1700-1721*, 1948).
70 Nekrich, 292–93, 296.
71 Nekrich, 308. According to the samizdat transcript, Raskat was from the IML.
72 Nekrich, 315. Probably Dmitrii Iakovlevich Telegin, from the Institute of Archaeology of the USSR Academy of Sciences.
73 Nekrich, 289. A military historian and war veteran, Viktor Aleksandrovich Anfilov had himself recently published a book on the beginning of the war (*Nachalo velikoi otechestvennoi voiny*, 1962). The samizdat transcript identifies him as being from the general staff.
74 Nekrich, 300.
75 Nekrich, 289.
76 Nekrich, 305. Vasilii Mikhailovich Kulish was yet another Second World War expert, who later on published a monograph on the "second front" of the Second World War (*Istoriia vtorogo fronta*, 1971).
77 Nekrich, 317, 319.
78 Nekrich, 310, 311.
79 Nekrich, 311–13.
80 Nekrich, 314.
81 Nekrich, 320.
82 Nekrich, 320–22.
83 See Chapter 3.
84 Nekrich, "Obsuzhdenie knigi A.M. Nekricha," 322.
85 Nekrich, 323.
86 Nekrich, 323.
87 Nekrich, 323–24.
88 Nekrich, 325–26.
89 Nekrich, 329.
90 Nekrich, 330–31.
91 Nekrich, 330, 333.
92 OKhDLSM, F. 333, sd. op. 32, u.d. 6.
93 L.V. Danilova, "Partiinaia organizatsiia Instituta Istorii AN SSSR v ideinom protvistoianii s partiinymi instantsiami, 1966-1968 gg," *Voprosy istorii* 12 (2007): 47; Markwick, *Rewriting History in Soviet Russia*, 75–110.
94 Markwick, "Catalyst of Historiography, Marxism and Dissidence," 581.
95 Markwick, 581–83.

96 Markwick, *Rewriting History in Soviet Russia*, 193.
97 Markwick, 113.
98 Markwick, 126. According to R.W. Davies, the discussions lasted until 1969. However, by 1966, "fierce onslaughts on the critical approach to collectivization" had already appeared in the party press. (R.W. Davies, "Soviet History in the Gorbachev Revolution: The First Phase," *The Socialist Register* 24 (1988): 38.)
99 Nekrich, *Forsake Fear*, 164.
100 Nekrich, 164.
101 RGANI, F. 5, op. 35, d. 212, l. 30–59.
102 Nekrich, *Forsake Fear*, 167–68.
103 Nekrich, 166–68.
104 Letter of S. Trapeznikov to the TsK CPSU, June 9, 1965. RGANI, F. 5, op. 35, d. 212, l. 27–29.
105 Nekrich, *Forsake Fear*, 169.
106 Nekrich, 171.
107 Nekrich, 171–74.
108 For the complete text, see Danilova, "Partiinaia organizatsiia Instituta Istorii AN SSSR...," 59–80.
109 Al'perovich, "Knigi imeiut svoiu sud'bu," 89.
110 Danilova, "Partiinaia organizatsiia Instituta Istorii AN SSSR...," 62.
111 Danilova, 68.
112 Danilova, 69.
113 Danilova, 72.
114 Danilova, 72.
115 Reference to Evgenii Vuchetich's article "*Vnesem iasnost'*," see Chapter 3.
116 Danilova, "Partiinaia organizatsiia Instituta Istorii AN SSSR...," 75.
117 Danilova, 52.
118 RGANI, F. 5, op. 35, d. 223, l. 63–71.
119 Ernst Genri (also known as Semen Rostovskii) was a Soviet secret agent in Germany in the 1930s, imprisoned in the early 1950s and subsequently rehabilitated. In the 1960s, he was famous as a writer and journalist. (Ia. S. Drabkin, "Ernst Genri - 'Nash chelovek v XX-m veke,'" *Novaia i noveishaia istoriia*, no. 4 (2004).)
120 AS n° 273, *Sobranie Dokumentov Samizdata*, vol. 4 (Munich: Samizdat Archive Association, 1973).
121 A. Artizov et al., eds., *Reabilitatsiia: kak èto bylo*, vol. II: Fevral' 1956-nachalo 80-kh godov. (Moscow: Izdatel'stvo "Materik," 2003), 485–87.
122 Medvedev Roy, *Politicheskii dnevnik*, March 1966, p. 1. (Archive of the History of Dissent in the USSR (1953–1987), Mezhdunarodnyi Memorial, F. 128 Roy Medvedev, Box 1.) The term "Presidium" then designated the Politburo. Medvedev also claims that the text circulated in "tens of thousands of copies throughout the country, was summarized in several Communist newspapers and was broadcast on British and American radio." (Ibid.)
123 Medvedev and Medvedev, *1925-2010. Iz vospominanii*, 70.
124 Roy Medvedev mentions several articles in the Italian Communist newspaper *L'Unità*, sympathizing with the letter of the 25, on March 19 and 27, 1966 (*Politicheskii dnevnik*, March 1966, pp. 6–8).
125 Arbatov, "Iz nedavnego proshlogo," 65.
126 Bovin, *XX vek kak zhizn'*, 153.
127 Arbatov, "Iz nedavnego proshlogo," 67–69.

128 Arbatov, 70–71.
129 V. Golikov et al., "Za Leninskuiu partiinost' v osveshchenii istorii KPSS," *Kommunist*, no. 3 (1969): 67–82. Although the second initials are missing, V. Golikov probably stands for Viktor Andreevich Golikov, Brezhnev's aide and speechwriter. This is confirmed by Roy Medvedev, who mentions that Golikov and Chkhikvishvili worked in the Central Committee apparatus, while the other two authors were scholars. (Roy Medvedev, *Faut-il réhabiliter Staline?* (Paris: Ed. du Seuil, 1969), 38.)
130 V. Golikov et al., 70.
131 V. Golikov et al., 70 (emphasis in the original).
132 V. Golikov et al., 72–73.
133 L.P. Petrovskii, "Open Letter to the TsK of the CPSU with a critique of historical publications rehabilitating Stalin," AS n°130, *Sobranie Dokumentov Samizdata*, vol. 2.
134 P.I. Iakir, "Open letter to the editor of the journal "Kommunist" in relation to its publications rehabilitating Stalin," AS n° 99, *Sobranie Dokumentov Samizdata*, vol. 1, 1.
135 R.A. Medvedev, "Is it possible today to rehabilitate Stalin?," open letter to the journal 'Kommunist,'" April 4, 1969, AS n°131, *Sobranie Dokumentov Samizdata*, vol. 2. This long letter was published in France the same year as a short book: Medvedev, *Faut-il réhabiliter Staline?*
136 Medvedev, *Lichnost' i èpokha*, 174.
137 Artizov et al., *Reabilitatsiia: Kak èto bylo*, II: Fevral' 1956-nachalo 80-kh godov.: 526.
138 [Roi] [Medvedev], *Politicheskii dnevnik. 1964-1970.* (Amsterdam: Fond imeni Gertsena, 1972), 586–88.

Chapter 3

1 Cécile Vaissié, *Pour votre liberté et pour la nôtre: Le combat des dissidents de Russie* (Paris: R. Laffont, 1999), 56–60.
2 See Nathans, "The Dictatorship of Reason."
3 Sergei Oushakine, "The Terrifying Mimicry of Samizdat," *Public Culture* 13, no. 2 (2001): 208.
4 Richard Pipes, "The Historical Evolution of the Russian Intelligentsia," in *The Russian Intelligentsia*, ed. Richard Pipes (New York: Columbia University Press, 1961), 52–58.
5 Pipes, 58–59.
6 Ludmilla Alexeyeva and Paul Goldberg, *The Thaw Generation: Coming of Age in the Post-Stalin Era* (Pittsburgh: University of Pittsburgh Press, 1993), 97.
7 Vladislav Martinovich Zubok, *Zhivago's Children: The Last Russian Intelligentsia* (Cambridge, MA: Belknap Press of Harvard University Press, 2009), 162.
8 Tromly, *Making the Soviet Intelligentsia*, 10–12.
9 Shlapentokh, *Soviet Intellectuals and Political Power*, 14–15.
10 Shlapentokh, 15–16.
11 Denis Kozlov, *The Readers of Novyi Mir. Coming to Terms with the Stalinist Past.* (Cambridge, MA; London: Harvard University Press, 2013), 18.
12 Kozlov, *The Readers of Novyi Mir.*
13 Ekaterina Surovtseva, *Zhanr "pis'ma vozhdiu" v Sovetskuiu èpokhu (1950-e-1980-e gg.)*, AIRO-Monografiia 24 (Moscow: AIRO-XXI, 2010), 42–43.
14 Surovtseva, 42.

15 On this term, and the courage needed to sign a collective letter of protest, see Alexeyeva and Goldberg, *The Thaw Generation*, 167-68.
16 Mikhail Meerson-Aksenov, "The Dissident Movement and *Samizdat*," in *The Political, Social and Religious Thought of Russian "Samizdat": An Anthologie*, eds. M. Meerson-Aksenov and N. Lupinin (Belmont: Notable & Academik Books, 1977), 32. Quoted in Philip Boobbyer, *Conscience, Dissent and Reform in Soviet Russia* (London: Routledge, 2005), 113.
17 Kozlov, *The Readers of Novyi Mir*, 19.
18 "Forty-three children of murdered Bolsheviks protest rehabilitation of Stalin," in *Samizdat: Voices of the Soviet Opposition*, ed. George Saunders (New York: Monad Press, 1974), 248-50.
19 Lev Kopelev, "Vozmozhna li reabilitatsiia Stalina?," in *Vera s slovo: Vystupleniia i pis'ma, 1962-1976 gg.* (Ann Arbor: Ardis, 1977), 31-35. Kochetov's novel *Chego zhe ty khochesh* ("What is that you want then?"), published in 1969, aroused particular criticism from anti-Stalinists for its overt pro-Stalinist tone. Kopelev mentions some of his earlier writings.
20 Kopelev, 33.
21 See Chapter 2.
22 Petrovskii, "Open Letter to the TsK of the CPSU…," 6.
23 Iakir, "Open letter to the editor of the journal Kommunist…," 3.
24 Medvedev, *Faut-il Réhabiliter Staline?*, 14-15.
25 Il'ia Gabai, Iulii Kim, and Petr Iakir, "K deiateliam nauki, kul'tury i iskusstva," in *Antologiia Samizdata: Nepodtsenzurnaia Literatura v SSSR 1950-e -1980-e*, ed. Viacheslav Igrunov, vol. 2: 1966-1973 (Moscow: Mezhdunarodnyi Institut Gumanitarno-Politicheskikh Issledovanii, 2005), 46-50.
26 Gabai, Kim, and Iakir, 50.
27 Lidiia Chukovskaia, "V gazetu 'Izvestiia'. Ne kazn', no mysl', no slovo (k 15-letiiu so dnia smerti Stalina)," in *Antologiia Samizdata: Nepodtsenzurnaia literatura v SSSR 1950-e -1980-e*, ed. Viacheslav Igrunov, vol. 2: 1966-1973 (Moscow: Mezhdunarodnyi Institut Gumanitarno-Politicheskikh Issledovanii, 2005), 129.
28 L.Z. Kopelev, "Why is a rehabilitation of Stalin impossible?", *Tagebuch*, Vienna, 1967. Reproduced in Lev Kopelev, *Vera v slovo: Vystupleniia i pis'ma, 1962-1976 gg.* (Ann Arbor: Ardis, 1977), 31-35.
29 G.Ts. Svirskii, "Transcript of a speech at an open Party meeting of the Moscow section of the Writers' Union of the USSR dedicated to the threat of rebirth of Stalinism and the problem of censorship," AS n°26, *Sobranie Dokumentov Samizdata*, vol. 1 (Munich: Samizdat Archive Association, 1973), 14.
30 G. Pomerants, "Moral make-up of a historical figure," AS n°479-b, *Sobranie Dokumentov Samizdata* vol. 16 (Munich: Samizdat Archive Association, 1976), 22. This samizdat text was adapted from a speech pronounced by Pomerants at the Institute of Philosophy on December 3, 1965.
31 Iakir, "Open letter to the editor of the journal "Kommunist…".
32 Iakir, 5.
33 Iakir, 11.
34 Chukovskaia, "Ne kazn', no mysl', no slovo," 129.
35 Chukovskaia, 129.
36 Petrovskii, "Open Letter to the TsK of the CPSU…"
37 Wilhelm Goerdt, "PRAVDA: Wahrheit (ISTINA) Und Gerechtigkeit (SPRAVEDLIVOST')," *Archiv Für Begriffsgeschichte* 12 (1968): 58-85.

38 Boobbyer, *Conscience, Dissent and Reform in Soviet Russia*, 97.
39 Vladimir Pomerantsev, "Ob iskrennosti v literature," *Novyi mir*, 1953, 220. Quoted in Boobbyer, 96.
40 Evgenii Vuchetich, "Vnesem iasnost'," *Izvestiia*, April 14, 1965.
41 Vuchetich. (Emphasis in the original)
42 Roy Medvedev, "Pis'mo gruppy vidnykh istorikov v gazetu 'Izvestiia'", *Politicheskii dnevnik*, June 1965. ([Medvedev], *Politicheskii dnevnik I*, 83.) (Emphasis in the original).
43 On *Political Diary*, see Chapter 5. Roy Medvedev, "O 'bol'shoi' i 'maloi' pravdakh," *Politicheskii dnevnik*, January 1967. This discussion is also reproduced in Medvedev, *On Socialist Democracy*, 195–201.
44 Medvedev.
45 Medvedev.
46 "Ob istoricheskoi pravde," November 30, 1966, Transcript. (HIA, A.M. Nekrich Papers, Box 62, Microfilm 1)
47 Ibid.
48 See Nanci Dale Adler, *Keeping Faith with the Party: Communist Believers Return from the Gulag* (Bloomington, IN: Indiana University Press, 2012).
49 Heer, *Politics and History in the Soviet Union*, 156–57.
50 OKhDLSM, F. 333, sd.op. 1, u.d. 74.
51 Sergei Mikoian, "Istoricheskaia publitsistika. Aleksei Snegov v bor'be za 'destalinizatsiiu,'" *Voprosy istorii*, no. 4 (April 2006): 69–74.
52 Artizov et al., *Reabilitatsiia: kak èto bylo*, II: Fevral' 1956-nachalo 80-kh godov.:524.
53 Roy Medvedev, *Khrushchev* (New York: Anchor Books, 1984), 67.
54 On contradictory accounts of this episode, see Smith, *Moscow 1956*, 33.
55 Medvedev, *Khrushchev*, 69. According to Kathleen Smith, until 1960. (Smith, *Moscow 1956*, 33.)
56 Mikoian, "Istoricheskaia publitsistika," 78.
57 Smith, *Moscow 1956*, 34.
58 See Chapter 4.
59 Anastas Ivanovich Mikoian, *Tak bylo: Razmyshleniia o minuvshem* (Moscow: Vagrius, 1999), 590.
60 Sergei Nikitich Khrushchev, *Khrushchev* (Moscow: Vagrius, 2001).
61 Mikoian, "Istoricheskaia publitsistika," 77.
62 Dobson, *Khrushchev's Cold Summer*, 201. See also Roy Medvedev's unpublished memoirs in German, which contain a chapter on Snegov (OKhDLSM, F. 333, sd.op. 1, u.d. 74).
63 Letter of A.V. Snegov to M.A. Suslov, April 24, 1965. RGANI, F. 5, op. 35, d. 211, l. 9–12.
64 Letter of A.V. Snegov to the Party Commission of the Moscow City Committee of the CPSU, n.d. (probably 1971), 13. Personal archive of Leonid Novak, courtesy of Kathleen Smith. Among them was A.V. Snegov, *Serdtse, otdannoe liudiam, Rasskaz o zhizni i deiatel'nosti Grigoriia Ivanovicha Petrovskogo* (Moscow: Izd. Pol. Literatury, 1964).
65 OKhDLSM, F. 333, op. 1, d. 74; Interview of R. Medvedev (1).
66 Letter of A.V. Snegov to M.A. Suslov…
67 Ibid. On Snegov and Suslov's mutual antipathy, see Mikoian, "Istoricheskaia publitsistika," 82.
68 Letter of P. Pospelov to the TsK, May 14, 1965. RGANI, F. 5, op. 35, d. 211, l. 28.
69 Letter of A.V. Snegov to the Party Commission…, 15.

70 "Vystuplenie na konferentsii starykh bol'shevikov sovmestno s rukovodstvom Instituta MARKSIZMA-LENINIZMA pri TsK KPSS," July 27–28, 1966. Archive of the History of Dissent in the USSR (1953–1987), Mezhdunarodnyi Memorial, F. 128 Roy Medvedev, Box 2.
71 "Vystuplenie na konferentsii...," 1.
72 "Vystuplenie na konferentsii...," 13.
73 OKhDLSM, F. 333, sd.op. 1, u.d. 74.
74 Artizov et al., *Reabilitatsiia: kak èto bylo*, II: Fevral' 1956-nachalo 80-kh godov.: 523.
75 Artizov et al., 521.
76 Artizov et al., 522.
77 Artizov et al., 523.
78 Artizov et al., 523.
79 Khrushchev, *Khrushchev*.
80 OKhDLSM, F. 333, sd.op. 1, u.d. 74.
81 Interview of R. Medvedev by L. Novak, January 2004, 13.
82 Leonid Petrovskii, "K 15-letiiu so dnia smerti. Borets protiv stalinizma. Pamiati A.V. Snegova (1.12.1989–18.09.1989)," Personal Archive of L.G. Novak, Courtesy of Kathleen Smith.
83 A. Sovokin, "Replika: Istoriia odnoi telegrammy," *Izvestiia*, July 10, 1965.
84 Sovokin.
85 According to the memoirs of I.L. Abramovich, "The author [of *Imenem Revoliutsii*] used in it the memoirs of Antonov-Ovseenko published in 1933, when it was forbidden to mention Smil'ga's name in print, and therefore Antonov-Ovseenko struck it out from his memoirs" (I.L. Abramovich, *Vospominaniia i vzgliady*, vol. 1: Vospominaniia (KRUK-Prestizh, 2004), 66). In 2014, in a conversation with me, Tat'iana Smil'ga, Ivar's daughter, still mentioned with bitterness A.V. Antonov-Ovseenko's attribution of the telegram to his father, rather than to Smil'ga, which she considered as an undue appropriation.
86 Antonov-Ovseenko, *The Time of Stalin*, 330.
87 F.N. Petrov, "V mire knig. Obraz revoliutsionnera," *Izvestiia*, July 18, 1965.
88 Letter of A.V. Antonov-Ovseenko to the editorial committee of the newspaper *Izvestiia*, July 15, 1965. Personal papers of A.V. A-O.
89 Antonov-Ovseenko, *The Time of Stalin*, 330.
90 Letter of A.V. Antonov-Ovseenko to P.N. Demichev, July 30, 1965; Letter of A.V. Antonov-Ovseenko to A.I. Mikoian, July 30, 1965. Personal papers of A.V. A-O.
91 "Pis'mo v redaktsiiu. Eshche raz ob odnoi telegramme," *Izvestiia*, № 206, August 31, 1965, 5.
92 Antonov-Ovseenko, *The Time of Stalin*, 330.
93 Letter by A.N. Tsitovich to L.I. Brezhnev, August 1965. Personal Papers of A.V. A-O.
94 Letter of L.A. Meerson to P.N. Demichev, September 14, 1965. Personal papers of A.V. A-O.
95 Letter by A.P. Ivanov to the Department of Publications of the Central Committee of the CPSU, September 19, 1965; Letter by M. Pokaliukhin, A. Strygin, S. Golovanov to F.N. Petrov, n.d. Personal papers of A.V. A.-O.
96 Letter by L.M. Ol'shanskaia and L.M. Stoliarova to the editorial committee of Izvestiia, September 15, 1965. Personal papers of A.V. A.-O.
97 Letter by Rudenko and Verkhovykh to the Department of Publications of the Central Committee of the CPSU, August 1, 1965. Personal papers of A.V. A.-O.
98 Antonov-Ovseenko, *The Time of Stalin*, 330.

99 Antonov-Ovseenko, 331–32.
100 Antonov-Ovseenko, 332–33.
101 RGANI, F. 5, op. 62, d. 70, l. 181–207.
102 Ibid., l. 185.
103 Ibid., l.187.
104 Ibid., l. 192–196.
105 Ibid., l. 195.
106 Ibid., l. 208–209.
107 Anton Rakitin, *A.V. Antonov-Ovseenko* (Leningrad: Lenizdat, 1975).
108 G.A. Deborin and B.S. Tel'pukhovskii, "V ideinom plenu u fal'sifikatorov istorii," *Voprosy istorii KPSS*, no. 9 (September 1967): 127–40. For the English translation, see G.A. Deborin and B.S. Tel'pukhovskii, "In the Ideological Captivity of the Falsifiers of History," in *June 22, 1941: Soviet Historians and the German Invasion*, ed. Vladimir Petrov (Columbia, SC: University of South Carolina Press, 1968), 271–302.
109 RGANI, F. 5, op. 35, d. 212, l. 27–29. See Chapter 2.
110 D.G. Nadzhafov, "Kollega, edinomyshlennik, drug," in *Otreshivshiisia ot strakha. Pam'iati A.M. Nekricha: Vospominaniia, stat'i, dokumenty*, ed. M.S. Al'perovich (Moscow: Institut Vseobshchei Istorii RAN, 1996), 102.
111 OKhDLSM, F. 333, sd.op. 32, u.d. 6.
112 Deborin and Tel'pukhovskii, "In the Ideological Captivity," 278.
113 Deborin and Tel'pukhovskii, 283–84.
114 Deborin and Tel'pukhovskii, 284.
115 Deborin and Tel'pukhovskii, 295.
116 Deborin and Tel'pukhovskii, 293.
117 Deborin and Tel'pukhovskii, 287.
118 Deborin and Tel'pukhovskii, 301.
119 Deborin and Tel'pukhovskii, 302.
120 Al'perovich, "Knigi imeiut svoiu sud'bu," 84.
121 Al'perovich, 84.
122 Al'perovich, *Otreshivshiisia ot strakha*, 151.
123 Al'perovich, 166–67.
124 Nekrich, *Forsake Fear*, 222.
125 Al'perovich, "Knigi imeiut svoiu sud'bu," 85.
126 Al'perovich, 85–86.
127 Al'perovich, *Otreshivshiisia ot strakha*, 191.
128 Al'perovich, 196–97. (Emphasis in the original)
129 Al'perovich, 197–98.
130 Al'perovich, 170.
131 Al'perovich, 168.
132 Al'perovich, 168–69.
133 Al'perovich, 171.
134 Al'perovich, "Knigi imeiut svoiu sud'bu," 86–87. Concerning the attempt to deprive Nekrich of his doctoral degree, see Nekrich, *Forsake Fear*, 224–28. See also the testimony of S.Z. Sluch, a key actor in this episode: S.Z. Sluch, "Nes'kol'ko vstrech," in *Otreshivshiisia ot strakha. Pam'iati A.M. Nekricha: Vospominaniia, stat'i, dokumenty*, ed. M.S. Al'perovich (Moscow: Institut Vseobshchei Istorii RAN, 1996), 114–20.
135 A Second World War veteran, General Grigorenko joined in the early 1960s an underground socialist group. As a result, he was incarcerated in a psychiatric hospital in 1964–65.

136　Petr Grigor'evich Grigorenko, "The Concealment of Historical Truth—A Public Crime: The Real Fate of the Armed Forces When Hitler Invaded," in *The Grigorenko Papers: Writings and Documents on His Case* (Boulder, CO: Westview Press, 1976), 12–50. In his memoirs, Grigorenko explains that this happened against his will, probably through his friend Sergei Pisarev, to whom he had lent the text, and who immediately began to copy it for circulation. Although Grigorenko asked to take back all copies, it was probably too late to stop further dissemination. (Petr Grigorenko, *Mémoires* (Paris: Presses de la Renaissance, 1980), 517–18.)
137　Grigorenko, "The Concealment of Historical Truth," 20.
138　Grigorenko, 23–24.
139　Grigorenko, 32–34.
140　This sentence is missing from the English version but is to be found in the Russian one (Petr Grigorenko, *Mysli sumasshedshego: Izbrannye pis'ma i vystupleniia Petra Grigor'evicha Grigorenko* (Amsterdam: Fond imeni Gertsena, 1973), 73.)
141　Grigorenko, 81. The English version cuts the sentence in half (p. 44).
142　Grigorenko, "The Concealment of Historical Truth," 47–48.
143　Nekrich, *Forsake Fear*, 208.
144　Andrei Sakharov, *Vospominaniia* (New York: Izd. im. Chekhova, 1990), 428.
145　Grigorenko, *Mémoires*, 519.

Chapter 4

1　Kozlov, *The Readers of Novyi Mir*, 2–6.
2　Zubok, *Zhivago's Children*, 168.
3　Dobson, *Khrushchev's Cold Summer*, 216.
4　Kozlov, *The Readers of Novyi Mir*, Chapter 7.
5　Kozlov, 7.
6　Evgenii Dolmatovskii, "Kniga, propavshaia bez vesti," *Literaturnaia gazeta*, January 20, 1988.
7　Aleksandr Isaevich Solzhenitsyn, *The Gulag Archipelago: 1918-1956*, vol. 3 (Glasgow: Harpers and Row Publishers, 1978), 526.
8　Dolmatovskii, "Kniga, propavshaia bez vesti."
9　Polly Jones, "Iurii Trifonov's Fireglow and the 'Mnemonic Communities' of the Brezhnev Era," *Cahiers du monde russe* 54, no. 1–2 (2013): 1–24.
10　Medvedev, *On Socialist Democracy*, 180.
11　Aleksandr Etkind, *Warped Mourning: Stories of the Undead in the Land of the Unburied*, Cultural Memory in the Present (Stanford, CA: Stanford University Press, 2013), 4.
12　Solzhenitsyn, *The Oak and the Calf*, 4.
13　Solzhenitsyn, 8–9.
14　Solzhenitsyn, 14.
15　See Kozlov, *The Readers of Novyi Mir*, Chapter 7. A selection of letters of readers have appeared in Tiurina, *Dorogoi Ivan Denisovich!..*.
16　Tiurina, *Dorogoi Ivan Denisovich!...*, 166.
17　Tiurina, 159–60.
18　Anna Skripnikova (1896–1974) was arrested five times between 1919 and 1952. After her rehabilitation, in 1959, she demonstrated her civic engagement by writing hundreds of letters to intercede in favor of former political prisoners, particularly

those who were unable to speak for themselves. (N. Popov, "Pamiat' Anny Petrovny Skripnikovoi," in *Pamiat': Istoricheskii Sbornik*, vol. 1 (New York: Khronika Press, 1978), 285–94.)

19   Tiurina, *Dorogoi Ivan Denisovich!...*, 146–49.
20   Aleksandr Isaevich Solzhenitsyn, *The Gulag Archipelago: 1918-1956*, vol. 1 (Glasgow: Harpers and Row Publishers, 1974), xii.
21   Solzhenitsyn, *The Gulag Archipelago*, 1978, 3:526.
22   Solzhenitsyn, *The Gulag Archipelago*, 1974, 1:xi; Solzhenitsyn, *The Gulag Archipelago*, 1978, 3:526.
23   See their correspondence in Tiurina, *Dorogoi Ivan Denisovich!...*, 133–38.
24   Solzhenitsyn, *The Gulag Archipelago*, 1978, 3:526.
25   In the latest Russian edition, which includes the full list, the number stated is 257. (Aleksandr Solzhenitsyn, *Arkhipelag GULag: 1918-1956 : opyt khudozhestvennogo issledovaniia* (Ekaterinburg: Izdatel'stvo "U-Factoriia," 2006), 13–18).
26   Solzhenitsyn, *The Gulag Archipelago*, 1974, 1: xi.
27   The *sharashka* was a prison compound for highly qualified specialists and scientists, where they benefited from improved living conditions and worked on special projects in their field of specialization. Solzhenitsyn himself spent several years of his camp term in a *sharashka*, an experience he describes in *The First Circle*.
28   Soljénitsyne, *Les invisibles*, 189–92.
29   Soljénitsyne, 193.
30   Solzhenitsyn, *The Gulag Archipelago*, 1974, 1:205; 213.
31   Solzhenitsyn, *The Gulag Archipelago*, 1978, 3:119.
32   Solzhenitsyn, 3: Chapter 7.
33   Solzhenitsyn, 3:289.
34   Solzhenitsyn, 3:462.
35   Tiurina, *Dorogoi Ivan Denisovich!...*, 157.
36   Tiurina, 143.
37   These memoirs were published after the fall of the Soviet Union under the title *Spohady* ("Memories") (Kyiv, Vydavnitstvo im. Telihy, 1996).
38   Tiurina, *Dorogoi Ivan Denisovich!...*, 222–24.
39   Solzhenitsyn, *The Gulag Archipelago*, 1974, 1:419–31.
40   Solzhenitsyn, 1:455.
41   Soljénitsyne, *Les invisibles*, 93–95; Interview of N. Levitskaia, June 19, 2012.
42   Interview of N. Levitskaia.
43   Interview of N. Levitskaia.
44   Interview of N. Levitskaia.
45   Soljénitsyne, *Les invisibles*, 93–105; Interview of N. Levitskaia.
46   Soljénitsyne, *Les invisibles*, 145–49.
47   Anna M. Garaseva, *Ia zhila v samoi beschelovechnoi strane: Vospominaniia anarkhistki* (Moscow: Intergraf Service, 1997), 6–7.
48   Soljénitsyne, *Les invisibles*, 181–82.
49   Garaseva, *Ia zhila v samoi beschelovechnoi strane*, 288.
50   Aleksandr Isaevich Solzhenitsyn, *Invisible Allies* (Washington, DC: Counterpoint, 1995).
51   Tiurina, *Dorogoi Ivan Denisovich!...*, 231.
52   Soljénitsyne, *Les invisibles*, 71.
53   Soljénitsyne, 72–80.
54   Solzhenitsyn, *The Oak and the Calf*, 80.

55 Soljénitsyne, *Les invisibles*, 151-52.
56 Solzhenitsyn, *The Oak and the Calf*, 90.
57 Michael Scammell, *Solzhenitsyn: A Biography* (London; Melbourne: Hutchinson, 1985), 511.
58 Nikolai Krylenko, *Za piat' let 1918-1922 gg.: Obvinitel'nye rechi po naibolee krupnym protsessam, zaslushannym v Moskovskom i verkhovnom revoliutsionnykh tribunalakh* (Moscow; Petrograd: Gosizdat, 1931); Martin Latsis, *Dva goda bor'by na vnutrennem fronte* (Moscow: Gos. izdatel'stvo, 1920); Andrei Vyshinskii, *Ot tiurem k vospitatel'nym uchrezhdeniiam: Sbornik statei* (Moscow: Sovetskoe zakonodatel'stvo, 1934).
59 Scammell, *Solzhenitsyn*, 523-25. The fourth copy, oddly enough, he entrusted to the *Pravda* safe.
60 Soljénitsyne, *Les invisibles*, 44.
61 This is apparent from an October 5, 1965 memorandum from the KGB reproduced in Scammell and Fitzpatrick, *The Solzhenitsyn Files*, 7.
62 Soljénitsyne, *Les invisibles*, 37-46. Solzhenitsyn had transferred his papers to Anichkova's apartment in June 1965. However, Teush failed to mention that during the summer, he had found several of Solzhenitsyn's works in his apartment and had entrusted them to a friend, Il'ia Zilberberg. The KGB raided both the Teushes' and Zilberberg's apartments on the same day.
63 Solzhenitsyn, *The Oak and the Calf*, 103.
64 Soljénitsyne, *Les invisibles*, 46-47.
65 Interview of E. Chukovskaia, June 20, 2012.
66 Elena Chukovskaia, Elena Tsezarevna: K iubileiu vnuchki Chukovskogo, *Radio Svoboda*, August 7, 2011, http://www.svoboda.org/a/24289634.html. The text of the review is reproduced in: Pavel Spivakovskii and T. V. Esina, eds., *"Ivanu Denisovichu" polveka: Iubileinyi sbornik, 1962-2012* (Moscow: Dom russkogo zarubezh'ia im. Aleksandra Solzhenitsyna / Russkii put', 2012), 20-21.
67 Chukovskaia, K iubileiu vnuchki Chukovskogo.
68 Soljénitsyne, *Les invisibles*, 117.
69 Soljénitsyne, 118-22.
70 The letter is reproduced in Leopold Labedz, ed., *Solzhenitsyn: A Documentary Record* (London: Allen Lane the Penguin Press, 1970), 64-69.
71 Labedz, 161.
72 Soljénitsyne, *Les invisibles*, 124; Interview of E. Chukovskaia.
73 Soljénitsyne, *Les invisibles*, 128-29.
74 Interview of E. Chukovskaia.
75 Soljénitsyne, *Les invisibles*, 130-32.
76 Soljénitsyne, 199-201.
77 Roy Medvedev, *Let History Judge: The Origins and Consequences of Stalinism*, Revised and expanded ed. (Oxford; New York [etc.]: Oxford University Press, 1989), xi-xii.
78 Roy Medvedev, *Let History Judge* (London: McMillan, 1972), xxxiii.
79 Medvedev, xxxiii.
80 Medvedev and Medvedev, *1925-2010. Iz vospominanii*, 7-9, 12.
81 "Triumf Tirana, Tragediia naroda. Beseda s D.A. Volkogonovym i R.A. Medvedevym," in *Surovaia drama naroda. Uchenye i publitsisty o prirode Stalinizma* (Moscow: Politizdat, 1989), 270; Interview of R. Medvedev (4), September 24, 2017.
82 Letter by D.Iu. Zorina to Roy and Zhores Medvedev, November 14, 1965. OKhDLSM, sd.op. 9, u.d. 252.

83 OKhDLSM, F. 333, sd.op. 1, u.d. 74; See introduction to Suren Gazarian, "Èto ne olzhno povtorit'sia: Dokumental'naia povest'," *Literaturnaia Armeniia*, no. 6, 7, 8, 9 (1988).
84 It was Zhores Medvedev who unsuccessfully tried to publish the book after moving to the West. (Communication of Zhores Medvedev, May 13, 2016).
85 Gazarian, "Èto ne dolzhno povtorit'sia"; Medvedev and Medvedev, *1925-2010. Iz vospominanii*, 110.
86 Interview of R. Medvedev (1).
87 OKhDLSM, F. 333, sd.op. 1, u.d. 74.
88 Interview of R. Medvedev by L. Novak, 8.
89 Letter by Lev Portnov to Roy Medvedev, September 2, 1964. OKhDLSM, F. 333, sd.op. 9, u.d. 252.
90 OKhDLSM, F. 333, sd.op. 1, u.d. 74.
91 Interview of R. Medvedev (1).
92 Interview of R. Medvedev (1).
93 Stephen F. Cohen, *The Victims Return: Survivors of the Gulag After Stalin* (Exeter, NH: PublishingWorks, 2010), 89.
94 Grigorii Pomerants, *Sledstvie vedet katorzhanka* (Moscow; Saint-Petersburg: Tsentr gumanitarnykh initiativ, 2014), 5.
95 Smith, *Moscow 1956*, 98.
96 Pomerants, *Sledstvie vedet katorzhanka*, 135–38.
97 Pomerants, 6. These numbers, of 19,840,000 arrested and 7,000,000 executed in prisons, do not correspond to the estimates of historians, however, who consider that no more than 700,000 people were executed during the Great Terror. On the controversy surrounding Shatunovskaia's very high numbers, see Chapter 8.
98 Pomerants, 7. In 1962 already, Shatunovskaia tried to bring Khrushchev's attention to the documents that her commission had uncovered, to no avail. ("Letter of O.G. Shatunovskaia to Khrushchev," May 22, 1962, in Artizov et al., *Reabilitatsiia: Kak èto bylo*, II: Fevral' 1956-nachalo 80-kh godov.: 372–74.) See Shatunovskaia's account of the disappearance of key documents in Olga Shatunovskaia, *Ob ushedshem veke. Rasskazyvaet Olga Shatunovskaia*, ed. D. Kut'ina, A. Broido, and A. Kut'in (La Jolla, CA: DAA Books, 2001), 353–56.
99 Medvedev, Interview (1).
100 Matthew E. Lenoe, *The Kirov Murder and Soviet History* (New Haven: Yale University Press, 2010).
101 Lenoe, 607.
102 Lenoe, 609.
103 Lenoe, 631.
104 Lenoe, 635–37.
105 Medvedev, Interview (1).
106 Zhores Medvedev, *Nikita Khrushchev* (Izdatel'stvo "Vremia," 2012), 164; Interview of R. Medvedev (1).
107 Interview of R. Medvedev (2), January 25, 2013.
108 "O Parvuse i ne tol'ko. Pervoe v zhizni interv'iu Tat'iany Evgenevny Gnedinoi, vnuchki Parvusa," *Laboratoriia fantastiki* (blog), http://fantlab.ru/article429.
109 Medvedev, Interview (1).
110 "O Parvuse i ne tol'ko"; "V Narkomindele. 1922-1939- Interv'iu s E.A. Gnedinym," in *Pamiat': Istoricheskii sbornik*, vol. 5 (Paris: Ed. La Presse libre, 1982), 357–93.
111 Medvedev and Medvedev, *1925-2010. Iz vospominanii*, 277; Interview of R. Medvedev (1).

112 This was the original title of the book later published under the title *The Rise and Fall of T.D. Lysenko*.
113 Medvedev and Medvedev, *1925-2010. Iz vospominanii*, 62.
114 Konstantin Simonov, *Glazami cheloveka moego pokoleniia: Razmyshleniia o I.V. Staline* (Moscow: Kniga, 1990), 256–69. On Vuchetich see Chapter 3.
115 Medvedev and Medvedev, *1925-2010. Iz vospominanii*, 62–63.
116 Medvedev and Medvedev, 65.
117 Medvedev and Medvedev, 70–75.
118 Probably the most well-known position in this controversy is Ernst Genri's letter to Ehrenburg, which circulated in samizdat in 1965, in which the journalist accused Ehrenburg of failing to condemn Stalin unequivocally in his memoirs. (Viacheslav Igrunov, ed., *Antologiia samizdata: Nepodtsenzurnaia literatura v SSSR 1950-e -1980-e*, vol. Vol. 1: do 1966 goda (Moscow: Mezhdunarodnyi Institut Gumanitarno-Politicheskikh Issledovanii, 2005), 335–44.)
119 Medvedev and Medvedev, *1925-2010. Iz vospominanii*, 76–83.
120 At the time, Zhores Medvedev had submitted for publication a short version of his study *Biology and the Personality Cult* and had met the editors for this purpose. However, the publication did not take place and he eventually published his book in the West in 1969. Medvedev and Medvedev, *1925-2010. Iz vospominanii*, 103.
121 Medvedev and Medvedev, 104–05.
122 Aleksandr Tvardovskii, *Novomirskii dnevnik*, ed. V.A. Tvardovskii and O.A. Tvardovskii, vol. 1 (Moscow: Prozaik, 2009), 510.
123 Tvardovskii, 1:509.
124 Medvedev and Medvedev, *1925-2010. Iz vospominanii*, 116.
125 Medvedev and Medvedev, 124.
126 Interview of R. Medvedev (2).
127 Medvedev, *On Socialist Democracy*.
128 Medvedev and Medvedev, *1925-2010. Iz vospominanii*, 127.
129 Medvedev eventually published these memoirs in the West in his journal "Twentieth century" (Dmitrii Vitkovskii, "Polzhizni," in *Dvadtsatyi vek*, ed. Roi Medvedev (London: T.C.D. Publications, 1976), 138).
130 See the Medvedev brothers' account of this episode: Zhores Medvedev and Roy Medvedev, *A Question of Madness* (New York: Knopf, 1971).
131 Medvedev and Medvedev, *1925-2010. Iz vospominanii*, 139.
132 In particular, such articles as "Ivan Denisovich, ego druz'ia i nedrugi," in *Solzhenitsyn i koleso istorii*, ed. Vladimir Lakshin (Moscow: Veche, 2008), 13–60.
133 See Chapter 7.
134 Interview of R. Medvedev (1).
135 Medvedev and Medvedev, *1925-2010. Iz vospominanii*, 88.
136 Medvedev and Medvedev, 86; Interview of R. Medvedev (1).
137 Medvedev and Medvedev, *1925-2010. Iz vospominanii*, 94–95. Solzhenitsyn had also tried to approach Starikov as he was interested in using his materials, but he was not interested in working in coauthorship and Starikov only begrudgingly agreed to lend him some materials. Solzhenitsyn acrimoniously commented on this episode in his memoirs, accusing Medvedev of having "forewarned" Starikov against him. (Soljénitsyne, *Les invisibles*, 292–94.)
138 Sakharov, *Vospominaniia*, 1990, 360.
139 Sakharov, 360.
140 Andrei Sakharov, *Trevoga i nadezhda*, 2nd ed. (Moscow: Inter-Verso, 1991), 27.

141 Georgii Shakhnazarov, *S vozhdiami i bez nikh* (Moscow: Vagrius, 2001), 191–92.
142 Medvedev and Medvedev, *1925-2010. Iz vospominanii*, 277.
143 Aleksandr Bovin, "Kurs na stabil'nost' porodil zastoi," in *L.I. Breznev. Materialy k biografii*, ed. Iurii Aksiutin (Moscow: Politizdat, 1991), 92–102.
144 Interview of R. Medvedev (3), January 22, 2017.
145 Interview of R. Medvedev (1).
146 Roy Medvedev, Manuscript "Pered sudom istorii," 1966, OKhDLSM, F. 333, sd.op. 9, u.d. 2, 8.
147 Medvedev, 8–9.
148 Medvedev, 9.
149 Medvedev, 12.
150 Medvedev, 44–54.
151 Roy Medvedev, *The Samizdat Register*, vol. 2 (London: Merlin Press, 1981), x. The number of years of incarceration mentioned varies from 24 to 26, perhaps depending on the inclusion of pretrial detention.
152 KGB report to the TsK of the CPSU, September 2, 1966, RGANI, F. 5, op. 58, d. 21, l. 1.
153 Medvedev, *The Samizdat Register*, 1981, 2:51–97.
154 KGB report to the TsK of the CPSU, September 2, 1966, RGANI, F. 5, op. 58, d. 21, l. 2–6.
155 KGB report to the TsK of the CPSU, l. 30–120.
156 Roy Medvedev, Manuscript "K sudu istorii," 1967, OKhDLSM, F. 333, sd.op. 9, u.d. 3.
157 Medvedev, 122.
158 Letter reproduced in Artizov et al., *Reabilitatsiia: Kak èto bylo*, II: Fevral' 1956-nachalo 80-kh godov.:474–75.
159 Roy Medvedev, Manuscript "K sudu istorii," 1967, OKhDLSM, F. 333, sd.op. 9, u.d. 3, 299.
160 Medvedev, 220. On Solzhenitsyn's (mis)use of Iakubovich's testimony, see Chapter 7.
161 Medvedev, 432.
162 Medvedev, 776–77.

Chapter 5

1 Iurii Andropov, "'Samizdat' preterpel kachestvennye izmeneniia.," *Istochnik. Dokumenty russkoi istorii*. 2, no. 9 (1994): 77.
2 R. Blekhman, "Bespamiatstvo," *22* VIII, no. 3 (1978): 249–53. Reproduced in *Summa. Za svobodnuiu mysl'*. (Saint-Petersburg: Izdatel'stvo zhurnala "Zvezda," 2002), 191.
3 Robert M. Slusser, "History and the Democratic Opposition," in *Dissent in the USSR: Politics, Ideology and People* (Baltimore: Johns Hopkins University Press, 1975), 334.
4 Denis Kozlov, "The Historical Turn in Late Soviet Culture: Retrospectivism, Factography, Doubt, 1953–91," *Kritika: Explorations in Russian and Eurasian History* 2, no. 3 (Summer 2001): 577–600.
5 See for instance Frederick C. Barghoorn, "Factional, Sectoral and Subversive Opposition in Soviet Politics," in *Regimes and Opposition*, ed. Robert Dahl (New Haven; London: Yale University Press, 1973), 57.
6 See for example Rudolf L. Tőkés, ed., *Dissent in the USSR: Politics, Ideology and People* (Baltimore: Johns Hopkins University Press, 1975).

7   Gordon Skilling, "Samizdat: A Return to the Pre-Gutenberg Era?," in *Samizdat and an Independent Society in Central and Eastern Europe* (Columbus, OH: Ohio State University Press, 1989), 17.
8   Oushakine, "The Terrifying Mimicry of Samizdat," 196, 202–03.
9   Ann Komaromi, "The Unofficial Field of Late Soviet Culture," *Slavic Review* 66, no. 4 (December 1, 2007): 606. (Emphasis in the original)
10 Komaromi, 610–11.
11 Friederike Kind-Kovács and Jessie Labov, eds., *Samizdat, Tamizdat, and beyond: Transnational Media during and after Socialism* (New York: Berghahn Books, 2013), 3.
12 The USSR's accession to the UCC, however, did not solve all of these issues and created new ones, as Friederike Kind-Kovács emphasized. (Friederike Kind-Kovács, *Written Here, Published There: How Underground Literature Crossed the Iron Curtain* (Budapest: CEU Press, 2014), 132.)
13 The NTS (Narodno-Trudovoi Soiuz, "the Union of the People and Workers"), founded in 1930, set as its goal the overthrow of the Soviet regime. Its publishing organs regularly edited works from samizdat without the consent of their authors.
14 Article 190-1, adopted in September 1966, thus forbade "the systematic diffusion, in oral form, of notoriously false allegations, denigrating the Soviet political and social system, as well as the preparation or diffusion, in manuscript form, printed or otherwise, of works of such content." Nevertheless, trumped-up criminal charges were also a frequent way of dealing with dissidents, especially after the signing of the Helsinki Accords in 1975.
15 Kind-Kovács, *Written Here, Published There*, 426.
16 Kind-Kovács, 138.
17 Abdurakhman Avtorkhanov, *Stalin and the Soviet Communist Party: A Study in the Technology of Power* (New York: Praeger, 1959).
18 Abdurakhman Avtorkhanov, *Memuary* (Frankfurt/Main: Posev, 1983).
19 Avtorkhanov, 528.
20 Avtorkhanov, 674.
21 He was among the early founders of the radio, then called "Liberation," in 1951, and later spoke on Radio Liberty under the pseudonym of "Professor Temirov." ("Chto bylo, to bylo. 'Ideia, vo imia kotoroi i smert' krasna.' Interviu s politologom Abdurakhmanom Avtorkhanovym," *Vek XX i mir*, no. 9 (1990), http://old.russ.ru/antolog/vek/1990/9/ideya.htm.)
22 Abdurakhman Avtorkhanov, *Staline au pouvoir* (Paris: Les Iles d'or, 1951).
23 Avtorkhanov, *Memuary*, 735.
24 Avtorkhanov, 721–23.
25 Avtorkhanov, *Stalin and the Soviet Communist Party*, Foreword.
26 Michael David-Fox, "Memory, Archives, Politics: The Rise of Stalin in Avtorkhanov's Technology of Power," *Slavic Review* 54, no. 4 (1995): 988–1003, https://doi.org/10.2307/2501404.
27 [Roi] [Medvedev], "O knige A. Avtorkhanova 'Tekhnologiia vlasti,'" in *Politicheskii dnevnik. 1964-1970.* (Amsterdam: Fond imeni Gertsena, 1972), 509–15. Avtorkhanov replied to this review fiercely in his 1976 edition of *Tekhnologiia vlasti*, accusing the Medvedev brothers of collaborating with the KGB. Abdurakhman Avtorkhanov, *Tekhnologiia vlasti*, 2nd ed. (Frankfurt/Main: Posev, 1976), 9.
28 Grigorenko, *Mémoires*, 520–21.
29 Grigorenko, 521. Grigorenko speaks of paying his own copy 50 rubles, and this was only the cost of the typist's work.

30 Gabriel' Superfin and Roy Medvedev both mentioned this rumor. (Communication of Gabriel' Superfin, March 10, 2012; OKhDLSM, F. 333, sd.op. 14, u.d. 31) Medvedev even claimed in a letter that his brother Zhores had measured such radioactivity, but the latter denied this. (Communication of Zhores Medvedev, February 8, 2018)
31 "Sudebnyi protsess v Leningrade 17-28 dekabria 1968 goda," *Khronika tekushchikh sobytii*, no. 5 (1968), http://hts.memo.ru/chr5.htm.
32 The quotes provided comes from a copy in Roy Medvedev's papers. (OKhDLSM, F. 333, sd.op. 6, u.d. 34)
33 "Dela Liubarskogo i Popova," *Khronika tekushchikh sobytii*, no. 28 (1972).
34 Avtorkhanov, *Tekhnologiia vlasti*, 34.
35 Avtorkhanov, 34–35.
36 Avtorkhanov, 5.
37 Avtorkhanov, *Memuary*, 744.
38 Apart from *The Technology of Power*, Avtorkhanov's work *The Enigma of Stalin's Death: Beria's Plot* (*Zagadka smerti Stalina*, 1976) was also broadly circulated, and to a smaller extent his *Origins of the Partocracy* (*Proiskhozhdenie partokratii*, 1973) and *Brezhnev's Strength and weakness* (*Sila i bessilie Brezhneva*, 1979).
39 Vladimir Voinovich, "K 100-letiiu Abdurakhmana Avtorkhanova," *Dosh* (blog), 2008, http://www.dosh-journal.ru/4(22)2008/1231168217.htm.
40 The title was added for publication abroad, in the 1970s. Informally, Medvedev and his readers referred to the journal as "the months," as the current month and year stood on the title page of each issue. (Roy Medvedev, "How Political Diary Was Created," in *An End to Silence: Uncensored Opinion in the Soviet Union, from Roy Medvedev's Underground Magazine Political Diary*, ed. Stephen F. Cohen (New York: Norton, 1982), 20.) This overview of *Political Diary* is based on the near complete collection of the samizdat journal from the archive of "Memorial" (Archive on the History of Dissent in the USSR, Organization "Mezhdunarodnyi Memorial," F. 128, Roi Medvedev, Boxes 1–2). The dates provided in this book are indicated according to the "Memorial" archive designation, with the publication reference added as well, if warranted.
41 Stephen F. Cohen, *An End to Silence: Uncensored Opinion in the Soviet Union, from Roy Medvedev's Underground Magazine Political Diary* (New York: W W Norton, 1982), 8.
42 See Chapter 4.
43 Medvedev, "How Political Diary Was Created," 17–18.
44 For an overview of the history of the *Chronicle*, see Cécile Vaissié, "La chronique des événements en cours. Une revue de la dissidence dans l'URSS brejnévienne," *Vingtième siècle. Revue d'histoire*, no. 63 (September 1999): 107–18.
45 Medvedev, "How Political Diary Was Created," 19.
46 Medvedev mentioned that this was the case for some of his essays on Soviet foreign policy, on the Six-Day War, "the Near-Eastern Conflict and the Jewish Question" or "Six points of view on Soviet-Chinese relations." ("Letter to Vladimir Pribylovskii, editor of the dictionary 'New political parties and organizations in Russia," OKhDLSM, F. 333, sd.op. 14, u.d. 31).
47 Medvedev, "How Political Diary Was Created," 19.
48 With the two latter he would sign in 1970 a common appeal to the Soviet leaders. (Roy Medvedev, Andrei Sakharov, and Valentin Turchin, "Appeal for a Gradual Democratization," in *Samizdat: Voices of the Soviet Opposition*, ed. George Saunders (New York: Monad Press, 1974), 399–412.)
49 Medvedev, "How Political Diary Was Created," 21.
50 Medvedev, 20.

51 Zhores Medvedev, "Potomok dekabrista - v 'Dvadtsatom veke' i 'Gulage,'" *2000.ua*, February 22, 2013, http://www.2000.ua/specproekty_ru/opasnaja-professija/glavy-iz-knigi-opasnja-professija/potomok-dekabrista--v-dvadtsatom-veke-i-gulage_arhiv_art.htm.
52 [Medvedev], *Politicheskii dnevnik I*; Roi Medvedev, *Politicheskii dnevnik II. 1965-1970*. (Amsterdam: Fond imeni Gertsena, 1975); Cohen, *An End to Silence*.
53 Medvedev believed that the first tamizdat publication of the journal had triggered the house search at his place in October 1971. (See Chapter 6). But Medvedev had carefully hidden his archive of the journal, and the KGB was only able to lay hand on some of Medvedev's current work material. (Interview of R. Medvedev (2).)
54 See Alexeyeva and Goldberg, *The Thaw Generation*, 57. Cases of demonstrative exit from the Party are mostly from the 1970s and 1980s—for example, Evgenii Gnedin (1979) and Mikhail Gefter (1982). In 1968, Aleksei Kosterin left the Party in protest against the invasion of Czechoslovakia, but only after he had been notified of his exclusion, and a few days before his death. Elena Bonner also returned her party card on the day she was summoned by the Moscow Party Committee to launch a procedure of exclusion (see Andrei Dmitrievich Sakharov, *Vospominaniia*, vol. 1 (Moscow: Prava cheloveka, 1996), 534–35.)
55 Yuri Glazov, *To Be or Not to Be in the Party: Communist Party Membership in the USSR* (Dordrecht: Kluwer Academic Publishers, 1988), 105–6.
56 Al'perovich, "Knigi imeiut svoiu sud'bu," 83.
57 RGANI, F. 89, op. 20, d. 84, l. 6–10. (HIA, Reel 1995).
58 Ibid., l. 41–45.
59 Ibid., l. 73–93.
60 Ibid., l. 6–8.
61 Ibid., l. 6.
62 Ibid., l. 8.
63 Ibid., l. 4–5.
64 Nekrich, *Forsake Fear*, 182–83.
65 "Mit Lagern machst Du uns nicht bange," *Der Spiegel*, March 20, 1967. (In his memoirs, Nekrich mistakenly mentions the date March 18 and slightly misquotes the article.)
66 Nekrich, *Forsake Fear*, 183–84.
67 RGANI, F. 89, op. 20, d. 84, l. 1–8. (HIA, Reel 1995).
68 Aleksei Bogomolov, "Istoriia kak izmena rodine," *Sovershenno sekretno* 8, no. 291 (August 2013), http://www.sovsekretno.ru/articles/id/3741/.
69 Bogomolov.
70 See, for example, Medvedev's April 1965 article in *Political Diary*: "Vnov' podnimaetsia vopros o Staline," in Medvedev, *Politicheskii dnevnik II*, 15.
71 Bogomolov, "Istoriia kak izmena rodine."
72 Bogomolov.
73 According to Nekrich, Moskalenko later denied having been contacted to write a review. His draft article was therefore used without his knowledge. (Nekrich, *Forsake Fear*, 198.)
74 Nekrich, *Forsake Fear*, 185.
75 Nekrich, 185.
76 Nekrich, 185–86.
77 Nekrich, 187–89.

78 N.N. Bolkhovitinov, "Pamiatnye vstrechi," in *Otreshivshiisia ot strakha: Pamiati A.M. Nekricha. Vospominaniia, stat'i, dokumenty*, ed. M.S. Al'perovich (Moscow: Institut Vseobshchei Istorii RAN, 1996), 51.
79 Nekrich, *Forsake Fear,* 193.
80 The KGB rapidly intercepted the letter, and on June 24, 1967, Iurii Andropov, freshly appointed head of this institution, wrote a report about it to the Central Committee. (Petrovskii, "Delo Nekricha," 1995, 534–35.)
81 Nekrich, *Forsake Fear*, 193–94.
82 Nekrich, 203; Bogomolov, "Istoriia kak izmena rodine."
83 Nekrich, 203.
84 Nekrich, 200; Bogomolov, "Istoriia kak izmena rodine."
85 Kulish, Dashichev and Anfilov were forced into retirement from the military, while Melamid and Slezkin were officially reprimanded. (Bogomolov, "Istoriia kak izmena rodine.")
86 Bogomolov, "Istoriia kak izmena rodine."
87 OKhDLSM, F.333, sd.op. 32, u.d. 6.
88 Nekrich, *Forsake Fear*, 211.
89 Nekrich, 200, 203, 209.
90 Slezkin, "Pamiati druga," 32.
91 See for examples L.I. Grintsberg's and N.N. Bolkhovitinov's testimonies in Al'perovich, *Otreshivshiisia ot strakha*, 47, 52.
92 OKhDLSM, F. 333, sd.op. 32, u.d. 6.
93 Slezkin, "Pamiati druga," 32; Al'perovich, "Knigi imeiut svoiu sud'bu," 90–91. Nekrich said that Danilov's retractation was a "great blow" to him (Nekrich, *Forsake Fear,* 205.)
94 Al'perovich, "Knigi imeiut svoiu sud'bu," 91.
95 Al'perovich, 92.
96 Al'perovich, 94.
97 Slezkin, "Pamiati druga," 33.
98 OKhDLSM, F. 333, sd.op. 14, u.d. 31. This was the initial title, which was changed to *Let History Judge* in later versions.
99 Roi Medvedev, *Neizvestnyi Andropov. Politicheskaia biografiia Iuriia Andropova*. (Moscow: Izd. "Prava cheloveka," 1999), 170.; Letter of Igor' Nikolaev to Roy Medvedev, December 11, 1967. OKhDLSM, F. 333, sd.op. 14, u.d. 31. In his biography of Andropov, Medvedev situates the events in early 1969, but unless Nikolaev was twice arrested for the same facts, primary sources indicate that the search and arrest took place in 1967, and the procedure of party exclusion and appeals in 1968. Nikolaev's incarceration is also mentioned (without a date) in Zhores Medvedev, *Kto sumasshedshii?* (London: Macmillan, 1971), 154–55.
100 Letter of Igor' Nikolaev to Roy Medvedev, November 9, 1968; Letter of Igor' Nikolaev to the Party Commission of the Leningrad City Committee, October 22, 1968. OKhDLSM, F. 333, op.d. 14, u.d. 31.
101 OKhDLSM, F. 333, sd.op. 14, u.d. 31.
102 Ibid.
103 RGANI, F. 89, op. 17, d. 49, l. 14. (HIA, Reel 1994).
104 OKhDLSM, F. 333, sd.op. 14, u.d. 31.
105 RGANI, F. 89, op. 17, d. 49, l. 10. (HIA, Reel 1994). (the same document, registered as RGANI F. 4, op. 20, d. 972, l. 92–95 is reproduced in Artizov et al., *Reabilitatsiia: Kak èto bylo.*, II: Fevral' 1956-nachalo 80-kh godov.: 518–20.)

106 RGANI, F. 89, op. 17, d. 49, l. 11–12.
107 Ibid., l. 13.
108 OKhDLSM, F. 333, sd.op. 14, u.d. 31.
109 Ibid.
110 Ibid.
111 Ibid.
112 Ibid.
113 RGANI, F. 89, op. 17, d. 49, l. 5. (HIA, Reel 1994).
114 Ibid., l. 6.
115 Medvedev, *Neizvestnyi Andropov*, 169.
116 RGANI, F. 89, op. 17, d. 49, l. 1–3. (HIA, Reel 1994).
117 Ibid., l. 1–2.
118 Ibid., l. 2.
119 Ibid., l. 2–3.
120 The report referred to a previous incident in Medvedev's party biography: in 1962, he had received a reprimand for the "unconscientious editing of a geography reader" (Ibid., l. 3). In 1988, Medvedev recounted this episode in a public lecture: as he worked as an editor, he had failed to adequately censor a chapter describing England in very flattering terms, instead of pointing to the evils of capitalism. ("Lecture on the theme: history teacher, history textbook," December 13, 1988, p 4. OKhDLSM, sd.op. 5, u.d. 44)
121 RGANI, F. 89, op. 17, d. 49, l. 5. (HIA, Reel 1994), l. 3.
122 Mikhail Zelenov, "Otzyv G.A. Deborina na tret'iu chast' rukopisi R.A. Medvedeva 'Edinolichnoe pravlenie Stalina'. 1969 g," *Acta Samizdatica / Zapiski o samizdate* 3 (2016): 127–32.
123 Zelenov, 129.
124 Zelenov, 131.
125 See Chapter 3.
126 OKhDLSM, F. 333, sd.op. 14, u.d. 31.
127 Ibid.
128 Ibid.
129 Medvedev, *On Soviet Dissent*, 28–29; OKhDLSM, F. 333, sd.op. 14, u.d. 31
130 Medvedev, 28.
131 OKhDLSM, F. 333, sd.op. 14, u.d. 31; Medvedev, *On Soviet Dissent*, 29–32.
132 Interview of R. Medvedev (3).
133 Interview of Z. Medvedev (2), April 12, 2018; Zhores Medvedev, "Istoriia s pechal'nym finalom," *2000.ua*, March 24, 2012, https://www.2000.ua/specproekty_ru/opasnaja-professija/glavy-iz-knigi-opasnja-professija/istorija-s-pechalnym-finalom_arhiv_art.htm.
134 Medvedev, *Neizvestnyi Andropov*, 170–71.
135 Interview of R. Medvedev (4); Interview of Z. Medvedev (1).
136 Soljénitsyne, *Les invisibles*, 225–26.
137 Medvedev, *Neizvestnyi Andropov*, 170. David Joravsky had himself published a book on Trofim Lysenko (*The Lysenko Affair*, 1970).
138 Medvedev, *On Soviet Dissent*, 28.
139 Soljénitsyne, *Les invisibles*, 161.
140 Olga Andreyev Carlisle and her husband had already acted as Solzhenitsyn's literary agents and edited the English translation of *The First Circle*. However, the couple's failure to get the translation of *Gulag* ready in time for a simultaneous publication in

English and Russian triggered Solzhenitsyn's wrath and caused the Carlisles' eventual withdrawal from the project. Carlisle's memoirs tell her version of the conflict (Olga Andreyev Carlisle, *Solzhenitsyn and the Secret Circle* (London; Henley: Routledge & Kegan Paul, 1978)). Solzhenitsyn's version appears in his memoirs of exile. (Soljenitsyne, *Le grain tombé entre les meules*, 175–231.)

141 Scammell and Fitzpatrick, *The Solzhenitsyn Files*, 209.
142 Scammell and Fitzpatrick, 225. Emphasis in the original.
143 Scammell and Fitzpatrick, 226–27.
144 Scammell and Fitzpatrick, 230.
145 Scammell and Fitzpatrick, 231.
146 In his memoirs, Solzhenitsyn throws doubt upon the official version of the suicide, suggesting Voronianskaia might have been murdered. (Soljénitsyne, *Les invisibles*, 85–89.) The KGB report, however, tells a different story: that Voronianskaia made a first suicide attempt, was hospitalized, and then killed herself. (Scammell and Fitzpatrick, *The Solzhenitsyn Files*, 247.)
147 Soljénitsyne, *Les invisibles*, 92.
148 Aleksandr Solzhenitsyn, *Letter to the Soviet Leaders* (New York: Harper & Row, 1974).
149 Scammell, *Solzhenitsyn*, 818.
150 Scammell, 818–19.
151 Scammell and Fitzpatrick, *The Solzhenitsyn Files*, 259–60.
152 Scammell and Fitzpatrick, 279.
153 Scammell and Fitzpatrick, 283.
154 Reference to the Solzhenitsyn Aid Fund in support of political prisoners and their families. All royalties from the *Gulag Archipelago* were deposited on a special bank account and transferred to this fund.
155 Scammell and Fitzpatrick, *The Solzhenitsyn Files*, 284.
156 See Michael Nicholson, "The Gulag Archipelago: A Survey of Soviet Responses," in *Aleksandr Solzhenitsyn : Critical Essays and Documentary Material*, ed. John B. Dunlop, Richard Haugh, and Alexis Klimoff, 2nd ed. (New York: Collier books, 1975), 477–500.
157 I. Solov'ev "Put' predatel'stva," *Pravda*, January 14, 1974. (Quoted in *Slovo probivaet sebe dorogu: Sbornik statei i dokumentov ob A.I. Solzhenitsyne: 1962-1974* (Moscow: Izd-vo "Russkii put", 1998), 439.)
158 "Solzhenitsyn's Counterattack," 45.
159 Lidiia Chukovskaia, "Proryv nemoty," Moscow, samizdat, February 4, 1974. (*Slovo probivaet sebe dorogu*, 455.)
160 Solzhenitsyn, *The Oak and the Calf*, 386–87.

Chapter 6

1 Medvedev, *On Socialist Democracy*, 215–16.
2 Andrei Sakharov, "A Letter to the Congress of the United States," in *Sakharov Speaks*, ed. Harrison E. Salisbury (London: Collins & Harvill Press, 1974), 212–15.
3 A.B. Bezborodov, *Fenomen akademicheskogo dissidentsva v SSSR* (Moscow: Rossiiskii Gosudarstvennyi Gumanitarnyi Universitet, 1998), 42.
4 Although the expression was coined for German writers who opposed the Nazi regime but chose to remain in the country after 1933, I think that the analogy to Soviet dissidents' situation is valid, insofar as both cases deal with passive or active resistance to an authoritarian regime.

5   In the Soviet Union, Jewishness was not considered a religion, but a "nationality" (*natsional'nost'*), indicated on the Soviet passport.
6   Liudmilla Alexeyeva, *Soviet Dissent: Contemporary Movements for National, Religious, and Human Rights* (Middletown, CT: Wesleyan University Press, 1985), 196; Mark Tolts, "Demography of the Contemporary Russian-Speaking Jewish Diaspora," in *The New Jewish Diaspora: Russian-Speaking Immigrants in the United States, Israel, and Germany*, ed. Zvi Gitelman (New Brunswick, NJ: Rutgers University Press, 2016), 23–24. See also Laurie P. Salitan, "Domestic Pressures and the Politics of Exit: Trends in Soviet Emigration Policy," Political Science Quarterly 104, no. 4 (1989): 671–87.
7   Alexeyeva, *Soviet Dissent*, 174.
8   See Anatoly Shcharansky, *Fear No Evil: A Memoir* (London: Hodder and Stoughton, 1989).
9   Medvedev, *On Socialist Democracy*, 215.
10 On the Helsinki monitoring groups, see Snyder, *Human Rights Activism and the End of the Cold War*. On the Moscow Helsinki group, see Goldberg, *The Final Act*.
11 Samuel Moyn, *The Last Utopia: Human Rights in History* (Cambridge, MA; London: The Belknap Press of Harvard University Press, 2010).
12 Benjamin Nathans, "The Disenchantment of Socialism: Soviet Dissidents, Human Rights, and the New Global Morality," in *The Breakthrough. Human Rights in the 1970s*, eds. Jan Eckel and Samuel Moyn (Philadelphia: University of Pennsylvania Press, 2014), 33–48; Nathans, "The Dictatorship of Reason."
13 Mark Hurst has examined these networks of support in Britain. Hurst, *British Human Rights Organizations and Soviet Dissent, 1965-1985*.
14 See for instance Abdurakhman Avtorkhanov, "R. Medvedev: Klevetnik ili provokator?," *Russkaia mysl'*, December 14, 1978.
15 See Chapter 3.
16 OKhDLSM, F. 333, sd.op. 9, u.d. 61.
17 Roy Medvedev, "Vozmozhno li segodnia reabilitirovat' Stalina? Otkrytoe pis'mo v zhurnal 'Kommunist,'" *Posev* 25, no. 6 (1969): 25–30; no. 7, 25–34; Medvedev, *Faut-il réhabiliter Staline?*
18 See for instance David Joravsky's introduction in Roy Medvedev, *Let History Judge: The Origins and Consequences of Stalinism* (London: MacMillan, 1972), x.
19 *V poiskakh zdravogo smysla*, 185–186. (OKhDLSM, F. 333, sd.op. 1, u.d. 30)
20 Ibid., 188–189. See for example "Russian historian disavows anti-Soviet article," *The New York Times*, April 26, 1970.
21 Medvedev and Medvedev, *1925-2010. Iz vospominanii*, 224–26.
22 Zhores Medvedev, *The Medvedev Papers: Fruitful Meetings between Scientists of the World, and, Secrecy of Correspondence Is Guaranteed by Law* (London; New York: Macmillan ; St. Martin's Press, 1971).
23 Medvedev, *Neizvestnyi Andropov*, 172. See Chapter 4.
24 He received the information through Ivan Abramov, who worked in the infamous "fifth directorate" of the KGB. Medvedev, *Neizvestnyi Andropov*, 176.
25 OKhDLSM, F. 333, sd.op. 9, u.d. 214.
26 *V poiskakh zdravogo smysla*, 19. (OKhDLSM, F. 333, sd.op. 1, u.d. 30)
27 Zhores Medvedev, "Novoe napravlenie issledovanii, novye knigi... i proshchanie s redaktorom 'Novogo mira,'" *2000.ua*, May 18, 2012, http://www.2000.ua/specproekty _ru/opasnaja-professija/glavy-iz-knigi-opasnja-professija/novoe-napravlenie-issl edovanij-novye-knigi--i-proschanie-s-redaktorom-novogo-mira_arhiv_art.htm.

28 *V poiskakh zdravogo smysla*, 123. (OKhDLSM, F. 333, sd.op. 1, u.d. 30)
29 OKhDLSM, F. 333, sd.op. 9, u.d. 214.
30 Ibid.
31 Ibid.
32 Ibid; OKhDLSM sd.op. 9, u.d. 219.
33 Medvedev, "Novoe napravlenie issledovanii, novye knigi…"
34 P. Priimak, "Prestupnik i svideteli," *Vecherniaia Moskva*, February 11, 1972.
35 Medvedev, *Neizvestnyi Andropov*, 176.
36 Hedrick R. Smith, *The Russians* (New York: Ballantine Books, 1977), 599.
37 Smith, 599–600.
38 His short unpublished memoirs are entitled "Roy Medvedev. A free scholar in a totalitarian society" (OKhDLSM, F. 333, sd.op. 5, u.d. 146).
39 Communication of Zhores Medvedev, May 17, 2016. The sale of coffee table books seems to have been a common way for dissidents in contact with Westerners to earn small sums of money.
40 Zhores considered that it was precisely in the field of the security of mail delivery that he was able to have an impact on the authorities through his essay "The Secrecy of Correspondence Is Guaranteed by Law." Over time, as the USSR was obliged to pay a financial compensation for lost registered letters, the letters stopped disappearing and were simply delayed. (Interview of Z. Medvedev (1).)
41 Letter from Roy to Zhores Medvedev, October 9, 1978. (OKhDLSM, F. 333, sd.op. 10, u.d. 6)
42 *V poiskakh zdravogo smysla*, 255. (OKhDLSM, F. 333, sd.op. 1, u.d. 30)
43 Letter from Roy to Zhores Medvedev, October 14, 1978. (OKhDLSM, F. 333, sd.op. 10, u.d. 6)
44 *V poiskakh zdravogo smysla*, 253. (OKhDLSM, F. 333, sd.op. 1, u.d. 30)
45 Interview of R. Medvedev (4).
46 For this second biography, he benefited from the support of Khrushchev's family, to whom Snegov introduced him. Khrushchev's son, however, later expressed his disappointment with the critical tone of the biography. (Khrushchev, *Khrushchev*.)
47 Interview of R. Medvedev (2).
48 Anna Ivanova, *Magaziny "Berezka": Paradoksy potrebleniia v pozdnem SSSR* (Moscow: Novoe Literaturnoe Obozrenie, 2017), 111–12.
49 Interview of R. Medvedev (2).
50 Ivanova, *Magaziny "Berezka,"* 115. After 1973, the Soviet Union joined the World Convention on Copyright and all Soviet authors published abroad were supposed to sign contracts with Western editors through the intermediary of VAAP. (Ivanova, 107–08.)
51 Letter from Roy to Zhores Medvedev, August 31, 1973. OKhDLSM, F. 333, sd.op. 10, u.d. 1.
52 *V poiskakh zdravogo smysla*, 119. (OKhDLSM, F. 333, sd.op. 1, u.d. 30)
53 Roy Aleksandrovich Medvedev, *Qui a écrit le "Don paisible"?* (Paris: Bourgois, 1975).
54 Sholokhov had spoken up against Daniel' and Siniavskii at their trial and in 1973 he signed an open letter of Soviet writers to *Pravda* condemning Sakharov and Solzhenitsyn.
55 Letter of Roy to Zhores Medvedev, April 7, 1975. OKhDLSM, F. 333, sd.op. 10, u.d. 3.
56 Ibid.
57 Ibid.
58 Letter of Roy to Zhores Medvedev, April 17, 1975. OKhDLSM, F. 333, sd.op. 10, u.d. 3.

59 *V poiskakh zdravogo smysla*, 122–123. (OKhDLSM, F. 333, sd.op. 1, u.d. 30)
60 Letter of Roy to Zhores Medvedev, October 9, 1976. OKhDLSM, F. 333, sd.op. 10, u.d. 4.
61 Ibid.
62 Letter of Roy to Zhores Medvedev, November 26, 1976. OKhDLSM, F. 333, sd.op. 10, u.d. 4.
63 *V poiskakh zdravogo smysla*, 256–257. (OKhDLSM, F. 333, sd.op. 1, u.d. 30)
64 "The Medvedev Case - An Official Warning, a Firm Rejection," *The Sun*, January 26, 1983.
65 Mikhail Agursky, "Victims of a Soviet Power Struggle," *The Jerusalem Post*, January 31, 1983.
66 This document appeared in *Izvestiia*, June 7, 1996. (Cited in Medvedev, *Neizvestnyi Andropov*, 178–80.)
67 Medvedev, 178–80.
68 Letters of Federal Chancellor Office to Ken Coates, March 10 and May 17, 1983. OKhDLSM, F. 333, sd. Op. 7, u.d. 6.
69 Margaret Jay, "The 'Careful Non-Conformist' and Andropov's New Broom," *The Listener*, February 3, 1983.
70 Medvedev, *Neizvestnyi Andropov*, 180.
71 Medvedev, 173.
72 Roi Medvedev, *Gensek s Lubianki (Iu. V. Andropov. Politicheskii portret)* (Nizhnii Novgorod: Izd. "Leta," 1993), 52. This is confirmed by Susanne Schattenberg, who writes that political repression through judicial prosecution actually decreased in the Brezhnev era. Schattenberg, *Leonid Breschnew*, 419.
73 Confidential letter of Roy to Zhores Medvedev, February 25, 1984, OKhDLSM, sd. op. 15, u.d. 15.
74 Letter of Roy to Zhores Medvedev, February 25, 1984, OKhDLSM, sd. op. 15, u.d. 15.
75 Letter of Roy to Zhores Medvedev, March 24, 1984, OKhDLSM, sd. op. 15, u.d. 15.
76 See Chapter 5.
77 Medvedev, *Neizvestnyi Andropov*, 180–81.
78 Nekrich, *Forsake Fear*, 270.
79 Nekrich, 233.
80 Nekrich, 232.
81 Nekrich, 241–43.
82 Markwick, *Rewriting History in Soviet Russia*, 216–19.
83 Markwick, 219–33. See also Nekrich's somewhat biased account: Nekrich, *Forsake Fear*, 236–38.
84 Nekrich, *Forsake Fear*, 224–28.
85 Nekrich, 230.
86 Nekrich, 219.
87 Nekrich, 264.
88 Aleksandr Nekrich, *Les peuples punis: La déportation et le sort des minorités soviétiques à la fin de la Seconde Guerre mondiale*, 371 (Paris: F. Maspero, 1982), 175–78.
89 Nekrich, 180–85.
90 Nekrich, *Forsake Fear*, 271.
91 Nekrich, 272.
92 Radio Free Europe Broadcast, June 13, 1978. (HIA, A.M. Nekrich Papers, Box 62, Audiotape 1).
93 Nekrich, *Forsake Fear*, 265274.
94 This is what appears from a letter of Roy Medvedev to his brother. (Letter of Roy to Zhores Medvedev, January 2, 1974. OKhDLSM, F. 333, sd.op. 10, u.d. 2)

95 Nekrich, 275–77.
96 These microfilms are still conserved in Box 62 of the Nekrich Papers at the Hoover Institution Archives.
97 The text of this call is reproduced in Nekrich, *Les peuples punis*, 171–72.
98 Nekrich, *Forsake Fear*, 278–80.
99 Letter of Roy to Zhores Medvedev, April 23, 1976. (OKhDLSM, F. 333, sd.op. 10, u.d. 4)
100 Ibid.
101 Letter of Aleksandr Nekrich to Michel Heller, August 16, 1976. (BDIC, F-delta rés 928 (8) (1) (2)).
102 Letter of Aleksandr Nekrich to Robert Drinan, March 30, 1977 (HIA, A.M. Nekrich Papers, Box 3, Folder 5).
103 Ibid.
104 Ibid.
105 Nekrich, Aleksandr, "Amerika, kakoi ia ee uvidel," 3. (HIA, A.M. Nekrich Papers, Box 18, Folder 10)
106 Letter of Aleksandr Nekrich to Michel Heller, November 9, 1976. (BDIC, F-delta rés 928 (8) (1) (4)).
107 Letter of Aleksandr Nekrich to Michel Heller, January 30, 1977. (BDIC, F-delta rés 928 (8) (1) (5)).
108 HIA, A.M. Nekrich Papers, Box 44, Folder 1. Nekrich thus received a grant of $2,000 in January 1977.
109 Letter of Aleksandr Nekrich to Michel Heller, January 30, 1977. (BDIC, F-delta rés 928 (8) (1) (5)).
110 Nekrich, "Amerika, kakoi ia ee uvidel," 4. (HIA, A.M. Nekrich Papers, Box 18, Folder 10).
111 Letter of Aleksandr Nekrich to Moisei Al'perovich, November 23, 1977. (M.S. Al'perovich, ed., "Pis'ma iz Bel'monta. K 85-letiiu A.M. Nekricha," *Novaia i noveishaia istoriia*, no. 3 (2005): 204–18.)
112 Although this project never evolved into a book, a chapter of *Utopia in Power* bears this title. (Michel Heller and Aleksandr Nekrich, *Utopia in Power: The History of the Soviet Union from 1917 to the Present* (New York: Hutchinson, 1986), 450–511.)
113 Financial statement, September 1, 1978. (HIA, A.M. Nekrich Papers, Box 3, Folder 5).
114 Letter of Robert Gordon to Robert Drinan, January 25, 1977. (HIA, A.M. Nekrich Papers, Box 3, Folder 5).
115 Letter of Aleksandr Nekrich to Robert Gordon, May 3, 1977. (HIA, A.M. Nekrich Papers, Box 3, Folder 5).
116 Letter of Robert Drinan to Aleksandr Nekrich, May 3 and 9, 1977. (HIA, A.M. Nekrich Papers, Box 3, Folder 5).
117 Letter of Patrick Coomey from the US Department of Justice to Aleksandr Nekrich, October 31, 1977. (HIA, A.M. Nekrich Papers, Box 3, Folder 5).
118 Letter of Abram Bergson et al. to Thomas O'Neill, December 1, 1977. (HIA, A.M. Nekrich Papers, Box 3, Folder 6). Edward Keenan and Robert Gordon also wrote a separate letter.
119 Memorandum of the Off-the-record Conversation Re: Case of Alexander Nekrich, December 13, 1977. (HIA, A.M. Nekrich Papers, Box 3, Folder 5). This provision was the "defector exemption" (section 212(a) (28) (I) (ii)): "An alien who has defected from the Communist Party and who since that defection is and has been, for at least five years prior to the date of application for admission actively opposed to the doctrine, program, principles and ideology of the Party may be admitted to the United

States if his admission would be in the public interest." (Photocopy of "Advance Operations Instruction, HIA, A.M. Nekrich Papers, Box 3, Folder 6).
120 Letter of Aleksandr Nekrich to Marshall Shulman, April 14, 1978 (HIA, A.M. Nekrich Papers, Box 3, Folder 5).
121 Letters of Dimitri Simes to Aleksandr Nekrich and to Irene Manekofsky, March 22, 1978. (HIA, A.M. Nekrich Papers, Box 3, Folder 5).
122 Letter of Aleksandr Nekrich to Joseph O'Neill, July 16, 1978. (HIA, A.M. Nekrich Papers, Box 3, Folder 5).
123 Ibid.
124 Letter of Sam Feldman to Aleksandr Nekrich, August 21, 1978. (HIA, A.M. Nekrich Papers, Box 3, Folder 4).
125 Letter of Donald Carlisle to Zbigniew Brzezinski, January 8, 1979. (HIA, A.M. Nekrich Papers, Box 3, Folder 6).
126 Letter of Donald Carlisle to Sam Feldman, January 8, 1979. (HIA, A.M. Nekrich Papers, Box 3, Folder 6).
127 Letter of Donald Carlisle to Zbigniew Brzezinski, January 8, 1979. (HIA, A.M. Nekrich Papers, Box 3, Folder 6).
128 Letter of Sam Feldman to Aleksandr Nekrich, January 25, 1979. (HIA, A.M. Nekrich Papers, Box 3, Folder 4).
129 Letter of Iurii Tuvin, n.d. (HIA, A.M. Nekrich Papers, Box 3, Folder 4).
130 Record of Sworn statement, January 25, 1979. (HIA, A.M. Nekrich Papers, Box 3, Folder 7).
131 Ibid.
132 Leonid Heller, ed., *Vmesto memuarov: Pamiati M.Ia. Gellera* (Moscow: Mik, 2000), 212, 330; Nekrich, *Forsake Fear,* 133.
133 Letter of Aleksandr Nekrich to Michel Heller, January 30, 1977. (BDIC, F-delta rés 928 (8) (1) (5)). (emphasis in the original)
134 Letter of Aleksandr Nekrich to Michel Heller, October 21, 1977. (BDIC, F-delta rés 928 (8) (1) (10)).
135 Letter of Aleksandr Nekrich to Michel Heller, June 21, 1979. (BDIC, F-delta rés 928 (8) (1) (37)).
136 Heller, *Vmesto memuarov*, 212.
137 Letter of Aleksandr Nekrich to Michel Heller, March 19, 1977. (BDIC, F-delta rés 928 (8) (1) (30)).
138 Letter of Michel Heller to Aleksandr Nekrich, May 17, 1979. (BDIC, F-delta rés 928 (8) (1) (33)).
139 Letter of Aleksandr Nekrich to Michel Heller, November 19, 1977. (BDIC, F-delta rés 928 (8) (1) (14)).
140 Letter of Aleksandr Nekrich to Michel Heller, December 29, 1977. (BDIC, F-delta rés 928 (8) (1) (15)).(emphasis in the original)
141 Ibid.
142 Heller and Nekrich, *Utopia in Power*, 11.
143 Heller and Nekrich, 11.
144 Heller and Nekrich, 732.
145 Heller and Nekrich, 9.
146 Letter of Aleksandr Nekrich to Michel Heller, November 12, 1977. (BDIC, F-delta rés 928 (8) (1) (11)). Leonid Heller confirmed that copies of the book were most certainly smuggled to the USSR (Communication from Leonid Heller, September 9, 2017).

Chapter 7

1. Tatyana Tolstaya, "The Grand Inquisitor," *The New Republic*, June 29, 1992, 29.
2. Alexander Solzhenitsyn, "Live Not by Lies," *Index on Censorship* 33, no. 2 (April 2004): 203–07.
3. "Aleksandr Solzhenitsyn Nobel Lecture," 1970, https://www.nobelprize.org/nobel_prizes/literature/laureates/1970/solzhenitsyn-lecture.html.
4. Solzhenitsyn, *The Gulag Archipelago*, 1974, 1:vi.
5. Solzhenitsyn, 1: x.
6. Quoted in Elisabeth Markstein, "Observations in the Narrative Structure of the 'Gulag Archipelago,'" in *Solzhenitsyn in Exile: Critical Essays and Documentary Materials*, ed. John Barrett Dunlop, Hoover Press Publication 305 (Stanford, CA: Hoover Institution Press, 1985), 179.
7. Medvedev, *Let History Judge*, 1972, xxv.
8. Antonov-Ovseenko, *The Time of Stalin*, xviii.
9. Antonov-Ovseenko, xviii.
10. Medvedev, *Let History Judge*, 1972, xvii.
11. Medvedev, xxxiv.
12. Medvedev, xi.
13. Medvedev, xiii.
14. According to Robert Slusser, the most biting critiques came from Merle Fainsod (*Book Week*, January 2, 1972, 4), and Leonard Schapiro (*Sunday Times*, London, March 26, 1972, 40).
15. Shatz, *Soviet Dissent in Historical Perspective*, 160.
16. Robert M. Slusser, "A Soviet Historian Evaluates Stalin's Role in History," *American Historical Review* 77, no. 5 (December 1972): 1393.
17. Slusser, 1393.
18. Medvedev, *Let History Judge*, 1972, 566.
19. Medvedev, 365.
20. Medvedev, *On Socialist Democracy*. The Russian and French language versions appeared in 1972 (Roi Medvedev, *Kniga o sotsialisticheskoi demokratii* (Amsterdam: Fond imeni Gertsena, 1972)).
21. Medvedev, *Let History Judge*, 1972, 554.
22. On the Lenin cult, see Nina Tumarkin, *Lenin Lives. The Lenin Cult in Soviet Russia*, Enlarged edition (Cambridge, MA; London: Harvard University Press, 1997).
23. For example in Roy Medvedev, *The October Revolution* (New York: Columbia University Press, 1979). Harrison Salisbury, however, still found this critique rather mild in his preface.
24. Boris Suvarin, "'Stalinizm' po Roiu Medvedevu," *Novyi Zhurnal*, no. 113 (1973): 192–211.
25. From Dzhugashvili, Stalin's real name.
26. Suvarin, "'Stalinizm' po Roiu Medvedevu," 194.
27. Suvarin, 194–95.
28. Suvarin, 198.
29. Suvarin, 209.
30. Suvarin, 208–09.
31. These are the names of the chapters 3 and 4 in Part III (Volume 2).
32. Aleksandr Isaevich Solzhenitsyn, *The Gulag Archipelago: 1918-1956*, vol. 2 (Glasgow: Harpers and Row Publishers, 1975), 632.

33 Solzhenitsyn, *The Gulag Archipelago*, 1974, 1:25.
34 Solzhenitsyn, *The Gulag Archipelago*, 1975, 2:10.
35 Solzhenitsyn, *The Gulag Archipelago*, 1978, 3:17.
36 Solzhenitsyn, *The Gulag Archipelago*, 1975, 2:615.
37 Solzhenitsyn, 2:615–16.
38 Elisa Kriza has pointed out the fallacy of Solzhenitsyn's representations of tsarist camps (*katorga*). (Elisa Kriza, *Alexander Solzhenitsyn: Cold War Icon, Gulag Author, Russian Nationalist?* (Stuttgart: Ibidem-Verlag, 2014), 246.)
39 Martin Malia, "A War on Two Fronts: Solzhenitsyn and the Gulag Archipelago," *The Russian Review* 36, no. 1 (1977): 48.
40 Malia, 52.
41 Malia, 52–53.
42 Malia, 54.
43 Malia, 56.
44 Malia, 60.
45 Malia, 63.
46 *V poiskakh zdravogo smysla*, 94. (OKhDLSM, F. 333, sd.op. 1, u.d. 30). Emphasis in the original.
47 Zhores Medvedev, "Iz vospominanii o Solzhenitsyne," in *1925-2010. Iz vospominanii*, ed. Roi Medvedev and Zhores Medvedev (Moscow: Izd. "Prava cheloveka," 2010), 145–207; Roi Medvedev and Zhores Medvedev, *Solzhenitsyn i Sakharov. Dva proroka.* (Moscow: Vremia, 2005).
48 Zhores Medvedev, *Ten Years after Ivan Denisovich* (New York: A.A. Knopf, 1973).
49 *Slovo probivaet sebe dorogu*, 458.
50 Medvedev and Medvedev, *1925-2010. Iz vospominanii*, 189.
51 See Roy Medvedev, "Problems of Democratization and Détente," *New Left Review* I, no. 83 (February 1974), http://newleftreview.org/I/83/roy-medvedev-problems-of-democratization-and-detente.
52 Vladimir Maksimov, "Otkrytoe pis'mo V.E. Maksimova brat'iam Roiu i Zhoresu Medvedevym," *Chasovoi*, no. 571 (1974): 18.
53 Medvedev, Interview (1).
54 Roy Medvedev, "On Gulag Volume One," in *Political Essays* (Nottingham: Spokesman Books, 1976), 61.
55 Medvedev, 62.
56 Medvedev, 63.
57 Medvedev, 67.
58 Medvedev, 70.
59 Medvedev, 68.
60 Roy Medvedev, "On Gulag Volume Two," in *Political Essays* (Nottingham: Spokesman Books, 1976), 77–88.
61 Medvedev, 81–82.
62 Medvedev, 83.
63 Medvedev, 85–86.
64 Medvedev, 86.
65 Roy Medvedev, "Solzhenitsyn: Truth and Politics," in *The Samizdat Register*, vol. 2 (London: Merlin Press, 1981), 297.
66 Medvedev, 2:298.
67 Medvedev, 2:299.
68 Medvedev, 2:299.

69 Medvedev, 2:301.
70 Medvedev, 2:313.
71 Medvedev, 2:317.
72 "Press-konferentsiia A.I. Solzhenitsyna," *Russkaia mysl'*, January 16, 1975, 6.
73 See Chapter 4. In the first English-language volume, Iakubovich published his essay on the Revolution "From the History of Ideas. Part I" (Roy Medvedev, ed., *The Samizdat Register*, vol. 1 (London: Merlin Press, 1977), 149–204.) and in the second, his essays on Kamenev and Zinoviev (Medvedev, *The Samizdat Register*, 1981, 2:51–97.)
74 Solzhenitsyn, *The Gulag Archipelago*, 1974, 1:403.
75 Solzhenitsyn, 1:405.
76 George Kennan considered Solzhenitsyn's rendition of the show trials the least successful element of the first volume, in particular his very "inadequate" treatment of Bukharin. (George Kennan, "Between Earth and Hell," in *Aleksandr Solzhenitsyn : Critical Essays and Documentary Material*, ed. John B. Dunlop, Richard Haugh, and Alexis Klimoff (New York: Collier books, 1975), 503.)
77 For comparison, see this document in Viacheslav Igrunov, ed., *Antologiia Samizdata: Nepodtsenzurnaia literatura v SSSR 1950-e -1980-e*, vol. 2: 1966–1973 (Moscow: Mezhdunarodnyi Institut Gumanitarno-Politicheskikh Issledovanii, 2005), 120–26.
78 Medvedev, "Potomok dekabrista - v 'Dvadtsatom veke' i 'Gulage.'" Although Solzhenitsyn had by then finished writing *The Gulag Archipelago*, he did include a mention of this document, which he stated was circulating in samizdat. (Solzhenitsyn, *The Gulag Archipelago*, 1974, 1:400.)
79 Medvedev, *Let History Judge*, 1971, 129–30.
80 Medvedev, "Potomok dekabrista - v 'Dvadtsatom veke' i 'Gulage.'"
81 Letter of Mikhail Iakubovich to Roy Medvedev, December 15, 1974. OKhDLSM, F. 333, sd.op. 9, u.d. 249.
82 Letter of Mikhail Iakubovich to V.M. Makotinskaia, February 7, 1974. OKhDLSM, F. 333, sd. Op. 9, u.d. 384.
83 Letter of Roy Medvedev to Mikhail Iakubovich, January 29, 1975. OKhDLSM, F. 333, sd.op. 9, u.d. 249.
84 Letter of Mikhail Iakubovich to Roy Medvedev, April 12, 1975. OKhDLSM, F. 333, sd.op. 9, u.d. 249.
85 Letter of Mikhail Iakubovich to V.M. Makotinskaia, January 3, 1974. OKhDLSM, F. 333, sd.op. 9, u.d. 384.
86 Medvedev, "Potomok dekabrista - v 'Dvadtsatom veke' i 'Gulage.'"
87 Medvedev, *The Samizdat Register*, 1981, 2: xi.
88 Medvedev, "Potomok Dekabrista - v 'Dvadtsatom veke' i 'Gulage.'"
89 Medvedev.
90 Medvedev.
91 See for instance the newest edition in Russian: Solzhenitsyn, *Arkhipelag GULag*, 370–72.
92 Soljenitsyne, *Le grain tombé entre les meules*, 394–97.
93 Letter of Roy to Zhores Medvedev, November 9, 1975. OKhDLSM, F. 333, sd.op. 10, u.d. 3.
94 Tomáš Řezáč, *Spiral' izmeny Solzhenitsyna*, ed. M. Pravdina (Moscow: Progress, 1978). See Solzhenitsyn's view on the book and Iakubovich's participation in it: A.I. Solzhenitsyn, "Ugodilo zernyshko promezh dvukh zhernovov. Ocherki izgnaniia. Chast' pervaia (1974–1978). Glavy 4–5.," *Novyi Mir*, no. 2 (1999).
95 Letter of Mikhail Iakubovich to V.M. Makotinskaia, March 26, 1980. OKhDLSM, F. 333, sd.op. 9, u.d. 384.

96 Letter of Mikhail Iakubovich to V.M. Makotinskaia, May 6, 1980. OKhDLSM, F. 333, sd.op. 9, u.d. 384.
97 Ibid.
98 This refers to an interview with Solzhenitsyn's aunt Irina Shcherbak in Georgievsk, in 1971. The writer claims that it was organized by the KGB to discredit him, as Georgievsk was then a city closed to foreigners. See Solzhenitsyn, *The Oak and the Calf*, 321–22, 508.
99 Letter of Roy to Zhores Medvedev, May 22, 1978. OKhDLSM, F. 333, sd.op. 10, u.d. 6.
100 See, for example, "Vetrov, on zhe Solzhenitsyn," *Voenno-Istoricheskii Zhurnal*, no. 12 (1990): 72–77.
101 Antonov-Ovseenko, *The Time of Stalin*, xvii.
102 Antonov-Ovseenko, xvii.
103 Antonov-Ovseenko, 231; Interview of A.V. Antonov-Ovseenko.
104 Interview of A.V. Antonov-Ovseenko.
105 Anton Antonov-Ovseenko, "Aleksei Snegov" (unpublished manuscript), n.d., Personal Papers of A.V. A.-O.
106 Interview of A.V. Antonov-Ovseenko. See Chapter 4.
107 "Ubiitsy Kirova," *Gudok*, April 11, 1989.
108 Ivan Gronskii, "Arest. Lager," ed. Svetlana Gronskaia, *Zvezda*, no. 5 (2008).
109 Dmitrii Mamleev, "Stalin - Gronskomu: 'Ne lez' ne v svoe delo!'," Izvestiia, June 13, 2006, http://izvestia.ru/news/315401; Gronskii, "Arest. Lager."
110 Interview of A.V. Antonov-Ovseenko.
111 Ivan Gronskii, *Iz proshlogo* (Moscow: 1991), 152. Quoted in "Gronskii (Fedulov) Ivan Mikhailovich," *Khronos* (blog), n.d., http://hrono.info/biograf/bio_g/gronski_im.html.
112 Antonov-Ovseenko, *The Time of Stalin*, 245.
113 "Fofanova," *Bol'shaia Sovetskaia Entsiklopediia*, 1978, 1969.
114 Antonov-Ovseenko, *The Time of Stalin*, 140.
115 Rakitin, "On bral zimnii." See also Chapter 1.
116 Interview of A.V. Antonov-Ovseenko.
117 Interview of A.V. Antonov-Ovseenko.
118 "Poedinok so vremenem."
119 Interview of A.V. Antonov-Ovseenko.
120 Interview of R. Medvedev (1).
121 Interview of A.V. Antonov-Ovseenko.
122 Interview of I. Levitan, June 23, 2012.
123 Cohen, *The Victims Return*, 9.
124 Cohen, 14.
125 Cohen, 21–22.
126 Antonov-Ovseenko eventually restored and published this work (Anton Antonov-Ovseenko, *Lavrentii Beria* (Krasnodar: Sovetskaia Kuban' Kontsern kurort, 1993)).
127 "Eshche odno svidetel'stvo politicheskogo syska," *Literaturnaia gazeta*, July 3, 1996.
128 "Eshche odno svidetel'stvo politicheskogo syska."
129 Julia Wishnevsky, "The Arrest of Antonov-Ovseenko: One Step Closer to a New Stalinism" (Radio Liberty Research RL 18/85, January 18, 1985), HU OSA 300-80-9, Box 25, File "Antonov-Ovseenko A. 1985-1994," Radio Free Europe/Radio Liberty Archive, Open Society Archive, Budapest. A year later, they reported that the charges against him were dropped, presumably after he agreed not to publish his biography of Beria. (Radio Liberty Research, December 17, 1985, HU OSA 300-85-13-14) Antonov-Ovs-

eenko's son, however, denied that his father had been arrested or exiled from Moscow, as some rumors had it at the time. (Interview of A.A. Antonov-Ovseenko.)
130 "Otets, syn, pravda istorii," *Moskovskaia pravda*, November 7, 1988.
131 Interview of A.V. Antonov-Ovseenko.
132 Antonov-Ovseenko, *The Time of Stalin*, xvi.
133 Antonov-Ovseenko, xvii.
134 Interview of A.V. Antonov-Ovseenko.
135 "Otets, syn, pravda istorii."
136 Anton Antonov-Ovseenko, "Aleksei Snegov" (unpublished manuscript), n.d., Personal Papers of A.V. A.-O.
137 *Pamiat'* was a tamizdat historical collection, five issues of which came out in the West between 1978 and 1982. Composed of documents, articles and memoirs about twentieth-century Russian and Soviet history, it was edited by a Moscow- and Leningrad-based underground editorial team, with Arsenii Roginskii acting as an informal editor in chief. The main author of this review was David Mironovich Batser, an old Menshevik, with some contribution from Roginskii. (Martin and Sveshnikov, *Istoricheskii Sbornik Pamiat'*, 134, 137–38.)
138 M. Dovner, "Lubok vmesto istorii," *Pamiat': Istoricheskii sbornik* 4 (1981): 442.
139 Dovner, 446.
140 Dovner, 446. The quotes are taken from Anton Antonov-Ovseenko, *Portret tirana* (New York: Khronika, 1980), 5–6.
141 Dovner, "Lubok vmesto istorii," 447.
142 Dovner, 447.
143 Dovner, 452–54.
144 Dmitrii Zubarev remembers that he and Roginskii were invited over by Antonov-Ovseenko, who asked to see materials from *Pamiat'*. Then he allegedly used them in his book without acknowledging the source. This, according to Zubarev, angered Roginskii, who decided to write a negative review of the book. Roginskii, however, has no recollection of these events. See Martin and Sveshnikov, *Istoricheskii Sbornik Pamiat'*, 195–96.
145 Martin and Sveshnikov, 196.
146 *Summa*, n° 5/6, 1980. Reproduced in *Summa. Za svobodnuiu mysl'*, 414.
147 Anton Antonov-Ovseenko, "The Survivor as Historian (Introduction) by Stephen F. Cohen," in *The Time of Stalin. Portrait of a Tyranny* (New York: Harper and Row, 1981), vii–xi.
148 Leo Van Rossum, "A. Antonov-Ovseenko's Book on Stalin: Is It Reliable? A Note," *Soviet Studies* 36, no. 3 (July 1984): 445–47.
149 Teddy J. Uldriks, "Review: The Time of Stalin: Portrait of a Tyranny by Anton Antonov-Ovseyenko," *Russian Review* 42, no. 3 (July 1983): 333–34.
150 On Solzhenitsyn's reception among Western historians, see for example Kriza, *Alexander Solzhenitsyn: Cold War Icon, Gulag Author, Russian Nationalist?*, 243–44.
151 Interview of A.V. Antonov-Ovseenko.
152 Solzhenitsyn, Aleksandr, "Interv'iu na literaturnye temy s N.A. Struve," *Vestnik Russkogo Khristianskogo Dvizheniia* (1977) 120: 1, 135. Quoted in Markstein, "Observations in the Narrative Structure of the 'Gulag Archipelago,'" 178.
153 Evgeniia Ivanova, "Predanie i fakt v sud'be 'Arkhipelaga Gulaga,'" in *Mezhdu dvumia iubileiami, 1998-2003: Pisateli, kritiki i literaturovedy o tvorchestve A.I. Solzhenitsyna: Al'manach*, ed. Nikita Alekseevich Struve (Moscow: Russkii put', 2005), 452.
154 Solzhenitsyn, *The Gulag Archipelago*, 1975, 2:7.
155 Antonov-Ovseenko, *Lavrentii Beria*, 9.

156 "Poedinok so vremenem."
157 Antonov-Ovseenko, *The Time of Stalin*, xviii.
158 "Otets, syn, pravda istorii."
159 Antonov-Ovseenko, *Lavrentii Beria*, 9.
160 "Otets, syn, pravda istorii."
161 Gabai, Kim, and Iakir, "K deiateliam nauki, kul'tury i iskusstva," 48.
162 Antoon De Baets, *Censorship of Historical Thought: A World Guide, 1945-2000* (Westport, CT: Greenwood Press, 2002).
163 De Baets, 4–5.

Chapter 8

1 Vladimir Shlapentokh, "Intellectuals Live in the Chosen Land: Gorbachev's Glasnost," in *Soviet Intellectuals and Political Power: The Post-Stalin Era* (London; New York: I.B. Tauris, 1990), 228–29.
2 *Materialy plenuma Tsentral'nogo Komiteta KPSS 27-28 ianvaria 1987 goda.* (Moscow: Politizdat, 1987).
3 Davies, "Soviet History in the Gorbachev Revolution," 40.
4 *Pravda*, February 14, 1987. Quoted in Davies, 40.
5 Roy Medvedev, *Sovetskii Soiuz. Poslednie gody zhizni.* (Moscow: Vremia, 2015), 106.
6 Medvedev, 107.
7 Alexis Berelowitch, "Des romans contre les tabous de l'histoire," in *A l'Est, la mémoire retrouvée*, ed. Alain Brossat (Paris: Ed. La découverte, 1990), 438.
8 Berelowitch, 435.
9 Berelowitch, 435.
10 Medvedev, *Sovetskii soiuz*, 111.
11 Medvedev, 109.
12 Medvedev, 111.
13 William B. Husband, "Secondary School History Texts in the USSR: Revising the Soviet Past, 1985-1989," *The Russian Review* 50, no. 4 (October 1991): 464.
14 Husband, 464.
15 Donald J. Raleigh, *Soviet Historians and Perestroika: The First Phase* (Routledge, 2016), x–xi.
16 Raleigh, xi.
17 *Moskovskie novosti* (1987), n°2, January 18–25, 8–9. Quoted in Raleigh, *Soviet Historians and Perestroika*, 5–8.
18 Husband, "Secondary School History Texts in the USSR," 465–66.
19 Husband, 467. See for example "Kruglyi stol: Istoricheskaia nauka v usloviakh perestroiki," *Voprosy istorii*, no. 3 (March 1988): 3–52.
20 John W. Boyer et al., "Perestroika, History, and Historians," *The Journal of Modern History* 62, no. 4 (December 1990): 787.
21 Boyer et al., 801–02.
22 Marc Elie, "Ce que réhabiliter veut dire. Khrouchtchev et Gorbatchev aux prises avec l'héritage répressif stalinien," *Vingtième siècle. Revue d'histoire.*, no. 107 (September 2010): 108–10.
23 Davies, "Soviet History in the Gorbachev Revolution," 43; Alec Nove, *Glasnost' in Action: Cultural Renaissance in Russia*, Rev. Ed (Boston; London [etc.]: Unwin Hyman, 1990), 45–46.

24 Medvedev, *Sovetskii soiuz*, 121–22.
25 Iurii Afanas'ev, "Perestroika i istoricheskoe znanie," in *Inogo ne dano: Perestroika: Glasnost', demokratiia, sotsializm: Sud'by perestroiki, vgliadyvaias' v proshloe, vozvrashchenie k budushchemu*, ed. Iurii Afanas'ev (Moscow: Progress, 1988), 492; Nove, *Glasnost' in Action*, 15–36.
26 Dietrich Geyer, ed., *Die Umwertung der Sowjetischen Geschichte* (Göttingen: Vandenhoeck & Ruprecht, 1991), 19.
27 Maria Ferretti, "Les archives entrouvertes," in *A l'Est, la mémoire retrouvée*, ed. Alain Brossat (Paris: Ed. La découverte, 1990), 449.
28 Ferretti, 460.
29 Davies, "Soviet History in the Gorbachev Revolution," 62–63; Nove, *Glasnost' in Action*, 32–33.
30 Ferretti, "Les archives entrouvertes," 462.
31 On these restrictions, see Geyer, *Die Umwertung der Sowjetischen Geschichte*, 23–24; Patricia Kennedy Grimstead, "Glasnost' in the Archives? Recent Developments on the Soviet Archival Scene," *The American Archivist* 52, no. 2 (Spring 1989): 214–36.
32 Davies, "Soviet History in the Gorbachev Revolution," 72.
33 Geyer, *Die Umwertung der Sowjetischen Geschichte*, 25.
34 Viktor Shibaev, "Arkhivnoe zakonodatel'stvo sovremennoi Rossii: Osnovnye tendentsii razvitiia," in *Arkhivy Rossii i Pol'shi: Istoriia, problemy i perspektivy razvitiia* (Ekaterinburg: Izd. Uralskogo universiteta, 2013), 107.
35 Medvedev, *Sovetskii soiuz*, 122.
36 Quoted in Husband, "Secondary School History Texts in the USSR," 460.
37 Husband, 470.
38 Husband, 480.
39 Medvedev, *Sovetskii soiuz*, 123.
40 Shlapentokh, *Soviet Intellectuals and Political Power*, 131–32.
41 Medvedev, *Sovetskii soiuz*, 123–25.
42 Nina Andreeva, "Ne mogu postupat'sia printsipami," *Sovetskaia Rossiia*, March 13, 1988.
43 This was an expression used by Nikolai Ezhov, head of the NKVD at the height of the Terror. An English equivalent would be: "One cannot make an omelette without breaking eggs."
44 "Printsipy perestroiki : Revolutionnost' myshleniia i deistvii," *Pravda*, April 5, 1988.
45 On the club phenomenon, see Carole Sigman, *Clubs politiques et perestroïka en Russie: Subversion sans dissidence* (Paris: Karthala, 2009). On the birth of Memorial, see Kathleen E. Smith, *Remembering Stalin's Victims: Popular Memory and the End of the USSR*, 2nd ed. [1st ed: 1996] (Ithaca, NY: Cornell University Press, 2009). Note that the organization "Pamiat'" was unconnected to the dissident historical collection of the same name mentioned in Chapter 7.
46 Smith, *Remembering Stalin's Victims*, 171.
47 Denis Paillard, "Figures de la mémoire: Pamiat' et Memorial," in *A l'Est, la mémoire retrouvée*, ed. Alain Brossat (Paris: Ed. La découverte, 1990), 374–75.
48 Paillard, 374–87.
49 Robert W. Strayer, *Why Did the Soviet Union Collapse ?: Understanding Historical Change* (Armonk, NY; London: M.E. Sharpe, 1998), 106.
50 Strayer, 102, 106.
51 Paul Hollander, *Political Will and Personal Belief: The Decline and Fall of Soviet Communism* (New Haven [etc.]: Yale University Press, 1999), 105.

52 Thomas Sherlock, *Historical Narratives in the Soviet Union and Post-Soviet Russia: Destroying the Settled Past, Creating an Uncertain Future* (New York: Palgrave Macmillan, 2007), 19–21.
53 Letter of Roy to Zhores Medvedev, March 9, 1986. OKhDLSM, F. 333, sd.op. 15, u.d. 17.
54 Letter of Roy to Zhores Medvedev, May 2, 1987. OKhDLSM, F. 333, sd.op. 15, u.d. 18.
55 Letter of Roy to Zhores Medvedev, July 22, 1987. OKhDLSM, F. 333, sd.op. 15, u.d. 18.
56 Letter from Roy to Zhores Medvedev, March 30, 1987. OKhDLSM, F. 333, sd.op. 15, u.d. 18.
57 Letter from Roy to Zhores Medvedev, May 27, 1987. OKhDLSM, F. 333, sd.op. 15, u.d. 18.
58 Letter from Roy to Zhores Medvedev, February 25, 1987. OKhDLSM, F. 333, sd.op. 15, u.d. 18.
59 Interview of R. Medvedev (3).
60 "Iz reki po imeni fakt," *Sobesednik*, no. 18 (April 1988): 12.
61 Letter of Roy to Zhores Medvedev, April 29, 1988. OKhDLSM, F. 333, sd.op. 15, u.d. 19.
62 Letter of Roy to Zhores Medvedev, May 5, 1988. OKhDLSM, F. 333, sd.op. 15, u.d. 19.
63 Interview of R. Medvedev (3).
64 Interview of R. Medvedev (3).
65 Letter of Roy to Zhores Medvedev, January 9, 1989. OKhDLSM, F.333, sd.op. 10, u.d. 12.
66 A discussion with Igor' Shafarevich: "Stalin i Stalinizm : Dve tochki zreniia," *Moskovskie novosti*, June 12, 1988; with Dmitrii Volkogonov: "Triumf tirana, tragediia naroda"; and with professional historians: "Trudnyi put' k pravde," *Nedelia*, 1988.
67 Stephen White, *Gorbachev in Power* (Cambridge: Cambridge University Press, 1990), 61. The essay on Galina Brezhneva, depicting her luxurious lifestyle and involvement in scandals and corruption, first appeared in the Western Press (see, for example, Roj Medwedew, "Die Brillanten der Madame Galina Breschnewa," *Der Spiegel*, no. 5 (1988).) and circulated in samizdat before appearing in the Soviet press. (Letter of Roy to Zhores, April 29, 1988. OKhDLSM, F. 333, sd.op. 15, u.d. 19).
68 Medvedev, *Sovetskii soiuz*, 129.
69 "Lektsii po problemam istoricheskoi nauki. 1988-1989" OKhDLSM, F. 333, sd.Op. 5, u.d. 44.
70 Letter of Roy to Zhores Medvedev, January 22, 1989. OKhDLSM, F.333, sd.op. 10, u.d. 12.
71 Letter of Roy to Zhores Medvedev, May 12, 1989. OKhDLSM, F.333, sd.op. 10, u.d. 12.
72 Letter of Roy to Zhores Medvedev, January 29, 1989. OKhDLSM, F.333, sd.op. 10, u.d. 12.
73 Letter of Roy to Zhores Medvedev, October 9, 1989. OKhDLSM, F.333, sd.op. 10, u.d. 12.
74 R.A. Medvedev and S.P. Starikov, *Zhizn' i gibel' Filippa Kuzmicha Mironova* (Moscow: Patriot, 1989); Roy Medvedev, *On Stalin and Stalinism* (Oxford: Oxford University Press, 1979); Medvedev, *Khrushchev*. Also published were: Roi Medvedev, *Trudnaia vesna 1918 goda* (Voronezh: Tsentral'no-chernozemnoe knizhnoe izdatel'stvo, 1990); Roi Medvedev, *O Staline i Stalinizme* (Moscow: Progress, 1990); Roi Medvedev, *N.S. Khrushchev. Politicheskaia biografiia* (Moscow: Kniga, 1990).
75 Medvedev, *Lichnost' i èpokha*.
76 Anton Antonov-Ovseenko, "Utverzhdenie zakonnosti (soldaty Leniniskoi gvardii. Ob Antonove-Ovseenko V.A.)," *Nauka i zhizn'*, no. 8 (1988): 40–48.
77 "Poedinok so vremenem."
78 See the author's justification in Anton Rakitin, *A.V. Antonov-Ovseenko* (Leningrad: Lenizdat, 1989), 5. The changes concern the section "The party's strength is its unity," 288–99.
79 Rakitin, 309–27.

80 "Otets, syn, pravda istorii."
81 Anton Antonov-Ovseenko, "Kar'era palacha," *Zvezda*, no. 9 (1988): 141–64; no. 5 (1989): 72–109; no. 11 (1989): 77–100; no. 7 (1991): 138–47; no. 8 (1991): 139–66.
82 "Poedinok so vremenem"; Interview of A.V. Antonov-Ovseenko.
83 "Otets, syn, pravda istorii."
84 Anton Antonov-Ovseenko, *Kar'era palacha* (Omsk: Omskaia pravda, 1991), 5.
85 Antonov-Ovseenko, 6.
86 A. Antonov-Ovseenko, "Beria: gody voiny," *Kommunist Tatarii* (1990) no. 3, 81–90; no. 4, 81–87; no. 5, 59–68; "Konets papy malogo," *Kommunist Tatarii*, no. 11 (1990): 51–61; "Beria," *Iunost'* no. 12 (1988): 66–84. Book version: Antonov-Ovseenko, *Kar'era palacha*.
87 Anton Antonov-Ovseenko, *Stalin bez maski* (Moskva: Vsia Moskva, 1990); Anton Antonov-Ovseenko, "Stalin i ego vremia," *Voprosy istorii*, no. 1–4 (1989): 6–11.
88 "Bez maski," *Vzgliad*, December 21, 1988.
89 "Poedinok so vremenem."
90 "Poedinok so vremenem."
91 "Nichego, krome pravdy," *Sobesednik*, December 23, 1988, 10.
92 Anton Antonov-Ovseenko, "Chitateliam Iunosti," *Iunost'* no. 3 (1990): 89.
93 See comment of V. Karnaushenko, presented as "a literary scholar," in Elena Chukovskaia, "Vernut' Solzhenitsynu grazhdanstvo SSSR," *Knizhnoe obozrenie*, August 5, 1988.
94 Liudmila Saraskina, *Aleksandr Solzhenitsyn* (Moscow: Izd. "Molodaia Gvardiia," 2008), 792.
95 Saraskina, 794.
96 Lev Voskresenskii, "Zdravstvuite, Ivan Denisovich!," *Moskovskie novosti*, August 7, 1988.
97 Chukovskaia, "Vernut' Solzhenitsynu grazhdanstvo SSSR."
98 "Otkliki na stat'iu Eleny Chukovskoi," *Knizhnoe obozrenie*, August 12, 1988, 6.
99 "Chitatel' i gazeta," *Knizhnoe obozrenie*, September 2, 1988, 4.
100 "Chitatel' i gazeta," 5.
101 Saraskina, *Aleksandr Solzhenitsyn*, 794–95.
102 *Pervyi s"ezd narodnykh deputatov. Stenograficheskii otchet.*, vol. 2 (Moscow: Izdanie Verkhovnogo Soveta SSSR, 1989), 362.
103 "Sergei Zalygin - Nachinaem s 'Arkhipelaga' - takaia volia avtora," *Moskovskie novosti*, July 16, 1989; Aleksandr Solzhenitsyn, "Nobelevskaia lektsiia," *Novyi mir*, no. 7 (1989): 135.
104 Saraskina, *Aleksandr Solzhenitsyn*, 797.
105 Aleksandr Solzhenitsyn, "Arkhipelag Gulag 1918-1956," *Novyi mir* 8 (1989): 7.
106 A thirteen-year-old thus complained that the journal had not gone on sale in his town and had been directly requisitioned to be distributed within the local Party Committee. (*Knizhnoe obozrenie*, December 8, 1989, 4.)
107 Selections of these letters appeared in "'Arkhipelag Gulag' chitaiut na rodine," *Nezavisimaia gazeta*, July 4, 1991, and "'Arkhipelag Gulag' chitaiut na rodine," *Novyi mir*, September 1991.
108 "'Arkhipelag Gulag' chitaiut na rodine," September 1991, 248.
109 "'Arkhipelag Gulag' chitaiut na rodine," 236.
110 Roi Medvedev, "O knige A.I. Solzhenitsyna 'Arkhipelag Gulag,'" *Pravda*, December 18, 1989; Roi Medvedev, "S tochki zreniia istorika," *Pravda*, December 29, 1989.
111 "'Arkhipelag Gulag' chitaiut na rodine," September 1991, 246.

112 "'Arkhipelag Gulag' chitaiut na rodine," 239.
113 "'Arkhipelag Gulag' chitaiut na rodine," 247. (Emphasis in the original)
114 "'Arkhipelag Gulag' chitaiut na rodine," 238.
115 Saraskina, *Aleksandr Solzhenitsyn*, 800–801.
116 TASS Press release, December 11, 1990. HU OSA 300-80-9, Box 596, File "Solzhenitsyn Aleksandr."
117 TASS Press release, September 17, 1991. HU OSA 300-80-9, Box 596, File "Solzhenitsyn Aleksandr."
118 Letters of Irina Alberti to Aleksandr Nekrich, February 3, 1982; April 16 [1986]; October 12, 1986. (HIA A.M. Nekrich Papers, Box 7, Folder 31) She had invited Nekrich to head the supplement after Michel Heller turned down the offer. On *Obozrenie*'s content, see "From the Editor," *The Russian Review* 42, no. 2 (April 1983).
119 Nataliia Iziumova, "SSSR i perestroika. Vzgliad iz-za okeana," *Moskovskie novosti*, October 8, 1989.
120 In October 1990, Nekrich successfully applied for a $104,000 grant from the National Endowment for the Humanities with a project entitled "Restructuring the Soviet past." (HIA A.M. Nekrich Papers, Box 36, Folder 10) In 1990, Nekrich also wrote two reports on the subject for the National Council for Soviet and East European Research. Earlier publications on the subject include Aleksandr Nekrich, "Perestroika in History: The First Stage," in *Perestroika and Soviet History*, ed. Mikhail Geller (London: Survey Ltd. in association with the Institute for European Defence & Strategic Studies, 1989); Aleksandr M Nekrich, "Perestroika, Current Trends and Soviet History Nationalities, Polish Church, Emigration - Old & New," *Survey: A Journal of Soviet and East European Studies* 30, no. 4 (1989).
121 Vladimir Todres, "Istoriia: tiazheloe moe remeslo," *Sobesednik*, October 1989.
122 Unsigned letter from Independent Publishing House "Wers" to Aleksandr Nekrich, August 22, 1987. (HIA A.M. Nekrich Papers, Box 9, Folder 8)
123 Communication of Leonid Heller, September 9, 2017.
124 Aleksandr Nekrich, *1941, 22 iunia* (Moscow: Pamiatniki istoricheskoi mysli, 1995), 3–4.
125 Vladimir Baburin, "Aleksandr Nekrich: 'Politika - èto istoriia, oprokinutaia v budushchee,'" *Megapolis-Express*, July 26, 1990.
126 Nekrich worked, among others, at the Central State Archive of the October Revolution (TsGAOR), the IML, and the Russian Center of Conservation and Study of Documents of Contemporary History (RTsKhIDNI). (HIA A.M. Nekrich Papers, Box 14, Folders 6-7)
127 Baburin, "Aleksandr Nekrich: 'Politika - èto istoriia, oprokinutaia v budushchee.'"
128 Alekansadr Nekrich, "Introduction," 4. (HIA A.M. Nekrich Papers, Box 23, Folder 8.)
129 Aleksandr Nekrich, *Pariahs, Partners, Predators: German-Soviet Relations, 1922-1941* (New York: Columbia University Press, 1997).
130 See obituaries by Elena Bonner, "Ukhodiat druz'ia... Umer Aleksandr Nekrich," *Izvestiia*, September 4, 1993, and L.V. Pozdeeva, "Pamiati A.M. Nekricha," *Novaia i noveishaia istoriia*, no. 2 (n.d.): 249–51.
131 "Tragicheskaia statistika," *Argumenty i fakty*, February 4, 1989, 5.
132 "Tragicheskaia statistika," 5–6. Adding up the separate categories produces a higher total, but the same person could suffer from repression more than once, and this number seems to have been Medvedev's "conservative" estimate. See also his estimates in an earlier article (Roi Medvedev, "Nash isk Stalinu," *Moskovskie novosti*, no. 48 (November 27, 1988): 8.)

133 "Major Soviet Paper Says 20 Million Died As Victims of Stalin," *The New York Times*, February 3, 1989. ; Robert Conquest, "Andrei Sakharov," in *Tyrants and Typewriters. Communiqués from the Struggle for Truth*. (Lexington, MA; Toronto: Lexington Books, 1989), 30–31.
134 E.F. Krinko and S.A. Kropachev, "Masshtaby Stalinskikh repressii v otsenkakh sovetskikh i sovremennykh rossiiskikh issledovatelei," *Bylye gody*. 26, no. 4 (2012): 90–93.
135 Courtois, *Le livre noir du communisme*, 8, 14. Stephen G. Wheatcroft brings up similar numbers for the Great Terror (Stephen G. Wheatcroft, "The Great Terror in Historical Perspective: The Records of the Statistical Department of the Investigative Organs of OGPU/NKVD," in *Anatomy of Terror: Political Violence under Stalin*, ed. James R. Harris (Oxford: Oxford University Press, 2013), 287–305.)
136 These letters are conserved at OKhDLSM, F.333, sd.op. 9, u.d. 98.
137 Letter of V.I. Zaguliaev to "Argumenty i Fakty," n.d. OKhDLSM, F.333, sd.op. 9, u.d. 98. Emphasis in the original.
138 V.K. Lygan, "Po sledam gazetnogo teksta," February 16, 1989. OKhDLSM, F.333, sd.op. 9, u.d. 98.
139 Letter of I.L. Kuravshov to "Argumenty i Fakty," n.d. OKhDLSM, F.333, sd.op. 9, u.d. 98.
140 Lygan, "Po sledam gazetnogo teksta."
141 Letter of A.I. Beliaev to "Argumenty i Fakty," April 6, 1989. OKhDLSM, F.333, sd.op. 9, u.d. 98.
142 Letter of G.M. Bugai to "Argumenty i Fakty," February 7, 1989. OKhDLSM, F.333, sd.op. 9, u.d. 98.
143 Antonov-Ovseenko, *The Time of Stalin*, 307.
144 Anton Antonov-Ovseenko, "Protivostoianie," *Literaturnaia gazeta*, April 3, 1991. He repeated the same numbers and accusations against Zemskov in a Radio Liberty broadcast on April 12, 1990 ("Beseda s Antonovym-Ovseenko o chisle zhertv stalinizma," HU OSA 300-80-9 Box 25, File Antonov-Ovseenko A. 1985-1994.)
145 See *Argumenty i Fakty* 1989, no. 45; 1990, no. 5, 35.
146 V.N. Zemskov, "Zakliuchennye, spetsposelentsy, ssyl'noposelentsy, ssyl'nye i vyslannye (statistiko-geograficheskii otchet)," *Istoriia SSSR*, no. 5 (1991): 151. (Emphasis in the original)
147 Zemskov, 151.
148 Krinko and Kropachev, "Masshtaby stalinskikh repressii," 91. See, for example, Lev Razgon, "Lozh' pod vidom statistiki," *Stolitsa*, 1992. Medvedev also estimated the number of prisoners to up to ten million. (See "Triumf tirana, tragediia naroda," 280.)
149 Nikita Petrov, "Roi Medvedev kak istorik-dissident," *Kontinent*, no. 68 (1991): 335–45.
150 Petrov, 344.
151 Letter of V.M. Alpatov to Roy Medvedev, February 5, March 14, May 9, 1989. OKhDLSM, F. 333, sd.op. 9, u.d. 304a.
152 E. Beltov, "Netochnostei, pozhalui, mnogovato… (Zametki na poliakh istoricheskikh ocherkov Roia Medvedeva)," n.d. OKhDLSM, F. 333, sd.op. 9, u.d. 297.
153 Sergei Konstantinov, "Istoriia s oshibkami," *Molodoi kommunist*, no. 10 (1989): 94–95.
154 Letter of L.A. Rozybakieva, April 25, 1989. OKhDLSM, F.333, sd.op. 9, u.d. 297.
155 Letter of I.S. Smirnova to "Znamia," n.d. OKhDLSM, F. 333, sd.op. 9, u.d. 296.
156 Letter of A.F. Kovalev to "Znamia," April 2, 1989. OKhDLSM, F. 333, sd.op. 9, u.d. 297.
157 Letter of Roy to Zhores Medvedev, November 7 and 12, 1989. OKhDLSM, F. 333, sd.op. 10, u.d. 12.

158 Letter of Roy to Zhores Medvedev, February 5, 1990. OKhDLSM, F. 333, sd.op. 10, u.d. 13.
159 OKhDLSM, F. 333, sd.op. 9, u.d. 216.
160 M. Krotov, M. Kholmskaia, and V. Chebotarev, "Roi Medvedev. Svobodnyi uchenyi v totalitarnom obshchestve." n.d., 18, OKhDLSM F.333, sd.op. 5, u.d. 146. This manuscript was actually written by Medvedev.
161 Zhores Medvedev, *Opasnaia professiia* (unpublished manuscript), Chapter 67; Medvedev, *Sovetskii soiuz*, 164. The official electoral law, however, did not limit the number of candidates and provided for a run-off if no candidate was elected in the first round. (*Zakon Soiuza Sovetskikh Sotsialisticheskikh Respublik o vyborakh narodnykh deputatov SSSR* (Moscow, 1988), 27–28.)
162 Medvedev, *Sovetskii Soiuz*, 165.
163 Letter of Roy to Zhores Medvedev, April 12, 1989. OKhDLSM, F. 333, sd.op. 10, u.d. 12.
164 Roy Medvedev, "Programma kandidata v narodnye deputaty SSSR," March 1989. OKhDLSM, F. 333, sd.op. 9, u.d. 216.
165 Letter of Roy to Zhores Medvedev, April 12, 1989. OKhDLSM, F. 333, sd.op. 10, u.d. 12.
166 Medvedev, *Sovetskii Soiuz*, 165.
167 Letter of Roy to Zhores Medvedev, April 30, 1989. OKhDLSM, F. 333, sd.op. 10, u.d. 12. Although Medvedev claimed not to have asked to be reinstated, his archive contains a letter from November 1988, in which he requests from the Party Control Committee the revision of his exclusion sentence. Whether it was sent or not is unclear. (Letter of Roy Medvedev to PCC, November 26, 1988. OKhDLSM, F. 333, sd.op. 14, u.d. 31.)
168 According to polls, eight in ten urban adults watched the broadcast "constantly" and only one percent did not watch it at all. (Scott Shane, *Dismantling Utopia: How Information Ended the Soviet Union* (Chicago: I.R. Dee, 1995), 148–49.)
169 Medvedev, *Sovetskii Soiuz*, 172.
170 *Pervyi s"ezd narodnykh deputatov. Stenograficheskii otchet.*, 2:198.
171 Petrov, "Roi Medvedev kak istorik-dissident," 335.
172 Medvedev, *Sovetskii Soiuz*, 196.
173 Medvedev, 208.

Conclusion

1 L. Bogoraz, V. Golitsyn, and S. Kovalev, "Politicheskaia bor'ba ili zashchita prav? Dvatsatiletnii opyt nezavisimogo obshchestvennogo dvizheniia v SSSR: 1965-1985," in A.T. Notkina, ed., *Pogruzhenie v triasinu (Anatomiia zastoia)* (Moscow: Progress, 1991), 503.
2 Interview of G. Khomizuri, January 19, 2013.
3 Martin and Sveshnikov, "Between Scholarship and Dissidence: The Dissident Historical Collection Pamiat' (1975-1982)"; Martin and Sveshnikov, *Istoricheskii sbornik Pamiat'*.
4 Bolton, *Worlds of Dissent*, 45.
5 Medvedev and Medvedev, *1925-2010. Iz vospominanii*, 269.
6 Gleb Morev, ed., *Dissidenty. Dvadtsat' razgovorov.* (Moscow: Izdatel'stvo ACT, 2017), 36.

Timeline of Events

1953

March 5: Death of Iosif Stalin.
March 27: Decree of Amnesty of the Supreme Soviet: liberation of Gulag prisoners condemned to sentences of up to five years.
June 26: Arrest of Lavrentii Beria.
December 23: Execution of Lavrentii Beria.

1956

February 25: Nikita Khrushchev's "Secret Speech" on the Consequences of Stalin's personality cult in front of the 20th Congress of the CPSU.
June 28: Workers' protests in Poznań, Poland.
June 30: Central Committee Resolution "On the Overcoming of the Personality Cult."
October 23–November 10: Hungarian uprising, followed by intervention from the Soviet Red Army.
December 19: Closed letter from the Central Committee "On the Reinforcement of Political Work of Party Organizations among the Masses and the Suppression of Outings of Anti-Soviet, Hostile Elements."

1957

March: Eduard Burdzhalov dismissed from the editorial board of *Voprosy istorii*.
June 18: Unsuccessful attempt by the "Anti-Party Group" (Molotov, Malenkov, Kaganovich, with Shepilov's support) to depose Khrushchev during a session of the Presidium of the Council of Ministers.

1961

October 17–31: 22nd Congress of the CPSU. Resolution to remove Stalin's body from the Red Square Mausoleum and to rename all cities named after him and his close accomplices.

1962

November 18: Publication of *One Day in the Life of Ivan Denisovich* by A. Solzhenitsyn.
December 18–21: All-Union Conference to Improve the Training of Scientific-Pedagogical Cadres in the Historical Sciences.

1963

December 28: *Novyi mir* nominates *One Day in the Life of Ivan Denisovich* for the 1964 Lenin Prize.

1964

October: Beginning of Roy Medvedev's samizdat *Political Diary*.
October 14: N. Khrushchev ousted from power by his political opponents, led by L. Brezhnev, A. Shelepin, and KGB chief V. Semichastnyi.
End of October: Solzhenitsyn sends to the West the manuscript of *The First Circle*.
November 20: Editorial meeting at "Politizdat" to discuss Anton Antonov-Ovseenko's book *In the Name of the Revolution*.

1965

April 14: Article by Evgenii Vuchetich "Let's Clarify [Things]" in *Izvestiia*.
May 9: Brezhnev's speech on 20th anniversary of Victory Day with mention of Stalin meets with applause.
June 21–23 and November 15–18: Meeting of the Ideological Commission to discuss the situation in the Humanities and Social Sciences.
July: Publication of A. Antonov-Ovseenko's *In the Name of the Revolution*.
September 9–12: Arrest of the writers Iulii Daniel' and Andrei Siniavskii.
September 11: Solzhenitsyn's unpublished works seized during house searches.
October: Publication of Aleksandr Nekrich's *June 22, 1941*.
December 5: "Glasnost' demonstration" on Pushkin Square.

1966

January 30: Article by Zhukov et al. "The High Responsibility of Historians" in *Pravda*.
February 10–12: Trial over Daniel' and Siniavskii.
February 14: Letter of twenty-five scientists, writers, and artists to L. I. Brezhnev against Stalin's rehabilitation.

February 16: Discussion of Nekrich's book at the Institute of Marxism-Leninism.
March 29–April 8: 23rd Congress of the CPSU.
August: A copy of the "short transcript" of the discussion of Nekrich's book at the IML is seized at the Polish-Soviet border.
December 28: The Politburo is informed that the "short transcript" of the IML discussion was broadcast on *Deutsche Welle* and featured in an article in the French magazine *Nouvel Observateur*.

1967

March 20: Publication in *Der Spiegel* of an article on Nekrich.
March 22: Central Committee Resolution entrusting the Party Control Committee with the investigation of the Nekrich case.
May: Distribution of Solzhenitsyn's *Letter to the Fourth Congress of the Writers' Union* to the Congress delegates and dissemination in samizdat.
May 22–June 28: Instruction of the "Nekrich case" and exclusion from the Party.
August: Roy Medvedev's manuscript *Pered sudom istorii* is seized during a house search in Leningrad.
September: Publication of Grigorii Deborin's and Boris Tel'pukhovskii's critique of *June 22, 1941* in *Voprosy istorii KPSS*.
September 19–21: R. Medvedev is summoned to the Party Control Committee.
September 24: Open letter of forty-three sons and daughters of repressed Communists against the rehabilitation of Stalin.
October: Letter by General Petr Grigorenko to the journal *Voprosy istorii KPSS* protesting against Deborin's and Tel'pukhovskii's article.
Early November: Letter of nineteen Soviet scholars in defense of A. Nekrich.

1968

Publication in the West of Solzhenitsyn's works *The First Circle* and *Cancer Ward*.
January 16: Speech of Grigorii Svirskii on censorship in front of the Writers' Union.
January: Open letter by Petr Iakir, Il'ia Gabai, and Iulii Kim "to those active in the field of science, culture and arts" against the restoration of Stalinism.
February: Open letter of Lidiia Chukovskaia to the newspaper *Izvestiia* on the fifteenth anniversary of Stalin's death.
June: Solzhenitsyn sends a microfilm of *The Gulag Archipelago* to the West.
August 21: Soviet military intervention in Czechoslovakia.
August 25: Demonstration on Red Square against the Soviet invasion of Czechoslovakia.
October 9–11: Trial over the participants in the Red Square demonstration.
December: Trial of Iurii Gendler, Lev Kvachevskii, and Anatolii Studenkov for spreading samizdat. First trial featuring A. Avtorkhanov's *Tekhnologiia Vlasti*.

1969

Early 1969: Elisabeth Markstein transmits Roy Medvedev's manuscript to the West.
February: Article "For a Leninist Party Spirit in the Treatment of Soviet History" by V. Golikov, S. Murashov, I. Chkhikvishvili, N. Shatagin, and S. Shaumian published in *Kommunist*. Zhores Medvedev is dismissed from his position in Obninsk for his correspondence with Western publishers.
March 2: Open letter by Petr Iakir to the journal *Kommunist* against Stalin's rehabilitation.
March 5: Open letter by Leonid Petrovskii to the TsK of the CPSU against Stalin's rehabilitation.
April 3: Open letter of Roy Medvedev to the journal *Kommunist* "Is it possible today to rehabilitate Stalin?"
April 22: The Party Control Committee threatens to handle A. Snegov's case in abstentia.
July–October: Attempt to deprive Nekrich of his doctoral degree.
August 7: Exclusion of Roy Medvedev from the Communist Party.
November 4: Expulsion of Solzhenitsyn from the Riazan section of the Writers' Union.
December 21: Commemorative article in *Pravda* on Stalin's ninetieth birthday.

1970

February: Aleksandr Tvardovskii resigns from his position as editor in chief of *Novyi mir*, after the dismissal of his editorial team.
March 19: Letter of Andrei Sakharov, Valentin Turchin, and Roy Medvedev to the Party Leaders and Government.
May–June: Attempt to lock Zhores Medvedev up in a psychiatric ward, averted by protests from the liberal intelligentsia.
October 8: Solzhenitsyn is designated as the laureate of the Nobel Prize for Literature.

1971

July: Publication by Zhores Medvedev of *The Medvedev Papers* (*Secrecy of Correspondence Is Guaranteed by Law* and *International Cooperation of Scientists and National Frontiers*).
July 11: Publication by Paris-based publisher YMCA-Press of Solzhenitsyn's novel *August 1914*.
October 12: Search of Roy Medvedev's apartment. Summons to the Public Prosecutor's Office by phone. Medvedev escapes and goes into hiding.
December 18: Death of A. Tvardovskii.
Late 1971: Publication of *Let History Judge*.

1972

January: Trial over Sh. in which Roy Medvedev is cleared of all charges.

1973

August 7: Zhores Medvedev is deprived of his Soviet citizenship (decree dated July 16, 1973).
August 23: Solzhenitsyn's typist Elizaveta Voronianskaia is arrested by the KGB.
August 27–September 1: Trial over Petr Iakir and Viktor Krasin and public recantation of their views.
August–September: Campaign against Solzhenitsyn and Sakharov in Soviet media.
September 5: Solzhenitsyn hears about Voronianskaia's suicide and her confession of the hiding place of *The Gulag Archipelago*. He sends his "Letter to the Soviet leaders" to the Soviet leadership.
December 28: Publication of the first volume of A. Solzhenitsyn's *The Gulag Archipelago* (Russian edition).

1974

January–February: Campaign against Solzhenitsyn in the Soviet media.
February 12–14: Arrest and forced expulsion of Solzhenitsyn from the USSR.
February: Solzhenitsyn's text "To Live Not by Lies" is launched into samizdat.
Summer: Creation of Solzhenitsyn's "Russian Social Fond of Assistance to the Persecuted and their Families," funded by royalties from *The Gulag Archipelago*.

1975

January: Medvedev creates the samizdat/tamizdat journal, *Dvadtsatyi (XX) vek* ("Twentieth Century").
March 14: Official warning issued to Medvedev by the Public Prosecutor's Office.
April: Second search of Medvedev's apartment.
December 10: Nobel Peace Prize awarded to Andrei Sakharov.

1976

April: Solzhenitsyn settles in Cavendish, Vermont, USA.
June 7: Emigration of Nekrich from the USSR.
October 28: Nekrich settles in Cambridge, Massachusetts.
November: New warning from the Public Prosecutor's Office to Roy Medvedev.

1979

May: Nekrich obtains a US residency permit.

1980

Publication by Anton Antonov-Ovseenko of *The Time of Stalin: Portrait of a Tyranny* (Russian edition).
January 22: Sakharov is sent to Gorkii in internal exile.

1982

Publication by A. Nekrich and M. Heller of *Utopia in Power: The History of the Soviet Union from 1917 to the Present* (Russian and French editions).
Late April or early May: House search at Anton Antonov-Ovseenko's apartment.
November 10: Death of Leonid Brezhnev. Iurii Andropov is elected general secretary of the CPSU.

1983

January 18: Roy Medvedev is summoned to the Public Prosecutor of the USSR's office and issued a warning. He gives a press conference to reject the warning.
April 8: Secret letter from the KGB to the Central Committee recommending Roy Medvedev's deportation.
April–May 1983: Austrian Chancellor Bruno Kreisky approaches the Soviet authorities and offers to take Medvedev in case he were allowed to emigrate.

1984

February 9: Death of Iurii Andropov. Konstantin Chernenko is elected general secretary of the CPSU.
February: Implementation of a system of constant surveillance of Roy Medvedev's apartment.
November: Second house search at Antonov-Ovseenko's apartment and rumors of his arrest.

1985

March 10: Death of Konstantin Chernenko. Mikhail Gorbachev is elected general secretary of the CPSU.
May: End of the surveillance of Medvedev's apartment.

1986

December 23: Sakharov allowed to return from his exile in Gorkii to Moscow.

1987

January: Central Committee Plenum during which Gorbachev advocates for the first time Glasnost.
February: Wave of liberation of political prisoners.

1988

February: Rightist oppositionists Nikolai Bukharin and Aleksei Rykov rehabilitated.
March 13: Nina Andreeva's letter published in *Sovetskaia Rossiia*.
April 5: Official rebuffal of Nina Andreeva's letter in *Pravda*.
Late April: Publication of a first interview of Roy Medvedev in *Sobesednik*.
June 10: Secondary school history examinations canceled.
July: Leftist oppositionists Grigorii Zinoviev and Lev Kamenev rehabilitated.
August: Call by Elena Chukovskaia in *Knizhnoe obozrenie* to restore Solzhenitsyn's Soviet citizenship. First Perestroika publication by Anton Antonov-Ovseenko.
September: Beginning of serialization of Antonov-Ovseenko's *Beria* in journal *Zvezda*.
October: Politburo vetoes the publication by *Novyi mir* of an announcement of the forthcoming publication of *The Gulag Archipelago*.

1989

January: Beginning of serialization of *Let History Judge* in *Znamia* under the title "On Stalin and Stalinism."
January 28: Founding Congress of Memorial society.
March 25: First round of the election to the Congress of People's Deputies.
April 9: Roy Medvedev elected People's Deputy.
May 25: Opening of the Congress of People's Deputies. Medvedev elected to the Supreme Soviet.
August: Beginning of serialization of *The Gulag Archipelago* in *Novyi mir*.
October: Publication of a first interview of Nekrich in *Moskovskie novosti*. First visit to Moscow since his emigration.
December 14: Death of Andrei Sakharov.

1990

June 12: Declaration of sovereignty by the Russian Soviet Federative Socialist Republic.
July: Roy Medvedev elected to the Central Committee of the CPSU.

1991

March 17: Union-wide referendum on the preservation of the USSR

August 19–21: Failed coup attempt by hardliners within the Communist Party leadership.

December 8: Signing of the Belovezha accords, which led to the dissolution of the Union of Soviet Socialist Republics.

Bibliography

Archival Material

Anton Vladimirovich Antonov-Ovseenko Papers, Personal Archive.
Archives of the Soviet Communist Party and Soviet state microfilm collection, 1903-1922: Russian State Archive of Contemporary History: copies conserved at Hoover Institution Archive, Stanford University, California (United States).
Michel Heller Papers, Bibliothèque de Documentation Internationale Contemporaine, Université de Nanterre (France).
Open Society Archive, Central European University, Budapest (Hungary); Radio Free Europe/Radio Liberty Research Institute.
Roy Medvedev Papers, Archive of the History of Dissent in the USSR (1953-1987), Mezhdunarodnyi Memorial, Moscow (Russia).
Roy and Zhores Medvedev Papers, Department of Conservation of Documents from Personal Collections (OKhDLSM), Moscow City Archive, Moscow (Russia).
Aleksandr Nekrich Papers, Hoover Institution Archive, Stanford University, California (United States).
Russian State Archive of Contemporary History (RGANI), Moscow (Russia).
Russian State Archive of Social-Political History (RGASPI), Moscow (Russia).

Interviews

Interview of A.A. Antonov-Ovseenko, September 22, 2017, Moscow (Russia).
Interview of A.V. Antonov-Ovseenko, June 29, 2012, Moscow (Russia).
Interview of E. Chukovskaia, June 20, 2012, Moscow (Russia).
Interview of G. Khomizuri, January 19, 2013, Moscow (Russia).
Interview of I. Levitan, June 23, 2012, Moscow (Russia).
Interview of N. Levitskaia, June 19, 2012, Moscow (Russia).
Interview of R. Medvedev (1), June 19, 2012, Moscow (Russia).
Interview of R. Medvedev (2), January 25, 2013, Moscow (Russia).
Interview of R. Medvedev (3), January 22, 2017, Moscow (Russia).
Interview of R. Medvedev (4), September 24, 2017, Moscow (Russia).
Interview of R. Medvedev by L. Novak, January 2004, Moscow (Russia).
Interview of V. Tikhanova, October 25, 2014, Moscow (Russia).
Interview of Z. Medvedev (1), May 29, 2014, London (United Kingdom).
Interview of Z. Medvedev (2), April 12, 2018, London (United Kingdom).

Memoirs and published primary sources

Abramovich, I.L. *Vospominaniia i vzgliady*. Vol. 1: Vospominaniia. 2 vols. Moscow: KRUK-Prestizh, 2004.
Afanas'ev, Iurii. "Perestroika i istoricheskoe znanie." In *Inogo ne dano: perestroika: glasnost', demokratiia, sotsializm: sud'by perestroiki, vgliadyvaias' v proshloe, vozvrashchenie k budushchemu*, edited by Iurii Afanas'ev, 491–506. Moscow: Progress, 1988.
Aksiutin, Iurii, ed. *L.I. Breznev. Materialy k biografii*. Moscow: Politizdat, 1991.
"Aleksandr Solzhenitsyn Nobel Lecture," 1970. https://www.nobelprize.org/nobel_prizes/literature/laureates/1970/solzhenitsyn-lecture.html.
Alexeyeva, Ludmilla, and Paul Goldberg. *The Thaw Generation: Coming of Age in the Post-Stalin Era*. Pittsburgh: University of Pittsburgh Press, 1993.
Al'perovich, M.S. "Knigi imeiut svoiu sud'bu." In *Otreshivshiisia ot strakha. Pam'iati A.M. Nekricha: Vospominaniia, stat'i, dokumenty.*, edited by M.S. Al'perovich, 79–97. Moscow: Institut Vseobshchei Istorii RAN, 1996.
Al'perovich, M.S., ed. *Otreshivshiisia ot strakha: pamiati A.M. Nekricha. Vospominaniia, stat'i, dokumenty.* Moscow: Institut Vseobshchei Istorii RAN, 1996.
Andropov, Iurii. "'Samizdat' preterpel kachestvennye izmeneniia." *Istochnik. Dokumenty russkoi istorii*. 2, no. 9 (1994): 77–78.
Antonov-Ovseenko, Anton. *Kar'era palacha*. Omsk: Omskaia pravda, 1991.
Antonov-Ovseenko, Anton. *Lavrentii Beria*. Krasnodar: Sovetskaia Kuban' kontsern kurort, 1993.
Antonov-Ovseenko, Anton."Protivostoianie." *Literaturnaia gazeta*, April 3, 1991.
Antonov-Ovseenko, Anton. *Stalin bez maski*. Moskva: Vsia Moskva, 1990.
Antonov-Ovseenko, Anton. "Stalin i ego vremia." *Voprosy istorii*, no. 1–4; 6–11. (1989).
Antonov-Ovseenko, Anton. *Teatr Iosifa Stalina*. Moscow: Gregorii Peidzh, 1995.
Antonov-Ovseenko, Anton. *The Time of Stalin. Portrait of a Tyranny*. New York: Harper and Row, 1981.
Antonov-Ovseenko, Anton. "Utverzhdenie zakonnosti (Soldaty Leniniskoi gvardii. Ob Antonove-Ovseenko V.A.)." *Nauka i zhizn'*, no. 8 (1988): 40–48.
Antonov-Ovseenko, Anton. *Vragi naroda*. Moscow: Intellekt, 1996.
Antonov-Ovseenko, Vladimir. *V semnadtstom godu*. 1st ed. Moscow: Gosudarstvennoe izdatel'stvo khudozhestvennoi literatury, 1933.
Arbatov, Georgii. "Iz nedavnego proshlogo." In *L.I. Breznev. Materialy k biografii.*, edited by Iurii Aksiutin, 61–92. Moscow: Politizdat, 1991.
"'Arkhipelag Gulag' chitaiut na rodine." *Nezavisimaia gazeta*, July 4, 1991.
"'Arkhipelag Gulag' chitaiut na rodine." *Novyi mir*, no 9, (1991).
Artizov, A., Iu. Sigachev, I. Shevchuk, and V. Khlopov, eds. *Reabilitatsiia: kak èto bylo*. Vol. II: Fevral' 1956-nachalo 80-kh godov. Moscow: Izdatel'stvo "Materik," 2003.
Avtorkhanov, Abdurakhman. *Memuary*. Frankfurt/Main: Posev, 1983.
Avtorkhanov, Abdurakhman. *Stalin and the Soviet Communist Party: A Study in the Technology of Power*. New York: Praeger, 1959.
Avtorkhanov, Abdurakhman. *Staline au pouvoir*. Paris: Les Iles d'or, 1951.
Avtorkhanov, Abdurakhman. *Tekhnologiia vlasti*. 2nd ed. Frankfurt/Main: Posev, 1976.
Baburin, Vladimir. "Aleksandr Nekrich: 'Politika - èto istoriia, oprokinutaia v budushchee.'" *Megapolis-Express*, July 26, 1990.
Bogoraz, L., V. Golitsyn, and S. Kovalev. "Politicheskaia bor'ba ili zashchita prav? dvatsatiletnii opyt nezavisimogo obshchestvennogo dvizheniia v SSSR: 1965-1985." In

Pogruzhenie v triasinu (anatomiia zastoia), edited by A.T. Notkina, 501–44. Moscow: Progress, 1991.
Bolkhovitinov, N.N. "Pamiatnye vstrechi." In *Otreshivshiisia ot strakha: pamiati A.M. Nekricha. Vospominaniia, stat'i, dokumenty.*, edited by M.S. Al'perovich. Moscow: Institut Vseobshchei Istorii RAN, 1996.
Bonner, Elena. "Ukhodiat druz'ia... Umer Aleksandr Nekrich." *Izvestiia*, September 4, 1993.
Bovin, Aleksandr. "Kurs na stabil'nost' porodil zastoi." In *L.I. Breznev. Materialy k Biografii.*, edited by Iurii Aksiutin, 92–102. Moscow: Politizdat, 1991.
Bovin, Aleksandr. *XX vek kak zhizn'*. Moscow: Zakharov, 2003.
Burlatskii, Fedor. "Brezhnev i krushenie 'ottepeli.'" In *L.I. Breznev. Materialy k Biografii.*, edited by Iurii Aksiutin, 102–45. Moscow: Politizdat, 1991.
Carlisle, Olga Andreyev. *Solzhenitsyn and the Secret Circle*. London; Henley: Routledge & Kegan Paul, 1978.
Chukovskaia, Elena. Elena Tsezarevna: K iubileiu vnuchki Chukovskogo. Radio Svoboda, August 7, 2011. http://www.svobodanews.org/a/24289634.html.
Chukovskaia, Elena. "Vernut' Solzhenitsynu grazhdanstvo SSSR." *Knizhnoe Obozrenie*, August 5, 1988.
Chukovskaia, Lidiia. "V gazetu 'Izvestiia'. Ne kazn', no mysl', no slovo (k 15-letiiu so dnia smerti Stalina)." In *Antologiia Samizdata: nepodtsenzurnaia literatura v SSSR 1950-e -1980-e*, edited by Viacheslav Igrunov, 2: 1966-1973:127–31. Moscow: Mezhdunarodnyi Institut Gumanitarno-Politicheskikh Issledovanii, 2005.
Cohen, Stephen F., ed. *An End to Silence: Uncensored Opinion in the Soviet Union, from Roy Medvedev's Underground Magazine Political Diary*. New York: W W Norton, 1982.
Danilova, L.V. "Partiinaia organizatsiia Instituta Istorii AN SSSR v ideinom protvistoianii s partiinymi instantsiami, 1966-1968 gg." *Voprosy istorii* 12 (2007): 44–80.
Deborin, G.A., and B.S. Tel'pukhovskii. "In the Ideological Captivity of the Falsifiers of History." In *"June 22, 1941": Soviet Historians and the German Invasion*, edited by Vladimir Petrov, 271–302. Columbia, SC: University of South Carolina Press, 1968.
Dovner, M. "Lubok vmesto istorii." *Pamiat': Istoricheskii sbornik* 4 (1981): 442–55.
"Eshche odno svidetel'stvo politicheskogo syska." *Literaturnaia gazeta*, July 3, 1996.
Fedorov, G. "A Measure of Responsibility." In *"June 22, 1941": Soviet Historians and the German Invasion*, edited by Vladimir Petrov, 264–270. Columbia, SC: University of South Carolina Press, 1968.
Gabai, Il'ia, Iulii Kim, and Petr Iakir. "K deiateliam nauki, kul'tury i iskusstva." In *Antologiia samizdata: nepodtsenzurnaia literatura v SSSR 1950-e -1980-e*, edited by Viacheslav Igrunov, 2: 1966-1973:46–50. Moscow: Mezhdunarodnyi Institut Gumanitarno-Politicheskikh Issledovanii, 2005.
Garaseva, Anna M. *Ia zhila v samoi beschelovechnoi strane: vospominaniia anarkhistki*. Moscow: Intergraf Service, 1997.
Gazarian, Suren. "Èto ne dolzhno povtorit'sia: dokumental'naia povest'." *Literaturnaia Armeniia*, no. 6, 7, 8, 9 (1988).
Gnedin, Evgenii. *Vykhod iz labirinta*. Moscow: Memorial, 1994.
Golikov, V., S. Murashov, I. Chkhikvishvili, M. Shatagin, and S. Shaumian. "Za Leninskuiu partiinost' v osveshchenii istorii KPSS." *Kommunist*, no. 3 (1969): 67–82.
Grigorenko, Petr. *Mémoires*. Paris: Presses de la Renaissance, 1980.
Grigorenko, Petr. *Mysli sumasshedshego: izbrannye pis'ma i vystupleniia Petra Grigor'evicha Grigorenko*. Amsterdam: Fond imeni Gertsena, 1973.

Grigorenko, Petr. "The Concealment of Historical Truth - A Public Crime: The Real Fate of the Armed Forces When Hitler Invaded." In *The Grigorenko Papers: Writings and Documents on His Case*, 12–50. Boulder, CO: Westview Press, 1976.

Gronskii, Ivan. "Arest. Lager." Edited by Svetlana Gronskaia. *Zvezda*, no. 5 (2008).

Heller, Leonid, ed. *Vmesto memuarov: pamiati M.Ia. Gellera*. Moscow: Mik, 2000.

Heller, Michel, and Aleksandr Nekrich. *Utopia in Power: The History of the Soviet Union from 1917 to the Present*. New York: Hutchinson, 1986.

Igrunov, Viacheslav, ed. *Antologiia samizdata: nepodtsenzurnaia literatura v SSSR 1950-e -1980-e*.Vol. 1: do 1966 goda. 3 vols. Moscow: Mezhdunarodnyi Institut Gumanitarno-Politicheskikh Issledovanii, 2005.

Khrushchev, Nikita Sergeevich. *The Crimes of the Stalin Era: Special Report to the 20th Congress of the Communist Party of the Soviet Union*. New York: The New Leader, 1956.

Khrushchev, Sergei Nikitich. *Khrushchev*. Moscow: Vagrius, 2001.

Kopelev, Lev. "Vozmozhna li reabilitatsiia Stalina?" In *Vera v slovo: vystupleniia i pis'ma, 1962-1976 gg.*, 31–35. Ann Arbor: Ardis, 1977.

"Kruglyi stol: istoricheskaia nauka v usloviakh perestroiki." *Voprosy istorii*, no. 3 (March 1988): 3–52.

Krylenko, Nikolai. *Za piat' let 1918-1922 gg.: obvinitel'nye rechi po naibolee krupnym protsessam, zaslushannym v moskovskom i verkhovnom revoliutsionnykh tribunalakh*. Moscow, Petrograd: Gosizdat, 1931.

Labedz, Leopold, ed. *Solzhenitsyn: A Documentary Record*. London: Allen Lane the Penguin Press, 1970.

Lakshin Vladimir , "Ivan Denisovich, ego druz'ia i nedrugi." In *Solzhenitsyn i koleso istorii*, 13–60. Moscow: Veche, 2008.

Latsis, Martin. *Dva goda bor'by na vnutrennem fronte*. Moscow: Gos. izdatel'stvo, 1920.

Maksimov, Vladimir. "Otkrytoe pis'mo V.E. Maksimova brat'iam Roiu i Zhoresu Medvedevym." *Chasovoi*, no. 571 (1974): 18.

Martin, Barbara, and Anton Sveshnikov, ed. *Istoricheskii sbornik Pamiat': Issledovaniia i materialy*. Moscow: Novoe Literaturnoe Obozrenie, 2017.

Materialy plenuma Tsentral'nogo Komiteta KPSS 27-28 ianvaria 1987 Goda. Moscow: Politizdat, 1987.

Medvedev, R.A. *N.S. Khrushchev. Politicheskaia biografiia*. Moscow: Kniga, 1990.

Medvedev, R.A. *Trudnaia vesna 1918 goda*. Voronezh: Tsentral'no-chernozemnoe knizhnoe izdatel'stvo, 1990.

Medvedev, R.A., and S.P. Starikov. *Zhizn' i gibel' Filippa Kuzmicha Mironova*. Moscow: Patriot, 1989.

Medvedev, Roi. *Gensek s Lubianki (Iu. V. Andropov. Politicheskii Portret)*. Nizhnii Novgorod: Izd. "Leta," 1993.

Medvedev, Roi. *Kniga o sotsialisticheskoi demokratii*. Amsterdam: Fond imeni Gertsena, 1972.

Medvedev, Roi. *Lichnost' i èpokha. Politicheskii portret L.I. Brezhneva*. Moscow: Izd. "Novosti," 1991.

Medvedev, Roi. *Neizvestnyi Andropov. Politicheskaia biografiia Iuriia Andropova*. Moscow: Izd. "Prava cheloveka," 1999.

Medvedev, Roi. *O Staline i stalinizme*. Moscow: Progress, 1990.

Medvedev, Roi. *Politicheskie portrety. Istoricheskie ocherki i stat'i*. Stavropol': Stavropol'skoe knizhnoe izdatel'stvo, 1990.

Medvedev, Roi. *Politicheskii dnevnik. 1964-1970*. Amsterdam: Fond imeni Gertsena, 1972.

Medvedev, Roi. *Politicheskii dnevnik II. 1965-1970*. Amsterdam: Fond imeni Gertsena, 1975.

Medvedev, Roi, and Zhores Medvedev. 1925-2010. *Iz vospominanii*. Moscow: Izd. "Prava cheloveka," 2010.

Medvedev, Roi. *Solzhenitsyn i Sakharov. Dva proroka.* Moscow: Vremia, 2005.
Medvedev, Roy. *Faut-il réhabiliter Staline?* Paris: Ed. du Seuil, 1969.
Medvedev, Roy. "How Political Diary Was Created." In *An End to Silence: Uncensored Opinion in the Soviet Union, from Roy Medvedev's Underground Magazine Political Diary,* edited by Stephen F. Cohen, 17–21. New York: Norton, 1982.
Medvedev, Roy. *Khrushchev.* New York: Anchor Books, 1984.
Medvedev, Roy. *Let History Judge: The Origins and Consequences of Stalinism.* London: MacMillan, 1972.
Medvedev, Roy. *Let History Judge: The Origins and Consequences of Stalinism.* Revised and expanded ed. Oxford; New York [etc.]: Oxford University Press, 1989.
Medvedev, Roy. "On Gulag Volume One." In *Political Essays,* 61–76. Nottingham: Spokesman Books, 1976a.
Medvedev, Roy. "On Gulag Volume Two." In *Political Essays,* 77–88. Nottingham: Spokesman Books, 1976b.
Medvedev, Roy. *On Socialist Democracy.* London [etc.].: MacMillan, 1975.
Medvedev, Roy. *On Soviet Dissent.* Columbia University Press, 1980.
Medvedev, Roy. "Problems of Democratization and Détente." *New Left Review* I, no. 83 (February 1974). http://newleftreview.org/I/83/roy-medvedev-problems-of-democratization-and-detente.
Medvedev, Roy. *Qui a écrit le "Don paisible"?* Paris: Bourgois, 1975.
Medvedev, Roy. "Solzhenitsyn: Truth and Politics." In *The Samizdat Register,* 2:295–323. London: Merlin Press, 1981.
Medvedev, Roy. *Sovetskii Soiuz. Poslednie gody zhizni.* Moscow: Vremia, 2015.
Medvedev, Roy. *The October Revolution.* New York: Columbia University Press, 1979.
Medvedev, Roy. ed. *The Samizdat Register.* Vol. 1. London: Merlin Press, 1977.
Medvedev, Roy. *The Samizdat Register.* Vol. 2. London: Merlin Press, 1981.
Medvedev, Roy, Andrei Sakharov, and Valentin Turchin. "Appeal for a Gradual Democratization." In *Samizdat: Voices of the Soviet Opposition,* edited by George Saunders, 399–412. New York: Monad Press, 1974.
Medvedev, Zhores. "Iz vospominanii o Solzhenitsyne." In *1925-2010. Iz vospominanii.,* edited by Roi Medvedev and Zhores Medvedev, 145–207. Moscow: Izd. "Prava cheloveka," 2010.
Medvedev, Zhores. *Kto sumasshedshii?* London: Macmillan, 1971.
Medvedev, Zhores. *Nikita Khrushchev.* Izdatel'stvo "Vremia," 2012.
Medvedev, Zhores. *Ten Years after Ivan Denisovich.* New York: A.A. Knopf, 1973.
Medvedev, Zhores. *The Medvedev Papers: Fruitful Meetings between Scientists of the World, and, Secrecy of Correspondence Is Guaranteed by Law.* London; New York: Macmillan; St. Martin's Press, 1971.
Medvedev, Zhores. *The Rise and Fall of T.D. Lysenko.* New York; London: Columbia University Press, 1969.
Medvedev, Zhores, and Roy Medvedev. *A Question of Madness.* New York: Knopf, 1971.
Medwedew, Roj. "Die Brillanten der Madame Galina Breschnewa." *Der Spiegel,* no. 5 (February 2, 1988).
Meerson-Aksenov, M., and N. Lupinin, eds. *The Political, Social and Religious Thought of Russian "Samizdat": An Anthologie.* Belmont: Notable & Academik Books, 1977.
Mikoian, Anastas Ivanovich. *Tak bylo: razmyshleniia o minuvshem.* Moscow: Vagrius, 1999.
Mikoian, Sergei. "Istoricheskaia publitsistika. Aleksei Snegov v bor'be za 'destalinizatsiiu.'" *Voprosy istorii,* no. 4 (2006): 69–84.

Morev, Gleb, ed. *Dissidenty. Dvadtsat' razgovorov.* Moscow: Izdatel'stvo ACT, 2017.
Nadzhafov, D.G. "Kollega, Edinomyshlennik, Drug." In *Otreshivshiisia ot strakha. Pam'iati A.M. Nekricha: Vospominaniia, stat'i, dokumenty.*, edited by M.S. Al'perovich, 95–113. Moscow: Institut Vseobshchei Istorii RAN, 1996.
Nekrich, Aleksandr. *1941, 22 iunia.* Moscow: Pamiatniki istoricheskoi mysli, 1995.
Nekrich, Aleksandr. *Forsake Fear: Memoirs of an Historian.* Boston; London: Unwin Hyman, 1991.
Nekrich, Aleksandr. *"June 22, 1941": Soviet Historians and the German Invasion.* Edited by Vladimir Petrov. Columbia, SC: University of South Carolina Press, 1968.
Nekrich, Aleksandr. *L'armée rouge assassinée: 22 Juin 1941.* Paris: B. Grasset, 1968.
Nekrich, Aleksandr. *Les peuples punis: La déportation et le sort des minorités soviétiques à la fin de la Seconde Guerre mondiale.* Paris: F. Maspero, 1982.
Nekrich, Aleksandr. ed. "Obsuzhdenie knigi A.M. Nekricha '1941, 22 Iunia' v Institute Marksizma-Leninizma pri TsK KPSS (Stenogramma)." In *1941, 22 Iunia*, 279–333. Moscow: Pamiatniki istoricheskoi mysli, 1995.
Nekrich, Aleksandr. *Pariahs, Partners, Predators: German-Soviet Relations, 1922-1941.* New York: Columbia University Press, 1997.
Nekrich, Aleksandr. Perestroika, Current Trends and Soviet History Nationalities, Polish Church, Emigration - Old & New." *Survey: A Journal of Soviet and East European Studies* 30, no. 4 (1989).
Nekrich, Aleksandr. "Perestroika in History: The First Stage." In *Perestroika and Soviet History*, edited by Mikhail Geller, 22–43. London: Survey Ltd. in association with the Institute for European Defence & Strategic Studies, 1989.
Noril'skii, Sergei. "Vlast' idei i uzi krovi." In *Kniga pamiati zhertv politicheskoi repressii Tul'skoi oblasti. 1917-1987.*, edited by S.L. Shcheglov, 3:18–26. Tula: GrifiK, n.d.
"O Parvuse i ne tol'ko. Pervoe v zhizni interv'iu Tat'iany Evgenevny Gnedinoi, vnuchki Parvusa." *Laboratoriia fantastiki* (blog). http://fantlab.ru/article429.
Pervyi s"ezd narodnykh deputatov. Stenograficheskii otchet. Vol. 2. Moscow: Izdanie Verkhovnogo Soveta SSSR, 1989.
Petrov, Nikita. "Roi Medvedev kak istorik-dissident." *Kontinent*, no. 68 (1991): 335–45.
Petrov, Vladimir, ed. "A Meeting of the Division of History of the Great Patriotic War of the Institute of Marxism-Leninism of the CC CPSU, February 16, 1966." In *"June 22, 1941": Soviet Historians and the German Invasion*, 246–61. Columbia, SC: University of South Carolina Press, 1968.
Pogudin, V. "Anton Rakitin. Imenem Revoliutsii... (Ocherk o V.A. Antonove-Ovseenko. M., Politizdat, 1965. 191 str." *Kommunist*, no. 12 (August 1965): 125–26.
Pomerantsev, Vladimir. "Ob iskrennosti v literature." *Novyi mir*, 1953.
"Press-konferentsiia A.I. Solzhenitsyna." *Russkaia mysl'*, January 16, 1975.
Rakitin, Anton. *A.V. Antonov-Ovseenko.* Leningrad: Lenizdat, 1975.
Rakitin, Anton. *A.V. Antonov-Ovseenko.* Leningrad: Lenizdat, 1989.
Rakitin, Anton, and A.V. Antonov-Ovseenko, ed. "On bral zimnii." *Novyi mir* 11 (November 1964): 200–212.
Řezáč, Tomáš. *Spiral' izmeny Solzhenitsyna.* Edited by M. Pravdina. Moscow: Progress, 1978.
Sakharov, Andrei. "A Letter to the Congress of the United States." In *Sakharov Speaks*, edited by Harrison E. Salisbury, 212–15. London: Collins & Harvill Press, 1974.
Sakharov, Andrei. *Trevoga i nadezhda.* 2nd ed. Moscow: Inter-Verso, 1991.
Sakharov, Andrei. *Vospominaniia.* New York: Izd. im. Chekhova, 1990.

Saunders, George, ed. *Samizdat: Voices of the Soviet Opposition*. New York: Monad Press, 1974.
Scammell, Michael, and Catherine A. Fitzpatrick, eds. *The Solzhenitsyn Files: Secret Soviet Documents Reveal One Man's Fight against the Monolith*. Chicago: Edition Q, 1995.
Shakhnazarov, Georgii. *S vozhdiami i bez nikh*. Moscow: Vagrius, 2001.
Shatunovskaia, Olga. *Ob ushedshem veke. Rasskazyvaet Olga Shatunovskaia*. Edited by D. Kut'ina, A. Broido, and A. Kut'in. La Jolla, CA: DAA Books, 2001.
Shcharansky, Anatoly. *Fear No Evil: A Memoir*. London: Hodder and Stoughton, 1989.
Simonov, Konstantin. *Glazami cheloveka moego pokoleniia: razmyshleniia o I.V. Staline*. Moscow: Kniga, 1990.
Slezkin, L.Iu. "Pamiati druga." In *Otreshivshiisia ot strakha. Pam'iati A.M. Nekricha: vospominaniia, stat'i, dokumenty.*, edited by M.S. Al'perovich, 11–38. Moscow: Institut Vseobshchei Istorii RAN, 1996.
Slovo probivaet sebe dorogu: sbornik statei i dokumentov ob A.I. Solzhenitsyne: 1962-1974. Moscow: Russkii put', 1998.
Sluch, S.Z. "Nes'kol'ko vstrech." In *Otreshivshiisia ot strakha. Pam'iati A.M. Nekricha: Vospominaniia, stat'i, dokumenty.*, edited by M.S. Al'perovich, 114–20. Moscow: Institut Vseobshchei Istorii RAN, 1996.
Soljenitsyne, Aleksandr Isaevitch. *Le grain tombé entre les meules: Esquisses d'exil. Première partie*. Paris: Fayard, 1998.
Soljénitsyne, Alexandre. *Les Invisibles*. Paris: Fayard, 1992.
Solzhenitsyn, A.I. "Ugodilo zernyshko promezh dvukh zhernovov. Ocherki izgnaniia. Chast' pervaia (1974-1978). Glavy 4-5." *Novyi mir*, no. 2 (1999): 67–140.
Solzhenitsyn, Aleksandr. "Arkhipelag Gulag 1918-1956." *Novyi mir*, 8 (1989): 7.
Solzhenitsyn, Aleksandr. *Arkhipelag GULag : 1918-1956 : opyt khudozhestvennogo issledovaniia*. Ekaterinburg: Izdatel'stvo "U-Factoriia," 2006.
Solzhenitsyn, Aleksandr. *The Gulag Archipelago: 1918-1956*. Vol. 1. Glasgow: Harpers and Row Publishers, 1974.
Solzhenitsyn, Aleksandr. *The Gulag Archipelago: 1918-1956*. Vol. 2. Glasgow: Harpers and Row Publishers, 1975.
Solzhenitsyn, Aleksandr. *The Gulag Archipelago: 1918-1956*. Vol. 3. Glasgow: Harpers and Row Publishers, 1978.
Solzhenitsyn, Aleksandr. *Letter to the Soviet Leaders*. New York: Harper & Row, 1974.
Solzhenitsyn, Aleksandr. "Nobelevskaia lektsiia." *Novyi mir*, no. 7 (1989): 135.
Solzhenitsyn, Aleksandr. *The Oak and the Calf*. Collins/Fontana, 1980.
Solzhenitsyn, Alexander. "Live Not by Lies." *Index on Censorship* 33, no. 2 (April 2004): 203–7.
Sovokin, A. "Replika: istoriia odnoi telegrammy." *Izvestiia*, July 10, 1965.
Spivakovskii, Pavel, and T. V. Esina, eds. *"Ivanu Denisovichu" polveka: iubileinyi sbornik, 1962-2012*. Moscow: Dom russkogo zarubezh'ia im. Aleksandra Solzhenitsyna / Russkii put', 2012.
"Stalin i Stalinizm : dve tochki zreniia." *Moskovskie novosti*, June 12, 1988.
Summa. Za svobodnuiu mysl'. Saint-Petersburg: Izdatel'stvo zhurnala "Zvezda," 2002.
Suvarin, Boris. "'Stalinizm' po Roiu Medvedevu." *Novyi zhurnal*, no. 113 (1973): 192–211.
Tiurina, Galina Andreevna, ed. *"Dorogoi Ivan Denisovich!..": Pis'ma chitatelei 1962-1964*. Moscow: Russkii put', 2012.
"Triumf tirana, tragediia naroda. Beseda s D.A. Volkogonovym i R.A. Medvedevym." In *Surovaia drama naroda. Uchenye i publitsisty o prirode Stalinizma*, 270–91. Moscow: Politizdat, 1989.

Tvardovskii, Aleksandr. *Novomirskii dnevnik*. Edited by V.A. Tvardovskii and O.A. Tvardovskii. Vol. 1. Moscow: Prozaik, 2009.
Uldriks, Teddy J. "Review: The Time of Stalin: Portrait of a Tyranny by Anton Antonov-Ovseyenko." *Russian Review* 42, no. 3 (July 1983): 333-34.
"V Narkomindele. 1922-1939. Interv'iu s E.A. Gnedinym." In *Pamiat': Istoricheskii sbornik*, 5:357-93. Paris: Ed. La Presse libre, 1982.
Van Rossum, Leo. "A. Antonov-Ovseenko's Book on Stalin: Is It Reliable? A Note." *Soviet Studies* 36, no. 3 (July 1984): 445-47.
Vuchetich, Evgenii. "Vnesem iasnost'." *Izvestiia*, April 14, 1965.
Vyshinskii, Andrei. *Ot tiurem k vospitatel'nym uchrezhdeniiam: sbornik statei*. Moscow: Sovetskoe zakonodatel'stvo, 1934.
XX s"ezd Kommunisticheskoi Partii Sovetskogo Soiuza. 14-25 Fevralia 1956 goda. Stenograficheskii otchet. Vol. I. Moscow: Gosudarstvennoe izdatel'stvo politicheskoi literatury, 1956.
XXII s"ezd Kommunisticheskoi Partii Sovetskogo Soiuza. 17-31 Oktiabria 1961 goda. Stenograficheskii otchet. Vol. II. Moscow: Gosudarstvennoe izdatel'stvo politicheskoi literatury, 1962.
Zakon Soiuza Sovetskikh Sotsialisticheskikh Respublik o vyborakh narodnykh deputatov SSSR. Moscow, 1988.
Zelenov, Mikhail. "Otzyv G.A. Deborina na tret'iu chast' rukopisi R.A. Medvedeva 'Edinolichnoe pravlenie Stalina'. 1969 g." *Acta Samizdatics / Zapiski o Samizdate* 3 (2016): 127-32.
Zemskov, V.N. "Zakliuchennye, spetsposelentsy, ssyl'noposelentsy, ssyl'nye i vyslannye (statistiko-geograficheskii otchet)." *Istoriia SSSR*, no. 5 (1991): 151-65.
Zhukov, E., V. Trukhanovskii, and V. Shunkov. "Vysokaia otvetstvennost' istorikov." *Pravda*. January 30, 1966.

Secondary Literature

Adler, Nanci Dale. *Keeping Faith with the Party: Communist Believers Return from the Gulag*. Bloomington: Indiana University Press, 2012.
Alexeyeva, Liudmilla. *Soviet Dissent: Contemporary Movements for National, Religious, and Human Rights*. Middletown, CT: Wesleyan University Press, 1985.
Bacon, Edwin. "Reconsidering Brezhnev." In *Brezhnev Reconsidered*, edited by Edwin Bacon and Mark Sandle, 1-21. Houndmills, Basingstoke: Palgrave Macmillan, 2002.
Banerji, Arup. *Writing History in the Soviet Union: Making the Past Work*. New York: Berghahn Books, 2008.
Barghoorn, Frederick C. "Factional, Sectoral and Subversive Opposition in Soviet Politics." In *Regimes and Opposition*, edited by Robert Dahl, 17-87. New Haven; London: Yale University Press, 1973.
Berelowitch, Alexis. "Des romans contre les tabous de l'histoire." In *A l'Est, la mémoire retrouvée*, edited by Alain Brossat, 430-43. Paris: Ed. La Découverte, 1990.
Beyrau, Dietrich. "Arcane and Public Spheres in the Soviet Union." In *Underground Publishing and the Public Sphere: Transnational Perspectives*, edited by Jan C. Behrends and Thomas Lindenberger, 99-142. Wien: Lit, 2014.
Bezborodov, A.B. *Fenomen akademicheskogo dissidentsva v SSSR*. Moscow: Rossiiskii Gosudarstvennyi Gumanitarnyi Universitet, 1998.

Bogomolov, Aleksei. "Istoriia kak izmena rodine." *Sovershenno sekretno* 8, no. 291 (August 2013). http://www.sovsekretno.ru/articles/id/3741/.

Bolton, Jonathan. *Worlds of Dissent: Charter 77, the Plastic People of the Universe and Czech Culture under Communism*. Cambridge, MA: Harvard University Press, 2012.

Boobbyer, Philip. *Conscience, Dissent and Reform in Soviet Russia*. London: Routledge, 2005.

Boyer, John W., Julius Kirshner, Iurii N. Afanas'ev, Mikhail A. Barg, Efim B. Cherniak, Viktor P. Danilov, Vladimir Z. Drobizhev, et al. "Perestroika, History, and Historians." *The Journal of Modern History* 62, no. 4 (December 1990): 782–830.

Cohen, Stephen F. "The Friends and Foes of Change: Reformism and Conservatism in the Soviet Union." In *The Soviet Union since Stalin*, edited by Stephen Cohen, Alexander Rabinowitch, and Robert Sharlet, 11–31. Bloomington, IN: Indiana University Press, 1980.

Cohen, Stephen F. "The Stalin Question since Stalin." In *An End to Silence: Uncensored Opinion in the Soviet Union, from Roy Medvedev's Underground Magazine Political Diary*, edited by Stephen F. Cohen, 22–50. New York: W. W. Norton & Co Inc, 1984.

Cohen, Stephen F. *The Victims Return: Survivors of the Gulag after Stalin*. Exeter, NH: PublishingWorks, 2010.

Conquest, Robert. "Andrei Sakharov." In *Tyrants and Typewriters. Communiqués From the Struggle for Truth*, 29–32. Lexington, MA; Toronto: Lexington Books, 1989.

Courtois, Stéphane, ed. *Le livre noir du communisme: crimes, terreur, répression*. Paris: R. Laffont, 1998.

Daniel', Aleksandr, and Larisa Bogoraz. "V poiskakh nesushchestvuiushchei nauki (dissidentstvo kak istoricheskaia problema)." *Problemy vostochonoi Evropy*, no. 37–38 (1993): 142–61.

David-Fox, Michael. "Memory, Archives, Politics: The Rise of Stalin in Avtorkhanov's Technology of Power." *Slavic Review* 54, no. 4 (1995): 988–1003.

Davies, R.W. "Soviet History in the Gorbachev Revolution: The First Phase." *The Socialist Register* 24 (1988): 37–78.

De Baets, Antoon. *Censorship of Historical Thought: A World Guide, 1945-2000*. Westport, CT: Greenwood Press, 2002.

Dobson, Miriam. *Khrushchev's Cold Summer: Gulag Returnees, Crime, and the Fate of Reform after Stalin*. Ithaca: Cornell University Press, 2011.

Dolmatovskii, Evgenii. "Kniga, propavshaia bez vesti." *Literaturnaia gazeta*, January 20, 1988.

Drabkin, Ia. S. "Ernst Genri - 'nash chelovek v XX-m veke.'" *Novaia i noveishaia istoriia*, no. 4 (2004).

Elie, Marc. "Ce que réhabiliter veut dire. Khrouchtchev et Gorbatchev aux prises avec l'héritage répressif stalinien." *Vingtième siècle. Revue d'histoire.*, no. 107 (September 2010): 101–12.

Etkind, Aleksandr. *Warped Mourning: Stories of the Undead in the Land of the Unburied*. Cultural Memory in the Present. Stanford, CA: Stanford University Press, 2013.

Ferretti, Maria. "Les archives entrouvertes." In *A l'Est, la mémoire retrouvée*, edited by Alain Brossat, 444–64. Paris: Ed. La découverte, 1990.

Fitzpatrick, Sheila. "Afterword: The Thaw in Retrospect." In *The Thaw: Soviet Society and Culture during the 1950s and 1960s*, edited by Eleonory Gilburd and Denis Kozlov, 482–91. Toronto: University of Toronto Press, 2013.

Geyer, Dietrich, ed. *Die Umwertung der Sowjetischen Geschichte*. Göttingen: Vandenhoeck & Ruprecht, 1991.

Glazov, Yuri. *To Be or Not to Be in the Party: Communist Party Membership in the USSR.* Dordrecht: Kluwer Academic Publishers, 1988.
Goerdt, Wilhelm. "PRAVDA: Wahrheit (ISTINA) und Gerechtigkeit (SPRAVEDLIVOST')." *Archiv Für Begriffsgeschichte* 12 (1968): 58–85.
Goldberg, Paul. *The Final Act: The Dramatic, Revealing Story of the Moscow Helsinki Watch Group.* New York: Morrow, 1988.
Griffiths, Franklyn, and Harold Gordon Skilling. *Interest Groups in Soviet Politics.* Princeton, NJ: University Press, 1971.
Heer, Nancy Whittier. *Politics and History in the Soviet Union.* Cambridge, MA: The MIT Press, 1973.
Hollander, Paul. *Political Will and Personal Belief: The Decline and Fall of Soviet Communism.* New Haven [etc.]: Yale University Press, 1999.
Hornsby, Robert. *Protest, Reform and Repression in Khrushchev's Soviet Union.* Cambridge: Cambridge University Press, 2013.
Hurst, Mark. *British Human Rights Organizations and Soviet Dissent, 1965-1985.* London: Bloomsbury Academic, 2016.
Husband, William B. "Secondary School History Texts in the USSR: Revising the Soviet Past, 1985-1989." *The Russian Review* 50, no. 4 (October 1991): 458–80.
Ivanova, Anna. *Magaziny "Berezka": Paradoksy potrebleniia v pozdnem SSSR.* Moscow: Novoe Literaturnoe Obozrenie, 2017.
Ivanova, Evgeniia. "Predanie i fakt v sud'be 'Arkhipelaga Gulaga.'" In *Mezhdu dvumia iubileiami, 1998-2003: pisateli, kritiki i literaturovedy o tvorchestve A.I. Solzhenitsyna: Al'manach,* edited by Nikita Alekseevich Struve, 449–57. Moscow: Russkii put', 2005.
Jones, Polly. "Iurii Trifonov's Fireglow and the 'Mnemonic Communities' of the Brezhnev Era." *Cahiers Du Monde Russe* 54, no. 1–2 (2013): 1–24.
Jones, Polly. *Myth, Memory, Trauma: Rethinking the Stalinist Past in the Soviet Union (1953-1970).* New Haven; London: Yale University Press, 2013.
Jones, Polly. "The Fire Burns On? The 'Fiery Revolutionaries' Biographical Series and the Rethinking of Propaganda in the Brezhnev Era." *Slavic Review* 74, no. 1 (Spring 2015): 32–56.
Kennan, George. "Between Earth and Hell." In *Aleksandr Solzhenitsyn: Critical Essays and Documentary Material,* edited by John B. Dunlop, Richard Haugh, and Alexis Klimoff, 501–11. New York: Collier books, 1975.
Kennedy Grimstead, Patricia. "'Glasnost' in the Archives? Recent Developments on the Soviet Archival Scene." *The American Archivist* 52, no. 2 (Spring 1989): 214–36.
Kind-Kovács, Friederike. *Written Here, Published There: How Underground Literature Crossed the Iron Curtain.* Budapest: CEU Press, 2014.
Kind-Kovács, Friederike, and Jessie Labov, eds. *Samizdat, Tamizdat, and beyond: Transnational Media during and after Socialism.* New York: Berghahn Books, 2013.
Kochetkova, Inna. *The Myth of the Russian Intelligentsia: Old Intellectuals in the New Russia.* London: Routledge, 2010.
Komaromi, Ann. "The Unofficial Field of Late Soviet Culture." *Slavic Review* 66, no. 4 (December 1, 2007): 605–29.
Kozlov, Denis. "The Historical Turn in Late Soviet Culture: Retrospectivism, Factography, Doubt, 1953–91." *Kritika: Explorations in Russian and Eurasian History* 2, no. 3 (Summer 2001): 577–600.
Kozlov, Denis. *The Readers of Novyi Mir. Coming to Terms with the Stalinist Past.* Cambridge, MA; London: Harvard University Press, 2013.

Kozlov, Vladimir, Sheila Fitzpatrick, and Sergei Mironenko, eds. *Sedition: Everyday Resistance in the Soviet Union under Khrushchev and Brezhnev*. Annals of Communism. New Haven: Yale University Press, 2011.

Krinko, E.F., and S.A. Kropachev. "Masshtaby stalinskikh repressii v otsenkakh sovetskikh i sovremennykh rossiiskikh issledovatelei." *Bylye gody*. 26, no. 4 (2012): 86–99.

Kriza, Elisa. *Alexander Solzhenitsyn: Cold War Icon, Gulag Author, Russian Nationalist?* Stuttgart: Ibidem-Verlag, 2014.

Labedz, Leopold. "The Structure of the Soviet Intelligentsia." In *The Russian Intelligentsia*, edited by Richard Pipes, 63–79. New York: Columbia University Press, 1961.

Lenoe, Matthew E. *The Kirov Murder and Soviet History*. New Haven: Yale University Press, 2010.

Leonhard, Wolfgang. "Politics and Ideology in the Post-Khrushchev Era." In *Soviet Politics since Khrushchev*, edited by Alexander Dallin, 41–71. Englewood Cliffs, NJ: Prentice-Hall, 1968.

Malia, Martin. "A War on Two Fronts: Solzhenitsyn and the Gulag Archipelago." *The Russian Review* 36, no. 1 (1977): 46–63.

Malia, Martin. "What Is the Intelligentsia?" In *The Russian Intelligentsia*, edited by Richard Pipes, 1–18. New York: Columbia University Press, 1961.

Markstein, Elisabeth. "Observations in the Narrative Structure of the 'Gulag Archipelago.'" In *Solzhenitsyn in Exile: Critical Essays and Documentary Materials*, edited by John Barrett Dunlop, 176–89. Hoover Press Publication 305. Stanford, CA: Hoover Institution Press, 1985.

Markwick, Roger D. "Catalyst of Historiography, Marxism and Dissidence: The Sector of Methodology of the Institute of History, Soviet Academy of Sciences, 1964-68." *Europe-Asia Studies* 46, no. 4 (January 1, 1994): 579–96.

Markwick, Roger D. *Rewriting History in Soviet Russia: The Politics of Revisionist Historiography, 1956-1974*. Basingstoke: Palgrave, 2001.

Martin, Barbara, and Anton Sveshnikov. "Between Scholarship and Dissidence: The Dissident Historical Collection Pamiat' (1975-1982)" *Slavic Review* 76, no. 4 (Winter 2017): 1003–26.

Moyn, Samuel. *The Last Utopia: Human Rights in History*. Cambridge, MA; London: The Belknap Press of Harvard University Press, 2010.

Nathans, Benjamin. "The Dictatorship of Reason: Aleksandr Vol'pin and the Idea of Rights under 'Developed Socialism.'" *Slavic Review* 66, no. 4 (December 1, 2007): 630–63.

Nathans, Benjamin. "The Disenchantment of Socialism: Soviet Dissidents, Human Rights, and the New Global Morality." In *The Breakthrough. Human Rights in the 1970s*, edited by Jan Eckel and Samuel Moyn, 33–48. Philadelphia: University of Pennsylvania Press, 2014.

Nicholson, Michael. "The Gulag Archipelago: A Survey of Soviet Responses." In *Aleksandr Solzhenitsyn : Critical Essays and Documentary Material*, edited by John B. Dunlop, Richard Haugh, and Alexis Klimoff, 2nd ed., 477–500. New York: Collier books, 1975.

Nove, Alec. *Glasnost' in Action: Cultural Renaissance in Russia*. Rev. Ed. Boston; London [etc.]: Unwin Hyman, 1990.

Oushakine, Sergei. "The Terrifying Mimicry of Samizdat." *Public Culture* 13, no. 2 (2001): 191–214.

Paillard, Denis. "Figures de la mémoire : Pamiat' et Memorial." In *A l'Est, la mémoire retrouvée*, edited by Alain Brossat, 365–87. Paris: Ed. La découverte, 1990.

Petrovskii, Leonid Petrovich. "Delo Nekricha." *Vechernii klub*, December 17, 1994.

Petrovskii, Leonid Petrovich. "Delo Nekricha." *Vestnik RAN* t. 65, no. 6 (1995): 528–39.

Pipes, Richard. "The Historical Evolution of the Russian Intelligentsia." In *The Russian Intelligentsia*, edited by Richard Pipes, 47–62. New York: Columbia University Press, 1961.

Pollack, Detlef, ed. *Dissent and Opposition in Communist Eastern Europe: Origins of Civil Society and Democratic Transition*. Aldershot: Ashgate, 2004.

Pomerants, Grigorii. *Sledstvie vedet katorzhanka*. Moscow; Saint-Petersburg: Tsentr gumanitarnykh initiativ, 2014.

Popov, N. "Pamiat' Anny Petrovny Skripnikovoi." In *Pamiat': Istoricheskii Sbornik*, 1:285–94. New York: Khronika Press, 1978.

Pozdeeva, L.V. "Pamiati A.M. Nekricha." *Novaia i noveishaia istoriia*, no. 2 (1994.): 249–51.

Radosh, Ronald, Mary R. Habeck, and Grigorij Nikolaevič Sevosťânov. *Spain Betrayed: The Soviet Union in the Spanish Civil War*. New Haven: Yale University Press, 2001.

Raleigh, Donald J. *Soviet Historians and Perestroika: The First Phase: The First Phase*. London: Routledge, 2016.

Rigby, T. H. "The Soviet Leadership: Towards a Self-Stabilizing Oligarchy?" *Soviet Studies* 22, no. 2 (1970): 167–91.

Salitan, Laurie P. "Domestic Pressures and the Politics of Exit: Trends in Soviet Emigration Policy." *Political Science Quarterly* 104, no. 4 (Winter 1989–): 671–87.

Saraskina, Liudmila. *Aleksandr Solzhenitsyn*. Zhizn' zamechatel'nykh liudei. Moscow: Izd. "Molodaia gvardiia," 2008.

Scammell, Michael. *Solzhenitsyn: A Biography*. London; Melbourne: Hutchinson, 1985.

Schattenberg, Susanne. "'Democracy or Despotism?' How the Secret Speech Was Translated into Everyday Life." In *The Dilemmas of De-Stalinization: Negotiating Cultural and Social Change in the Khrushchev Era*, edited by Polly Jones, 64–79. London: Routledge, 2009.

Schattenberg, Susanne *Leonid Breschnew: Staatsmann und Schauspieler im Schatten Stalins. Eine Biographie*. Köln: Böhlau Verlag, 2017.

Shane, Scott. *Dismantling Utopia: How Information Ended the Soviet Union*. Chicago: I.R. Dee, 1995.

Shatz, Marshall S. *Soviet Dissent in Historical Perspective*. Cambridge; London: Cambridge University Press, 1980.

Sherlock, Thomas. *Historical Narratives in the Soviet Union and Post-Soviet Russia: Destroying the Settled Past, Creating an Uncertain Future*. New York: Palgrave Macmillan, 2007.

Shibaev, Viktor. "Arkhivnoe zakonodatel'stvo sovremennoi Rossii: osnovnye tendentsii razvitiia." In *Arkhivy Rossii i Pol'shi: istoriia, problemy i perspektivy razvitiia*, 106–20. Ekaterinburg: Izd. Ural'skogo universiteta, 2013.

Shlapentokh, Vladimir. "Intellectuals Live in the Chosen Land: Gorbachev's Glasnost." In *Soviet Intellectuals and Political Power: The Post-Stalin Era*, 224–79. London; New York: I.B. Tauris, 1990.

Shlapentokh, Vladimir. *Soviet Intellectuals and Political Power: The Post-Stalin Era*. London; New York: I.B. Tauris, 1990.

Sigman, Carole. *Clubs politiques et perestroïka en Russie: subversion sans dissidence*. Paris: Karthala, 2009.

Skilling, Gordon. "Samizdat: A Return to the Pre-Gutenberg Era?" In *Samizdat and an Independent Society in Central and Eastern Europe*, 3–18. Columbus, OH: Ohio State University Press, 1989.

Slusser, Robert M. "A Soviet Historian Evaluates Stalin's Role in History." *American Historical Review* 77, no. 5 (December 1972): 1389–98.
Slusser, Robert M. "History and the Democratic Opposition." In *Dissent in the USSR: Politics, Ideology and People*, 329–53. Baltimore: Johns Hopkins University Press, 1975.
Smith, Hedrick R. *The Russians*. New York: Ballantine Books, 1977.
Smith, Kathleen E. *Moscow 1956. The Silenced Spring*. Cambridge, MA; London: Harvard University Press, 2017.
Smith, Kathleen E. *Remembering Stalin's Victims: Popular Memory and the End of the USSR*. 2nd ed. [1st ed: 1996]. Ithaca, NY: Cornell University Press, 2009.
Snyder, Sarah B. *Human Rights Activism and the End of the Cold War: A Transnational History of the Helsinki Network*. Human Rights in History. Cambridge: Cambridge University Press, 2011.
Stephen G. Wheatcroft. "The Great Terror in Historical Perspective: The Records of the Statistical Department of the Investigative Organs of OGPU/NKVD." In *Anatomy of Terror: Political Violence under Stalin*, edited by James R. Harris, 287–305. Oxford: Oxford University Press, 2013.
Strayer, Robert W. *Why Did the Soviet Union Collapse ?: Understanding Historical Change*. Armonk, NY; London: M.E. Sharpe, 1998.
Surovtseva, Ekaterina. *Zhanr "pis'ma vozhdiu" v sovetskuiu èpokhu (1950-e-1980-e gg.)*. AIRO-Monografiia 24. Moscow: AIRO-XXI, 2010.
Thatcher, Ian D. "Brezhnev as a Leader." In *Brezhnev Reconsidered*, edited by Edwin Bacon and Mark Sandle, 22–37. Houndmills, Basingstoke: Palgrave Macmillan, 2002.
Tőkés, Rudolf L., ed. *Dissent in the USSR: Politics, Ideology and People*. Baltimore: Johns Hopkins University Press, 1975.
Tolts, Mark. "Demography of the Contemporary Russian-Speaking Jewish Diaspora." In *The New Jewish Diaspora: Russian-Speaking Immigrants in the United States, Israel, and Germany*, edited by Zvi Gitelman, 23–40. New Brunswick, NJ: Rutgers University Press, 2016.
Tromly, Benjamin. *Making the Soviet Intelligentsia: Universities and Intellectual Life under Stalin and Khrushchev*. Cambridge; New York: Cambridge University Press, 2014.
Tumarkin, Nina. *Lenin Lives. The Lenin Cult in Soviet Russia*. Enlarged ed. Cambridge, MA; London: Harvard University Press, 1997.
Vaissié, Cécile. "La chronique des événements en cours. Une revue de la dissidence dans l'URSS brejnévienne." *Vingtième Siècle. Revue d'histoire.*, no. 63 (September 1999): 107–18.
Vaissié, Cécile. *Pour votre liberté et pour la nôtre: le combat des dissidents de Russie*. Paris: R. Laffont, 1999.
White, Stephen. *Gorbachev in Power*. Cambridge: Cambridge University Press, 1990.
Willerton, John P. "Patronage Networks and Coalition Building in the Brezhnev Era." *Soviet Studies* 39, no. 2 (1987): 175–204.
Zubok, Vladislav Martinovich. *Zhivago's Children: The Last Russian Intelligentsia*. Cambridge, MA: Belknap Press of Harvard University Press, 2009.

Index

Abramov, Ivan   144
Abramovich, I. L.   225 n.85, 239 n.24
Abuladze, Tengiz   184
Academy of Pedagogical Sciences   23, 116, 125, 140, 141
Academy of Sciences   32, 43, 53, 54, 77, 78, 99, 128, 145, 146, 153
Action for Soviet Jewry   150
Adamova-Sliozberg, Ol'ga   87
Adler, Nanci Dale   224 n.48
Afanas'ev, Iurii   185, 187, 250 n.25
Agursky, Mikhail   143
Akhmatova, Anna   184
Aksiutin, Iurii   217 n.4, 218 nn.20, 22, 232 n.143
Alberti, Irina   253 n.118
Aleksandrov, V. S.   17, 218 nn.27, 30
Aleksandrov-Agentov, Andrei   57
Alekseeva, Liudmila (Alexeyeva, Ludmilla)   63, 117, 222 n.6, 223 n.15, 235 n.54, 239 nn.6, 7
Alexander Herzen Foundation   116
Alfred Knopf   129
All Stalin's Men (Medvedev)   71, 140, 191
All-Union Agency on Copyright (VAAP)   141
All-Union Bureau of Mensheviks   105, 168
"All-Union Conference to Improve the Training of Scientific-Pedagogical Cadres in the Historical Sciences"   12, 44, 69
All-Union Society of the Blind   15, 73
Alpatov, Vladimir   200
Al'perovich, M. S.   76–8, 117, 212 n.15, 219 n.56, 221 n.109, 226 nn.120–3, 125–34, 235 n.56, 236 nn.78, 91, 242 n.111
Andreeva, Nina   187–8, 190, 198, 250 n.42, 262
Andreyev, Leonid   91, 129
Andreyev, Vadim   91

Andreyev-Carlisle, Olga   129, 237–8 n.140
Andropov, Iurii   30, 36, 42–3, 104, 109, 125, 129–31, 140, 142–4, 175, 206, 232 n.1, 236 nn.80, 99, 261
Anfilov, Viktor Aleksandrovich   49–50, 220 n.73, 236 n.85
Anichkova, Natal'ia Milevna   89–90
anti-Communism   160, 206, 209
anti-cosmopolitan campaign   148
anti-Semitism   101, 126
anti-Sovietism   35, 40–1, 52, 54, 72, 92–3, 113, 118, 121, 129–30, 136, 141, 143, 175, 207
anti-Stalinism/Stalinists   2, 5, 11–12, 37, 39–40, 42, 48, 53–4, 55–6, 58–9, 61–2, 64–7, 69, 71, 76, 80–1, 98, 101, 113, 114, 115, 122, 131, 135, 145, 155, 176, 177, 181, 184, 187–8, 191, 194, 204, 205–6
Antonov-Ovseenko, Anton Antonovich   214 n.26
Antonov-Ovseenko, Anton Vladimirovich   5, 8, 12–22, 36, 65, 71–4, 81, 84, 98, 158–9, 172–81, 183, 192–3, 199–200, 204, 213 nn.14, 15, 17–24, 214 nn.25, 26, 31, 32, 35, 37–8, 40, 42–5, 49, 215 nn.59–60, 64, 65, 225 nn.85–6, 88–90, 92, 98, 226 nn.99–100, 107, 244 nn.8–9, 247 nn.101–6, 112, 114, 116–17, 119, 121, 126, 248 nn.129, 131–4, 136, 144, 147, 249 nn.157, 159, 251 n.76, 252 nn.81, 84–7, 92, 254 nn.142–4, 257, 261–2
Antonov-Ovseenko, Vladimir   13–14, 15–22, 73–4, 173, 192, 213 nn.12, 14, 16, 214 nn.26, 28
APN (Soviet News Agency Novosti)   136, 169–71
Aralov, Semen   74

Arbatov, Georgii 40, 42–3, 57, 217 n.4, 218 n.25, 221 nn.125, 127, 222 n.128
Argumenty i Fakty 185, 197, 199
Artizov, A. 221 n.121, 222 n.137, 224 n.52, 225 nn.74–8, 230 n.98, 236 n.105
Astaurov, Boris 136
Austrian Communist Party 128
Avtorkhanov, Abdurakhman 111–14, 207, 233 nn.17–20, 22–5, 27, 234 nn.34–8, 239 n.14, 258

Baburin, Vladimir 253 nn.125, 127
Bacon, Edwin 40, 217 n.2
Baltiitsev, V. A. 196
Banerji, Arup 212 n.4
Barghoorn, Frederick C. 232 n.5
Before the Tribunal of History. See Pered sudom istorii (Medvedev)
Behrends, Jan C. 211 n.8
Bek, Aleksandr 101
Beliaev, A. I. 254 n.141
Beltov, Eduard 200, 254 n.152
Berdiaev, Nikolai 113
Berelowitch, Alexis 249 nn.7–9
"Berezka" shops 140–1
Bergson, Abram 151, 242 n.118
Beria, Lavrentii 12, 70, 96, 175, 191–2, 256
Berlin crisis 126
Bernshtein, Ans 88
Bertrand Russell Peace Foundation 143
Beyrau, Dietrich 211 n.8
Bezborodov, A. B. 238
Biology and the Personality Cult (Medvedev) 30, 100
Bison, The (Granin) 184
Blekhman, R. 232 n.2
Bodalsia Telenok s Dubom (Solzhenitsyn) 93
Bogomolov, Aleksei 235 nn.68–9, 71–2, 236 n.86
Bogoraz, Larisa 205, 211 n.6, 255 n.1
Bolkhovitinov, N. N. 236 nn.78, 91
Böll, Heinrich 140
Bolshevik Party 105, 126
Bolsheviks 13–14, 19, 67, 98, 166, 186
Boltin, Evgenii 47–8, 52, 75, 118, 121
Bolton, Jonathan 208, 211 n.5, 255 n.4

Bonner, Elena 117, 235 n.54, 253 n.130
Boobbyer, Philip 67, 223 n.16, 224 nn.38–9
"bourgeois propaganda" 129–30, 207
Bovin, Aleksandr 42, 57, 104, 136, 218 n.20, 221 n.126, 232 n.143
Boyer, John W. 249 nn.20–1
Brandeis University (MA) 150
Brest Fortress, The (Smirnov) 83–4
Brezhnev, Leonid 1–2, 4, 32, 39–40, 42–3, 47, 56–9, 62, 65, 71–2, 77, 119, 121, 128, 130, 136, 142–4, 184, 190, 192, 201, 206, 217 n.3, 222 n.129, 225 n.93, 257, 261
British foreign policy during the Second World War (Nekrich) 34
British Policy in Europe 1941-1945 (Nekrich) 145
British Second World War 147
Broido, A. 230 n.98
Bryl', V. V. 195
Brzezinski, Zbigniew 152, 243 nn.125, 127
Bugai, G. M. 199, 254 n.142
Bukharin, Nikolai 12, 17, 23, 55, 106, 161, 168, 174, 186, 262
Bunin, Ivan 184
Burdzhalov, Eduard 41, 256
bureaucratism 29, 149
Burlatskii, Fedor 42–3, 218 nn.22–3
By Right of Memory (Tvardovskii) 184
"The Calf that butted heads with the Oak." *See Bodalsia Telenok s Dubom* (Solzhenitsyn)

Cancer Ward, The (Solzhenitsyn) 93, 130, 193, 196
Carlisle, Donald 151, 243 nn.125–7
Carlisle, Olga Andreyev. *See* Andreyev-Carlisle, Olga
Carter, Jimmy 135
censorship 2, 5, 9, 13, 26, 31–2, 34, 49, 52, 56, 66, 68–9, 71, 79, 80–1, 83, 85, 93, 109, 120, 131, 136, 140, 158, 181, 204, 207
Censorship of Historical Thought (de Baets) 181
Central Commission on Rehabilitation 97

Central Committee   41–3, 48, 52, 54, 56,
    58, 63, 71, 74, 83, 99, 104, 106, 109,
    112, 118–21, 123–6, 128, 129–30,
    131, 136, 143, 145, 147, 173, 203,
    206
Central Committee Department
    of Science and Higher
    Education   16–17, 19–20, 30
Central Committee International
    Department   30
Central Committee Plenum   39, 184
Central Committee Resolution (June
    1956)   45
Central Party Archives (TsPA)   18, 21
Central State Archive of the October
    Revolution and Socialist
    Construction (TsGAOR)   18
Chalidze, Valerii   174
Chebotarev, V.   255 n.160
Chebrikov, Viktor   143
Chekotillo, Andrei   18, 214 n.42
Chernenko, Konstantin   43, 144, 261
Chicherin, Georgii   99
Children of the Arbat (Rybakov)   184, 189
China and the superpowers
    (Medvedev)   140
Chkhikvishvili, I.   57, 222 n.129, 259
Chronicle of Current Events, The   113,
    115, 126
Chukovskaia, Elena (Liusia)   8, 90, 93–4,
    194, 229 nn.66–7, 74, 262
Chukovskaia, Lidiia   66–7, 93, 223 nn.27,
    34–5, 238 n.159, 258
Chukovskii, Kornei   56, 93
City Party Committee of Kraslava   18
Civil War   103, 166
    Russian   188
    Spanish   13, 16–17
    in Ukraine   20, 70, 95
Coates, Ken   143
Cohen, Stephen F. (Steve)   42, 97, 114,
    116, 139, 150, 174, 178, 218 nn.15,
    17–18, 230 n.93, 234 nn.40, 41, 247
    nn.123–5
Cold War   76, 110, 149, 158, 209
collective petitions   64
*Collectivization of Agriculture in the USSR
    1927-1932, The* (Sidorov)   53
Collins&Harvill   170

commemoration   67, 69, 147, 208
commemorative publications   15–17
Committee of Veterans of the October
    Revolution for the Tambov and
    Riazan regions   17
communism   12, 29, 112, 115, 133, 146,
    152, 159, 164, 167
Communist Party   7–8, 11, 13, 15, 17,
    23–4, 26–7, 29–31, 37, 40–3, 45–6,
    56–9, 62–3, 67, 72–4, 75, 77, 80, 95,
    105–6, 111–12, 116–32, 136, 145–6,
    149–50, 152, 158, 161, 169, 176,
    183, 203, 206, 208
"Complete works" (Lenin)   71
"The Concealment of Historical Truth Is a
    Crime against the People!"   79
Conference on Security and Cooperation
    in Europe (CSCE)   134
conformism   61–2, 81
Congress of People's Deputies of the
    USSR   192, 194, 203–4
Congress of the Italian Communist
    Party   192
Congress of the Soviet of Workers' and
    Soldiers' Deputies   13
Conquest, Robert   147, 172, 198
conservatism   53
Coomey, Patrick   242 n.117
cosmopolitism   32
Council of "Memorial"   200
Courtois, Stéphane   198, 213 n.11
Crimean Tatars   147

Dallin, Alexander   147, 218 n.21
Dal'nii, Boris   18, 214 n.45
Daniel', Aleksandr   211 n.6, 240 n.54,
    257
Daniel', Iulii   47, 61, 66, 135, 176
Danilov, V. P.   53, 54–6, 99, 122, 138, 145,
    186, 214 n.37, 221 nn.108, 110–14,
    116–17
Danilova, L. V.   220 n.93
Dashichev, Viacheslav   49–50, 220 n.67,
    236 n.85
David-Fox, Michael   112, 233 n.26
Davies, R. W.   249 nn.3, 23, 250 n.32
de Baets, Antoon   181, 249 n.162
Deborin, Abram   32, 75, 219 n.37, 226
    nn.108, 112–19, 258

Deborin, Grigorii   48–52, 75–9, 118, 121–2, 126–7
"declaration of 46"   13, 19, 192
Demichev, Petr   73, 136, 225 n.94
Department of Agitation and Propaganda (Central Committee)   123–5
Department of Historical Sciences (Academy of Sciences of the USSR)   146
Department of Russian Philology (Wroclaw University)   197
Der Spiegel   119
de-Stalinization   1–3, 11, 22, 25–6, 31–7, 39–40, 54, 58, 65, 66, 67, 69, 77, 85, 92, 104, 183, 206, 208
  bipartisan systems   42–6
  decade of upheavals   40–2
  23rd Party Congress   46–7
Deutsche Welle   118, 120
Diachkov, A. B.   195
Dictatorship of Consciousness, The (Shatrov)   184
District Executive Committee (*raikom*)   142
Djilas, Milovan   113
Dobson, Miriam   212 n.6, 217 n.8, 224 n.62, 227 n.3
Doctor Zhivago (Pasternak)   61, 176, 184
Dolmatovskii, Evgenii   84, 227 nn.6, 8
Dorfman, Joel   152
Dostoevsky, Fedor   194
Dovner, M.   248 nn.138–43
Drabkin, Iakov   55, 99, 221 n.119
Drinan, Robert   150, 242 nn.102, 114
Druzhba narodov   184, 191
Druzhinin, N. M.   77–8
Dubina, K. K.   218 n.31
Dudintsev, Vladimir   101, 184
Dudko, S.   196
Dunlop, John B.   238 n.156, 246 n.76
Dybenko, Pavel   72–3
Dzhemilev, Mustafa   147, 148

Eckel, Jan   239 n.12
Editorial Publications Council of the USSR   145
education   7, 41, 55, 63, 71
Education Department (Moscow City Committee)   124–5

Ehrenburg, Il'ia   90, 99, 101
Ekibastuz camp mutiny (1952)   88
electoral law   202
Elie, Marc   249 n.22
emigration   133, 147–8
émigré journals   111, 136, 139
Ericson, John   147
Esenin-Vol'pin, Aleksandr   2, 61, 135
Esina, T. V.   229 n.66
ethnic Germans   134, 198, 199
Etkind, Aleksandr   85, 227 n.11
Èto ne dolzhno povtorit'sia (Gazarian)   96
Eurocommunism   115, 209
European Communist Parties   111
Evgenov, Semen   18
Evtushenko, Evgenii   214 n.39
"Experiment in Literary Investigation"   179
Ezhov, Nikolai   250 n.43

Far from the Crimean Mountains: Anatomy of a Deportation (Muzafarov)   147
fascism   66, 112, 164
FBI (Federal Bureau of Investigation)   112
Feast of the Victors (play by Solzhenitsyn)   92–3
February Revolution   96
Fedorov, G.   36, 217 nn.135, 136
Fedoseev, Pavel   74
Feldman, Sam   243 nn.124, 126, 128
Ferretti, Maria   186, 250 nn.27–8, 30
"Fiery Revolutionaries" (biography series)   19
"figure of silence"   55–6
Finno-Soviet war   153
Fireglow. See Otblesk kostra (Trifonov)
First Circle, The (Solzhenitsyn)   87, 91–3, 193, 196
Fitzpatrick, Catherine A.   212 n.16, 218 n.16, 229 n.61, 238 nn.141–5, 151–3, 155
Fitzpatrick, Sheila   217 n.8
Fofanova, Margarita Vasil'evna   173
Fomina, Liudmila   213 n.22
"For a Leninist Party Spirit in the Treatment of Soviet History"   57, 65
Ford Foundation   150
Forsake Fear (Nekrich)   150, 155, 197

Fremdenpass   149–51
French Communist Party   161
Frolov, Evgenii   99, 114
From Prisons to Educative Institutions (Vyshinskii)   92
"From the History of Ideas" (Iakubovich)   170, 171
Frunze, Mikhail   126
Fukel'man, Sergei   15, 213 n.18
Further, further, further (Shatrov)   184

Gabai, Il'ia   66, 113, 180, 223 nn.25–6, 249 n.161, 258
Gaidar, Egor   196
Gaponenko, L. S.   54
Garaseva, Anna   90, 228 nn.47, 49
Garaseva, Tat'iana   90
Gavrilov, Ivan   23, 95
Gazarian, Suren   95–6, 137, 230 nn.83, 85
Gdlian, Tel'man   203
Gefter, Mikhail   53, 99, 145, 235 n.54
Geller, Mikhail. *See* Heller, Michel
Gendler, Iurii   258
Genri (Henri), Ernst (Rostovskii, Semen or Khentov, Leonid)   56, 101, 221 n.119, 231 n.118
German attack on Soviet Union   34–5, 49
German-Soviet pact. *See* Ribbentrop-Molotov pact
Gershuni, Vladimir   87–8
Gestapo   27
Geyer, Dietrich   250 nn.26, 33
Ginzburg, Abram   168
Ginzburg, Evgeniia   87, 101, 103, 109, 184, 193
Gitelman, Zvi   239 n.6
Gladnev, I. N.   119, 123
"Glasnost"   61, 66, 158, 183–9, 192–4, 198, 204
Glavlit   33, 121
Glazov, Yuri   235 n.55
Gnedin, Evgenii   50, 52, 99, 121, 219 n.56, 220 n.65, 235 n.54
Goerdt, Wilhelm   223 n.37
Gogol, Nikolai   194
Goldberg, Paul   211 n.4, 222 n.6, 223 n.15, 235 n.54
Golikov, Filip   35, 119

Golikov, Viktor   43, 49–50, 52, 57–8, 65, 222 nn.129–32, 259
Golitsyn, V.   255 n.1
Golovanov, S.   225 n.95
Gorbachev, Mikhail   104, 144, 183–7, 189–90, 193, 195, 197, 202–4, 208, 261–2
Gordon, Robert   150, 242 nn.114, 116, 118
Grani   111
Granin, Daniil   184
Great Patriotic War   32, 42, 52, 68, 75, 118, 121, 126
Great Terror   23, 26–7, 41, 52, 65, 103, 160, 174
Great Terror, The (Conquest)   172
Griffiths, Franklyn   217 n.3
Grigorenko, Petr Grigor'evich   79–81, 113, 227 nn.136–42, 145, 233 nn.28–9, 258
Grintsberg, L. I.   236 n.91
Gronskii, Ivan Mikhailovich   173, 247 nn.108, 111
Grossman, Vasilii   92, 184, 193
"Group on Soviet Peasantry"   53
Guber, A. A.   77
Gulag   5, 14, 23, 42, 51, 69, 83–4, 86, 96, 101, 103, 106, 121, 152, 154, 162, 163–4, 166, 168, 174, 176, 179, 194, 196, 199
Gulag Archipelago, The (Solzhenitsyn)   1, 28, 83, 85–94, 107, 111, 114, 117, 128–30, 135, 157–8, 162–71, 177–9, 189, 193, 195–6, 204–5

Habeck, Mary R.   213 n.13
Half a life. See Polzhizni (Vitkovskii)
Harper&Row   170
Harris, James R.   254 n.135
Harvard Russian Research Center   149, 196
Haugh, Richard   238 n.156, 246 n.76
Haupt, Georges   128
Heer, Nancy Whittier   69, 212 n.5, 218 n.14, 224 n.49
Heller, Leonid   197, 243 nn.132, 146
Heller, Michel (Geller, Mikhail)   149, 152–4, 242 nn.101, 106–7, 109, 112, 243 nn.133–40, 142–6, 253 nn.118, 120, 261

Helsinki Accords   134–5
Helsinki Watch   4, 134
"Heroic Fortress"   84
Herzen, Alexander   161
"The High Responsibility of Historians"   46, 55
Historical-Archival Institute   196
historical scholarship   12, 41, 44–5, 47, 49, 55, 58, 69, 106, 185–6
"History of a Telegram"   72
History of the Communist Party of the Soviet Union, The (Stalin)   41, 46, 71
History of the Great Patriotic War of the Soviet Union, The (Pospelov)   45–6
"History of the Leadership of the CPSU"   207
Hitler, Adolf   51, 75–6, 79
Hokkaido University   152
Hollander, Paul   189, 250 n.51
Hornsby, Robert   212 n.1, 217 n.9
House of Writers   190
House on the Embankment, The (Trifonov)   103
human rights   6, 61, 81, 115, 134–5, 194, 205, 209
Hungarian Revolution   41
Hurst, Mark   211 n.4, 239 n.13
Husband, William B.   185, 249 nn.13–14, 18–19, 250 nn.37–8

Iadov, Vladimir   99
Iakir, Iona   51
Iakir, Petr   51, 54, 58, 65–7, 113, 141, 180, 222 n.134, 223 nn.23, 25–6, 31–3, 249 n.161, 258–60
Iakovlev, Aleksandr   185, 190
Iakovlev, I. I.   18, 214 n.44
Iakubovich (Yakubovich), Mikhail   105–7, 167–71, 246 nn.73, 81–3, 95, 247 n.96
Iakubovskaia, I.   56
Iampol'skii, Boris   103
Ianin, A.   17–18, 214 n.40
Iasnyi, V. G.   19
"I Cannot Forsake My Principles"   187
Ideological Commission of the Central Committee   43, 45–6

Ideological Department of the Central Committee   16, 99, 123, 126
Igrunov, Viacheslav   223 nn.25, 27, 246 n.77
Il'ichev, Leonid   16, 30
Imenem Revoliutsii (Antonov-Ovseenko)   18, 21, 72–3
IML (Institute of Marxism-Leninism)   17–18, 39, 41, 47–8, 52, 55, 58, 61, 65, 71, 74, 78, 99, 117–21, 123–4, 126–7, 209
Immigration Services   151–2
Impatience (Trifonov)   103
inner emigration   135–45, 154–5
Inseparable Twins, The. See Nochevala tuchka zolotaia (Pristavkin)
Institute of Eastern Studies   200
Institute of General History   122
Institute of History   17, 32, 48, 50–1, 53–6, 75, 78, 99, 118, 121–2, 145–6, 147–8
Institute of Military History   185
Institute of Research for Polytechnic Teaching, Production Teaching, and Professional Orientation   23
Institute of the World Workers' Movement   99
Institute of World History   145, 152
intelligentsia   7–8, 37, 41–3, 42, 45, 56, 57, 58, 59, 61–2, 76, 80, 83, 94, 99, 101, 105, 115, 127, 146, 155, 169, 187, 206
   anti-Stalinist protest letters   65–67
   old cultured   62–5
   theory of two truths   67–9
Interregional Deputies' Group   203
In the Name of the Revolution. See Imenem Revoliutsii (Antonov-Ovseenko)
In the Year 1917 (Antonov-Ovseenko)   18
Into the Whirlwind (Ginzburg)   103, 109, 184
Invisible Allies (Solzhenitsyn)   90
Ioffe, Nadezhda   174
Iron Curtain   111, 116, 135, 136, 139, 140, 153, 165
Istoriia SSSR   78, 199
Italian Communist press   56
Iudin, Pavel   45, 219 n.38
Iunost'   192–3

Iurasov, Dmitrii   187
Ivanov, A. P.   225 n.95, 240 nn.48, 50
Ivanov, Nikolai   203
Ivanov, S. N.   19
Ivanova, Anna   140
Ivanova, Evgeniia   179, 248 n.153
Iziumova, Nataliia   253 n.119
Izvestiia   16, 21, 68, 72–3, 119, 142, 173
Izvestiia TsK KPSS   187

Jackson and Vanik amendment   133
Jay, Margaret   241 n.69
Jones, Polly   19, 84, 214 n.50, 215 n.51, 217 nn.8, 10–11, 218 n.13, 227 n.9
Joravsky, David   128–9, 159, 239 n.18
June 22, 1941 (Nekrich)   32, 34–7, 39, 47–9, 54, 75, 119–22, 126, 146, 197

Kady District Case   89
Kaganovich, Lazar'   65, 97, 172, 256
Kagarlitskii, Boris   194
Kaiser, Robert   116
Kamenev, Lev   12, 17, 23, 55, 106, 126, 161, 170, 186, 246 n.73, 262
Kapitsa, Petr   136
Karaulov, Andrei   201
Karbe, Iurii   87
Kariakin, Iurii   194
Karnaushenko, V.   252 n.93
Katyn Affair   175
Kaverin, Veniamin   101
Kazhdan, Aleksandr   152
Keenan, Edward   149, 242 n.118
Kengir camp uprising (1954)   88
Kennan Institute   150
KGB (Committee of State Security)   1, 30, 36, 56, 91, 92, 98, 106, 109, 112–13, 116, 125, 128, 129, 131–2, 133, 135–9, 141, 142–4, 154, 171, 174–5
Kholmskaia, M.   255 n.160
Khomizuri, Georgii   207, 255 n.2
Khronika Press   174
Khrushchev (Medvedev)   140, 191
Khrushchev, Nikita   1–4, 11–12, 15–16, 19, 21–3, 26, 29–34, 39, 41–7, 53, 55–6, 58, 64–5, 67, 70–2, 114, 160–1, 186, 192, 205–6, 212 n.4, 217 n.1, 224 n.60, 225 n.79, 230 n.98, 240 n.46, 256–7

Khrushchev, Sergei   83, 85, 91, 96–9, 104
'Khrushchev's zeks'   97
Khrushchev: The Years in Power (Medvedev)   116, 140
Khvostov, Vladimir   33, 44, 54, 118, 218 n.28
Kim, Iulii   66, 113, 180, 223 nn.25–6, 249 n.161, 258
Kim, M. P.   20
Kind-Kovács, Friederike   111, 233 nn.11–12, 15–16
Kirilov, G.   214 n.43
Kirov, Sergei   23, 26–7, 97–8, 105, 107, 126, 160, 173, 174, 199
Kiseleva, E. V.   196
Klimoff, Alexis   238 n.156, 246 n.76
Klimova, Natal'ia   90
Klimovich, G. S.   195
Knizhnoe obozrenie   194
Kochetkova, Inna   7, 212 nn.11, 13
Kochetov, Viacheslav   65, 223 n.19
Kolyma camp   89–90, 95, 97
Kolyma Tales (Shalamov)   184
Komaromi, Ann   110, 233 nn.9–10
Kommunist   21, 57–8, 66, 78, 114, 127, 136
Kommunist Tatarii   192
Komsomol   14, 50, 117
Komsomol'skaia pravda   190
Kondrat'ev, Viacheslav   194
Konev, I. S.   119
Konrad, N. I.   77
Konstantinov, Sergei   254 n.153
Kopelev, Lev   65, 66, 87, 90, 128, 223 nn.19, 20, 28
Koplenig, Johann   128
Korean War   126
Korneevna, Lidiia   93
Korolev, F. F.   116
Kosterin, Aleksei   235 n.54
Kosygin, Aleksei   191
Kotelenets, A.   31
Kovalenko, M. S.   195
Kovalev, A. F.   201, 254 n.156
Kovalev, Sergei   205, 255 n.1
Kozlov, Denis   63–4, 83, 109, 232 n.4
Kozlov, Vladimir   217 n.8, 222 nn.11–12, 223 n.17, 227 nn.1, 4–5, 15
Krasin, Iurii   104
Krasin, Viktor   113, 141, 260

Krasnaia niva 173
Krasnaia zvezda 16, 21
Krasnopevtsev, Lev 218 n.13
Krasnopevtsev Affair 41
Kreisky, Bruno 143, 261
Kremlin wall 12
Krinko, Evgenii 198, 200, 254 nn.134, 148
Kriukov, I. 194
Kriza, Elisa 245 n.38
Kropachev, Sergei 198, 200, 254 nn.134, 148
Krotov, M. 255 n.160
Krupskaia, Nadezhda 173
Krylenko, Nikolai 73, 92, 107, 168–9
Kuchkin, Andrei 46, 219 nn.41, 42
Kudriashov, P. 214 n.32
kulaks 12, 94, 105, 195, 197, 198–9
Kulish, Vasilii Mikhailovich 50, 52, 220 n.76, 236 n.85
Kuravshov, Ivan 198, 254 n.139
Kurchatov Institute of Atomic Energy 202
Kut'in, A. 230 n.98
Kut'ina, D. 230 n.98
Kvachevskii, Lev 258

Labedz, Leopold 152–3, 212 n.14, 229 nn.70, 71
Labov, Jessie 233 n.11
Lakshin, Vladimir 102, 138
La révolution d'octobre était-elle inéluctable? (Medvedev) 140
Larin, Iurii 174
Larina, Anna 174
Last Five years 1918-1922. Indictment Speeches for the Greatest Trials Heard by the Moscow and Supreme Revolutionary Tribunals, The (Krylenko) 92
Latsis, Martyn 92
"legalist strategy" 2, 61, 135
Lenin (Ul'ianov) Vladimir Il'ich 16–17, 19, 26, 29, 51, 53, 72–4, 95, 105, 106, 123, 126, 130–1, 159, 161–4, 166–7, 175, 184, 187, 189, 193
Leningrad University 22
Leninism 54, 98, 155
Leninism and Western Socialism (Medvedev) 140

Lenin Prize 84, 91, 96
Lenin's Mausoleum 12, 51
Lenizdat 74
Lenoe, Matthew E. 98, 230 nn.100–4
Leonhard, Wolfgang 218 n.21
Let History Judge 71, 85, 111, 114–16, 128, 135–6, 138, 140, 144, 158–62, 168, 172, 174–6, 178, 180, 191, 200, 205
  collaborative writing 94–104
  questioning taboos 104–8
Let History Judge (Medvedev) 30, 67, 81
"Let's Introduce Clarity" 68
"Letter of the twenty-five" 56, 101
letter-pamphlets 64
"Letters to an Unknown Person" (Iakubovich) 106
"Letter to the Fourth Congress of the Writers' Union" (Solzhenitsyn) 91, 93, 195
"Letter to the Soviet Leaders" (Solzhenitsyn) 130
letter types 64
Levitan, Inna 174, 247 n.122
Levitskaia, Nadezhda 8, 89, 228 nn.42–4
Levitskii, Grigorii 89
liberalization 11, 41, 42, 134, 184
Lieberman, Sanford 151
Life and Death of Philip Kuzmich Mironov, The (Medvedev) 103, 192
Life and Fate (Grossman) 92, 184
Ligachev, Egor 188, 203
Likholat, A. V. 17, 214 n.35
Lindenberger, Thomas 211 n.8
"A literary miracle" 93
"literature-centrism" 83
Literaturnaia gazeta 199
Litvinov, Maxim 99, 216 n.110
Liubarskii, Kronid 113
Livre noir du communisme (Courtois) 198
Loginov, Vladlen 19, 196
London National Institute for Medical Research 140
Lukianov, Anatolii 203
Lupinin, N. 223 n.16
Luxemburg, Rosa 161
Lygan, Vladislav 254 nn.138, 140, 198–9
Lysenko, Trofim 22, 24, 30, 89, 101, 128, 165

McCarran Internal Security Act   151
Maiorov, M. S.   19
Maiskii, Ivan M.   32, 216 n.110
Makarov, F. F.   123, 125
Makeev, Aleksei   88
Makhno, Nestor   20, 199
Makotinskaia, V. M.   246 nn.82, 85
Maksimov, Vladimir   165, 245 n.52
Malenkov, Georgii   65, 256
Malia, Martin   163–4, 212 n.11, 245 nn.39–45
Mamleev, Dmitrii   247 n.109
Mandel'shtam, Nadezhda   101
"manifesto of anti-Perestroika forces"   188
Markstein, Elisabeth   128, 244 n.6, 259
Markwick, Roger D.   3, 7, 11, 211 nn.3, 9, 212 n.3, 217 nn.10, 12, 219 n.61, 220–1 nn.94–8, 241 nn.82–3
Martin, Barbara   211 n.1, 212 n.17, 248 nn.144–5, 255 n.3
Marx, Karl   189
Marxism   52, 53, 55, 75, 79, 115
Marxism-Leninism   27, 32, 50, 57, 69, 161–4, 191
Medvedev, Aleksandr   22, 23
Medvedev, Roi/Roy   4–8, 11–13, 36, 42–3, 52, 56, 58, 65, 68–70, 70–1, 72, 75, 81, 84–5, 94–108, 111, 113–17, 121–9, 131, 133–4, 138, 146, 148, 155, 158–9, 162, 168–75, 180–1, 183, 187, 189–92, 195, 198, 200–4, 206, 208–9, 212 n.15, 215 nn.67–9, 71–4, 76–84, 216 nn.85–95, 97–8, 100–2, 104, 218 n.19, 221 nn.122–4, 222 nn.129, 135–6, 223 n.24, 224 nn.42–5, 53, 55, 62, 225 nn.70, 81, 227 n.10, 229 nn.77–80, 230 nn.85–6, 91–2, 99, 105, 107, 109, 111, 231 nn.113, 115–17, 119, 121, 124–31, 135–7, 232 nn.142, 144–51, 153, 156–7, 159–62, 234 nn.30, 32, 40, 43, 45–50, 235 nn.52–3, 236 nn.99, 100, 237 nn.115, 120, 129–30, 132, 134–5, 137–8, 238 n.1, 239 nn.9, 17, 21, 23, 240 nn.33, 35, 41, 43, 51, 53, 55, 241 nn.58, 60, 67, 70–5, 77, 94, 242 nn.99, 244 nn.7, 10–13, 18–21, 23, 245 nn.47, 50–1, 54–68, 246 nn.69–71, 78–80, 83–4, 86–90, 247 nn.99, 120, 249 nn.5–6, 10–12, 250 nn.24, 39, 41, 251 nn.53–9, 61–5, 70–5, 252 n.110, 254 n.157, 255 nn.5, 158, 162–7, 169, 172–3, 257–62
  arrest   136–8
  establishing modus vivendi   138–45
  liberal Marxist truth   159–62
  review of *The Gulag Archipelago*   165–7
  writing for Communist Party   22–31
Medvedev, Zhores   8, 22, 24–5, 95, 100, 104, 116, 128, 136–8, 140–1, 154, 164–5, 170–1, 212 n.15, 216 nn.96, 99, 229 n.82, 230 nn.84–5, 106, 111, 231 nn.113, 115–17, 119–21, 124–5, 128, 130–1, 135–7, 232 n.142, 234 n.30, 235 n.51, 236 n.99, 237 n.133, 239 nn.21–2, 27, 240 nn.39–41, 43, 51, 55, 241 nn.58, 60, 62, 74–5, 94, 242 n.99, 245 nn.47–8, 50, 247 n.99, 251 nn.53–8, 61–2, 65, 70–3, 254 n.157,   255 nn.5, 158, 161–3, 165, 167, 259–60
Medvedev Papers, The (Medvedev)   136
Meerson, L. A.   225 n.94
Meerson-Aksenov, Mikhail   64, 223 n.16
Melamid, Daniil Efimovich   49–50, 220 n.68
Memorial   188, 191, 194, 202
Men, Aleksandr   194
Mensheviks   19, 94, 107
Mikoian, Anastas   15–17, 70, 72–3, 97, 191, 213 n.24, 214 n.31, 35, 38, 224 n.51, 56, 59, 61, 225 n.90
Minister of the Interior   97
Ministry of Defense   119
Ministry of Education   187
Ministry of Foreign Affairs   139
Ministry of Health   141
Ministry of Interior   92
Mironenko, Sergei   217 n.8
Mironov, Filip   103
Mironovich, David   248 n.137
"mnemonic communities"   84
Moldavian Republic   43
Molodoi kommunist   200
Molotov, Viacheslav   65, 99, 256

monopolism   29
moral consciousness   64
"The moral make-up of a historical figure" (Pomerants)   66
Morev, Gleb   255 n.6
Morning Star   148
Morozov, Pavel (Pavlik)   198
Moscow City Archive   8
Moscow City Party Committee   54, 97, 124, 128
Moscow Institute of Red Professors (IKP)   112–13
Moscow Pedagogical Institute   14
Moscow State Institute of Historian-Archivists   185
Moscow State University   77, 148
Moskalenko, K. S.   119, 235 n.73
Moskovskaia pravda   192
Moskovskie novosti   184–5, 194, 196
Moskovskii komsomolets   21
Most Favored Nation status   133
Moyn, Samuel   134, 239 nn.11, 12
"multistructuredness"   53
Murashov, S.   57, 259
Museum of the Revolution   48
Muzafarov, Refik   147

Nadzhafov, D. G.   226 n.110
Narodno-Trudovoi Soiuz (NTS)   111
Nathans, Benjamin   135, 211 n.2, 222 n.2, 239 n.12
National Endowment for Humanities   150–1
Nauka   36, 75–6, 78, 120–1
Nauka i zhizn'   21
Nazi Germany   35, 43, 112, 167, 194
Nazism   112, 184
Nazi-Soviet pact. *See* Ribbentrop-Molotov Pact
Nechkina, M. V.   77–8
Nekrich, Aleksandr   5–8, 12–13, 31–7, 39, 43, 46–55, 58–9, 61, 65, 69, 75–8, 80–1, 85, 99, 111, 117–24, 126–8, 132, 134–5, 145–55, 183, 196–7, 207, 212 n.15, 216 nn.105–9, 111–14, 116, 118, 120–1, 123–6, 217 nn.127–34, 219 nn.37, 45, 51–5, 57, 60, 62, 220 nn.64–91, 221 nn.99–100, 102–3, 105–7, 224 n.46, 226 nn.124, 134, 227 n.143, 235 nn.64, 66, 74–7, 236 nn.79, 81–4, 88–9, 93, 241 nn.78–81, 84–91, 93, 242 nn.95–8, 101–2, 105–11, 115, 119, 243 nn.120–2, 128, 133–5, 137–40, 142–6, 253 nn.118, 124, 126, 128–9, 257–9, 261–2
"Nekrich Affair"   4, 7, 34, 48, 62, 120, 122, 145, 205, 209
   campaign of letters   76–9
   Grigorenko letter   79–81
   treacherous attack   75–6
Nenarokov, Al'bert   196
neo-Stalinism/Stalinists. *See* Stalinists
NEP (New Economic Policy)   105, 185
Neva   195
Nevskii, V. I.   73
"New Direction"   53
New York Times, The   116, 131, 138, 198
Nicholson, Michael   238 n.156
nihilism   44
Nikiforov, N. A.   18
Nikolaev, Igor'   123, 125, 236 nn.99, 100
900 days: The Siege of Leningrad, The (Salisbury)   172
NKID (People's Commissariat of Foreign Affairs)   50, 99
NKVD (People's Commissariat of Internal Affairs)   15, 22, 27–8, 51, 70, 95–6, 99, 107, 112, 199
Nobel Committee   93
Nobel Prize   61, 93, 141, 157, 167, 195
Nochevala tuchka zolotaia (Pristavkin)   184
Notes from the Kolyma (Shalamov)   109
Notes on the Civil War (Antonov-Ovseenko)   18
Nouvel observateur   118
Novaia i noveishaia istoriia   78
Novak, Leonid   224 n.64, 230 n.88
Novyi mir   19, 21, 36, 56, 63, 68, 78, 83, 85, 90–1, 92–3, 100, 101–2, 115, 145, 173, 185, 192, 193, 195, 196
Nuremberg Trial   164

Oak and the Calf, The (Solzhenitsyn)   102
Obninsk Palace of Culture   69
Obozrenie   196

October Revolution 13, 15–18, 22, 65, 72, 74, 95–6, 107, 115, 129–30, 154, 159–60, 166, 173, 177, 184, 188, 192
October Revolution, The (Medvedev) 140
October Revolution Museum 70
Ogonek 184
Oktiabr' 185
Old Bolsheviks 15–16, 18, 25, 48–9, 51–2, 56, 62, 64, 69–74, 80, 81, 84, 94–6, 95, 97, 98, 99, 103, 104, 106, 107, 114, 125, 128, 137, 161, 167, 172, 173, 176–7, 181
Old Man, The (Starik) (Trifonov) 103
Old Menshevik 167, 169–70
Ol'shanskaia, L. M. 225 n.96
One Day in the Life of Ivan Denisovich (Solzhenitsyn) 83–5, 87–8, 90–1, 93, 231 n.132
O'Neill, Joseph 150, 243 n.122
O'Neill, Thomas 151, 242 n.118
"One word of truth shall outweigh the whole world" (Solzhenitsyn) 157
On Socialist Democracy (Medvedev) 102, 116, 133, 136–7, 140, 160
On Soviet Dissent (Medvedev) 140
On Stalin and Stalinism (Medvedev) 140, 191–2, 200
"On the Cult of Personality and Its Consequences" (report) 11, 15, 23, 26, 30, 33, 36, 40–1, 65, 70, 99, 131, 205–6
Open Society Archives 8
Order of Socialist Labor 173
Ordzhonikidze, Sergo 126
Orthodox Church 166
Orthodox Russophile 5
Osnos, Peter 139
Ostpolitik 134
Ostrovitianov, Konstantin 46
Otblesk kostra (Trifonov) 84, 103
Oushakine, Sergei 61, 110, 222 n.3, 233 n.8
Oznobishin, Dmitrii 17

Paillard, Denis 250 nn.47–8
Pakhtusova, Nina 129
Pamiat' (historical collection) 177–9, 207
Pamiat' (movement) 188
Pankratova, Anna 41

Pan-Russian Society of Safeguard of Historical Monuments and Culture 188
Pariahs, Partners, Predators: Soviet-German Relations 1922-1941 (Nekrich) 197
Parvus, Alexander 99
Pasternak, Boris 61, 184, 193
patronage networks 40
Pavlinchuk, Valerii 115
PCC (Party Control Committee) 24, 71–2, 75, 97, 119–24, 128
Pechora Gulag camp 15
Pel'she, Arvid 72, 120–1, 128
People, Years, Life (Ehrenburg) 101
People's Commissar for Justice 13
Pered sudom istorii (Medvedev) 26, 30, 31, 123, 126
Perestroika 2, 4–6, 104, 106, 117, 155, 171, 181, 183–9, 194, 196, 197, 200, 204–5, 208–9
Perova, G. Ia. 124–5, 127
Petliura, Semen 70
Petrov, F. N. 225 nn.87, 95
Petrov, Nikita 200, 254 nn.149–50, 255 n.171
Petrov, Vladimir 217 n.135, 219 n.62, 220 n.65
Petrovskii, Leonid 34, 48, 50–2, 58, 65, 67, 72, 99, 118, 120, 174, 216 nn.115, 122, 219 nn.56, 63, 222 n.133, 223 nn.22, 36, 225 n.82, 236 n.80, 259
Philip Mironov and the Russian Civil War (Starikov) 140
Piatakov, Georgii 106
Pimenova, T. P. 215 n.65
Pipes, Richard 62, 212 nn.11, 14, 222 nn.4, 5
Pisarev, Sergei 227 n.136
Platonov, Andrei 184
Plisetskaia, Maia 56
pluralism 29
Podvoiskii, Nikolai 74
Pogudin, V. 21, 215 n.62, 63
Pokaliukhin, M. 225 n.95
Policy of British Imperialism in Europe, October 1938-September 1939, The (Nekrich) 33

Politburo   40, 56, 57, 58, 65, 120, 121, 127, 129, 130–1, 144, 185, 188, 193, 203, 207
Political Diary (Medvedev)   58, 68, 102, 111, 114–17, 137, 140–1
Political Portrait of L.I. Brezhnev (Medvedev)   140
political repression   1–6, 12, 15, 23, 28, 65, 66, 67, 70, 73, 80–1, 99, 108, 135, 142, 144, 158, 160, 164
Politizdat   19, 21, 30–1
Politov, Z. N.   20
Pollack, Detlef   7, 211 n.7
Polytechnic Education   23
Polzhizni (Vitkovskii)   102
Pomerants, Grigorii   66, 97, 223 n.30, 230 nn.94, 96–8
Pomerantsev, Vladimir   68, 224 n.39
Ponomarev, Boris   30, 36
Popov, N.   228 n.18
Popular Front   13
Portnov, Lev   96, 230 n.89
Portret Tirana (Antonov-Ovseenko)   65, 172–8, 192–3, 199, 205, 214 n.25, 248 n.25
Posev   111, 136
Pospelov, Petr   71, 121, 146, 224 n.68
post-Stalin era   12, 32, 64, 83, 88, 117, 155, 161
POUM (Workers' Party of Marxist Unification)   13
Powell, David   151
Poznań protest (June 1956)   41
Prague Spring   81, 115, 125, 133, 146
Pravda   42, 46, 67, 131, 142, 158, 165, 188, 195
Pravdina, M.   246 n.94
Pribylovskii, Vladimir   234 n.46
Priimak, P.   240 n.34
Pristavkin, Anatolii   184
Problems in the Literary Biography of Mikhail Sholokhov (Medvedev)   140
Pro-Fascist Politics of English Imperialists in Europe (Nekrich)   32
"Progress, Coexistence and Intellectual Freedom" (Sakharov)   104
Pronman, Izmail   88
"prophylactic" methods   132, 154

Prosveshchenie   191
protest letters   56, 63–7, 81
Provisional government   13
Publications Committee   48, 56
Public Prosecutor's Office   142
public rehabilitation   15–17, 43, 65
Punished Peoples, The (Nekrich)   146, 148, 150, 197
Puzyrev, Oleg   54, 75

Question of Madness, A (Medvedev)   136–7
Questions of CPSU History. See *Voprosy istorii KPSS*
Questions of History. See *Vosprosy istorii*
Quiet Flows the Don (Sholokhov)   140, 141

Rabinowitch, Alexander   218 n.17
Rabochee slovo   195
"Radio Liberty"   112, 114, 136, 209
Radosh, Ronald   213 n.13
Raleigh, Donald   185, 249 nn.15–16
Raskat, M. Ia.   49
Razumova, Kseniia   202–3
Reagan, Ronald   190
Rebuilding Russia (Solzhenitsyn)   196
Red Army   34–5, 51, 52, 76, 79
Red Square   133
Red Wheel, The (Solzhenitsyn)   91–2, 129
"Reflections on Progress, Peaceful Coexistence and Intellectual Freedom" (Sakharov)   125
refuseniks   134
Regional Party Committee of Grodno   118
Rekunkov, Aleksandr   143
religion   166
Repentance (1987)   184
Requiem (Akhmatova)   184
Reshetovskaia, Natal'ia   94
Reuters Agency   148
revisionism   2, 41, 58–9, 65, 83, 185
Revolutionary Military Council   13
Řezáč, Tomáš   171, 246 n.94
Ribbentrop-Molotov Pact   35, 50–2, 76, 80, 107, 153, 197, 203
Rigby, T. H.   217 n.3
"R. Medvedev from Moscow"   136

Roginskii, Arsenii 198, 207, 248 nn.137, 144
Rostovskii, Semen. *See* Genri, Ernst
Rostropovich, Mstislav 90
royalties 111, 141, 209
"Roy Medvedev as a Historian-Dissident" (Petrov) 200
Rozybakieva, Lemara Abdullaevna 201, 254 n.154
Rubin, Lev 87
Rudenko 225 n.97
Russia at War 1941-1945 (Werth) 45
Russian Social Democratic Labor Party (RSDRP) 13
Russian Soviet Federative Socialist Republic (RSFSR) 5, 13, 192
Russkaia mysl' 196
Russophiles 187–8, 191
Rybakov, Anatolii 184, 189
Rybakov, Boris 145
Rykov, Aleksei 23, 106, 168, 186, 262

Sakharov, Andrei 56, 80, 99, 103–4, 115, 125, 133, 135–6, 141, 143, 148, 155, 165, 189, 203, 213 nn.138–40, 227 n.144, 234 n.48, 235 n.54, 238 n.2, 259–62
Salisbury, Harrison 172
Salitan, Laurie P. 239 n.6
Salvadó, Francisco J. Romero 213 n.13
samizdat 5, 8–9, 30, 39, 48, 50, 52, 56, 64, 71, 80, 90, 91, 102, 103, 108, 109–10, 112–18, 123, 125–6, 131, 136–7, 141, 158, 165, 167, 207
Samizdat Register (Medvedev) 170
Samsonov, Aleksandr 120, 121
Sandle, Mark 217 n.2
Saraskina, Liudmila 252 nn.94–5, 101, 104, 253 n.115
Saunders, George 234 n.48
Scammell, Michael 130, 212 n.16, 218 n.16, 229 nn.57, 59, 238 nn.141–5, 149–53, 155
Schattenberg, Susanne 39, 217 nn.1, 6, 8, 241 n.72
Sdobnov, S. I. 119
Second World War 32–4, 100, 119, 153, 160, 167

Secrecy of Correspondence Is Guaranteed by Law and *International Cooperation of Scientists and National Frontiers* (Medvedev) 136
Secretariat of the Writers' Union 195
Secretary of State on Soviet Affairs 151
Secret Speech. *See* "On the Cult of Personality and Its Consequences" (report)
Section of History of the Great Patriotic War 47
Section of Methodology 53, 145
Section of Social Sciences 53
self-censorship 4, 13, 33, 155, 161
self-criticism 29, 32, 52, 184
Semenov, Nikolai 87
Semichastnyi, Vladimir 118, 257
17th Party Congress 97–8, 172
Sevost'ânov, Grigorij Nikolaevič 213 n.13
Shafarevich, Igor' 194, 251 n.66
Shakhnazarov, Georgii 30, 57, 104, 232 n.141
Shalamov, Varlam 87, 101, 109, 184, 193
sharashka 87
Sharlet, Robert 218 n.17
Shatagin, N. 57, 259
Shatrov, Mikhail 184
Shatunovskaia, Ol'ga 70, 97–8, 172, 177, 199, 230 nn.97–8
Shatz, Marshall 159, 212 n.10, 244 n.15
Shaumian, S. 57, 97, 259
Shauro, Vassilii 126
Shcharanskii, Anatolii 134, 239 n.8
Shcheglov, S. L. 213 n.16
Shcherbak, Irina 247 n.98
Shchunkov, V. 46, 219 n.44
Shelepin, Aleksandr 43, 92, 257
Shelest, Petro 58
Shepilov, Dmitrii 256
Sherlock, Thomas 189, 251 n.52
shestidesiatniki 63
Shevarnadze, Eduard 203
Shibaev, Viktor 250 n.34
Shlapentokh, Vladimir 183, 187, 212 n.12, 222 nn.9–10, 249 n.1, 250 n.40
Shmidt, O.Iu. 213 n.10
Sholokhov, Mikhail 140–1, 240 n.54

Short Course on the History of the Communist Party (Bolsheviks) (Stalin)   11–12, 45–6, 53, 71
"short transcript"   118, 121, 123
Shtrakhov, A.   54
Shulman, Marshall   151, 152, 243 n.120
Shvernik Commission   97–8
Sidorov, Arkadii   53
Sigman, Carole   250 n.45
Simes, Dimitri   151, 243 n.121
Simis-Kaminskaia, Dina   152
Simonov, Konstantin   84, 99–101, 231 n.114
"Sincerity in Literature" (Pomerantsev)   68
Siniavskii, Andrei   47, 61, 66, 92, 135, 176, 240 n.54, 257
Sino-Soviet dispute   115
Six-Day War   134
6th Party Congress   71
"sixtiers' generation." *See shestidesiatniki*
Skilling, Harold Gordon   110, 217 n.3, 233 n.7
Skrypnikova, Anna   87, 227–8 n.18
Slavutskaia, Wilhelmina   128
Slezkin, Lev   50, 121, 216 n.117, 236 nn.93, 97
Slusser, Robert   109, 159, 232 n.3, 244 nn.14, 16
SMERSh   99
Smil'ga, Ivar   72–3, 225 n.85
Smil'ga, Tat'iana   225 n.85
Smirnov, Sergei   83–4
Smirnova, Iia   201, 254 n.155
Smith, Hedrick   116, 138, 240 n.36–7
Smith, Kathleen   70, 217 n.7, 224 nn.55, 57, 230 n.95, 250 n.46
Snegov, Aleksei   51–2, 69–72, 74, 96–7, 121, 172, 176, 224 nn.62–4, 66–7, 69, 225 n.82
Snyder, Sarah B.   211 n.4, 239 n.10
Sobesednik   190, 196
socialism   29, 33, 40, 42, 47, 49, 55, 58, 76, 101, 105, 126, 134–5, 153, 160, 162, 166, 169, 184, 189
socialist cesarism   126
Socialist Realism   68
social sciences   55, 184

Soldiers Are Made, Not Born (Simonov)   100
Solovki camp   89–90
"Solzhenitsyn Affair"   130
Solzhenitsyn/Soljénitsyne/Soljenitsyne, Aleksandr   1, 5–8, 28, 63, 81, 83–95, 99, 102, 108, 111, 114, 128–32, 135, 137, 143–4, 154–5, 157–9, 162–71, 176–7, 179–81, 183, 193–6, 204, 206, 208, 212 nn.17, 18, 227 nn.7, 12–14, 228 nn.20–2, 24–6, 28–34, 39–41, 45–6, 48, 50, 52–4, 229 nn.55–6, 60, 62–4, 68–9, 72–3, 75–6, 231 n.137, 237–8 nn.136, 139–40, 238 nn.146–8, 160, 244 nn.2–5, 32, 245 nn.33–8, 246 nn.72, 74–6, 91, 94, 247 n.98, 248 nn.152, 154, 252 n.105, 257–60
Solzhenitsyn's Spiral of Treason (Řezáč)   171
Solzhenitsyn's Writers' Union's membership   194
Soroka, O. V.   142
Souvarine, Boris   161, 244 nn.24, 26–30
Sovetskaia Rossiia   188
Soviet Army State Archive   197
Soviet Constitution Day   61
Soviet-Finnish war   35
Soviet Foreign Trade Ministry   140
Soviet Jews emigration   134, 146, 149
Soviet Ministry of Communications   139
Soviet News Agency. *See* APN
Soviet science   24–5
Sovokin, A. M.   72–3, 225 nn.83–4
Spivakovskii, Pavel   229 n.66
Stalin, Iosif   1–2, 13–14, 16, 85, 95, 98, 99, 107, 109, 113, 131, 168, 175, 179, 180–1, 191, 197, 218 n.13, 219 n.37, 256, 258–9
  biography   172
  commemorative events   58
  crimes   12, 24, 26, 28–9, 41–2, 51, 55, 62, 66–7, 69–70, 99, 104–5, 125, 158–60, 163–4, 166, 172, 183, 186, 190
  death   32, 49, 62, 216 n.110
  deportation of ethnic groups   147
  era   5–6, 11, 28–31, 32, 37, 40–2, 44, 53, 55, 67, 85, 111–12, 114, 115,

124–5, 146, 155, 162, 166, 167, 172, 176, 188, 208
evaluation of Kamenev   106
foreign policy   80
guilt   48
military command   36
murder of wife   178
opposition to Lenin's course   71
personality cult   11, 20, 23, 26–9, 31, 35, 39, 41, 43–7, 49–50, 52, 55–6, 58, 65, 78, 104, 106, 126, 160–1, 176
rehabilitation   4, 39–40, 42, 47, 56, 59, 62, 64–6, 77, 81, 101, 119–20, 127, 205
responsibility   50, 79, 97, 100, 159
rule   29
struggle   105, 126
"suspicious deaths"   173
wartime mistakes   31
Staline au pouvoir (Avtorkhanov)   112
Stalinism   12, 14, 22–30, 34, 40, 42, 55, 66, 70, 83, 96, 98, 101, 103–5, 112, 120, 140, 155, 158–62, 164–6, 177, 184, 186
Stalinists (neo-Stalinists, pro-Stalinists)   1, 37, 39–40, 42–3, 47, 57–9, 64, 65, 66, 68–9, 100, 115, 131, 136, 138, 145, 160, 166, 187, 206–7
Stalin unmasked   193
Stanford Hoover Institution Archives   8
Starikov, Sergei   103, 251 n.74
Stasova, Elena   16, 18–20, 73, 106
Stepakov, Vladimir   16, 47, 118, 123–6, 131, 214 n.34
Stern   171
Stoliarova, L. M.   225 n.96
Stoliarova, Natal'ia   90–1, 94, 101
Stolypin, Petr   90
Strayer, Robert   189, 250 nn.49–50
Strumilin, S. G.   77–8
Strygin, A.   225 n.95
Studenkov, Anatolii   258
subjectivism   44, 65
Superfin, Gabriel'   209, 234 n.30
Supreme Court of the Republic   14
Surovtseva, Nadezhda   89
Surovtseva, Ekaterina   64, 222 nn.13, 14
Susi, Arnold   88

Suslov, Mikhail   47, 71–4, 123–5, 131, 136, 224 nn.63, 67
Suvarin, Boris. *See* Souvarine, Boris
Sverdlov, Andrei   52
Sverdlov, Iakov   52, 72–3
Sveshnikov, Anton   211 n.1, 248 nn.144–5, 255 n.3
Svetlova, Natal'ia   90, 94
Svirskii, Grigorii   66, 223 n.29, 258
"Sworn Statement"   151

Tales from the Kolyma (Shalamov)   87
Tambovskaia Pravda   18
tamizdat   5, 8–9, 110–11, 117, 128, 131, 142, 146, 162, 167, 170, 172, 174, 177, 207, 209
Tartakovskii, A. G.   77–8
Teatral'naia zhizn'   201
Technology of Power. *See Tekhnologiia vlasti*
Tekhnologiia vlasti (Avtorkhanov)   111–14
Telegin, Dmitrii Iakovlevich   49, 52, 220 n.72
Tel'pukhovskii, Boris   49–50, 75–6, 78–9, 118, 121–2, 220 n.69, 226 nn.108, 112–19, 258
Tendriakov, Vladimir   56, 101
Tenno, Georgii   88
Ten Years after Ivan Denisovich (Medvedev)   165, 194–5
Ter-Akopian, Norair   99
testimonies   84–5, 87–90, 95, 96, 97, 98, 100, 107, 125, 157–8, 161, 168, 172, 173–4, 177–80, 181, 204, 207
Teush, Suzanna   92
Teush, Veniamin   92
Thaw   53, 62, 64, 85, 101, 147, 184–5, 186, 205
Tikhanova, Valentina   213 nn.16, 18, 214 n.27
Tikhomirov, B. N.   200
Tikhonov, Nikolai   43
Time of change: an insider's view of Russia's transformation (Medvedev)   140
Time of Stalin: Portrait of a Tyranny, The (Antonov-Ovseenko). *See Portret Tirana*
Timiriazev Agricultural Academy   22

Tiurina, Galina Andreevna   212 n.16, 227 nn.16–17, 228 nn.19, 35–6, 38, 51
Todres, Vladimir   253 n.121
Tőkés, Rudolf L.   232 n.6
To live not by lies (Solzhenitsyn)   195
Tolmachev Military-Political Academy   22
Tolstaya, Tatyana   157–8, 244 n.1
Tolstoi, Lev   194
Tolts, Mark   239 n.6
Tomskii, Iurii   14, 19, 106, 174
Tomskii, Mikhail   174
Trapeznikov, Sergei   16–17, 40, 43–7, 54, 56–7, 59, 104, 118–19, 122, 126, 131, 146, 207, 214 n.34, 218 nn.26, 32, 35, 221 n.104
Trifonov, Iurii   84, 100, 103
Triumph and Tragedy (Volkogonov)   185
Tromly, Benjamin   63, 218 n.13, 222 n.8
Trotsky, Lev   1, 12–13, 16–17, 19–20, 55, 105–6, 126, 161, 174–5, 194
Trotskyism/Trotskyist   16–17, 19–20, 73, 89
Trukhanovskii, V.   46, 219 n.44
"Truth about the present day"   136
Tsitovich, A. N.   225 n.93
Tsukanov, Georgii   57
Tübingen University   152
Tucker, Robert   150, 172
Tukhachevskii, Mikhail   173
Tumarkin, Nina   244 n.22
Turchin, Valentin   115, 136, 234 n.48, 259
Tuvin, Iurii   243 n.129
Tvardovskii, Aleksandr   63, 68, 83, 91–3, 96, 99–103, 115, 145, 184, 231 nn.122–3, 259
Twentieth Century (*XX vek*) (Medvedev)   106, 140–1, 148, 167, 170
20th Party Congress   1, 12, 15, 20, 26–7, 36, 40, 47, 52, 55–6, 58, 61–2, 65, 70, 76, 78, 96, 127, 173, 175, 177, 206, 208
22nd Party Congress   1, 11–12, 23, 30, 36, 42, 45, 51, 55–8, 61, 65, 70, 78, 83, 85, 98, 127, 155, 206
23rd Party Congress   1, 36, 46–7, 54, 55, 59, 61, 65, 101, 119

"Twilight of the Stalin Era"   150
Two Years of Struggle on the Inner Front: Popular Overview of the Activity of the Cheka (Latsis)   92

Uchpedgiz   23
Ulam, Adam   151
Uldriks, Teddy J.   178, 248 n.148
uncensored texts   5, 110–11
underground publishing   109–17
Under the Banner of October (Antonov-Ovseenko)   18
Union of Councils for Soviet Jews   151
Union of Soviet Writers   66, 92
Universal Copyright Convention   111
Universal Postal Union   139
US Army Russian Institute   112
USSR Council of Ministers   48, 56
Utopia in Power (Heller)   150, 153–4, 196–7

V.A. Antonov-Ovseenko (Antonov-Ovseenko)   65
Vaissié, Cécile   222 n.1
Vakhrameev, A.   217 n.135
Van Rossum, Leo   178, 248 n.148
Vavilov, Nikolai   89
Verkhovykh, Vasilii   98, 172–3, 225 n.97
Vertogradskaia, Elena   88
"Vetrov"   167–71
Vitkovskii, Dmitrii   87, 102, 231 n.129
Vlasov, Vasilii   89
Vneshposyltorg   140
Voenno-istoricheskii zhurnal   78
Voinovich, Vladimir   114, 234 n.39
Volkogonov, Dmitrii   185, 193, 251 n.66
Volobuev, Pavel   146, 185
Voprosy istorii KPSS   41, 71, 75, 78–9, 193
Vorkuta Gulag   15
Voronianskaia, Elizaveta   90–1, 129–30, 238 n.146, 260
Voroshilov, Kliment   65
Voskresenskii, Lev   194, 252 nn.96–7
Vosprosy istorii   41
Vuchetich, Evgenii   34, 68–9, 75, 100, 221 n.115, 224 nn.40–1, 257
Vyshinskii, Andrei   92

Wagner, Robert   149
Washington Post   116, 139
Wehrmacht   35
Werth, Alexander   45–6
Western Communist parties   56–7, 143
Wheatcroft, Stephen G.   254 n.135
White, Stephen   251 n.67
White Robes, The (Dudintsev)   184
Wielgohs, Jan   7
Willerton, John P.   217 nn.3, 5
Wishnevsky, Julia   247 n.129
World Congress of Historians   145
World History (Nekrich)   33
Wroclaw University   197

XX vek. See Twentieth Century

Yeltsin, Boris   203

Yergin, Daniel   151
YMCA-Press   130

Zaguliaev, V. I.   198, 254 n.137
Zalygin, Sergei   193, 195
Zelenov, Mikhail   237 n.122–4
Zemskov, V. N.   199–200, 254 nn.146–7
Zhukov, Evgenii   45–6, 46–7, 55, 65, 146, 148, 218 n.33, 219 nn.44, 46–7, 257
Zinoviev, Grigorii   12, 23, 55, 106, 126, 161, 170, 186, 246 n.73, 262
Znamia   84, 184, 191, 201
Zorina, Dora   95, 229 n.82
Zubarev, Dmitrii   248 n.144
Zubok, Vladislav   63, 83, 222 n.7, 227 n.2
Zubov, Nikolai   87
Zvezda   192